BLUTIGE FINGER

"„Die Geschichten, die ich blutend erzähle"

BY CECIL HICKS

Blutige Finger – Die Geschichte, die ich blutend erzähle

ISBN (Rated RC Paperback): 979-8-9921714-6-4

Erstveröffentlichung in den Vereinigten Staaten.
Rated RC – Reality Check.
Blutige Finger und Die Geschichte, die ich blutend erzähle sind Marken des Autors.

Besuchen Sie: www.BlutigeFinger.com

Cover und Innengestaltung vom Autor.
Gedruckt in den Vereinigten Staaten von Amerika.
Leser:
Diskretion wird empfohlen.

Reife Gespräche
Sie allein können entscheiden, ob Sie die geistige Reife besitzen, dieses Buch zu kaufen und zu lesen.

Für den Jungen, der niemals sicher war.
Für den Mann, der es fast nicht geschafft hätte.
Und für jeden, dem man je gesagt hat, er solle still sein.
So klingt Überleben

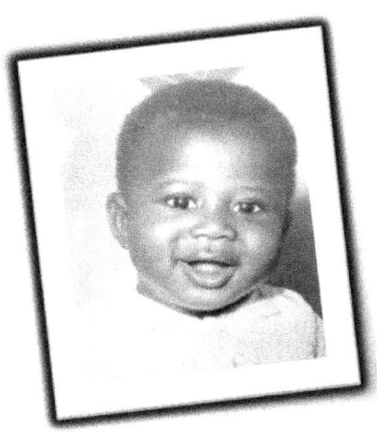

Dieses Baby auf dem Foto weiß, dass viele Menschen ihn für mein promiskuitives Verhalten und die Entscheidungen, die er nach dem Missbrauch im Alter von vierzehn Jahren getroffen hat, verurteilen werden.
Er ist sich auch der Konsequenzen bewusst, seine Gedanken, Meinungen und Erfahrungen in diesem Buch offenzulegen.
Einige Kapitel wirst du faszinierend, abstoßend, spannend oder nachvollziehbar finden.
Er versichert dir, dass er nichts zurückgehalten hat.
Verdammt!! Es fühlt sich unglaublich befreiend an, sich endlich keinen Dreck mehr darum zu scheren, was andere denken. Probier's mal aus – und danke mir, wenn du mich siehst.

VOM AUTOR

Bevor wir eintauchen, lass mich dir die Wahrheit direkt sagen.

Dieses Buch ist ein wilder Mix aus den schmerzhaften Wahrheiten meines Lebens, Gedanken, die mir um drei Uhr morgens durch den Kopf gingen, und ein paar erfundenen Geschichten, die ich einfach erzählen wollte. Einige Kapitel sind brutal ehrlich. Manche sind übertrieben, um einen Punkt klarzumachen – oder einfach, um dich zum Lachen zu bringen, wenn du es am wenigsten erwartest. Und einige dieser Geschichten stammen aus den Ecken meines Kopfes, in denen der kleine Junge, der ich einmal war, noch immer lebt – gefangen im Körper dieses 65-jährigen Mannes.

Ja, manchmal übernimmt dieser Junge die Kontrolle.
Er redet, wie er will, fühlt, was er fühlt, und sieht die Welt durch die Augen eines Kindes, das nie ganz geheilt ist. Wenn ich also abschweife oder von Schmerz zu Humor, zu etwas Sexuellem oder schlicht Wildem springe – das ist kein Zufall. Es ist Teil davon, wie ich das Leben verarbeitet habe. Wie ich damit umgegangen bin. Wie ich überlebt habe.

Das hier ist nicht nur ein Buch über Trauma.
Es ist ein Buch über mich. Meine Gedanken, meine Meinungen, meine Fehler, meine Fantasien und meine Fakten. Manche von euch werden sich in diesen Seiten wiederfinden. Manche werden lachen. Manche werden sich unwohl fühlen. Und manche – so hoffe ich – werden sich ein bisschen weniger allein fühlen, in der dunklen Ecke, in der sie gerade sitzen.

Wie auch immer – danke, dass du liest.

Danke, dass du einer Stimme wie meiner zuhörst, die nicht immer ins Schema passt.
Mein Wunsch ist einfach:
Dass irgendetwas in diesen Seiten dir hilft, zu heilen, zu lachen – oder vielleicht einfach wieder etwas zu fühlen.

Das ist meine Wahrheit.
Blutige Finger und alles.

—Cecil Hicks

BLUTIGEFINGER.COM

VORWORT one

Cecil und ich waren über mehrere Jahre enge Freunde. Als er mir erzählte, dass er den Wunsch habe, Autor zu werden, war ich ehrlich gesagt nicht besonders überrascht. Er hat in seinem Leben schon so vieles getan – er hat eigene Unternehmen geführt, ein Musikvideo produziert und eine beeindruckende Dokumentation über Polizeigewalt geschaffen – um nur einiges zu nennen.

Er war schon immer jemand, der offen seine Meinung sagt, selbst über Themen, vor denen andere lieber schweigen würden – aus Angst, was Freunde oder Familie denken könnten, wenn sie ihr wahres Ich zeigen.

Als ich erfuhr, dass das Thema des Buches seine eigenen sexuellen Erfahrungen betreffen würde, wusste ich, dass er sein ganzes Herz hineinlegen und etwas schaffen würde, das ehrlich und roh ist – ganz zu schweigen davon, dass es ein großer Erfolg werden würde. Nachdem ich mehrere Kapitel während des Schreibprozesses lesen durfte, empfinde ich nun noch größere Bewunderung für meinen Freund und wünschte, ich wäre so mutig wie er. Leider habe ich einen Beruf, bei dem eine Verbindung zu dieser Art von Inhalten meiner Karriere sicher nicht zugutekäme. Bin ich in einem der Kapitel erwähnt? Vielleicht nicht (siehe meine vorherige Aussage über den Job). Aber eines weiß ich mit Sicherheit – ich bin unglaublich stolz auf meinen Freund, dass er etwas so Persönliches teilt, ohne Angst vor dem Urteil anderer.

Lies das Buch – du wirst mir zustimmen.

VORWORT two

Dieses Buch wird Leben verändern. Es wird Millionen von Lesern dazu inspirieren, wieder ein Buch in die Hand zu nehmen, zu lesen und diese Geschichten mit ihren Freunden, Familien und Nachbarn zu teilen. Es wird Leser, die seit Jahren kein Buch mehr angerührt haben, dazu bewegen, eine Leidenschaft für Romantik zu entwickeln und ihre eigenen sexuellen Wünsche oder Fantasien zu entdecken. Es wird Ehen retten und Liebesaffären entfachen. Es wird kreative Seelen dazu bringen, ihre eigenen Geschichten zu erzählen. Es ist ein einzigartiges Memoir – mit expliziten Details, geprägt von besonderen Vorlieben und dunklen Geheimnissen.

Cecil Hicks ist ein unheilbarer Romantiker, der versucht, seine dunklen, erotischen Wünsche zu stillen. Nach Jahren, in denen er dieses sinnliche, dunkle Leben geführt hat, entschied er sich, seine Erfahrungen zu teilen. Ich bin sicher, dass es andere gibt, die ähnliche Erlebnisse hatten, aber nie darüber gesprochen haben – geschweige denn darüber geschrieben. Die meisten Menschen haben Fantasien, aber nur wenige haben sie je ausgelebt.

Cecil ist ein Perfektionist, und deshalb hat er sein Herz und seine Seele in das Schreiben dieses Memoirs gesteckt. Erlebe erneut die Sinnlichkeit, die Romantik und das Drama von Cecil Hicks. Entdecke Cecils dunkle Geheimnisse und erotischen Vorlieben. Begegne seinen leidenschaftlichen, sexuellen Abenteuern. Es gibt kein anderes Buch wie dieses! Dieses Buch ist für ein erwachsenes Publikum bestimmt.

Aufgrund meines Berufs kann ich nicht öffentlich mit diesem Inhalt in Verbindung gebracht werden. Leider kann ich meinen Namen nicht preisgeben, da dies meiner Karriere – und jedem, der mit mir in Verbindung steht – schaden würde.

Inhaltsverzeichnis

JUST KEEPS HAPPENING
PASSIERT IMMER WIEDER

MASSAGE ENVIOUS
MASSAGE-NEIDISCH

MUST BE THE DOG N ME
MUSS DER HUND IN MIR SEIN

MY GAY AZZ COUSIN
MEIN SCHWULER COUSIN

MY MOMMA BEATRICE HICKS
MEINE MUTTER BEATRICE HICKS

MY SHAFT, U DAMN RIGHT
MEIN SCHAFT, VERDAMMT RICHTIG

NO SUCH THANG
SO WAS GIBT'S NICHT

OH NO, NOT AGAIN
OH NEIN, NICHT SCHON WIEDER

PEEP SHOW BOOTH
PEEP-SHOW-KABINE

PIMPIN' AIN'T EZ
ZUHÄLTER SEIN IST NICHT EINFACH

PINE HILLS FLORIDA
PINE HILLS, FLORIDA

REAL FATHER & LIFE LESSONS
ECHTER VATER & LEBENSLEKTIONEN

JUST A SECOND

NUR EINEN MOMENT

In diesem Buch steckt die Weisheit, die das Universum dem Autor gegeben hat – zu deinem Vergnügen, zu deiner Verbindung. Es ist köstlich geschrieben und zutiefst nachvollziehbar, ganz gleich, wie alt du bist, was du glaubst, welche Hautfarbe du hast oder welchen Status du trägst. Er hat dich im Blick.

Bevor du in irgendeinen Teil dieses Buches eintauchst – und ja, du kannst ruhig hin und her springen, wenn du willst – wisse nur eines:
Alles kommt von einem missbrauchten Kind.
Egal welches Kapitel. Egal welches Thema.
Alles beginnt dort.

Es mag manchmal so wirken, als sei der Autor vom Titel abgeschweift.
Ist er nicht.

Hier ist, was du vielleicht nicht verstehst:
Wenn jemand etwas Traumatisches erlebt – verändert das alles.
Jede Entscheidung, jede Idee, jede Beziehung.
Was für dich „riskant" oder „verrückt" aussieht, kann sich für jemanden wie ihn völlig normal anfühlen.

So geht er damit um.
So sieht Überleben aus.
Hätte er anders werden können? Wer weiß.
Vielleicht, wenn er einen nicht-missbrauchten Zwilling hätte, könnten wir vergleichen.

Aber diese Version von ihm?
Mit der wirst du jetzt gleich Bekanntschaft machen.

Lach. Weine. Schaudere. Fühle dich verbunden.
Lass ihn jung in seinem Ton sein, roh in seiner Wahrheit und wild
in seiner Vergangenheit.
Du bist nicht zufällig hier.

Oh – und diese Version?
Das ist das Remix.

Vanilla Sheets hat es nie so erzählt.

Excerpt Reviews from *Vanilla Sheets* (First Edition)

☆☆☆☆☆
Authentically Bold
This book wins — authored with raw emotion.

☆☆☆☆☆
You NEED to read this!
Refreshing to hear a grown man speak the truth.

☆☆☆☆☆
A Must-Read — Pure and Honest Life Experiences
Vanilla Sheets is honest, raw, bold, and emotional.

☆☆☆☆☆
Must-Read Book
This was incredible. You've got to read this book.

☆☆☆☆☆
Great Read. Inspiring. Sensual. Erotic.
This book is amazing — full of stories that entice your desires.

„Über das Vorder- & Rückcover.

Die Wahrheit beginnt, bevor Seite Eins überhaupt aufgeschlagen wird."

[FRONT COVER]

That **blutige Hand** dripping down the wall ain't decoration, it's the past still reaching, still trying to drag me forward. Below it, three versions of me sit in plain sight — the **Baby**, still **unschuldig**, the **Junge**, already scarred, and the **Mann** seated on the throne he had to carve out of survival. That throne isn't about royalty, it's a crown made of **Schmerz**, rage, and scars. The older me towers above, shades on, hat tilted, wrapped in colors of **Rot, Schwarz,** and **Grün** — daring you to look away, daring you to deny the truth. Even the words carry a message: the English title haunts the German edition, reminding you this story bleeds across **Grenzen**, across **Sprachen**.

[BACK COVER]

Then comes the **Flur**, long, narrow, dark — the kind of silence that screams in every language. At the end, a faint **Licht** waits, but in the foreground a **Junge** stands with jeans dirty, afro tight, fists clenched. He doesn't run. He doesn't flinch. He's ready. That boy is me, staring into the **Schatten**, refusing to fold beneath the weight of faceless **Hände** stretching above him, too heavy for any child to bear. But he clenches harder. He refuses harder. And right there is the warning: **Schmerz, Überleben, Prophezeiung.** You don't even have to open to Chapter One — the cover already told you, the cover already warned you.

It's Me, Cecil

Ich bin's, Cecil

There is One Thing I Need You To Keep in Mind...
Es gibt eine Sache, die du dir merken musst ...

Das hier geht nicht um Weiß, Schwarz, Braun, Asiatisch oder
irgendein Kästchen auf einem Bewerbungsformular.
Es geht nicht um Sonntagskleidung, Politik oder wer gerade auf
irgendeiner verdammten Plattform im Trend liegt.

Es geht um Entscheidungen.
Die Art, die dich mit einem Flüstern hineinzieht und dich auf allen
Vieren wieder herauskriechen lässt.
Die Art, die sich gut anfühlt – bis du dich darin verlierst.

Es geht um Wege.
Nicht die, die du geplant hast – sondern die, auf denen du landest,
wegen dem, wem du vertraut hast, mit wem du geschlafen hast
oder wem du geglaubt hast, dass er auf deiner Seite ist.

Es geht um Schmerz.
Die Art, der egal ist, was deine Absichten waren.
Die Art, die einzieht, ihre Koffer auspackt und dich herausfordert,
um sie herum zu heilen.

Es geht um Schweigen.
Die Art, die du dir nicht ausgesucht hast – aber mit der du
trotzdem leben musstest.
Die Art, die dich gelehrt hat, zu lächeln, während du innerlich
untergehst.

Es geht darum, was ich überlebt habe ...
Was ich nur anspreche, wenn es jemand anderen davor bewahren
kann, so tief zu fallen wie ich.
Das hier bittet nicht um deine Zustimmung.

Und es wartet ganz sicher nicht auf deine Erlaubnis.

Denn die Wahrheit in diesen Seiten?
Sie interessiert sich nicht dafür, mit wem du schläfst, wen du
verlassen hast oder wer dich verlassen hat.
Sie kümmert sich nicht darum, welche Freunde du verloren oder
welche Geheimnisse du begraben hast, nur um deine Maske
geradezuhalten.

Manchmal wissen Menschen nicht einmal mehr, wie sie dorthin
gekommen sind, wo sie jetzt stehen.
Ich habe mich entschieden zu vergessen.
Nicht, weil ich schwach bin –
sondern weil Heilung bedeutet, manche Türen zu schließen, ohne
sie zuzuschlagen.

Diese Geschichte wurde nicht für dein Wohlbefinden geschrieben.
Sie wurde geschrieben, damit die Wahrheit endlich irgendwo
sitzen und atmen kann.
Sie braucht nur einen Platz, den sie Zuhause nennen kann.

Danke ...

All Kitties Are Not the Same

Before you reach down into your panties and start playing with your clit with your index finger,

(characters taken from the audiobook)

Royal – A sista **(R)**
David - white narrator. **(D)**
Chrissy – Black chick **(BC)**
& Cecil, that image on the right **(C)**

I want you to keep in mind, I have slept with a lot of women—and there hasn't been one time I treated the person I was with like the last one. Ain't no f**king way. And here's why:

Every woman's body is unique in every imaginable aspect from head to toe.

So now that I've made that perfectly clear, here's the reason I titled this chapter: *All Kitties Are Not the Same.*

Cecil leaned forward.
"By the way," he said, "I'd like to introduce a few characters throughout this chapter who I believe will help tell the story better. Cool?"

David spoke up first. "When I meet a woman for the first time in public, we should meet halfway—if the attraction is mutual. Most times, I don't mind driving closer to wherever she's comfortable. My reason is simple: I want her to feel safe when we meet."

"Wait just a second!" Royal cut in sharply.
David glanced over. "What's up?"
Royal folded her arms. "I've got a few things to say to the women listening to this chapter."

Cecil raised an eyebrow. "You mean, right now?"
"Yes, Cecil. Right now."
He nodded. "Sure, not a problem. Go right ahead."

"There are a few details you're leaving out," she said. "And I'm not sure if that's unintentional or deliberate."

"Would you just go ahead and say whatever the hell it is?"
"Don't rush me!"
"Alright then, what do you want to say?"

Royal turned to the reader. "Yes, ladies—make sure you've got some mace in your purse and keep a hand on it."

Cecil squinted. "Wait, why?"
"Because men get a little too touchy-feely when you first meet!"
"I know exactly what you mean. I don't do s**t like that."

"I'm not talking about you, obviously. Anyway, continue."

David picked back up. "There are some insecure people out there catfishing each other, so just be careful, that's all I'm saying."

He paused.

"That wasn't the case when I met a Black woman named Shay who lived in Riverdale, Florida."

He leaned back, the memory sharpening in his mind. "I drove to her city to make things easier for her. I asked Shay to choose the place, and she gave me directions. Honestly, it was an easy decision to drive those two hours—our phone conversations, the photos, the vibe—it all lined up. I trusted her judgment and met her at a bar near her house."

Royal cut in, eyebrow raised. "Umm... why you referring to her ethnicity?"

David held up a hand. "If you just shut up for a couple of paragraphs, you'll understand why."

"Okay," Royal said, sitting back. "This is going to be interesting."

David continued. "I arrived at the address she gave me and backed into a parking spot so I could see her enter the lot. When Shay finally showed up, I watched as she got out of her car.

She looked to be in her early fifties and was dressed so damn sexy—just the way I like a woman."

He smirked. "We'd already talked about sex before meeting up, and based on our conversations, I figured things between us would be exceptional. She had a slim build and small tits, but she made up for it with a cute face, firm legs, and a dope-ass personality. We vibed hard at the bar."

He leaned forward slightly. "What I really liked about her was that she bought a round of Jell-O shots after I got the first round.

Some women exploit thirsty men—hinting they want drinks but never offering to buy one themselves."

He shrugged. "I always sit back and watch a woman's behavior because, honestly, I don't play that shit."

He glanced at the reader. "Quick side note: I added this detail on February 1, 2025. Before we started drinking those shots, we sat at a round table near the bathroom. As she got tipsy and less aware of her surroundings, I noticed a few dudes coming out of the men's room and looking her way."

He raised his eyebrows. "At first, I thought it was because she was fine as hell. But there was another reason. REMEMBER THAT SHORT DRESS I told you Shay was wearing earlier?"

He smirked again. "Well, at some point I had to hit the restroom, and when I came out, I figured out what those men were looking at—I could see her red panties under the table."

Cecil shook his head, chuckling. "Me being the protective type, I told her she should turn to face me so she wouldn't keep giving these random dudes a show."

Royal nodded. "Well, that was nice of you."

"Thanks," David said.

He hesitated, then added, "Just a moment. I've never felt the need to take advantage of a woman while she's intoxicated... WAIT. FK! I just caught myself in a lie while writing this on November 12, 2024. 'Intoxicated Neighbor' was the second person I ever wanted to take advantage of."

David leaned in again. "On April 1, 2025, another lady I was dating came to mind. I think I already mentioned her in another chapter. Anyway, it was always fun sleeping with her while she was drunk. And if you're listening to this audio or reading these words—don't judge me. It is what it is. At least I'm admitting it."

He laughed. "And if that answer didn't satisfy you, here's the truth: sometimes it was just fun to bust a nut and roll over—no need to eat her out so she could get hers." Cecil chimed in. "Wait, that was back in the day though!"

He nodded. "These days, there's no need to wait until a woman is intoxicated—it's TOO DAMN easy to get pussy. And besides, why the hell would I risk getting prosecuted by a jury of so-called peers who don't look like me in a courtroom?" Royal raised an eyebrow. "Right, and then be sentenced, sent to prison, and passed around like a blunt from Jamaica by a gang of white supremacists?"

"Exactly. That sure in da-hell ain't something I wanna be a part of."

Royal teased, "With that big ass you got, you might as well delete yourself on the bus to prison. Your first clue will be the other men on the bus winking and licking their lips."

Cecil laughed. "Oh! You got jokes!"

"Yep, I sure do," Royal said, grinning. "And I'm listening for the next time I get to interrupt."

David rolled his eyes. "Okay!! Enough. Back to Shay in Riverdale."

He took a breath. "When we left the bar, Shay felt comfortable enough to invite me to her home. As the evening wore on, she thought it was too late for me to drive back, so she asked me to spend the night. That touched me—I felt it. And I expected it." He tapped the table. "See, a thirsty, immature man will always behave childishly on a first date—either being too touchy or expecting sex. A mature, well-rounded gentleman takes his time and benefits from patience."

"In this case, there was absolutely no reason for me to ask for pussy right away. I liked her enough to wait for the right moment."

He added, "When I walked into her home, Shay led me to the space where she felt most comfortable."

WHAT I'VE
LEARNED FROM THIS CHAPTER:

Cecil sat forward again. "Most men assume that what worked with their last partner will work with the next. But ladies, you and I know that ain't true. When I was in the lifestyle, I always asked women about their preferences—their experiences, their views on sex. And to this day, I still hear horror stories that blow my mind."

"You know what trips me up the most? When men say: 'All my previous girlfriends didn't have a problem with it.' That's some ignorant shit. Just because it worked for one, doesn't mean it works for all." Chrissy chimed in. "And if you're a woman listening right now, and he says that to you after your first time together—then I'm blaming you if you gave him a second chance." Royal added, "I don't understand how some of y'all stay in sexless relationships—especially when the sex is terrible. If you used to enjoy it, why settle now? I'm not talking about couples dealing with health issues. I'm talking about people just giving up."

Cecil shrugged. "Hell, which might happen to me one day. But I tell you what—I'll still be eating and fingering her pussy. That's just me.""Peace.

AOL Daze

You Got Mail

I am dedicating this chapter to those who are fifty years old and above.

Cecil: Remember when AOL was available and your computer would produce that static sound, and you would eagerly await the opportunity to connect online. Getting internet access would take at least three to five minutes. "Ain't that a bitch". Back then, it was harder to find dating and kink sites. Naturally, I could not find anything I was interested in on AOL. That's why chat rooms were so convenient for me.

In the privacy of your own home, just search for an intriguing subject, choose a chat room with people in it, and then introduce yourself. When I searched for chat rooms, I was frequently unaware that people lived in my city and sometimes were my neighbors. For this reason, exchanging photos was not a good idea.

Adam: Damn... Cecil!! ...You got a bad case of A.D.D ...and if any of ya'll are wondering what A.D.D. is ...it means attention deficit disorder. in otherwards "It's like trying to pray in church and suddenly wondering if you left the oven on, then picturing your neighbor naked, then realizing the pastor just said 'Amen' and you missed the whole sermon.

Cecil:" Alright...Back to the "chapter" oh!! and by the way...thanks for the A.D.D. explanation. so I don't have to repeat myself again when it happens.

Adam: I got you Cecil, would you mind finishing the rest of the chapter.

Cecil: After going to bed and leaving my chat room available to join I would then read the messages I had received. Every message I received came from married, white, gay, and bisexual men or from people who were discreetly interested in hooking up. I started participating in chat rooms because I found it tedious to sit in front of the computer and wait for someone to join in. After a profile appears in my chat room I would search for their profile, and then leave a message, saying. I noticed your username in the chat room last night. Can I assist you with anything There was only one time when I thought my neighbor was being aggressively friendly, when he asked "what time" my wife was coming home.
"

Black Cock" or "Black Man Available" are chat room titles I chose because it was arousing to see white men who wanted to suck my cock, which was how another one of my neighbors discovered me. I wanna say this before I continue with this chapter. Just like my neighbor, there are a lot of men around us who have bi-sexual tendencies but are afraid to admit it. Just saying. You know damn well I ain't lying, right? So ladies, check the back of your man's draws after he says he's playing poker with the guys. Ah huh I said it and it's to late to take it back now!!

Any chat room title containing the word "black" attracted white men FROM ALL OVER THE WORLD! If you are a white Christian or white nationalist, don't rip your swastika off the sleeve of your favorite shirt, for what I just said. In fact, all I am doing is exposing what most white men secretly and privately want to do with black men.

It is common for white men, such as your neighbor, best friend, father, uncles, brother, coach, football players, entertainers, ministers, and even priests, to have a lustful desire for black men's cock in their mouths or asses.

Do not hold me over a cross-burning fire for revealing this fact; it is well known.

Part Two

I just had another A.D.D. moment.
"Back to the chapter"!!

At some point, an idea popped into my head to start another chat room with one of the titles I mentioned earlier but make it available for the white down low cock suckers to join while I sleep. After leaving my chat room titled "Black Cock for White Boys," I would then wait for all the messages to start pouring in. I knew every message I received would come from married, white, gay, and bisexual men or from people who were discreetly interested in hooking up with black alpha males.

That's why I stopped participating in chat rooms; I found it tedious to sit in front of the computer and wait for someone to join even though I was nowhere near the computer. Additional thought: on 10/05/2024, Posting my chat room to attract white men to suck my cock was like putting one of those mosquito light catchers outside while sitting on your porch.

What does white closet bottom males have in common with mosquitos when it relates to black men? Well, remember those Bug zappers with ultraviolet light? Well, those sonsabitches could not resist that got damn light, right? Did you just laugh? I hope so because I thought it was funny enough to write it. Just so you know, I am not trying to be a comedian; I just have twisted thoughts I like sharing occasionally. When I woke up the following morning, I could always see the screen names of whoever entered my chat room, whether they had left a message. Since I could see who entered my chat room while I was sleeping, I would copy and paste their names into the AOL search bar and look for their profile.

Once I found the profile, I would leave a message saying I noticed your username in the chat room last night. Can I assist you with anything? After doing that, I started finding white men who loved servicing black men. Servicing means sucking or doing whatever black men desire. Sometimes they would respond back, saying they would like to suck my black cock. And some had changed their screen names by the time I responded. Do you, the listener, honestly think I am going to say no to a hot, wet mouth in exchange for the palm of my hand?

Fuck that shit! Bob: I will take the hot mouth behind curtain number two, please. After being molested, by my GAY ASS COUSIN!!, all my interactions with men I asserted my dominance over them. Wait, are you still judging me?

I don't care if you are male or female listening to this; just imagine being horny, like a dog in heat, and someone wanting to lick your clit or suck your cock with no reciprocation after a few conversations online. You may not admit it to me, but I can read your thoughts. If you smile, then that tells me everything I need to know about you!!!

"By rejecting someone like me, you're only deceiving yourself." Some of the men. I spoke to on AOL were typically men in high-profile or corporate roles who desire this type of fantasy. We would exchange cell phone numbers to take it to the next level. Their desire to be humiliated and be taught how to lick and suck a black man's cock and balls turns them on, surpassing anything they have ever "EXPERIENCED".

On July 7, 2024, I added this part in this chapter. I nearly forgot about this one couple I met residing in DeLand, FL. I met them in a chat group I created on AOL. I initially had a lengthy conversation with the husband before we exchanged cell phone numbers. Let us call him the gatekeeper, and I will explain what a gatekeeper is right now. In my interpretation, a gatekeeper is an individual who possesses the authority to determine who has the right to fuck his wife and who does not.

After two weeks had passed, he finally asked me to meet him. He told me to meet him at a gas station in Deland, Florida, near where he lived. I vividly remember being excited to meet him and wanting to be on time. I did not want to ruin things before I had the chance to meet his wife.

He met me at the gas station to make sure I was an actual person and to know what kind of car I drove. It seems important to him. I can relate to that because if I had pulled up in a beat-up old car, I am sure he would have said no, it is not happening. We sat in our cars and conversed, and he finally asked me to follow him. Reflecting, I was very naïve or trusting to follow a stranger to his home that I had never met. Did you just ask yourself, "Is this a white couple?

I hope you did not because that means you are not paying attention. I am laughing as I dictate this part of the chapter for you to read. My laughter comes from the fact that I was not naive; instead, I was as crazy as a crack addict, consuming alcohol, and smoking cigarettes near a gas station. Are you shaking your head right now? Because you should be while reading this part of the chapter. So here goes.

I followed him for about 30 minutes into a wooded area— yes, that's right, a wooded area— and then into an alley behind his home. I could have easily found myself with a group of white supremacists wanting to deep fry my black country trusting ass in a B.B.Q. pit for stupid peoples like me.

I did not see any cross-burnings or Confederate flags along the way, so I felt ok. Honestly, DeLand, FL, is known to harbor racist white people. Even though this period of my life occurred more than 20 years ago, not a damn thing has changed. He opened the gate so that we could drive into his backyard. We parked, and he asked me to wait in my car momentarily.

I am not sure why, but I did not feel suspicious. So, I waited patiently. He did not enter the main house directly because he also had a garage in his backyard that he had converted into a guesthouse. He stayed there for a short while, which made me nervous. Just as I was about to turn on the ignition, he came out, walked up to my car, and asked me to enter his guest house. I can tell you are paying attention because you are asking yourself questions.

Like, Cecil, what were you thinking? And to be honest, obviously, I was not. I am still laughing, and we will continue the rest of this story. Upon entering, I encountered his wife, whom I had never seen in a picture. Fortunately, she was attractive, and she and I sat down for a while and talked. Her husband said he would return, leaving us alone for a while. We must have been alone for about an hour, and that's when she trusted me enough to tell me what was happening. She revealed that her husband had a fantasy about her fucking black men. He will check in on us occasionally to see if we are getting along. She and I were getting along fine, and he left us alone again. This time, she told me a bit more, which made sense. He did this because he was having an affair and wanted something on her in case she divorced him.

She found out from some receipts left around the house and in his pants pockets. She also mentioned that she had been aware of his affair for over a year and had not said anything. I asked her why, and what she told me next made me concerned for my safety. She confided in me that she feared him and had no other options because he owned everything they had created together, including businesses, different ventures, and their home. She was also aware that he was hiding some of their money in an offshore account he thought she knew nothing about.

She found all of this by hiring a big-time private investigator. She could only pull this off without her husband's knowledge when her father gave her the money. At this point, I became angry because she seemed nice, just in a bad situation trying to make her husband happy.

She also mentioned that her husband had sexual preferences that she was not prepared for. Of course, my ears perked up like someone using one of those silent dog whistles and I asked well, what was it? She is hesitating and I was patient before she finally finished what she wanted to tell me. Cecil, there was one evening he wanted me to put my fist and arm in his ass. I asked her how she felt about it and her facial expression was of disgust.

The third time he visited us, I mentioned that I had a great conversation with her and would like to see her again. She and I agreed this would be my final visit, as I did not want to contribute to his repulsive behavior.

I am a hypocrite because, while this was happening, I was also married. At least I mentioned this before you gave it any thought. Ain't that a bitch? 10/18/2024 These kids now days don't have a clue of what we thought was THE SHIT back in the day, do they?

Anotha Sucka

I want 2
THANK YOU
for reading this book.

B efore you read this chapter, you must understand how difficult it was for Cecil to write about it.... So, here goes!

S O, be patient as he attempts to remember every little detail, okay? Additionally, if you read the entire chapter, you may think I am lying regarding the specifics of this chapter.

LET ME JUST SAY THIS:

If I had received any of the promises made to me by this person I am going to tell you about, I would not have been here to tell this story. I will also take a slightly different approach to tell you this story, beginning with the end instead of the beginning that will leave you saying, "YOU HAVE GOT TO BE KIDDING ME!!,"Before you start reading my explanation on how I nearly fell for the "CON ARTIST BITCH", that lived in St Augustine Florida. I need you to close your eyes and Imagine meeting someone on a well-known dating site.

This person who you see with your eyes closed told you they see untapped potential in you and wanted to invest in your dreams. In addition, ask for a list of what you need to achieve your goals.

I assured Beth over the phone that I would have that list ready for her when we meet face to face. If someone you have never met said what you just read, would you trust them or disregard their claims? I disregarded caution because I believe everyone is speaking the truth; otherwise, I might as well not trust anyone. I wanted to be confident and take advantage of a once-in-a-lifetime opportunity. So, I started to work on the list she mentioned.

Wait!!! Are you curious how long I have known Beth? So, are you? If so, it is none of your damn business and keep reading, okay! I don't like impatient people, "ARE YOU ONE OF THEM"? If that's the case, read another chapter and make this your last one.

SO, BUCKLE UP!

Because this chapter is all over the place, the memories popped into my head, down my arm, and into my finger, and I was typing it out for you to read. This won't be in chronological order. So, kiss my ass if I lose you at any point because I warned you before you started. Let us start with the $1.8 million home, followed by the Rolls Royce and then the Mercedes 12V, "shall we"!?

I worked with a guy named Jay for several years at a very established company in Altamonte Spring, Florida. I won't mention the name of that company in this chapter. He introduced me to his wife, Shelly, a real estate agent for CWB.

The entire time I was with her, she never made me feel as if she did not believe me when I mentioned the area and the price, I was willing to pay. She would have had every right to question where the money came from, especially when she knew the company I was working for and the pay rate. Let me just say this: I was ecstatic when I finally contacted Shelly to start searching for a home. In fact, I asked her to manage all my real estate transactions since I was planning to purchase more properties. She began researching enthusiastically within the pricing range and the neighborhood I was interested in. I had mentioned looking for what was available in the Alaqua Lakes area. I promise you there is not one home for under a million. After a few days, she called to tell me about several homes she thought I might be interested in viewing.

I wish I could remember the exact date and time we started house hunting, but that part's a blur. What I *do* remember are the three properties I walked through—and out of all of them, only one stuck. After some back-and-forth negotiations that nearly had me flipping a damn table, I closed the deal on a fully furnished home in Alaqua Lakes, Florida, for $1.8 million.

It contained six bedrooms, five bathrooms, and a theater room with a drop-down screen big enough to make Netflix feel like a red-carpet event. The furnished office came with a sleek desk, matching chair, built-in bookcases, and flooring that tied the whole room together like it was designed by somebody's interior decorator cousin. Now listen—don't shake your head—but I *really* wanted to keep that office furniture.

That setup was worth over $17,000. I know, I know... but I would've appreciated it. Seriously. The office alone was the size of a living room within a 15,000-square-foot home. I wanted to keep the office furnished just the way I had seen it. The kitchen had a Stainless Steel Thermador Freedom Refrigerator, with French doors that blended in with the cabinets right next to it. I Googled the cost of that refrigerator and that muthafucka, can cost up to "$20,000"!! Damn! The island that was in the middle of the kitchen was "SO DAMN BIG!!" that by the time I finished walking around it.. I would need a breathing apparatus over my face. I know. I know. I am EXAGGERATING, a little bit!

But you just imagined it, didn't you? Before I end this paragraph talking about the kitchen, imagine needing to wear roller skates to get around it while cooking. Does that help? Each bathroom had a walk-in shower and a double-marble vanity.

Don't you dare laugh or smile about what I am about to say next. When I looked down at the toilet there was a device on the side I had never seen before. I had to ask what that was and why there was a straw-looking thing in the middle of the water. The person I was with started laughing and told me she would tell me later. How in the hell was I supposed to know that it cleans the crack of your ass without toilet paper. Okay, "YOU CAN STOP LAUGHING NOW"! Seriously!! Say Reader!!!, I finally tried a bidet, and I did not like the feeling, just saying. I had flash backs of my "Gay Ass Cousin" See how trauma can come back to haunt you, unexpectedly?

It came with a five-car garage with flooring that matched the walls and ceiling. The cabinets to store your tools etc. is something I can't put into words right now. When I saw it, I planned to keep it completely furnished, which would cost me an additional

$120,000. From what I remember, this house was slightly over 10,000 square feet. Rumor had it that a few celebrities lived in this neighborhood, which also piqued my interest. Most importantly, it was a guarded community, which I found impressive.

You and I both know what it is like when those Jehovah Witnesses knock on your door unexpectedly. That's not happening in this neighborhood; I can promise you that. Remember Halloween? No kids are knocking on the door, either.

Best of all, no one shows up unannounced. Trick-ah-treaters were also not allowed in this gated community, which to me was another extra benefit I was looking forward to.

Oh My God!!! I had a thought while rewriting this section of the chapter on August 22, 2024. I just remembered something that may or may not be funny. We shall see, right?

After signing on the dotted line for the house I was considering buying, I was driving an old green pickup. So, I can only imagine how ridiculous it looked driving around in a white, wealthy community and looking at million-dollar houses. Pulling up in front of their house I bet reminded them of that classic television sitcom "The Beverly Hillbillies." Country as hell in a beat-up truck!!

Damn!! I found myself in a strange state of disconnection, feeling distant from reality, money, life, and the people I care about. In addition, before the real estate bubble, I planned to pay cash for two investment houses worth over half a million dollars. Please understand that I have no plans to write anything further about the house purchase. This was just additional info that wasn't included in "Vanilla Sheets."

Next, I remember driving from Orlando to Tampa to pay cash for a Rolls Royce, valued at around $240,000, previously driven by Johnnie Cochran. I can still see the salesman's expression when I mentioned wanting to buy the car. He had a slight sneer on his face, and I knew why, but I did not care that he was just another white boy who thought I was a drug dealer. Given his commission, he would not contest the purchase. Side note: I don't blame the salesperson for thinking I was a drug dealer or prostitute. Every movie and TV show I have watched consistently depicts us negatively in Hollywood. The question I still ask myself today, what dah hell was I thinking? I digress.

I wish I could remember who connected me to a vehicle broker representing numerous NBA players in Orlando. This individual was well-connected, and he vouched for us, saying that the Mercedes-Benz dealership only needed my signature to drive off the lot with a Mercedes 12V worth $178,000 for me and a red Mercedes-Benz SL 400 Roadster for her worth over $78,000.

After a few weeks had passed, they contacted me because Beth had not made a payment to the dealership. They demanded I return both automobiles after owning them for a few weeks. So, I drove to the dealership in the Mercedes 12VE, handed them the keys, and walked away. I told the dealership where they could find the Mercedes Roadster and gave them the address, and I assume they found it and towed it back to the dealership. After that, I never heard back from the vehicle broker who connected us with the dealership. Damn!! Fortunately, this did not escalate into an arrest case against me. I would like to take a moment to apologize to anyone who remembers and participated in this transaction. I am sure there were some awkward, unbelievable moments during this transaction.

Nonetheless, I must admit that while driving the Mercedes 12V. I felt like a baller, as in, I was acting like my shit did not stink, as my mother would say. Seeing how others perceived me when I drove a Mercedes 12V was always intriguing. I have included additional information here, even though it may not be necessary. On the interstate, I decided to test the speed of my 12V Mercedes.

With my eyes closed it felt like I had driven five miles in 30 seconds. Equally important, I never felt or heard a single gear shift, engine noise, or external disturbance. Now I understand why those of you who own one are such spoiled brats. Another day, I was driving through a nearby area and found speed bumps. The first time I drove over them at 25 mph, I could not believe what had happened. So, I pulled a U-turn and drove over them again at 45 mph. I felt no speed bumps at all. I had only driven one new truck in my life, so driving my Mercedes 12V was an entirely new level of luxury. Next, don't laugh, but fuck it; you can laugh if you want. I also considered buying a red Ford F-650 Super Truck for around $150,000.

Damn!! Was I materialistic, or what? Did you just nod your head, yes? Honestly, I don't blame you, one bit. Worse, I never considered how suspicious it would have looked when my house was only worth $79,000.

Here I am, driving a $178,000 Mercedes and intending to purchase a Ford F-650 Super Truck, all while residing in a black and Puerto Rican community with a small number of white residents. You know, the kind of neighborhood where nobody cares about their lawns while there are broken-down cars in the front yard. Besides, I could not understand why they never had their cars towed away. Another time, I remember having the Mercedes parked in front of my house, and numerous police officers stopped to check my license plate.

Fortunately, the address and license plate matched my own. They would have forced themselves through the front door with weapons drawn if there were inconsistencies. I did not understand why they did it then, but now I know why. I am confident that the police suspected I was A narcotics dealer. Even in 2024, their attitude remains unchanged. I recall one afternoon stopping by when I had quit working, and Beth was with me, making all these promises. I am laughing right now because I remember the expressions on my coworkers' faces. Nobody said anything unpleasant to my face about her since they all understood where I was coming from. I will discuss this later in the chapter. Even though I was materialistic, I wanted to help coworkers create businesses or achieve whatever goals they had set for themselves.

One man I used to work with, Jem, called me at least once or twice a day when he felt I had made some money. He told me a terrible, made-up story about his wife's health concerns while also expressing a desire to create a church. If he had seen my face on the phone, he would have cussed me out.

At the time, I would have trusted Joel, a coworker I addressed in a chapter named "Friends: How Many of Us Have One," and formed a business with him. Again, I would have regretted it since if a man can cheat on his wife with two lovely children and have a baby with another woman, what would stop that no-conscious lying ass porch negro from stealing from me? Not a dang thang!! Am I correct or wrong? Seriously!

Obviously, none of what you read above transpired, and here is why. Twenty-five years ago, I used a dating service named Match.com. I have nothing terrible to say about the site right now, nor will I say anything soon. Beth contacted me but did not include a photo of herself on her profile. Note that this is usually required;

otherwise, I won't respond. When Beth contacted me, I chose to talk to her.

She and I communicated on the phone for several weeks, leading me to believe, "she was genuine." So, after we chatted back and forth, I offered to meet, and she agreed. I wanted to drive to St. Augustine, but Beth visited me instead. After, she called to say she was on her way, which pleased me because our communication was excellent.

Shortly after Beth arrived, I looked out the window while Beth sat inside her car for a few minutes. Without appearing eager, I decided to sit back, relax, and wait till she knocked on the door. Upon opening the door, the woman's lack of attraction shocked me. First, she was shorter and heavier than her profile indicated, with one leg wrapped in some material. Despite our several weeks of chats and her driving from Daytona, Florida, I wasn't about to tell her to go home. Under my breath, I admitted that it was my fault for not asking for a photo before we met. As she walked past me, I politely asked her to come in and take a seat. (Just a second.) I am glad she did not turn around and look at my disgusted expression. I'm being respectful while describing Beth, because she is someone's daughter. I regret using the word disgusted and would like to clarify that it meant I did not find her attractive.

While sitting, she looked around my house, which made me uneasy. It appeared to me she was taking a visual snapshot while staring down the hallway into my bathroom. I chose to show her my house instead of my bedroom, and I also did not find her attractive, what's so ever! Before our meeting, I informed her that I operated a delivery service and parked my truck beside my house. She asked if she could see it, and I said absolutely. She complemented my home and business, and I felt better. She unexpectedly said she wanted to help me with business on her first visit.

I was stunned and did not know what to say except thank you. I asked why, and she responded that you have a business, a lovely home, and still employed. Beth also said that I should concentrate on your business instead. I am going to stop right here because the bottom line is that she was a scammer.

Let me explain how Beth managed to almost defraud me. I met her mother and stepfather in their home in St. Augustine and most of her family. They did not give me any indication that she was on medication. I spent the night at her house once and even went to dinner with her family; there were no red flags. So, when she said she was coming into some money, I did not think much of it.

This is not word-for-word, but it gives you an idea of what she told me and convinced me she was telling the truth. She opened a folder and showed me some clauses between her attorney and the hospital.

Though I did not read the paperwork, there were no red flags. After about three weeks, Beth called to say she had paid off my $79,000 home loan, and I was speechless. I even called the one eight hundred number, and they confirmed the debt was zero. How did she get my account information in the first place? Therefore, instead of conducting a thorough investigation, my excitement overshadowed my responsibility to follow up. Are you still reading this?

Go ahead and shake your head because what I say next will blow your mind. She also wrote me a check for $500,000, which I deposited into my bank then. While all of this was happening, I honestly thought someone would have tapped me on the shoulder and slapped my dumb gullible ass back to reality when this was going on. I called that bank twice daily to see if it had cleared yet.

Each time I called, the answers were the same: no, Mr. Hicks, the money has not cleared her bank, and I said OKAY. Do not ask me what I was thinking; I am shaking my head also as I tell you this story. Now, I saved the best for last because I trusted the information that Beth had told me. When this happened, I had just turned in my notice and walked away from the job I'd worked at for 36 years.

On August 23, 2024, at 9:19 PM, I added what you're about to read. I am hesitant to tell you the rest of this messed-up chapter. At this very moment, I'm breathing heavy questioning whether I should even keep telling you this story.

But I'm gonna go ahead and describe my experience. Maybe it'll give you an idea of where my head was.

Okay... I just took a deep breath.
Here's the rest of the story.

And I'll end this chapter by saying—I don't regret my experiences. Every single one of them helped shape me into the person I am today. It also helped me identify my friends—*or so I thought*.

After the incident, every one of them revealed who they really were. And for that reason alone, I'm grateful that none of what you just read ever materialized. Because if she had been honest If she had truly given me everything you just read about, I would've been a materialistic person than the one authoring this book. That whole situation humbled me. Next time I find myself in anything remotely like it, I'll move differently. My goals, my attitude toward life, even how I view wealth—all shifted.

My circle of friends shrunk faster than a bunch of men at a bachelor party with no alcohol, no food, and not a single naked girl to throw money at. I would've blown through the money she offered me. Quick. And based on some of the things I *haven't* told you yet and more than likely I would've ended up overdosing on cocaine. I also knew I would have gone to one of P. Diddy's parties when I thought I had all that money. Whoa!! I am not saying I would have done anything perverted, well maybe I would have but there would have been women in compromising positions. When this did not happen, many people laughed behind my back. It shocks me that people would desire someone else to fail. Like a movie once said, I am still standing, trying to improve and learn from my mistakes. Before you move on to the next chapter, let me explain why I was an easy target and what I have discovered about myself. I was raised around pimps and hustlers my entire teen life.

As I have said in "Pimpin' Ain't Easy," the white man knew precisely what they were producing when it came to black entertainment. The allure of cars, women, clothes, and jewelry convinced us that this symbolized success. It is wasteful spending that has carried over into what is happening right now. If you think I am kidding, just watch some of my videos on YouTube and anywhere social media platform.

I was influenced by all the stereotypical movies written and produced by white or Jewish men. They also glorified pimps and hustlers back in the day wearing fur coats, jewelry etc.

I am going to mention this again: if you take a moment and reflect on all the movies today, black folks are nothing but drug dealers who hate themselves and are not trying to improve their situation. Women will sell their soles for fortune and fame regardless of ethnicity. Just ask a music mogul who has sacrificed himself for fame. This is why I can understand the addiction to fame and money. Peace!

Everybody Plays the Fool Sometimes
The Main Ingredient

THE MAIN INGREDIENT
Arr. and cond. by Bert De Coteaux

An Ingredient Production L.T.D.
Produced by Silvester & Simmons
Production Supervised by Buzz Willis

STEREO
74-0731
APKS-5795

Giant
Enterprise,
BMI

3:22

**EVERYBODY PLAYS
THE FOOL**
(from the ''Bitter Sweet'' album)
(Clark-Bailey-Williams)

Authoritative Vs Degrading

BITCH!! DO YOU KNOW WHAT TIME IT IS?

I f you are a married couple and still having sex, I would like to offer one of my favorite things to do in a car.

And here is one of many different sexual acts you can do while in the car with your partner. Without her knowledge, I would plan a day together that would involve taking a long trip somewhere I planned. I would enter our closet and choose what I wanted her to wear. That also includes her accessories, believe it or not. I am also paying attention to her body language and facial expressions. This will let me know if she is excited about my plans. If she seemed excited, I would ask her to prepare snacks for this trip. I want her to feel she is also involved in the planning process. I bet you totally missed what I am trying to convey to you.

Allow me to break this down for you, okay? Asking her to prepare the snacks allows her to think about where we are going and what I have planned for her. In other words, she will be mentally stimulated and excited while preparing our snacks. Now that that has all been done, it is time to take that trip I have planned. Once she gets into the car and buckles up, it won't be long before I give her a look (like "The Rock.") as in, are you ready for what I have planned? When we travel together and expect the journey to last several hours, I will ask her to tease me while she removes her dress; the slower, the better.

Missy was the last person I told to do this for me. As she followed my every instruction, her enjoyment was evident from the red flush on her face. Let me give you a visual: her face was close to the color of a strawberry. Seriously! I can read your mind. Do you believe I exclusively date white women as you are reading this chapter? Well, I am not answering that question in this chapter. I mentioned why in another chapter called "**Pimpin' Ain't Ez**."

AUTHORITATIVE.

.

Back to Missy. Her shyness turned me on, so telling her to remove her dress in a firm, growling voice also turned her on. Wait!! No, the bat fuck you did not just ask yourself how I knew talking to her like that would turn her own. The reason I knew was because she was shaking nervously with excitement, with a devilish grin and most importantly I could visually see her panties were wet. Damn, you just asked yourself, how did I know she was wet, right? Because I asked her to open her legs, and I could see it. Does that answer your question? I hope so.

Now, can I continue? I knew Missy had never been asked to do anything like this because she blushed when I originally asked her when we first met. I spoke to Missy authoritatively, not demeaning; there is a clear distinction between the two. If you are a male reading this and don't know the difference, let me give you another example. Baby, take your pants off slowly, lean back, and play with your pussy. You better not cum until I tell you to. Now place your index finger inside your pussy and then pull out your finger and stick and put it in my mouth. Hey reader, yea you with this book in your hand, you betta not say that's nasty either, because you read it anyways, you could have stopped, right? And if you honestly thought I stopped there I told her to stick your wet cum- filled fingers in her mouth the way I like; you know what Daddy likes! Damn, you are turning me on. Now, which one is better? Obviously, this way, right?

DEGRADING...

Dumb ass bitch, just pull down your damn pants, will ya? Can't you just do what the hell I tell you without repeating myself? Damn, you are slow as shit, bitch! Wait! Everything depends on how she prefers to communicate sexually. You are the one who knows, so choose wisely, or it could be misinterpreted. I know this will be hard to believe. In my 66 years, I have never spoken to anyone like what you just read I don't do that shit because my mother raised me to be kind and a gentleman.

Being in this type of relationship was back in the day. Being sixty-five, I am mentally different these days and prefer to keep it that way. I have had enough women in my car and van back in the day who took off their panties from under their dresses, so from the waist down, they were obviously naked. I really don't need an energy drink if I am playing with my girlfriend's clit while I am driving. Listening to her in the car playing with herself while not looking over is also a nice tease.

During the entire time she is playing with her pussy, you might want to take a break. If you are one of those old asses married couples who have been together for so long that you have forgotten how to have fun, it is time to spice things up. I can't tell you how often I have met a woman over fifty without these experiences. It is unfortunate that, as a couple, you both develop the habit of fucking in bed and not anywhere else in the house. What a waste of years you two have been together.

How do two freaky-ass people end up just having sex in the bedroom? If you both decide to continue having sex in the bedroom, that's fine, I suppose. However, if you both still harbor sexual fantasies, it is essential to discuss them. I would not want to be in a relationship where every time I considered or initiated sex, all I heard was, "We need to wait until we get home.

" I can assure you that a person who consistently hears the phrase "wait till we get home" will eventually find someone who will say yes, let us go for it. This section is dedicated to all the men who, despite having a beautiful woman at home, still feel the urge to engage in sexual activity and fabricate lies about their relationships. You vanilla folks need some serious counseling. Swinging is unique in that it involves a mutual decision between two mature adults to engage in sexual activity with others. However, if a man, despite having an attractive wife or girlfriend at home, still feels the need to engage in sexual activity and, as I mentioned earlier, lies about it, it clearly indicates a lack of self-love, and there are consequences for such behavior.

If you are a male reading this right now, please check your attitude and give me a minute with an open mind. If you are a woman who feels compelled to share this, please do so. Ladies, keep this in mind. A man's ego will usually keep him from listening to you. This is the essence of my message to men.

It's no way in hell you can call yourself a man who has a freaky significant other that will suck and swallow your cum with a smile, gag on your cock till tears run down her eyes, beg to be slapped on her face with your cock and balls against her face, pull her hair.

At the same time, you can also stick your cock or dildo in her in the ass, and you mean to tell me you still feel the desire to sleep with another woman, seriously? She will let you do all the above because she trusts you. And man to man, if you are getting bored with your partner, at least try some role-playing. Spend some time together at a strip club clothing outlet or an adult novelty store in your city.

Alternatively, utilize your creativity to discover something you believe would pique her interest on the internet. Oh, I failed to mention earlier that if, by chance, she has had a few children, she may not feel sexy anymore, so tread lightly. If necessary, search Google or Bing for sexy clothes or garments for her. Hopefully, the time you put into this idea won't go unrewarded. If she notices your effort, who knows? Imagine her as a stranger and create a unique name if she is game.

THIS CHAPTER TAUGHT ME A LOT ABOUT MYSELF.

I have seriously tried to reflect since the day I started dating, and I have never intentionally talked to any woman or person in a demeaning way. It does not matter if the conversation concerns a known individual or a stranger; I won't tolerate such behavior. Suppose a man feels comfortable speaking to a woman in a demeaning manner. In that case, I will hold the woman or women responsible for allowing and enduring such behavior.

However, it is crucial to consider the woman's or man's upbringing and experiences. Too often, a woman or women will stay in an abusive relationship unnecessarily, and I attribute that also to their parents, but that's just me. Sometimes, a person can say something demeaning without even realizing it.

I want to also discuss unintentional demeaning behavior, also known as microaggression.

This part of the chapter unexpectedly entered my mind on 08/24/2024. Allow me to elaborate. okay? When a person unknowingly speaks to another person in a demeaning way, it is because of the environment they grew up in. I vaguely recall my childhood, when my father treated my mother more like a servant than a wife. Of course, that seemed normal at the time, even though it wasn't. Five days before my birthday, 08/24/2024, I am appalled to reflect on it. I don't know why my father spoke to her like that, and every time my mother just cried a little and shut the door, I could not see her. Unknowingly, this can also occur when the family does not know better. For some, it is just a way of life.

Can you relate? I surely hope you, as the reader, can't relate to what I just said. And if you can, I would like to apologize on their behalf, even though they don't deserve it. Additionally, the men I am referring to have been players for their entire lives. Given the current trend of women gravitating towards attractive men, it is not surprising that these players have such a mindset.

There was this one time when I was at a nightclub here in Florida with a male friend I knew. All he had to do was stand against the door, and women would stop what they were doing and speak to him. All he had to do was nod and smile, and they would give him their number. Of course, he kindly accepted.

Back in high school, I met a guy named WB, and I am sure you will recognize him. He did not need to do anything to entice women to give him their numbers. Most of those girls gave him money, bought clothes, and anything he wanted. There needed to be more time to decide how to treat each individually.

Finally, they possess superior knowledge and show no concern! If the women don't intend to rectify the situation, why should they be concerned? Let us stray from the topic for a moment. I once worked as a delivery driver for a furniture company in the Orlando, Florida, area. I witnessed a man yelling and pushing a woman against a wall. My natural instincts kicked in immediately, and I yelled, "

Hey, don't lay another hand on her, or else I will call the police. The only reason I am mentioning this to you right now is for one reason and one reason only no one has the right to be demeaning or threatening towards another person, and I don't give a damn about who you are.

As I was proofreading this on 01/07/2025, a thought popped into my head that I'd love to share with you. I'd love to hear if it resonates with you, so just let me know, alright? It's important for two mature, loving adults to always communicate without raising their voices or being disrespectful to each other. It can be tough to break that cycle, especially based on how your parents raised you both.

In any relationship I've been in, I never lose respect for myself by raising my voice. If you're dating someone who feels the need to know everything you're doing, that's definitely a red flag.

I really don't care about how they look or what they have down there; it's just not worth the hassle. I'm confident in saying this based on my experience!

There was a time when I encountered some experiences that nearly made me question my self-respect. I'm proud of who I've become, and there's no way I'm letting anyone take that away from me. That should be part of your daily wellbeing routine. Peace!!

.

Backstabbing MF'S

They Smile In Your Face
The Backstabbers – O'Jays

WARNING:

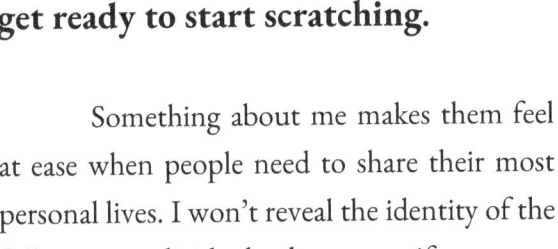

I have A.D.D, so be patient while reading this boring chapter. I just may bounce all over the place like fleas on a dog. So, get ready to start scratching.

Something about me makes them feel at ease when people need to share their most personal lives. I won't reveal the identity of the following individuals; however, if you are familiar with me personally, you might be able to figure out who the hell I am referring to effortlessly. I would not confirm the identity of the person I am referring to. I am going to share a true story that has deeply affected me. It is important to share.

As this book demonstrates, I have always been a freaky person. I avoid discussing this with friends, coworkers, and acquaintances, fearing judgment, and misinterpreting my decisions. If I were to disclose anything about myself, it would be because I felt safe and trusted the person. At this point in my life, it should come as no surprise that I don't give a damn any longer, right? Continue reading, please. One morning, I felt comfortable telling a coworker named Joel something private. I decided to describe one sexual exploration story from my childhood (involving a dog).

He was the first and only person I had ever related this story to in fifty years. As soon as I was halfway through the story, it became clear that he wasn't who I thought he was. I expected Joel to say something like, "Wow! Man! How long ago was that?" This would have allowed me to provide a detailed explanation; however, he deceived me, causing me to feel ashamed, uncomfortable, and embarrassed, and I immediately shut down. A friend of mine said: I guess you messed around and found out that whatever you feel is personal information, you should not even trust who you think is your best friend.

Honestly, I would have to agree with him. I knew things about him without judgment, and yet he could not, or would not, treat me the same way I treated him with respect. Since then, I have learned that you should not call anyone a best friend unless you know they won't judge you and are willing to take your secret to the grave with them. It is hard to believe that this was the same mutha sucka individual who had been unfaithful to his wife and openly flaunted his affair among his coworkers, even though he was completely transparent about it.

Despite having a lovely wife and children who loved him and behaved well at home, he shamelessly indulged in extramarital affairs. Consequently, he had a child with an unmarried coworker. This man, or, I should say, child, has absolutely no sense of morality under any circumstances. More than likely, he lied to the side piece of ass for a while too. However, she eventually realized he would not abandon his wife for her.

This mutha-sucka ended up getting his side piece of ass, pregnant!! Not only did he flaunt his affair among his coworkers, but he got her pregnant. Any self-respecting man who loved himself would not feel the desire to sleep around, period! I should know because I have cheated also. And before you call me a hypocrite, I did not have a successful real estate business., kids and a submissive wife at home waiting for me to return home safely. I know, ladies, cheating is wrong, period. I get that totally. There is a time when you can't be selfish when you are the primary provider.

I remember one morning before I realized what was happening when they would go around the side of the aisle and talk. I was skeptical then. While working with Joel, they always smiled and grinned when they saw each other before I realized what was happening. I have never been around anyone like Joel who does not disguise their affair.

Damn, I just realized why I am so pissed off about his affair. It reminds me of my own dysfunctional family. The lies and cheating were so disgusting and blatant when I was growing up. When he was expected to pick up his child from the side piece's location, he brought that child around his wife and children. Bold mutha fucka huh? It is like shitting in the living room while your wife and kids watch.

Then, expect them to ignore it and not have a say in the stench in the house. Men like this will eventually get what they deserve. Let us make it sooner than later.

If you happen to still be married TO THE SAME WOMAN Joel, that's why I added you in this chapter, bitch!!! I am sure THE KIDS privately talked about it and understood their mother wasn't or had not been pregnant. I'm sure they were perplexed and inquisitive about the identity of the baby their father brought home suddenly.

Unless he was honest about his affair with his kids, which I am sure he wasn't, they will have many unanswered questions. Regarding the publication date of this book, we will have to wait and observe the long-term impact of his actions on the level of maturity his children attain. There wasn't a single instance in which I made Joel feel awful about his lack of judgment or what he was doing to his family.

Despite this, he condemned me for something I had done fifty years ago, which I consider a terrible betrayal and a humbling experience. You can only tell if a friend is real or phony once you are open enough to tell them something extremely private. His response caused me to withdraw from others even more. Another friend of mine once said: You can never trust anyone like him. Frank was another negro who I worked with at the exact location.

He made some offensive remarks behind my back at a time when I was experiencing the lowest point in my life. Indeed, he was also a friend of mine. I will explain my mistake in the following paragraph.

** I am adding this part of the chapter below now because it will all make sense after reading this paragraph. So, just hang in there before I continue talking about Frank. I once thought I was on the verge of striking it rich, which led me to take a leap of faith and leave my job behind. Unfortunately, it turned out to be fraud.

I was deceived about someone's wealth, which led to the unraveling of the situation. Once I realized it was fraud, I asked someone from upper management about returning to work. I was extremely fortunate that the person I spoke to allowed me to return as if I had not quit my job. I will forever be grateful, and I will never forget him. I dive deeper into this topic in a chapter named. "Anotha Sucka", if you have not already, read it.

Let's return to my so-called "friend" named Frank, who couldn't resist kicking me while I was down after hearing I was returning to work. Keep in mind, you may already have a friend like Frank, but you will only realize it once it is too late. Only haters like him will step out of the gutter infested with maggots if they think they have something on you.

They are waiting patiently for your demise, and that's their moment to gloat. Do you recall the paragraph mentioned? The Scam I fell victim to? I still intend to discuss this in my upcoming chapter, "Another-Sucka." I quit my job of thirty plus years, because of this scammer. And also, because I thought she wanted to help me with my business and pay off my home. Anyway, it was all a lie, and I had to ask for my job back.

When Frank heard, I was returning to work, he showed his true colors. There was this one morning at his job during breaktime, where he was already plotting his revenge to humiliate me while everyone was in the break room. He was saying messed-up shit about me, which made everyone around him laugh about my return.

It is assholes like Frank that give the work friends a bad name if you know what I mean. I should have anticipated this, as he frequently lacks a positive outlook. Frank may not necessarily agree with me for saying this in this part of the chapter. Still, honestly, if he were a positive person and loved himself, he would not talk badly about me or anyone else.

In fact, he was talking so badly about me in the breakroom at work that a manager overheard him and had to walk in and tell him to shut up. Like buzzards, people like him attach their claws to a branch and wait for you or someone else to fail.

It makes them feel better about themselves, I suppose. Even when this same asshole disclosed that he had previously smoked crack, I refrained from making any disparaging remarks. He was also comfortable enough to tell me he messed around behind his wife's back, usually while she was at work. That gave me the impression that he would not hesitate to meet this woman, a friend of mine. She was game, and she trusted me enough to invite Frank over. He walked in, liked what he saw, played with her pussy a little bit with one of his fingers, and left. I was like, are you kidding me?

That's it. All fluff, no action. Suppose you are a male reading this part of the chapter and have fantasized about being in a ménage trios. In that case, it won't be easy when you have never been in that situation. Anyway, I have met Frank's wife a few times. Even then, I kept his secrets because it was no one else's business, nor what he did with anyone else.

It is funny how this same person was the first one to kick me while I was down and out, but at the same time, he told me his private shit and expected me to never repeat his private stories. So, if you are reading this chapter, Mr., here is a toast to you. I hope she reads this, bitch number two!! When I occasionally see him working, I am always cordial. I will smile and say to myself, what a piece of shit he is.

Despite these thoughts, I have never shared any details of his private life with anyone before this book. I will refrain from mentioning the real names of Frank or Joel; they know who the hell they are. Hopefully, Frank's wife will forgive him even after reading this book.

THIS IS AN UPDATE WRITTEN ON, MAY 2, 2024

I realized I neglected to mention this in my previous memoir, which was published on December 8, 2022. Yes, was another moment in time when Frank did the unthinkable:

One day, while working on the front end, we would check out the ladies and yell out a number as they stood in our checkout lines. If he or I said 3 (three), that meant to check out the third lady in our lines. Anyway, there was this one black woman I was checking out (in other words, flirting with), and she was also checking me out. Regrettably, she was in his lane while he rang up her purchases. When I smiled, she smiled back, and I was hoping she would come over to introduce herself.

She decided to ask Frank who I was and what my name was. I only know this because Frank turned around and briefly glanced at me.

At this point, her direct gaze indicated that he was conversing with her. After Frank finished ringing up her merchandise, she simply turned around, as if we were not flirting, and walked away. I wasn't sure what had happened, and I was curious to know what he had said to her. Frank finally admitted the truth when I asked him about the black woman who came through his line. He asked her if she had gone to a Frankie, Beveryly, and Maze concert, and she admitted yes.

He mentioned that I had brought a white girl to that concert; that was all the information she needed to hear. She turned around and walked away without looking back, and I never saw her again. I became so enraged that I resolved to exact my revenge one day. This is the same bitch ass mutha fucka who asked if I dated black women but sabotaged my chance to date a black woman.

Go figure. If you are wondering why I decided to add this update now, here is a simple explanation. I felt a unique connection with that customer, unlike any other woman who had shopped at the company where I worked for over 40 years. And because Frank is a hater and a pussy blocker; he destroyed the possibility of me dating her. Frank's big mouth will always remain a mystery, won't it?

Since I am rewriting this on 08/07/2025 a thought came to me that I could easily add to Franks hating mentality. He would be that same nigga singing we shall overcome with all the slaves while carefully listening to what the slave our planning and run and tell the slave owner, "hey boss they planning on leaving this great place I call home boss, get my drift?

Porch niggas!!

This individual changed the direction of my journey; do you understand? Be careful what you share with someone—if you have already told them something confidential. Bottom line: Only one person can judge another, and that's the almighty person above. Besides that, no one else on this planet has the right to judge someone based on their personal discretion. I began to realize that most people have their own agendas.

You must follow your own path because there will always be someone around who will disagree and try to derail your ideas and dreams. I know that not everyone will understand or buy this book, and that's okay; I am doing this for myself.

Currently, I have two close female friends named Sara and Lynn. Sara and I once dated, but now we are nonsexual friends, a status we both find appealing. We talked about our escapades—hers and mine. When she talks about the men, she is sleeping with, it does not faze me because I enjoy listening to her talk about them. Real friends stay connected one way or another and make sure the other is doing okay. To me, that's real love and friendship. Here is an update on my friendship with Sara. She is no longer someone I would call my friend. If you ask me, does she know this, I will have to say, NO!!!

My reason is simple, because if I told her how I feel about something she did, she would turn it around and make me the bad person just for mentioning it. So, FUCK THAT! I'll just keep it to myself. Since the first book was written, I have had no reason to ever talk to the two niggas that I mentioned in this chapter. One of them read my book, and I did not know it. When I texted Joel about it, he confirmed he had read it. The tone in his voice told me everything I needed to know, and, I must have pinched a nerve. But that wouldn't have happened if the Mutha-fucka had simply been an honest man with his wife, or more accurately, with all parties involved, right?

Should he choose to read this version of the memoir? I have always believed that best friends support each other through tough times and secrets shared. Something Joel or Frank, don't know anything about. My choice of friends significantly influences my relationship with my family. When I think about it, I have abandonment anxiety.

So, I keep choosing friends who share my family's characteristics, but none of us are close. Go figure. I forgot to mention what happened to Lynn, didn't I? Well, she and I don't communicate anymore, either. Once she found someone to date, that was it. I attempted to reach out to her several times, but once again, I found myself calling her more than she calls me. However, as I mentioned previously, some individuals only exist in your life for a specific period, not for the entirety of your existence. I am willing to accept that.

Just pause for a moment; there was another individual I mistakenly believed to be my friend, only to discover later that he wasn't. This is my final thought: many of you call someone your friend, but the only way to find out is to act like you need them. Then, sit back and wait to see if they are willing to help you in any way possible. This seems like a game, but it is better to apologize than to find out your "friend" won't help you.

With half a hand, I can count on my friends. Isn't it amusing that many of you refer to yourselves as friends to someone? Yet, you need to figure out which individuals can maintain a connection with, that's genuine. The moral of this story is to enjoy whoever comes into your life if they seem genuinely interested. By the way, since rewriting this book, I have realized that some people come into your life for a segment of it, not the rest of it. I have struggled to find someone who supports me as much as I support them. This will be my final paragraph regarding Backstabbing Co-Workers.

They will work side by side with you, laugh with you and sometimes seem genuine. But!!! the moment you hit rock bottom or tell them about the darkest moment in your life they turn that against you. My suggestion would be, don't trust anybody at your workplace. I know this from experiences I have already shared with you. Obviously, what they have done affected me in such a philosophical way as I included them in this book purposely. You know who the hell they are if you know me personally. These two mutha-fuckas I mention in this chapter are the reasons I do not have male friends today.

I DEDICATE THIS IMAGE TO THE 2 BITCHES I USE TO WORK WITH.

Bad Boys and Good Girls

I t's fascinating to me how women often gravitate, towards individuals with a bad boy mentality, as this mindset usually equates to being a "manipulative person"!

Bad boys typically exhibit a carefree attitude, have at least two other women in their lives for several reasons, and occasionally engage in sleeping with another woman. This is the playbook I am about to reveal and discard, as I no longer employ any of these strategies. Ladies!!!, if you see a good-looking man with his shit together, you can be sure that he is sleeping with another woman and if I am going to be politically correct or another man somewhere nearby. "When I say he has his shit together", ...I mean he has charisma, and he takes care of himself both emotionally and physically.

He can make you laugh out loud and hold your interest without bringing up sleeping with you. He also has good taste in clothes, a roof over his head, and a nice car. Once more, I am positive... that, this Mofo has at least one fuck friend within a half hour drive. **(I am certainly aware I repeated myself just said it differently for a reason)** If he invites you to come over to his place, you may find some evidence of another woman, if you are looking for it. Keep in mind, if you happen to see anything that makes you uncomfortable say something about it.

But!!! that all depends on the type of relationship you have with him also. Otherwise, mind your own damn business. When I am at a park people watching, there are often times I could tell when a girl has low self-esteem. Now!!! I have been known to be wrong but not that often. The low self-esteem woman or girl, usually ends up with a boy or man, that I am about to describe:

These girls believe that a guy wearing saggy pants, sporting a fake gold grill in his mouth, and driving a car with gold thirty-inch rims is the epitome of a gentleman. How about those bad boys who have on-wife-beater T-shirts, but don't have a toilet to shit in while living with, their mommas? Some girls may find such attire appealing, and that is perfectly acceptable. Still, I find it challenging to comprehend the attraction behind it. I seriously consider these types of girls to be hood rats! There is someone for everyone, and that is fine; it is their preference.

I understand, seriously I do. A trusted man should strive to be brutally honest from the beginning and, under no circumstances, lie about anything. If a woman is interested in knowing if you are sexually active, your response should be "Yes, particularly if it involves someone you are sleeping with occasionally." In addition, keep your romantic relationship intact. Do not say whatever you think she wants to hear. If you are a fake ass mutha fucka, you will make life difficult for every man who enters her life after you deceive her. Any woman who is considering the idea of getting married with a single male, she should inquire about his past sexual relationships.

Wait! Wait! Wait! I am not talking about a kid jacking off while looking at a centerfold model in a "Dirty Magazine," either. If he says it has been within a month, I will say that is an honest man. As the woman, you must figure out if you still want to be involved with him or decide to hook up with him occasionally as a booty call. I reiterate that regardless of your preference, it is crucial to consider that he has at least one or two women nearby, with whom he occasionally engages in sexual activity.

Please refrain from attempting to establish a relationship with this narcissistic asshole, as you are under the impression that you will be the sole woman in his life.

I am sure he knows of some decent pussy within a ten- to fifteen-mile radius of his residence. The chances of him not seeing someone else is rare. It could also be a warning or, should I say, a sign of behavioral problems or, he PREFERS MEN! I have never been able to understand how women could consider a long-lasting relationship with a bad boy.

LADIES! Before getting involved with this type of man, I am certain YOUR instincts are screaming aloud, WHAT THE FUCK ARE YOU DOING!! "He's going to screw me over at some point or another." If your claim is supported by evidence, pack up and leave. He knows you won't because, either he is supporting your dreams or his dick and tongue is so good, you stay longer than you should have.

Here is my list of characteristics that a man with confidence should possess.

- He is committed and made some mistakes but has learned from them.

- Frequently, they have had a rough or traumatic past, which has caused them to build up resilience.

- People don't care what others think; they value themselves more.

- The individual possesses a robust moral compass, demonstrating ethical compassion and a genuine desire to contribute to the betterment of society.

- They remain confident in themselves and their goals and are not intimidated by others' success or attention.

- Confident men are not scared to say no and mean it; they know when to say no and stick to it. They won't back down from their principles or put up with rudeness.

- Their unwavering determination to tolerate only what they deserve attracts others. It propels them to success in all aspects of their lives.

- They prioritize their time better because they don't shift their boundaries, which makes others value their time and attention more.

- They take criticism and comments very seriously, trying their hardest to learn from them instead of letting them get to them.
  - They evaluate its veracity and welcome constructive criticism.
  - If it is spiteful and inaccurate, it merely highlights the insecurity and resentment of the person making it.
- They can use it as a free evaluation to improve if it is accurate and worthwhile. A fully self-assured man embraces criticism rather than running from it.
- Being in the present allows people to change things and impact on those around them rather than dwelling on the past or the future.
- Does not check his cell phone while having sex.
- Explains himself so that he is not misunderstood.
- Expresses his feelings and allows himself to be vulnerable.
- Never has a problem of a woman expressing herself.

Focusing on the present, individuals actively strive for personal development and proceed to the subsequent task, ensuring they recognize the gravity of the situation. They accept responsibility for their actions, keep promises, and show respect for others' time. He maintains the general mindset of a self-assured man willing to acknowledge his mistakes and strive to make apologies.

He believes he controls his life, the actions of others don't affect his happiness, and he won't make excuses for his mistakes. The confidence that a person can complete activities and reach goals is known as self-efficacy, and accountability supports it. The man who is sure of himself talks with a certain amount of self-assurance. He wants to know your thoughts, not how you react or agree. He has the standard, measured flow you see in old Hollywood legends. Self-assured guys don't flinch when other people look at them. They are rarely aggressive and usually friendly.

On the other hand, they give off an air of confidence and calm neutrality that does not ask for or expect anything from others. They also don't look down often, especially when someone looks at them or walks by. They keep their eyes straight!

Self-assured guys don't flinch when other people look at them. They are rarely aggressive and usually friendly. On the other hand, they give off an air of confidence and calm neutrality that does not ask for or expect anything from others.

Confident men use precise, meaningful gestures to emphasize their points. They don't gasp, hoot, or hoot and holler at the first sign of surprise or shock, and they don't use phrases like "holy crap," "damn man," and other juvenile terminology. As I noted in the previous point, a confident man is poised and avoids excessive or erratic movements. He knows his direction and does not ask for permission or approval from anybody. Ladies, if a monogamous relationship is your preference, there is no way in hell you are going to change him, until he is ready to change for himself.

You have a couple of choices: you can either shut up and keep seeing him or move on. Here is my thought: if you have a gut feeling that makes you uncomfortable early in the relationship, why stress about something you don't have control over? Is that one man worth all that? Ladies! let us keep it real with one another "SHALL WE"?? If a guy looks attractive to you, other women will look at him, too. More than likely, they are thinking to themselves, "He's fuckable."

He may not be married, but he is sleeping with another woman somewhere. (I know I know I know but some of ya'll need to hear it or read it several times before it sinks in) If he discloses his sexual involvement to you before you fuck him, then you should appreciate his honesty. It gives you an opportunity to make a choice of what is going to work best for your current situation. When women don't ask the question, they usually don't want to hear the truth.

A confident man can appreciate directness; ask if it is important to you. He is entitled to ask you the same question and receive an honest answer. I have realized that some women can turn off their sexual desires for months and, in some cases, years. That all depends on how the earlier relationship ended. Hey ladies, take your time before getting involved with a man, keep things simple, and only engage with someone honest from the start. More than likely, not everything will be ideal; just evaluate what is important to you and your journey going forward. Earlier in my life, I had juggled five or six women at a time. T here is one thing I never did was lie about it. Fortunately, no one ever specifically asked me how many women I was seeing at the same time. If someone had asked, I would have been honest. I always told the truth, and sometimes it pissed off the woman who asked. I often thought to myself, "Well, damn, you asked me." From my perspective, a trustworthy man is typically a nerdy, big, fat, and unhealthy eater. He earns below-average money, has four inches of erect cock, and rarely cleans his own ass. Yes, I can assure you that he only engages in sexual activities with prostitutes.

So, if you want to get involved with that sucka, rest assured that he won't be out there slinging his cock around like the married man I mentioned in another chapter. He will worship the ground, you, walk on. I have had my fair share of encounters with attractive women, and when I do, I always keep in mind that they might be involved with someone else. I have always said that if she is giving me some of her attention, which is all I need. I don't give a damn who else she is fucking or hanging out with; I am okay with being among the men she likes fucking or visiting.

I don't want or need to be all up in her business if she is giving me the pussy, or better yet, the ass too. And what about these jealous bitch-ass mutha fucka's with attractive girlfriends? You know, the ones when another man is walking towards them, he reaches out for her hand, then pulls her closer to put his hand her waist or back pocket. That shit right there has insecurities written all over it in plane site. Ladies, you have officially been warned and thank me later.

Because I just saved your life or kept you from a beating you may never recover from. I've seen it happen so many times when I approach a couple. To me, that says they might as well swap lower body parts in that relationship. How can a man be with an attractive partner and think nobody should look at her? From my perspective, if I'm not the right fit for this woman, that's fine—I'll find someone else. I don't think I'm all that for every woman. In fact, I know I'm not What I don't understand is men who lack confidence in their relationships. Guys—be honest. When you first met the woman, you're with right now, did you find her attractive?

If yes, do you really expect other men to ignore her just because she's with you now??As far back as I can recall, I did not deliberately seek out someone who did not pique my interest. Here is another thing I can't understand: if you are the man having sex with her, why should it matter what she wears if it is sexy and classy? If either one of you has jealous tendencies, please seek a therapist as soon as possible.

Two times in my life, I have felt jealousy creeping into my head. As soon as I realized it, I checked myself, and it did not happen again. I have one more thought that I would like to share with you. I knew a white woman who had the physique of a black woman, based on the assumption that most black women have large asses. We were at a movie theater, and she bought popcorn because I had already purchased the tickets. As she was leaving, I noticed two women glancing at her and conversing among themselves. Do you think I became jealous?

The answer is hell no. In fact, I looked at the two women, and I smiled. My white woman's ass was phat. I never told her why I bought tight-fitting jeans for her. Sometimes, I intentionally let her walk ahead of me, and I am sure you know why. And if you don't, I will tell you why, because she had this big, juicy PHAT ass. I even saw a man get slapped by the woman he was walking with. No, I don't have jealousy issues, obviously. Peace!

Big Clitoris & Black Freak

I met a white woman named Lexie, who lived in Florida and was married to a truck driver.

By the way, from time to time when I refer to the race of the woman, I am purposely keeping you from wondering if she is or is not, white or black. He was okay with his wife occasionally searching for black men on the Internet, who would come to their apartment and fuck her.

After a few discussions back and forth, she invited me to visit her. And before the door was shut and locked, LEXIE! warned me about her huge clit and pussy lips right away, while I stood there like a deer in headlights.

I thought it was odd and unnecessary. It immediately became apparent to me why Lexie needed to warn me as I entered her apartment. Excuse me a minute, here is the jacked-up part about this story you are reading. Everyone she encountered laughed or became shocked, turned around, and exited her apartment expeditiously.

And to add insult to injury, she could hear their car tires screeching, just to hurry and leave her apartment development like at a drifting car show that white people tend to go to. Did you laugh, or at least smile? Thanks!! I stepped in and sat on the couch. She was reluctant, so we talked briefly to help her feel comfortable.

Face-to-face communication is fundamentally different from phone communication. Lexie's body language said everything I needed to know. I asked her to stand in front of me, but she hesitated. I was okay with that because I understood where it came from. She finally stood up and removed her dress; her face was red "LIKE A FIRETRUCK"! I admit when Lexie lowered her dress to the floor and showed me her pussy lips.

My mouth and eyes turned into that character Jim Carrey plays in the MASK! Oh my God, it turned me on like you would not believe! She had the most enormous pussy lips and clit I had ever seen on a woman. Despite its apparent freak of nature beyond anything I have ever seen, its uniqueness captivated me. As I already stated, there is something wrong with me. Her enormous, thick, sloppy-looking pussy lips turned me on, and she became even more turned on. She was willing to try anything after seeing how open-minded I was.

While there, I reached for my phone from my front pocket and contacted another strange black lady named Natasha, whom I had met online. I invited her to join me at Lexie's house. When Natasha walked in, I did not waste any time and urged Lexie to remove Natasha's clothing. It was quick because Natasha wore a sundress with no underwear or bra. I instructed Natasha to face Lexie so that she could hoist her dress up and over her head with her arms in the air. Lexie and I both became thrilled as soon as Natasha's dress passed her nipples. I told Natasha and Lexie to start eating each other's pussy, and they did so without hesitation.

While they were on the floor, a thought occurred to "me". I directed them both to lie down on their backs while I obtained the double-headed dildo. I packed one, just in case. I pushed one end into Natasha and the other into Lexie, my palm in the center of the dildo moving back and forth, fucking both of their pussies simultaneously. She lived in a hallway with her apartment right in the middle, so I am confident the neighbors heard everything.

They both wanted to suck my cock, which surprised me. Unbelievably, I started to feel shy. I knew Lexie had a good time because she contacted her husband while he was still driving and told him about our evening together. I am sure he was jacking off while she was telling him what occurred.

That was the first and only time I had ever done it. I never saw either woman again, but I had such vivid recollections. Me, Lexie and Natasha had a good time. I most certainly believe there are women who fuck themselves with double-headed dildos. By the way, if you don't have an imagination, let me help if, that's okay. It's a dildo with a shape of a cock head on both ends.

Take out your favorite lube and use it on both ends. Now, slowly put one end of that dildo in your pussy and the other end of it, in your ass. And, if you happen to be a talented little "BITCH! you should be able to fuck yourself and have an orgasm. Excuse me! I just turned myself on writing this last sentence for you to read. "GO FIGURE"!!

IF ANY OF THE LADIES READING THIS NEED HELP, OR IF YOU NEED ASSISTANCE HOLDING THE DILDO, YOU KNOW WHERE TO FIND ME.

Saving the best for last, since I did not mention this earlier, I never saw them again. I told Lexie and Natasha to get on the floor and bend over doggie style in a commanding firm "ALPHA VOICE". I had them turn in the opposite direction with the bottoms of their feet touching. Then, I commanded Lexie and Natasha to arch their backs like a threatened cat and place their elbows on the floor. That's when I pulled out a different double-headed dildo. Of course, I lubed up both ends of the dildo as I previously mentioned and slid one end into Lexie's ass and the other into "Natasha's "pussy".

I used one hand wrapped around the middle of the dildo and I played them both with it. I will admit it: There was a lot of screaming and hollowing in that small apartment. Sometimes, I wish I knew where all these ideas originated from. Back then, I wasn't watching porn to obtain these ideas, and neither were my parents nor my homosexual cousin. I am confident that whoever reads this has accomplished more than I have.

One day, I aspire to host a conference with just the freakiest people on earth, all under one roof, one love. Women reading this chapter will find this section especially relevant. Nobody should ever make you feel ashamed of your body under any circumstances. You must remember that no two bodies are identical unless you are twins. Even so, there may be slight differences.

When meeting someone for the first time and you have something about yourself that makes you uncomfortable, tell them immediately. Otherwise, you may experience what Lexie experienced with a lack of body confidence. Oh, and the bottom line is that women should love and embrace the aging process. If you are over fifty, shit changes that you either have control over or don't.

Hold your head up and don't give a damn what anyone is thinking. Those are the same people who are insecure about themselves in other areas. Oh, there is one thing I almost forgot to mention... Peace!

Busted

B

y The Way: I dedicate this chapter to those who are over fifty years old. Because on 01/02/2025:

I just remembered something embarrassing I will share with you. Yes, you who else is reading this right now huh? There was this one late evening I thought my first wife was sleeping and I decided to sneak out of the bed and then, our bedroom. I opened the door and closed it behind me.

If she had one eye open watching me, she would swear that I was up to no good. "Well, "I was". sort of".

I was hornier than a male dog with his cock still in the female's dog's ass and can't pull out until someone throws cold water on me. I thought to myself damn!! Why does our computer room have to be so far away from our bedroom, which means I am going to have gently pull the covers off me while trying not to wake her up just to tip toe out?

While still in the bed I faced her one last time to be sure she was sound asleep. This should be relatable if you have a sneaky husband who wanted to eat a candy bar at 2 o'clock in the morning while on a diet. I was able to get up, close the door and walk into the computer room without a change in her snoring pattern.

While in the room I turned down the volume on the computer because AOL had that loud static sound that I already referred to in the AOL DAYS chapter. I am going through all of this just because I wanted to watch some porn on the computer. Before sitting down on the computer chair and getting all worked up, for some reason I decided to check to see of my wife was still sleeping or not one last and final time.

Of course, she was snoring at a level I would not have been able to sleep anyways. Wait just a second, just imagine having a handheld snoring noise monitor close up to her face and that monitor stayed in the red continuously?

WELL? Yea that's exactly what I said that night DAMN!!!I closed the bedroom door again and quietly tiptoed back into the computer room. I searched the internet for a while using searchable keywords like cock in ass or black cock white bitche's and just like a genie waving the wand I found something worth jacking off to.

Of course, it was some black dude fucking a white bitch in the ass while she had both hands on her ass cheeks. And there was a white man sitting on a chair watching his wife being used like curbside furniture. She was tossed around a few times and then thrown into the dumpster truck. *Do you like my metaphor?*

That black dude looked like he was balls deep in her ass and I liked that. Just as I pulled down my underwear and lubed up the palm of my hand, reached for my cock, guess who poked her head through the door and busted me?

That's right, my wife whom I thought was snoring like the sound of a freight train. I CAN'T emphasize enough how embarrassing that was when it happened. I could see she was disappointed, and she didn't ask me why. We never talked about it afterwards and just acted as if it had never happened. Peace!

Can You Handle The Truth

AN ADULT CONVERSATION

I'm going to make this a quick read because a lot of you so-called liberal-minded women are the most judgmental.

I have mentioned this a few times in previous chapters, but this time I am not holding back. Most of you don't understand, I am not the only male on this fucking planet that has done some of the fucked up shit you have read or about to read or listen to.

There are many freaky ass mother fuckers like myself that wait until your ass is at work to do their freaky shit. By the time you bring your ass home, no wonder he's not attacking you once you walk in from work. That's all been taken care of either by himself or he cheated on your ass. When I watch porn and some of fucked up shit I kack'off to, I know damn well I ain't the only one, seriously!! Otherwise, the shit I like watching would not be available, right?

Here you are trying to fucking judge me when more than likely you want to try some of the shit you hear about. You are in denial, I bet, right? If you are a single man or woman, there is some shit out there that I would not want to be a part of, and that's saying a lot. After this chapter, calm your ass down and prepare yourself for some real talk, not some watered-down, vague ass publication. In this book, there is no way in hell I would share what I have seen with my own eyes at the parties I have attended. Ladies, there are a lot of men who will not come forward and admit the freaky shit they are into.

That's because you may have said something about feaky shit that made him choose not to mention it. Example: You are watching television and you saw or heard something about what he's into. He heard you say how disgusting that was, and coincidentally, that's exactly what he's into. I know damn well he ain't going to utter one damn word now, will he? I can honestly say that everything you just read or listened to was me once upon a time —a man scared to death of opening up and letting anyone in. That's no longer the case, is it? Take care for now...

Chocolate Starfish

S end this part of the chapter to a friend that may be considering being poked in their ass or poking someone in their asses.

Finally, ---here is my technique. Once you have had a mature conversation about anal sex, make damn sure your nails are clean and trimmed. Don't dare go from ass to pussy, and that includes your fingers, cock, toes, butt plug, dildo, bat, or bottle.

Let us ensure that anything you remove from her ass does not end up in her pussy unless you thoroughly clean it first. If you don't thoroughly wash whatever you use, it could lead to an infection like a U.T.I. or even worse. And if she tenses up, don't let that be the deciding factor to stop having fun. The rest of this chapter is based on trust. Otherwise, don't even think about it. Back to "Chocolate Starfish": As you eat her pussy, gradually play with her ass with only one finger, start very slowly without penetrating.

Eating the pussy and playing with her ass with your fingers should be a pleasurable distraction, with lubrication on your fingers. As she relaxes the "ANXIETY" she had about anal sex will start to fade. But (no pun intended) only if she has not had any trauma from anal sex from a previous relationship. Continue licking her pussy and slowly inserting one finger inside her ass.

You will know if you are doing this correctly when she "cums" --or squirts all over your face. As I previously mentioned she will have that look of embarrassment all over her face, which is normal, as far as I am concerned. Keep listening and looking for clues from how she responds to your actions, and you will know if she is enjoying it. Continue eating the pussy and eventually insert two fingers into her ass slowly. Once you have inserted your two fingers into her ass up to the second joint, begin moving in a circular motion, just like before. Continue licking that clitoral area until you can get three fingers into her ass, up to the second knuckle. I am sure you are wondering, "Why do you need three fingers to reach the second knuckle?" Three fingers should match the width of your cock.

Suppose you use my secret handy-dandy circular motion. In that case, it will stretch the opening of her ass, preparing her for anal penetration. Lubricating her ass is the key; I can't stress that enough. If you are as nasty as I am, then shit on your cock won't faze you. Just clean it up with soap and water and stick it back in.

But if fresh, hot shit grosses you out, then I suggest you wear a condom. This technique works best if your cock is under five inches in girth; if you are thicker, you will have to stretch the asshole more. Some women are okay with that; others are not. I have even known women who preferred girth over the length of the cock because they like their asses stretched out. They even go as far as to insert their own hands into their asses. For me, I have never gone more than four fingers, knuckles deep, into a woman's ass.

You might even run across a woman who enjoys fisting. I have never personally met one, but I am sure they are out there with the other mythical creatures of the world. Four fingers up, their ass seems insane to me, but who am I to say what is insane? That's my technique for having anal sex with someone who trusts you. If she is willing to try anal, then take your time, go slow, use lubrication, and keep building trust. Move one, two, and three fingers in a circular motion, preparing and stretching the asshole.

I have succeeded with this method; who knows what else she will do? If you are wondering what I have learned from this chapter, then here it is. Some years ago, I was talking to a lady on the phone who felt comfortable enough to say she loved anal sex. But, Later, told me she could not enjoy talking about it, because of a negative experience with a selfish man she was dating. I became inquisitive as to what that negative experience was.

Later in our conversation, she was comfortable enough to tell me what happened to her. To be honest with you, when she told me what happened, I became outraged, as I could not believe someone could do such a thing to another person. There was no lubrication, no preparation, and "NO" "WARNING"... before entering her ass. Her anus remains off-limits to this day, and nothing can enter it, not even a finger. Damn shame, right?

By the way, here is my definition of

"Chocolate Starfish"

"Chocolate starfish" is a slang term people sometimes use to describe the shape and appearance of a person's backside — specifically, the rear exit.

WHY THE NAME?

Well, if you've ever seen a starfish, it has a puckered center and radiating folds — and for some folks, that's what the human body's, uh, final frontier looks like from a certain angle. Add in the brown tone, and boom — someone decided to call it a "chocolate starfish. "It's crude, it's visual, and it definitely isn't found in any medical textbook — but it's been floating around in jokes, lyrics, and locker-room humor for decades.

Crack Epidemic

One Hit Wonder

Angel Dust ain't got wings—it's got shackles. It drags people out of their homes and into alleys, turns mothers into hoe's and father's into abusers, while risking their children being taken away and placed in foster care.

Every hit is another empty seat at a family table during the holidays, another promise broken, another future smoked away. Being straight up, If you honestly think this drug only hurts the user, you ain't seen souls it's taken with very puff.

This is going to be a short chapter, because sometimes you just want to know how it happened, right? Well, here goes. In my early twenties, I ran a mobile DJ service. Just before one weekend, a female neighbor called me to DJ one of her parties. I showed up early to set up my equipment, and later I walked into the kitchen. That's when I noticed two guys, about my age, bagging up something on the counter. I asked what it was, and they told me it was Angel Dust. Here's my description of that drug: Phencyclidine—better known as PCP—on the streets they called it Angel Dust. Trust me when I say there's nothing angel about it.

To me, it's a made-up name for something that yanks your mind out of reality and tosses you into a hole that's not easy to climb out of. One hit, and the world becomes an illusion. Breathing? Restricted—like someone kneeling on your chest on May 25, 2020. PCP doesn't just mess with your head—it hijacks your body. Blood pressure spikes like you're sprinting through the Boston Marathon. And in the middle of all that, people on dust can turn fearless, violent, or straight-up detached—like zombies fresh out of 28 Days Later. Many who experimented with it were never the same afterward. Me? I was one lucky mofo. Allow me to give you the 411.

While those guys were bagging it up, I asked why the tiny Ziplock bags and how much they went for. One guy smirked, looked at his buddy, and said, "Twenty bucks." I remember saying, "Damn—for that tiny bag?" They both busted out laughing. Nobody had arrived at the party yet, so curiosity kicked in. I asked if I could try some.

One guy gave me a strange look, then glanced at his friend. Finally, they said, "Sure, go ahead, roll yourself up one. You're the DJ." Do you remember Zigzags? They had some nearby, so I started rolling like it was herbs, you get my drift. One of the guys quickly said, "WHOA, YOUNG, WHOA! Brah, that's angel dust, not herbs." "I know," I said, and kept rolling. It came out fat—like a nine-month pregnant woman. The look they gave each other should've been my warning. But not me. I thought I could handle anything. After a few puffs, my vision went weird—like I was staring into one of those carnival funhouse mirrors.

The two guys were talking to me, but it felt like they were miles away, even though they were just an arm's length away. To this very day, I've never experienced anything like that again. All of a sudden, I felt like I needed something from my car. I opened the front door, and my car looked like it was parked three blocks away—even though it was sitting right there in front of the garage. I hurried back inside, shut the door, and called a good friend of mine. That's all I remember—just making that call, not what I said.

Weeks later, I called him up, laughing, and asked about it. He paused and asked me what I'd smoked or snorted before calling him that night. I said, "Why?" He hesitated, then told me: "Man, you weren't making any sense. You were talking about flying elephants. And you were slurring your words like you were drunk."

When he finished, I was in disbelief. That was the first and last time I ever touched that stuff. Man, a lot of friends I graduated with lost their lives, families, and souls messing with that addictive poison. Once he mentioned the elephant, I was scared straight. If you're wondering, why I even bothered writing this chapter—here's why. The fact you're reading this means more than words on a page. I could've easily ended up a crackhead like Chris Rock in New Jack City. And yes, I know you just pictured his crusty white lips in that movie.But here I am—66 years old—and I haven't had an illegal substance in my body since that night. One last thing, and it's important: sometimes, even now, my skin feels like something's crawling on me. Out of nowhere, I'll look at my arm like there's a bug on me—but nothing's there.

Since I've been straight-up with you about everything else, I might as well say that too. The universe must've known ahead of time that I had a story in me worth telling. This felt right to include—and I'll never mention it again.

Peace!!

Crazy Azz Latina Chick

Loca Azz Latina De Pollo

I decided to allow you to narrate this particular chapter, and I hope that's okay with you. He searched and heard 100 plus voices and thought yours would complement his story. So, with no more delays choose a voice in your head and read with it. Something different, right?

While working in Altamonte Springs, a five-foot-tall Puerto Rican chick named Lisa flirted with me.

Every time we saw each other, we flirted with eye contact. She was cute, short, and thick, and we looked forward to seeing each other every morning while she delivered and stocked the floral cooler. I used to work as a forklift driver in the food department, and her flower stand was near one of my aisles. I tried to drive my forklift in the same vicinity whenever I saw her.

Our talks were real, and I always enjoyed watching her come down the main aisle with her huge, juicy ass and a shopping basket full of beautiful flowers. Her husband occasionally accompanied her, depending on the number of flowers sold the previous day. Obviously, while her spouse was present, she would not flirt with me. It was always strange for us to sneak around Lisa's husband, Joe. We smiled every time he turned his back because we had a secret we did not want to be exposed. Unlike most co-workers, I did not need to flirt to catch her attention.

I have always been confident, and I recognized that aggressively flirting with her would make you appear to be a thirsty and weak ass mutha fucka. At some point, my back was so terrible that I had to miss a few months of work. I will admit that while I was at home healing, I missed flirting with her. I did not know her cell phone number then, so I could not text or call her. Never mind that she is married, which reminds me of Billy Paul's song "Me and Mrs. Jones." That will always be our song.

While I was at home from back pain, I had no idea Lisa was missing me; after a few weeks, she realized something was wrong. She kept asking others where I was, and someone at work gave her my phone number. Lisa contacted me and said they missed me and wanted to know if I was okay. Eventually, Lisa asked if she might come to see me. I did not mind, given I had not seen her in a long time.

Oh, she was a cutie and a tiny woman to kiss! Lisa could not have been no taller than 4'8" in height but made up for it with her smile, personality, and big ass. I knew something would happen during her first visit alone with me. One thing led to another, and before long, we were kissing. If I knew then what I know now, I would have licked Lisa's pussy. My skills today would have messed her head up. I had a shy, conservative demeanor back then. Without licking her pussy, I must have been doing something she enjoyed. Below, I will explain why "she must have liked it." We used to fuck around in Lisa's bed while her husband was away. Still, she also started acting strangely toward me because she would unexpectedly show up at my house.

Let me explain below; you will know what I mean. She would drive from wherever she came from then walk right up to my door without calling, texting. This woman (note I am calling her a bitch now) is married and shows up at my fucking doorstep. Admit it right now, only crazy ass bitches do that kinda shit!! This type of person would burn down your house with you inside and sit right outside and wait for you to come running out. Okay, enough, you get the idea.

I hate that shit then, and I still do today. Lisa continuously showed up unexpectedly at my house while I was away making deliveries for a business I ran. Pay attention to what I will say next: Lisa called me while I was away and said she was knocking on my door, but there was no answer; she rang the doorbell again, and there was still no answer.

Then she decided to call me and say, "I am at your door; allow me in." Are you reading this section and scratching your head? If you are not, you should be. I asked Lisa if she had seen my truck around the side of my house, to which she replied, "Well, no." Then there's a strong chance I'm not home," I remarked cynically. She assured me she would wait for me in her car, then arrogantly encouraged me to hurry. What the hell huh?! I mentioned that it would take a while and that I had no idea when I would return. **Dear reader,** as I write this, I am telling myself that I was acting like a little bitch back then. I am saying this because I should have told that bitch to take her married ass home.

Furthermore, I should have refrained from explaining my actions. Lisa did not seem to care and stated she would wait anyhow.

That bitch stayed two hours at my front door before finally leaving. She was acting that way even without eating her pussy, so I must have been doing something she did not get at home. Can you believe she was upset because I did not stop my deliveries? "I thought to myself bitch, you're acting like you're single and shit," I should have started with this and lured you in she was adventurous and enjoyed trying new things.

She once expressed a desire to have sex in the backyard, even though I did not have a tall wall. If someone had been strolling by, they could have easily spotted us, given the presence of some kids residing nearby.

And those same lazy ass's kids could easily climb over my wall rather than walk around the corner into the neighborhood. Following her suggestion, we spread a blanket on the grass and started having intimate moments. Why am I being polite suddenly? I meant we started fucking. It was enjoyable, although I worried about the red ants I knew were in my yard. I knew I had red ants in my backyard and was afraid that those ants would crawl up on my ass or hers. I nutted quickly, and we hurried back inside the house. Never mind the that someone could see us from the other side of the low-ass wall. While out on deliveries, Lisa called again while I was away from home, saying she had brought a friend and was waiting for me. I had another full load of furniture on my trailer and a busy day ahead of me.

I desperately wanted to quit making deliveries and go home, but I could not. I could not believe my luck, and I was pissed off like you can't imagine. I imagined her girlfriend as fine as she was, and I could have had both.

We eventually stopped seeing each other because she was married, and I needed to focus on my delivery business rather than fucking two hungry, thirsty Puerto Rican bitches. When I think about it, I am grateful I had the foresight to recognize that she had some boundary issues. Her behavior could have caused me to lose my business and full-time job. What woman in her right mind would advise a man to cease what he is doing when he has a business to run?

What woman in her right mind would wait in front of someone's house for two hours? And what woman in her right mind would fuck around where she sleeps? This chapter emphasizes the need for husbands to care for their wives, as previously discussed.

So, if you are a woman reading this part of the chapter and the man you are with has an eating disorder and refuses to eat that pussy, you know what to do, right? You should either take care of yourself or find someone who will. I will drop the mic right now and say, "Peace!"

Cuckold Relationships

C onsidering this happened twenty years ago, my memories were vividly clear while writing this chapter.

STARING:

Roy – The Husband
Jackie – The Wife
Cecil - You know.
Royal – You Already Know

Taken Str8 from the audiobook.

(CECIL) Keep in mind that this lifestyle you are about to read may come as a surprise to many vanilla folks of all ethnicities. Any couple that chooses this lifestyle also has a bond, unlike your typical couple next door. In fact, most couples who take part in this lifestyle would never be willing to admit it to anyone. After the warning I just gave you, it is time to buckle up. I was a freak back then and still am a freak today, well, sort of. Yes, I know I am a lot older, but so what? No matter the race, age, or background, once a freak, always a freak. You don't just wake up and become less freaky; there is no cure or holy water for it. Do not even think about your Minister tapping you on the forehead, and it is gone.

From my personal experience, white folks were always the freakiest ones in all my experiences. Innocent during the day and behind closed doors will do some shit that will mess your head up and make you say, "Oh Hell Naw! That's why I need you to remember all the couples I dominated were white and freaky people. Wait, hold on a second; should I be more politically, correct? Instead of calling y'all white, should I say Caucasian or European Americans? Fuck it, I will say it; I don't know what to call you mofo's have the time. Throughout my adventurous, lustful life, I have had the opportunity to meet two interracial couples. In these instances, the male was always white, and the woman was black.

I have shared my thoughts on this in a separate chapter, so I won't elaborate further. At these cuckold parties, I have not encountered any black couples at any events that I have been to, nor have I found a single black woman. I can just assume black folks are like Homie the Clown In Living Color they " Don't Play Dat Shit." Besides, black men and women folks are stingy and don't share their significant other.

Now, I am not saying it does not exist because it does; it is just that I have not been fortunate to discover where they are located. I digress, so let us discuss Mr. and Mrs. Collins, a cuckold couple who lived in Melbourne, Florida. We first connected on the internet, and after five conversations on our mobile phones, Roy, the husband, decided to send me revealing photographs of his wife, Jackie. It was as if he had been waiting for me to ask.

I gave him a thumbs-up symbol because I found her to be fine and that's usually how things heat up. I must be careful when searching for couples like Mr. and Mrs. Collins online because most are single men posing as couples. Those mutha sucka's asked me a bunch of sexual questions so they could jack off to my answers. Da hell with that shit! If I wanted to start at 1-900, I would have. Knowing my skills, I would be exceptionally good at it, too.

(Cecil) Keep reading, and you will understand why I can back it up. Nevertheless, I would use my list of serious series of questions so I can detect and sort through the bullshit and eliminate the Cuckold posers quickly. Serious couples looking for someone like me would ask my age? Age is important to them because most white couples in the Cuckold community are in their fifties and very private people.

A younger man would not understand their relationship's dynamics, which could cause problems with their privacy. Once a mature woman gives them some of their pussy, a younger man would become emotionally involved.

They would not maintain their agreement or confidentiality if they were emotionally unstable. I have seen it happen, and it is messy. Just ask August Alsina. Just so you know, I am not saying that The Smiths relationship was a Cuckold relationship, just to be precise. What I just said was for entertainment purposes only to make a point. Other questions would also be exactly where I resided.

How long have I been using this website? Have I fucked someone's wife? Do I have a spouse, or am I single? After I informed him at the time that I was married, he gave me a thumbs up in response. Even though I was married, he knew I would not fall in love with his wife and was less likely to have diseases.

Royal crossed her arms and snapped.

"Wait just a damn minute— you mean to tell me you were cheating on your second wife too? Well? No response is a response. Go ahead, cheating-ass muthafucka. Tell your damn chapter!"

Cecil raised his hands.
"Damn, Royal—this was all back in the day."
She rolled her eyes.
"I don't care, Cecil."

He exhaled.
"You're right. I knew what I was doing was wrong... and I did it anyway."

Royal smirked.
"Finally. The fucking truth."

Cecil shook his head, trying not to laugh.
"Can I continue now?"

Royal waved her hand.
"Yes, okay. Carry on... but I'm still judging you."

(Cecil) In addition, he knew that a married man would be discreet and mature enough to understand their lifestyle. Would you believe this mutha-fucka had the audacity to inquire about my cock's exact dimensions? Most men would be offended, but not me. It was okay because I knew why he asked. Roy wanted to avoid me bringing a Vienna sausage to a party when the host already had one. Get my indirect meaning? It was only natural for me to answer his question because I had nothing to lose. Trust me when I say that if our chats had not been honest, I would have chosen not to answer any of his questions and prevented him from contacting me in the future.

In any case, Roy, the husband, invited me to visit their house after he had become confident with our ability to communicate through our mobile phones. Meeting couples that live in gated communities is not something I am accustomed to doing. The fact that I must provide ID upon my arrival is one of the primary reasons.

After giving the security guard my name, I proceeded to their residence. I will confess that this was nicer than anywhere I had ever lived. I felt insecure again because the Ferrari and Harley were in the garage. When I arrived and entered the driveway, it was time to put my insecurities behind me. After getting out of my car, I walked towards the front door and rang the doorbell. Jackie, wearing a white miniskirt without panties, smiled as she opened the door. I immediately gave her a thorough eye examination from head to toe.

In case you were wondering, Jackie's miniskirt barely covered her ass cheeks. "Fuck it," I will tell you. There is no way she could bend over and pick up anything without exposing her pussy lips. I did not mention what I wanted her to wear before my arrival, so she must have been aware that I liked slutty attire. I remember saying to myself, "Is she some kind of mind reader? After closing the door, Jackie turned around and approached me. Jackie reached for my hand as we walked towards the living room. I suddenly had the desire for her to bend over while I sniffed her pussy as if I were a junkyard dog in heat. Just visualize me humping air after sniffing her pussy.

Did you imagine it? Watching her walk before me, I thought, "I'll fuck this bitch later in the evening." Jackie had a broad grin the entire time I was there as if she were prepared to lick these three hundred pounds of a pure, sweetened chocolate black man.

Jackie and I sat on the couch, positioning our bodies directly facing Roy. Since this was the first time we met in person, Roy wanted to talk with me before formally presenting me to Jackie. Roy informed me that he had made sure his wife, Jackie, was dressed in a sexy outfit for me. On top of that, her shoes complemented her dress. While she was sitting down next to me, I asked her to stand up and model her outfit. That was my way of setting the mood and why I was there. I know when to turn on the heat in most situations like this. I try to pay attention to the couple's body language, as well as the subtle eye contact that exists between them. After having a brief conversation with Roy and Jackie, I became aware of a possibility that would allow me to advance to the next level.

I stood up, looked directly at Roy, and said, "Okay, enough of this talking; I need you to sit in your favorite chair, and don't you fucking move or say one word until I say so." Roy sat down in the chair like a well-behaved boy and did not even bother to inquire about the reason for his order. I then instructed Jackie to stand up and face Roy in a firm voice. She followed the instructions, just like the fine-ass white bitch she was. Afterward, I instructed Jackie to "Look into the eyes of your husband, and don't say a single word unless I give you permission to do so."

The following is what I said to Roy: "We are going to do something directly in front of you, and I'm sure you are going to love watching us do it." Neither Jackie nor her husband made any kind of comment while Jackie was standing before her husband. I stood up, stepped behind her, and slowly unzipped her little white dress. My next step was to unzip her dress, and I instructed her to remove her shoes and then reach out to grip her husband's hand for balance.

It should be no surprise that she did not have stockings on, considering she wasn't wearing panties. How about this? Jackie asked. The entire time I was present, Jackie wore a stainless-steel butt plug with a Cosplay Foxtail. Oh! my bad. You don't know what the hell I am talking about, do you? Close by is an idea of what it looks like, and just so you know, it goes inside the "asshole."

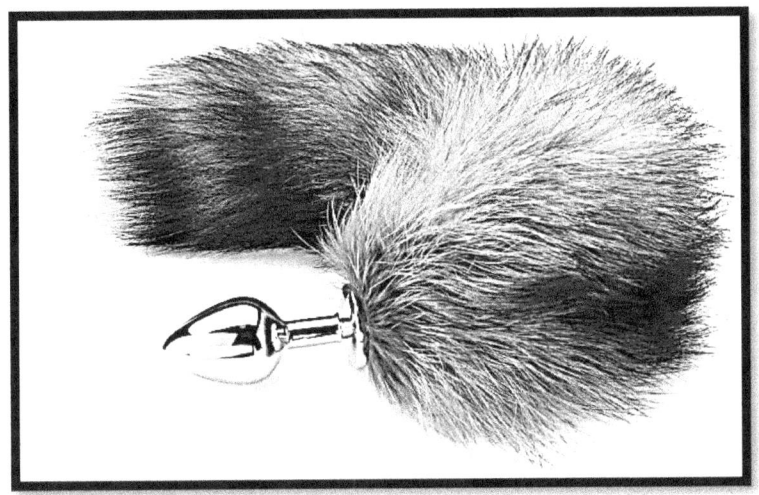

You just said what to yourself, right? I did also when I was first shown to me by a lady I was dating. I did not notice it when she opened the door. That would have been my clue that Jackie was a freak, and I would have looked for it.

The fact that she was sitting down and leaning to the side with a butt plug in her ass does not come as a surprise.

You may be wondering, "How did I determine that she wore a stainless-steel cosplay foxtail butt plug in her ass?" She stood before her husband, struggling to maintain her balance, and leaned over to remove her shoes. Jackie stood before me, looking down at her husband and excitedly shaking. I was positioned directly behind her. Roy's cock on the outside of his pants was another sign of his arousal. At this point, I decided to bring the intensity of this unique situation to its maximum.

Therefore, as Jackie was standing before her husband, I instructed her to raise her arms so I could take off her dress. I flung her dress onto the couch, intending to expose her naked, white, curved body in front of both her husband and her backside in front of me. I remember vividly looking at the back of her neck, shoulders, the curve of her back, the crack of her ass, thighs while she shivered in excitement. To calm her down, I gave a light slap on the ass and whispered, "Do you trust me? She nodded her head yes with a lustful smile.

As I placed my hands on her shoulder and turned her around, I gazed into Jackie's eyes as if she were a white slave I now owned and paid cash at a slave auction. I took a moment to stand back and observe the situation. I was impressed by her body, and at the same time, I appreciated the cellulite that was on her stomach and legs. It was because of this that I found her to be naturally appealing.

After that, I gently turned around and walked behind her once more. As I did so, I reached my hands around her from behind and lightly squeezed her nipples. Occasionally, I would break from playing with Jackie's nipples to allow my fingers to slowly move down and across her stomach until I reached her clitoral area. While playing with her clitoris, I slowly and softly moved in a circular pattern with my index finger. Just so you know, I washed my hands and clipped my field-down nails just in case you were wondering. When I barely touched her clitoris, she squirted on the floor, causing it to flow down her legs a release I am used to watching.

As I watched it gushing out of her, I could not help but feel a sense of accomplishment. When I realized she was about to cum, I abruptly stopped. Typically, I would refer to this as orgasm denial, but some vanilla folks may consider it teasing. Not only am I denying the wife an orgasm, but I am also manipulating Roy's mind. Roy remained seated in his chair, observing my playful manipulation of his wife's thighs, titties, and clitoris.

By placing my fingers inside her pussy, I stimulated her in a way that her eyes rolled around inside her eyes as if she were possessed. Roy stood up, concerned because he had never seen Jackie respond that way with her clit being stimulated. I confidently told James to sit there because I got this. "You're my bitch now," I whispered in Jackie's ear as I repeatedly inserted two fingers into her pussy.

As I was removing my fingers from her pussy, I observed that her cum was creamy and thick, indicating that she was completely wet and excited. After that, I instructed her to turn around and face me, allowing me to gently insert my fingers back into her pussy, which was already covered in cum.

I then took those same two fingers and placed them into both of our mouths while I was facing her. I wanted to be sure that every drop of cum wasn't wasted, so I made her lick each finger carefully until I was satisfied. What I just did to another man's wife was so sexy, and only in the United States of America is it possible for an ol school brotha like myself to do something like that.

At that moment, I thought to myself, "This white man consented to me entering his home, where he observed a nigga standing exactly behind his wife, playing around with her pussy." At this point, her pussy was wet, and cum was pouring down both of her inner thighs and down to the floor. I said aloud, "Oh my god! Jackie, you have created a puddle that covers the floor! "Take a moment to close your eyes and let your imagination run wild. If you read this entire book, you will find out another person squirts like Jackie.

The husband assumed she had finished squirting, but excitement caused her to release more. Just like before, I reached down and mopped up the squirt that was running down her thighs. Then I turned her to face me so that we could lick my fingers together while kissing each other passionately.

After two hours, I was hungry, and the husband asked if I wanted anything to eat. I said, "That's not a question you should ask me. Tell Jackie to ask me the same question. " **Roy told his wife,** "Honey, ask Cecil what he wants to eat. "**Jackie asked,** "Is there anything else besides eating and fucking my pussy that I can prepare for you,

Sir?" I said, "Not at this very moment; maybe after I make your husband watch me fuck you again, and after I pull out, he can clean the both of us up with his mouth."

(CECIL)
This chapter?
Yeah... it's kinda like "Under the Cover," right?

And yet—Here we are again...
With another white couple who wants their wife to be fucked by a Black man. Another time, she called her husband while he was at work. I overheard Jackie saying,

"Guess who's with me."
Roy didn't even hesitate,
"I know who you're with. You're with Cecil, right?"
Jackie grinned,
"Yep. We're going to the beach for a little while."

CECIL: Establishing trust is usually necessary for this type of unique situation to happen. Otherwise, I would have had to wait until Roy came home from work to go to the beach with her alone. Unexpectedly, Roy wanted to talk to me on the cell phone for a second. He wanted the details of my plans for Jackie at the beach.

I said, "It's not about my plans for Jackie, but how you will benefit from what I do to her." I told him to imagine me playing with Jackie's pussy while you are focused on work.

I articulated it in a manner that would captivate him, but my demeanor wasn't cordial. Right after I said it, he knew how to hang up the phone and waited until he came home to hear all the juicy details later.

So, while at the beach, I was playing with Jackie's pussy in the car; she was squirting all over my hands and leather seats. Damn it! I was having so much fun playing with her pussy and making her squirt that I forgot to occasionally look up and check out the surrounding areas.

I looked up finally, damn it! I looked over her shoulder and spotted a police car.

I don't remember seeing it when we arrived despite being on the other side of the parking lot. I could tell the officer wasn't watching what Jackie and I were doing; I was relieved.

Consider the following scenario: A white woman is parked in a parking lot with her back against the door, and a nigger (that's with a hard R) is in the car playing with a pale white sexy woman's pussy. Just go ahead and envision it. It would be up to her to explain to the police officer that we were familiar with each other, and everything was okay.

Unfortunately, I had to think that way initially. In fact, at any given moment, that officer could have easily driven over and asked what we were doing in an empty parking lot. Also, imagine if that officer decided to make some assumptions and called for backup. Luckily, the police never came over, and I kept playing with her pussy. I am uncertain why we lost touch, as they were a nice couple to have fun with. Role playing can be fun when there is trust between all parties involved.

Ending Note: People from different financial and ethnic backgrounds can secretly participate in the Cuckold lifestyle without detection, which has always made it exciting.

They don't share their private lives with anyone or participate in public events. I can promise you that cuckold couples can be your best friends or family members, and no one would know. People often avoid open discussions about the cuckold lifestyle, fearing misinterpretation from their peers.

There is absolutely nothing wrong with this lifestyle. It is three consenting adults fulfilling their fantasies together. No one is under coercion, and all involved have knowingly made a choice to fulfill a burning desire with someone who understands the lifestyle. Ignorant people often criticize this lifestyle. Peace!

By The Way, what you decided to do in the privacy of your own home, car, backyard, mobile home, in an alley, in your friends' bathroom, hotel or motel is your mutha fucking business, right? YOU DAMN RIGHT, SOLID.

INTERRACIAL CUCKOLDING:

A Layered Power Dynamic
When cuckoldry involves a white husband, a white wife, and a Black man (the bull), the situation is more than just sexual — it's loaded with history, race, taboo, and psychological complexity.

Behind Closed Doors
(Especially here in America):
I. HISTORICAL TENSIONS

The image of a Black man sleeping with a white woman has deep roots in America's racist and violent history, where Black men were lynched or criminalized over accusations — sometimes completely false — of sleeping with white women.

In a twisted flip, modern consensual interracial cuckold fantasies fetishize the very thing that used to terrify white supremacy: a Black man dominating a white woman, while the white husband watches or gives permission.

2. REVERSING POWER ROLES

The Black man is often cast as the dominant figure — sexually superior, confident, and in control.

The white husband, meanwhile, takes on a submissive, even humiliated role — watching his wife get pleasured in a way he supposedly can't.

This reverses historical power dynamics — the white man (traditionally seen as the dominant one) steps back while the Black man takes the lead.

It's an erotic but deeply symbolic shift in dominance — playing on centuries of racial tension, guilt, and taboo.

3. THE WHITE WIFE'S ROLE

She becomes the bridge between both men — often seen as the one choosing the Black man for his "forbidden," "superior," or "undeniable" sexuality.

Her arousal is often tied to doing something taboo — crossing a racial line that society once forbade.

FANTASY VS. FETISH VS. FETISHIZATION
There's a fine line between:

Erotic fantasy (something imagined, consensual, and fun),

Fetish (a repeated turn-on based on a certain trait), and

Fetishization (reducing someone solely to their race or body parts).

A Black man might be desired only for having a big dick or being "dominant" — not for his personality, humanity, or individuality. That's when it crosses from fantasy into dehumanizing territory.

In your book, you're walking the line between personal truth, sexual storytelling, and cultural commentary — so you're in a perfect position to explore and even critique this kind of dynamic.

Why Some White Men Fantasize About This
Loss of control turns some people on — watching someone else do what they "can't."

Some white men feel guilt or curiosity about race and power, and this is a way to "give over" control to a Black man in a safe, controlled setting.

Others get turned on by the idea of their wife being "taken" or "claimed" by someone society deems more virile or dangerous — the Black bull fantasy feeds that

Dirty Magazines

G il Scott-Heron's "The Revolution Won't Be Televised" Just so you know, I used the chapter's title to lure you in. Therefore, "I DARE YOU!!" to keep reading.

WARNING:

Do, do you find yourself easily triggered and disgusted by black men sleeping with white women but still enjoy watching interracial porn? Do you have a family member who is racist? Lately, have you shown hatred towards black people? Do you say nigger among your family and peers? Have you confronted a black family with aggression lately? Does it make sense to vandalize a black family's home because it is nicer than yours?

Have you ever said that they must be drug dealers? As a bank teller, are you suspicious of all African Americans' deposits? When a black person is driving a nice car, do you immediately assume they are selling drugs? Why can't a black family move into an all-white neighborhood? Have you ever said, Go back to Africa as a white person? Does taking down and moving the Confederate statues make you angry? Would you, as a white person, prefer segregated schools?

Are you familiar with the words to the Black National Anthem, Lift Every Voice, and Sing as a white person? Honestly, I don't, either, seriously. I should know the words but struggle to memorize them because I never had to sing it. As a white man, have you ever called a black woman a nigger? Do you follow black men as they jog in their own neighborhoods? Are you scared when approached by a black man? Do your parents refer to black people as niggers? Do you think it is necessary to call the police on a black child who is selling lemonade? Have you intentionally promoted a white person with no qualifications over a black person with qualifications?

Have you intentionally promoted a white person with no recommendations over a black person with recommendations? Have you asked or felt the need to ask a black person to prove they live in your neighborhood? Do you think all black teenagers are drug dealers and gang members? Have you ever tried to touch a black woman's hair without permission? Have you ever said this to a black person?

You can articulate your words very well. Have you unknowingly told a black person, "You seem intelligent?" Have you accused an underage black child of stealing your cell phone and then tackled him while he was with his father? Have you ever said that Black people don't deserve reparations, right? White women, are you jealous of black women's natural beauty and dark skin? Have you ever asked a black person, "Where were you born?"

People ask this question because they have not adjusted their intelligence and ignorance to understand our ability to overcome all obstacles and succeed. Is a black person currently managing you? Did you complain more because that person was black? At your job, are there black people in management? Have you consciously used your white privilege to your benefit? Do you say, "I don't see color"? Were you angrier with the George Floyd protestors than the white rioters on January 6? Do you still wear your MAGA hat proudly? Which part of the Make America Great era are you talking about? As a security guard in a major department store, do you intentionally follow more black people than white people, and why?

Do you instill hatred in your children? In front of your children, do you refer to black people as niggers? Do you, as a teacher, consciously or subconsciously ignore your black students? Do you honestly believe "ALL LIVES MATTER"? When you hear someone say, Black Lives Matter, do you feel propelled to say, ALL LIVES MATTER? Have you ripped down any signs that relate to BLM? When a white person wears a BLM shirt, does it irritate you? Which irritates you more—a black person wearing a BLM shirt or a white person?

When a black person does not allow your ignorance to upset them, does that irritate you? Do you live in Boston? Are you a white parent who discourages your children from listening to rap music? How would you feel, as white parents, if a black woman drowned your child in a pool under her supervision?

Would you demand a full investigation? Why were the charges against Amy Cooper dismissed? Even with evidence of lying to the police department on video? Have you aborted a black fetus? If black people were visually armed with a gun in a right-to-carry state, are you okay with that? Is your daughter fucking a nigger, and do you no longer talk to her? As a white woman, have you secretly fucked a black man? As a white woman, are you afraid to tell your current racist husband that you fucked a nigger? As a white woman, do you glance at black men's crotches? As a white woman, have you ever indulged in self-pleasure while fantasizing about fucking black men under duress? Do you subconsciously refer to black people as "niggers"?

As a realtor, are you consciously biased toward black clients? As a loan officer, have you intentionally given a higher interest rate to black clients? As a white doctor, are you secretly racist? As a white nurse, do you intentionally ignore black patients?

As a white police officer, do you deliberately pull over black drivers more than white drivers? Have your children exhibited compassion toward black children, and have you immediately suppressed this behavior as a white parent? Are you disgusted when you see interracial relationships and mixed children? You are aware that white male slave owners were the ones who bred interracial children with black women during slavery, right? The white male slave owners should have encouraged their black slaves to continue breeding among themselves, but none of them did. But instead, they were creeping out in the middle of the night, raping their own black female slaves.

In fact, in most cases, white male slave owners ignored their white wives, crying and begging for some cock. Just saying. Damn! That black pussy must have been good enough to ignore their own wife's white, pink pussy, right? We will never know, will we? Furthermore, tread lightly when calling me a nigger until you have researched your entire family history as far back as you can. For this reason, you might as well do it right now with Ancestry.

"Did you know that regardless of your perceived European heritage, you may have a black relative in your lineage? It is a fascinating aspect of our diverse and interconnected world!". The questions above directly and indirectly connect to the chapter "Dirty Magazines."

I am trying to persuade you to think from my point of view. In fact, I wanted to ask an authentic white person about the above questions, if they exist. The rest are just provocative, unanswered questions.

Alternatively, I wanted to take a break from writing about sex. I am preparing for you what you are about to read by presenting many questions I pondered as a teenager and now as an adult. If any of the above questions resonate, skip this chapter. As a colored boy growing up in Southeast San Diego, white men strategically and psychologically indoctrinated me and my peers into believing that black women are inferior to white women. I have a question for all you spoiled, milk-colored-looking white folks: has a black person ever made you feel inferior in the entertainment field, in school classrooms, or, in fact, period?

Or did your own insecurities make you feel inferior? Did you say something? Speak up. Allow me to convey my message to you in another way. White people have never portrayed black people positively on television or in dirty magazines since the early eighties.

All white people did it then, and to this day, they bombard our visuals with stimulating stereotypical negative images of black people on social media and news sources. How can a black baby, who eventually grows into an adult, cease to favor white women over black ones? How is it possible for a young, impressionable black teenager to consider the opinions of black women other than my mother? Why do racist white people become irate when a black man engages in sexual activity with white women?

Let us dive deeper into this topic, shall we? I only see white women in commercials, television, movies, and, of course, dirty magazines. Plant the seeds in black men's heads and dress them with white imagery. Black men crave, fantasize, and lust after white women. Look for movies or series starring black women in leading, solid, and positive roles on any significant streaming channel. I can tell you right now that the pickings are slim. Movie producers and commercial makers, y'all are not slick. You even dare to cast only black people as co-stars in significant roles. When black entertainers are in starring roles, we are liars, cheaters, wife-beaters, and drug dealers. While you are researching what I just said, be prepared to find us in demeaning roles. The last thing I am going to say before you read the rest of this chapter is: Why do white television producers always have niggas dancing at the beginning of the show?

Let us get into it: Dirty Magazines. Do you remember adult magazines and bookstores? Have you ever been inside one? Back then, you had to be at least eighteen years old to enter. I was a fourteen-year-old who looked eighteen at the time. Even then, I was able to go inside the Pussy Theatre in downtown San Diego to watch Deep Throat, starring Linda Lovelace. If you are a millennial, I am sure you are unfamiliar with adult magazines and the movies I have mentioned, due to the prevalence of the Internet.

So, if you want a trip back to the days of adult magazine stores, sit back and keep reading.

The World-Famous Body Shop, a shabby strip and adult magazine club/store in San Diego, California. The same company owned them and made significant revenue from them. How did I discover adult bookstores? I often walked past an adult bookstore and saw nothing but fat men inside. Additionally, the men smoked cigarettes, and if I planned to go inside, I might as well wait until there was no one smoking. As I strolled by the bookstore, I noticed a dense crowd of obese men crammed inside like Vienna sausages in a can.

In fact, I could see the cigarette smoke coming from the adult bookstore, like an early morning fog across the street from a Chinese food joint my family enjoyed eating at. I ain't stupid! My dad obviously wasn't either because he hid his choice of dirty magazines from my mom under the mattresses, which I later discovered. Back then, my parents referred to stores that sold adult magazines as "dirty magazines."

Let me explain how I discovered dirty magazines existed. Downtown San Diego had adult bookstores on every corner, it seemed. Back in my inquisitive teen years, the main entrance was wide open enough for curious underage fuckers like me to glance inside. That's what I thought, anyway.

NIGHT ONE:

In one of the adult bookstores, I mentioned earlier, three-quarters were wrestling, sports, and news-related magazines. However, a black curtain across the front blocked off this slightly open, mysterious area in the bookstore's back. In front of that black curtain were big, bold letters that read, Adults Only." I made sure the sign did not specify what age to enter. That made me even more curious.

Finally, after an evening without my parents, I was determined to walk into that adult store across from my parents' favorite Chinese restaurant. I did not have a car then, so I caught the bus everywhere I had to go. My destination was the adult bookstore in downtown San Diego. I arrived later that evening and walked in.

After walking past the curtain, I glanced in and realized what was back there. When people say curiosity killed the cat, I wanted to walk through the curtain badly but chose not to enter at the last second. I feared the cashier would have had me arrested because I was underage, even though the cashier had never asked me for ID.

Instead, I looked like a homeless kid picking up magazines. I ended up buying a WWF magazine instead. I overpaid, especially since I wanted something else. I left the bookstore frustrated and without the magazine I wanted. Let us just say I had not gone through the black curtain.

NIGHT TWO:

I walked back into the same bookstore and felt like the cashier from the night before remembered me. That was my subconscious guilt playing tricks on me. I acted like I had been his only customer the night before. Anyway, hopefully, with a change of clothes, he won't remember me. I was determined to walk in front of the cashier and head towards the black curtain this time.

The closer I got to the black curtain, the more nervous I became. And like that song by Johnny "Guitar" Watson, "Ain't That a Bitch?" Guess what? I bought another WWF magazine; went home and decided to try the following week. Yet again, I went home with blue balls and no adult magazines.

Even though I bought something each time, I wanted to avoid taking a chance at the cashier calling the police. With two WWF magazines, I could put them to good use, so I donated the magazines to my high school.

NIGHT THREE:

Next week has arrived, and it is time to get on the bus and return to the bookstore. This time, I stopped and had a conversation with the cashier. I did this to see if the cashier remembered me from the previous week. Nope, he did not! The whole time he talked, I thought about the adult section. During that boring conversation with the cashier, another customer walked up. It was time to finally walk towards the black curtain.

And guess what? I did it, y'all. I walked through the black curtain, which was only for adults. There were six men and one underage teenager in that room with their backs turned. Guess who that underage teen was. So, I turned my back toward them too. Not one of the six guys in that room said anything.

It was so quiet you could hear a mouse walking across the carpet. It was weird, and that's all I am going to say. Now that I am in the adult magazine room, all the magazine covers feature naked white women. Every magazine I picked up featured white women flaunting their tits and spreading their legs, revealing their shaved pink pussies and flat asses.

In fact, as a black teenager, I found the sight of white women spreading their legs and exposing their pussy's sexy ass hell!! "Here's just a sample of the magazines that shaped my teenage imagination — all featuring white women, all sending the same message about what was 'desirable': Barely Legal, Beaver Hunt, Club, High Society, Jugg's, Penthouse Forum, Playboy, Screw, Swank, Adam Film World, Chic, Gallery, Genesis, Oui, Perfect 10, Score.

And let me tell you, Hustler? That one was in a category of its own."

Here are some adult magazines featuring white, naked women on their front covers: These magazines include Barely Legal, Beaver Hunt, Club, High Society, jugs, Penthouse Forum, Playboy, Screw, Swank, Adam Film World, Chic, Gallery, Genesis, Oui, Perfect 10, and Score. Ladies and gentlemen, Hustler magazine stands out as the most racist of all.

Even now, I can vividly recall a cartoon that initially made me laugh, but I quickly came to regret it. It was a cartoon of a watermelon patch with a scarecrow. A Klansman was on the scarecrow. Did you just laugh or smile? Either way, I would not blame you because I did. Anyway, it was time to leave and come back another day. I did not make any purchases then, as I was unaware of the high cost of adult magazines. It did not bother me that I did not have enough money after paying for the bus.

INTERMISSION FROM THE SUBJECT:

Or Take a Pee Break / Grabe Some Snacks / Whatever!

I will take you to downtown San Diego, where all the adult bookstores are. Furthermore, I want to elaborate on why I am fascinated by white women and their origins. My deep interest in and understanding of white people was shaped by firsthand experiences and similar sources.

In addition to adult magazines, there were beauty ads, news anchors, nurses, doctors, cashiers, store managers, warehouse managers, bus drivers, principals, and teachers. I reiterate that magazines like Seventeen, Cosmopolitan, Vogue, Fashion, Bop, Mademoiselle, Easyriders, Rolling Stone, Life, People, Teen Beat, Us Weekly, Glamour, and Harper's Bazaar, among others, contributed to my craving for white women.

Hello, reader. Search Google for all the magazines mentioned above from the early 1980s. Straight up, all you are going to see are white women on the front, center, and back pages. If, by chance, she has a dark complexion, you will find her on the back of the magazines. Mixed-race people, or, should I say, redbones, are usually with another white woman. It is messed up, isn't it? Black women come in various shades, so why did they not highlight them?

Furthermore, faced with a multitude of naked white women in front of me, I was uncertain about which one to choose. After thirty minutes, I finally chose a magazine and walked towards the cashier. The magazine I ended up paying for was the most racist magazine of them all, Hustler. The women they selected to feature in their magazine were mostly blonde and slim. I say "slim" because there is a stark contrast when I reflect on and compare what is on social media. That makes those magazines appear PG-rated. Right?

On March 9, 1959, we even had White Ken and Barbie. And it wasn't until 1967 that they rolled out the first black Barbie, named Francie. This doll, up until the 1990s, had white features. In the eighties, all the superheroes were white men and women, such as Batman, Bionic Woman, Wonder Woman, The Incredible Hulk, Masters of the Universe, The Pumaman, The Return of Captain Invincible, Super Fuzz, Supergirl, Flash Gordon, The Incredible Hulk, and The Invisible Man. You get the idea.

Most commercials had white people front, back, and center. Another fact is that the major television shows starred white people. The television shows coming up were the ones I grew up watching religiously. What is even more problematic is that white people continue to dominate radio and television shows, a fact that's blatantly obvious and not disguised. I will go into greater detail about each of the highlighted shows. I want you to understand why black men and women over the age of seventy have a "Yassa boss" mentality. Hollywood has significantly contributed to us by starring in typical black shows and movies.

On that note, buckle up. I am about to list all the television shows that exclusively feature white men and women.

Wait!! When I mention black shows, most of the cast is white and written by a white person, like all these classic shows below.

- **All in the Family:** One Negro family as neighbors. Benson works as a black butler for a group of white people.

- **The Cosby Show** Negros expressed dissatisfaction with, claiming it lacked realism. The father was a doctor, and the mom was a lawyer living in a nice home. The parents were not divorced, and they frequently argued, cheated, lied, and cried before bedtime. Too positive. Isn't that messed up? As I mentioned earlier, Hollywood conditioned our minds.
-
- **Chico and the Man** - Comedy—had at least two major Negro co-stars.
- **Different Strokes** - Comedy A wealthy businessperson in New York adopted the concept. Keyword: adopted.
- **Welcome Back, Kotte** - Comedy/OMG! One co-starred as a Negro, alongside six other actors who were not black.
- **What's Happening** - Comedy/Whoa! Eight Negros, including one non-Black, are in starring roles.
- **Facts of Life** - Comedy/One Negro female actress and twenty-five mutha-fucking non-Negros.
- **The Flip Wilson Show** - featured comedy and drag, but he also starred in his own show with special guests who were always white people. Written by white people,
- **Good Times** – is a comedy/all-negro film with a positive vibe in the ghetto.
- **The Jeffersons** - Comedy features two male Negro actors, four female Negro actresses, and three white men. The portrayal of a

lazy Negro as a house cleaner is particularly notable. Yet another stereotypical role. If you were viewing this program in a different country, you would notice that we are boisterous and employ lazy Negros as house cleaners. Why hire Negro people, right?

-

- **Sanford and Son** - is a comedy with about two Negros who own a junkyard. A father-and-son duo.

- **Room 222** - Comedy I am just going to say there were Negros in starring roles in the hood.

- **That's My Mama** - Comedy/All-Negro Cast: I am not saying another word. Mod Squad: Serious/Action with one Negro actor. Now check out all the damn shows listed below. The shows highlighted were either action or non-comedic, and we now compare the number of black shows to white shows.

When I was growing up, all my mommy watched were shows starring white people in leading roles. With only one television in the house, guess what I was watching? That's right, white people, all damn day with no breaks. Right now, thinking about it makes me angry. We only had a sprinkle of Negro shows available to watch back in the day. As a Negro child (that's what we called ourselves back in the early 1960s), what am I supposed to think of my culture? More information: I am using the word "Negro" above because, back in the day, that's how white folks referred to us, sometimes worse.

HERE IS A LENGTHY LIST OF SHOWS THAT STARRED WHITE PEOPLE, WAIT, I MEANT EUROPEAN AMERICAN'S:

*Highlighted were my favorite.

American Girls, The Andy Williams Show, and The Bad News Bears were among the shows featured. **Baretta**, Don Knotts, The Don Rickles Show, Eight Is Enough, The Betty White Show, and **The Beverly Hillbillies** are some examples of popular white television shows. Bewitched, Get Christie Love! **Get Smart, Gomer Pyle of USMC, The Gong Show, Green Acres**, Gunsmoke, Happy Days, Hawaii Five-0, **Here's Lucy,** Hogan's Heroes, and I Dream of Jeannie. Ironside, It Takes a Thief. The series includes **Kojak,** Kung Fu, Little House on the Prairie, and more. Love, American Style: these shows include The Mary Tyler Moore Hour, The Mary Tyler Moore Show, M*A*S*H, Mission: Impossible, Mork & Mindy, My Three Sons, **The New Andy Griffith Show**, The Odd Couple, Operation Petticoat, The Partridge Family, Quincy M.E., The Rockford Files, The Six Million Dollar Man, Rowan & Martin's Laugh-In, and The Sonny and Cher Comedy Hour. Starsky and Hutch, The Waltons, Taxi, and **The Wild Wild West** are some examples. WKRP in Cincinnati. The program lineup includes Bonanza, The Brady Bunch, The Brady Bunch Variety Hour, Cannon, The Carol Burnett Show, Charlie's Angels, Chips, Columbo, **Dallas**, Donny, and Marie. We have Dragnet, The Dukes of Hazzard, 20/20, 60 Minutes, Adam-12, and Alice.

See how white brainwashing works? My observations of the 21st century demonstrate that nothing has changed.

White people, white movies, and white cartoons dominated my life around the clock. Allow me to refer to what I said earlier in this chapter. No wonder why I was always fascinated by or wanted to be white.

The idea of self-hate has been ingrained in my generation and seems to be deeply rooted. But I digress. I was sidetracked by my ADD my bad!

NIGHT FOUR / THIS SHOW IS CUMMING TO A CONCLUSION:

As usual, I caught the bus, and this time, I had enough money to take it to the bookstore and return home. I am all set to buy my first adult magazine. When I walked in, the same cashier was there again, and it looked like he still needed to change his clothes. He must have been the owner, sleeping somewhere in the back room. Again, I engaged in a casual conversation with the cashier.

Just as he was talking, another customer walked up. That's when I walked away, heading towards the black curtain again. This time, it felt different for me. It felt natural because I had been there so many times before. I entered the room by sticking one hand through the black curtain. Finally, I was inside the adult magazine room.

I had a brain overload malfunction; there were too many choices, and I wasn't sure which one to pick up first. Hell, I wasn't sure which one was nastier. After about thirty minutes, I had a magazine in my hand and walked towards the cashier. The magazine I chose was Hustler, with more classless women inside.

When I say classless, I am referring to how they look compared to what I am used to seeing in a professional setting. If you were one of the women featured in that magazine, I would like to apologize for what I said, okay? I like that when you buy a magazine, the cashier places it in a brown bag. I felt at ease, knowing no one knew what I had inside.

When the bus dropped me off in the back of my house, I looked to see if Mom was home. I knew she was there because I could see the light through the kitchen window, so I had to be careful. I opened the door very slowly and was surprised. My momma was sleeping, so I sneaked past her and headed straight for my bedroom.

I opened the bag again and pulled out my first dirty magazine featuring white women. It was pussy, ass, and titties on every page I turned. I was so excited to finally have my own adult magazine that if you had been a fly, you would have landed on my shoulder to watch me jack off. I was shooting cum all over the place.

One evening, I had an idea: why not find a photo of a girl looking up at me? To my surprise, there was one nude centerfold when I opened the magazine. I placed the magazine with the nude white girl face-up. Let me give you a visual. My pants and underwear were down by my ankles, with my cock in my hand. Everything is set, and my mom is snoring. I lubed up my cock and started jacking off as if the white girl in the magazine were watching me.

Damn! I shot a load of hot, fresh cum all over the white chick's face in the magazine. Mom must have heard me coming and asked if I was okay, and I responded with a "yes" and cleaned up myself. I closed the magazine, sat with Mom for a while, and had small talk.

Eventually, I got up and went back into my bedroom so that I could bust another nut all over the face of the white girl waiting for me in my bedroom. Damn!! That wasn't going to happen, and I will tell you why. I did not clean up the cum from the magazine. Once it dried, the pages adhered to each other. Fuck! Cumming on the pages without cleaning it meant I needed to buy more magazines from my favorite bookstore. The cashier knew my name this time but wasn't watching me closely like the others. I needed more than one magazine, so I decided to steal three.

Yes, I did say steal, and I did not stutter. I made my move and shoved three magazines into my jacket. Once I tucked those magazines into my coat, I swiftly tried to pass the cashier. He stopped me dead in my tracks because I was walking faster than usual.

While standing on the podium, he looked directly at me and said, "Put those magazines back, Cecil." I was shocked and asked myself, how in the hell did he know? Are you asking yourself if I took those magazines back? Yes, I did indeed take those magazines back. After that, I gave up trying to buy and steal dirty magazines. I thanked the cashier for not calling the police on me. He smiled and said, "I understand why you were trying to steal them."

He also said, "I remember my first dirty magazine I stole from a local bookstore. However, I found myself in a juvenile detention center, and I did not want that to happen to you. That's all I needed to hear to make an informed decision.

That same evening, I decided to go home and salvage the ones I have already bought it. Out of the three sticky magazines, none were salvageable. Oh well, peace! If you are a European American I have just one question to ask before you go. Before I listed all the black sitcoms here in this chapter, which ones did you grow up watching? Well, that settles that, right? Peace!

By the way,

Did you understand the message I was trying to convey to you in this chapter?

Doing It in Dah Park

On Our Way To The Park

I Remember this one young, slim lady named Tina from fifteen years ago. While she worked in the deli department at Publix, we dated briefly.

That's what I will say for now, and hopefully, she is reading this book. Let me tell you a little bit about Tina. I was a player when I met her, and she wanted a committed relationship. I had a lot on my plate when we first met, but it was fun being with her.

One of my memory cells just kicked in, so allow me to take you back to fifteen years ago.

One day, I called her unexpectedly and asked if she wanted to go for a ride with me. Tina responded yes, but like most women, she kept asking me where she and I were going. It became annoying, but all I had to do was look at her in a certain way, and she would know not to ask anymore. I smiled when Tina finally stopped asking me. She asked what I was smiling about. I said, "I can't tell you."

I said to myself, "Good girl." I like a woman who cares enough to STFU and listen, allowing me to lead...

While in my car,... I told her we were going to a park in Altamonte Springs Florida. I mentioned this park had a nature walk, and she and I were going to walk along the path. I parked and walked towards the park. I could not help but notice the strange expression she kept giving me. I saw her "up to no good" expression when she looked at me. I said, "What is up? I see a devilish grin on your face, and YOU! can't hide it either." While headed to the park there were other couples surrounding us as we walked towards the park, Tina leaned over and whispered, "I want to let you know I'm not wearing any panties underneath this dress."

TIME OUT, READER.

I don't care whether you are a male or a female reading this part of the chapter; how could you "stop yourself from "CUMMING" in your underwear after hearing someone say that to you? ... So I whispered in her ear, "why are you teasing a junkyard dog in heat?" I said with a devilish grin. She repeated it again, "I'm not wearing any panties."

I simply shook my head and tried not to think about it as we walked across the street towards the park.

By the way, If you have not been able to put this book down, thank you. As honest as I was with you, I could not help myself and had only one thought pounding in my head. While on my nature walk with Tina, I stopped and looked around to the right, left, and to the back of me, like I was a hooded daytime burglar opening a window, and did not make another move until, I felt comfortable enough that no one was around. There were wooden rails along the way and I told her to put both hands on the rail, in a commanding firm voice. And, Like a "good girl",... she did it without questioning, "why"! If I had been a police officer, she would have been the perfect obedient suspect.

So, I might as well treat her like one. I stood behind her and lifted her dress up. When she looked over her shoulder and smiled, it was as if she knew what I had planned.

'I STOPPED FOR A SECOND, AND SMILED AND SAID TO MYSELF, "SHE'S SO DAMN NAUGHTY AND 'I LIKE IT!!.PEACE!

ON OUR WAY LEAVING THE PARK

Dominant/ Submissive Romance

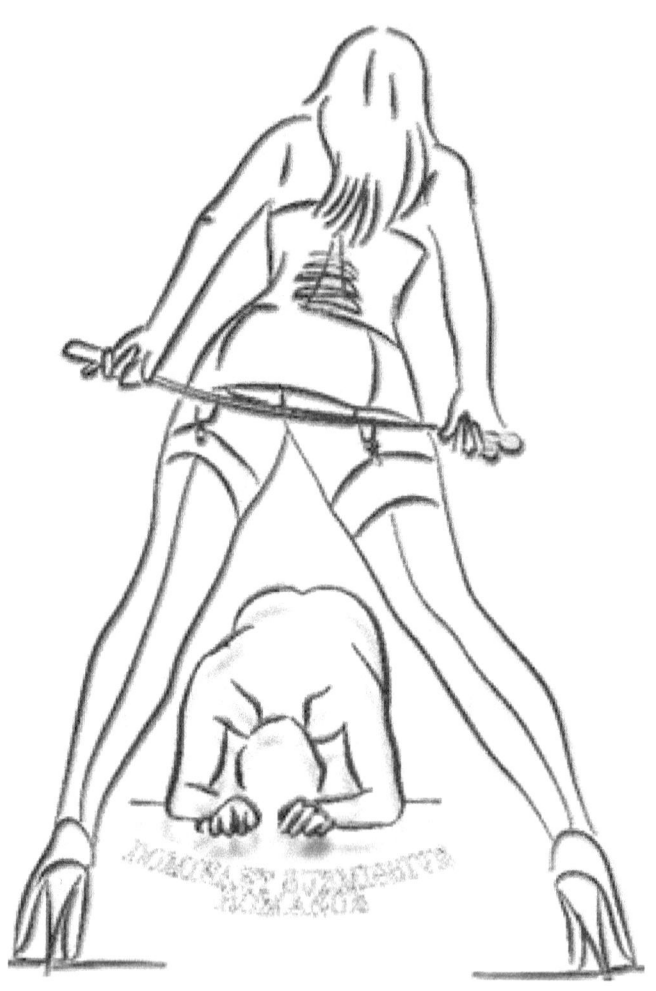

B efore I discuss my personal opinions and experiences in this chapter, I am not, nor do I claim to be, an expert on the subject. Now that I have made that "perfectly clear"! let's continue.

This was updated and added on August 16, 2024. I am sure you have your own definition of submissive, which is okay; I have always known that I prefer sexually submissive women, and I found this out by dating one of the women in one of my chapters. I would like to share what being submissive means to me and has always meant.

As a Dom, I want you to know that I am first a gentleman. You have to understand that I am completely focused on what is best for you, even if I am the one in charge and making all the decisions. Doing this frequently demands me to be unselfish; if you can't manage this dynamic, this relationship is not for you. A submissive must have complete faith in me and the decisions I make to relinquish all control and power to me. With each decision I make, you will be rewarded for trusting me to build your confidence. Everything I do is for one reason and one reason only, It pleases me with you being submissive.

In contrast, a submissive woman enjoys pleasing her spouse and has a "nurturing attitude"! If you are a woman reading this section, I am writing this for you: I know it is difficult for you to completely submit to a man. **Repeat: you will always be in control regardless of what he brings to the table financially, emotionally, or physically.**

It is okay to be fussy under these circumstances and submit to a person who values you and knows how to nurture, cherish, and respect you. To be the "dominant," I must be a man of integrity in the relationship. This means I should accept and admire your submission, which includes valuing your thoughts, opinions, and life goals. I will express my gratitude with something as simple as saying, "Thank you." I learned that showing and expressing my thanks allows you to offer your mind, body, and soul freely and happily.

You should only submit yourself when you can contribute emotionally and financially, not when you are emotionally insecure, unstable, or physically harmed by a previous relationship. Most women don't always take the time to get to know the man before submitting themselves. Later, he may treat her as if she is a doormat after establishing trust. Submission is meaningless if his words and deeds don't match.

You should know that fucking your partner is different from surrendering your love for him, no matter how excellent, the sex is. Let me be clear: "I am not referring to a woman who will passively accept unfair treatment.

"Regrettably, some women grew up watching their mothers in abusive marriages from a young age. I imagine that growing up in such a toxic environment would instill in them the belief that this is how men express their love. I am here to tell you that no one should ever treat a woman like a filthy, chained-up animal in the backyard. It is never acceptable, and I don't care how wealthy he or she is in their social status. Ladies, you are unique and deserve respect.

Under the right sexual circumstances, your partner's degrading behavior can be as sexy as hell; in other words, you enjoy the humiliation. "In this situation, finding someone who truly understands your needs will be very challenging, and rare."

So, don't settle for strangers fulfilling your fantasies until your partner is fully aware. In summary, individuals treat women as passive objects and hold the belief that they have the right to engage in any behavior, such as lying, cheating, physical abuse, and treating them as less than human. That behavior does not indicate an alpha male or Dom. He is a cowardly, self-centered individual who requires some introspection. So, let us not confuse the beautiful term "love" with "The Burning Bed."

The ideal man should recognize and cherish a woman who embodies traditional Southern values, which are becoming increasingly rare among today's women. Most women confuse being a submissive wife or girlfriend with giving up their independence.

Now I am going to discuss what flogging means to me:

"YOU DON'T JUST SWING A FLOGGER—
YOU EARN THE RIGHT TO."

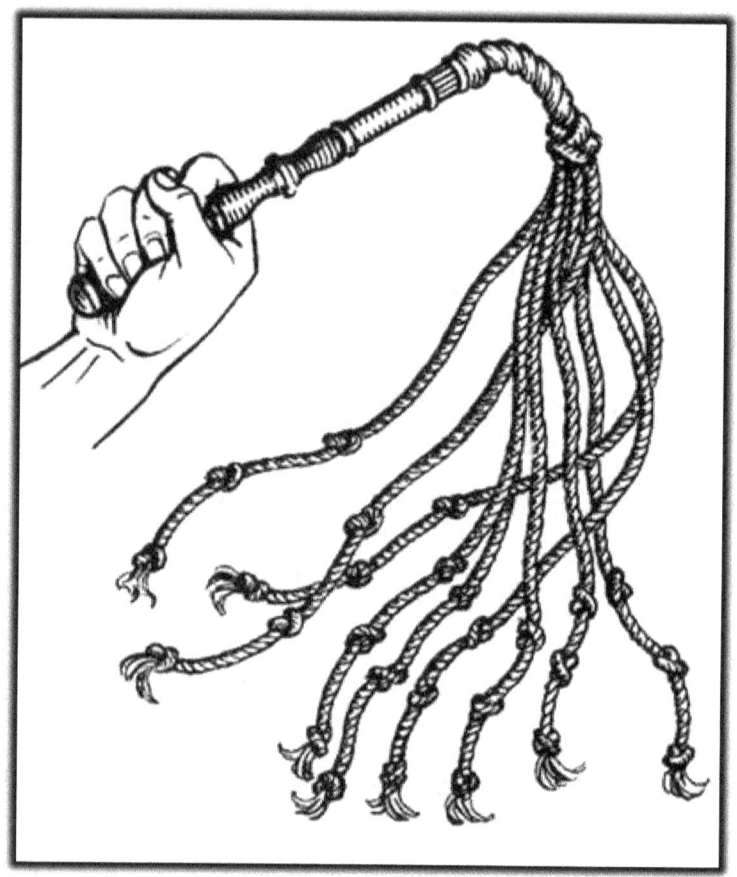

Respecting the safe word, you agreed on should be the number one rule when flogging starts pushing past what someone can take. If you're vanilla and have no clue what a flogger is, buckle up.

Flogging—also called flagellation—is the art of striking someone with a leather whip-like tool that's built for more than just looks. It can start soft, like a teasing warm-up, or hit hard enough to leave you wearing bruises like souvenirs. Those tails? They're not all the same. You've got fur for a sensual drag, leather and suede for that sting-meets-thud combo, rubber and silicone for a sharper bite, and even ball chains when you want the sound to make someone's skin crawl before you even touch them.

Me? I only pick up a flogger if my partner lights up at the thought of it—because the best kind of impact play is the kind that has them craving the next swing before the last one's even faded.

UNDERSTOOD?

Respecting the safe word you both have created should be his or her primary concern when flogging becomes too harsh to bear. I know you are vanilla, but if you don't know what a flogger is, let me explain. Flogging, or flagellation, involves striking someone with a leather flogger. The intensity of the flogging can vary, ranging from a gentle warm-up to a severe impact that causes bleeding. Floggers can have tails made from various materials, such as fur, leather, suede, rubber, silicone, and ball chains. I only use a flogger if my partner finds the experience stimulating.

A BDSM CROSS—usually a St. Andrew's Cross is basically a giant X or T frame built to lock someone in place.

BDSM CROSS

Arms and legs stretched out, nowhere to go. It's not about religion, it's about control. The dominant gets full access front or back—for whatever's been agreed to: flogging, teasing, or just making sure the submissive remembers exactly who's in charge.

There is a strategy, and if the women can tolerate extreme pain, I will execute it by flogging their backs, thighs, and asses. Typically, white ladies love this type of situation. Friends would ask me how I could flog a woman without feeling guilty. I tell them that, in my mind, I tell myself it is a form of retaliation for all the times white men raped black women during slavery.

At least for me, it is, and it takes place in a regulated, trusting atmosphere, a situation that black women did not experience during slavery. Every time I flog a white woman and hear her scream; it is not from pain but from pleasure.

I have always wondered why white women find enjoyment in being flogged, particularly by black men. In their minds, they may believe they deserve it in a strangely beautiful way. Again, it is all about trusting and ensuring the person is relaxed and appreciates it.

There was one big girl I knew, and she had lost weight since the last time I saw her. Unless she comes forward, I am not going to mention any names. After reading this book, I wanted to tell her that I photographed her enormous ass-bending-down doggie style (which I have since removed).

With every ounce of my strength, I was flogging the hell out of her massive white ass, and she simply laughed. She wasn't aiming her laughter at me; it was a response to the immense pain she was going through.

She realized that was beyond anything she had ever experienced and something she had wanted for quite some time. In BDSM, we refer to this as subspace, in which she is in a trance-like ecstasy while experiencing tremendous emotions, "simultaneously!" However, she was unable to find anyone to provide it, until I came into her life. I flogged her ass until it was a deep shade of purple.

She was ecstatic about the experience and immediately entered the bathroom to inspect her bruised ass.

Regardless of how hard I flogged her; she never sobbed or said the safe word. After that, I decided to raise my game, so one day at work, I came across a wooden paddle for a barbecue. Unfortunately, I never got to try it with her, but that's how things go sometimes. Another time, I shackled a white girl to her own bed frame, and I flogged her. Her pussy was moist with expectation, indicating that she enjoyed being flogged. I constantly used specific words to put her at ease, so that I knew what she desired.

And, as I mentioned earlier, she was always in command. When I am flogging a lady for the first time, and she says, "Stop," everything I am doing ceases. This is when trust comes in. Something about bondage and servitude fascinates me.

I have seen the Fifty Shades films, which are more of a fantasy than a realistic story. In the subsequent film, he transitions from dominant to submissive. That caused him to switch. What I will say next may not sit well with you as an Alpha female reading this, but when the perfect man for you enters your life and genuinely earns your obedience, you should only kneel to him in the privacy of your home when he arrives after establishing a solid bond with your submissive.

It is important to thoroughly explain kneeling rather than expect it. Kneeling is appropriate at certain times and places. For instance, she might kneel right before playtime or upon his return from work.

Let me reminisce: Six years before the publication of this book, I remember a white girl cooking dinner for me while watching television in her favorite chair. I was at her house, not mine, so it did not matter. She kneeled before me, extending her arms while holding the plate. She was submissive and different than anyone I had ever met. She served me first and then sat down next to me on the floor to eat her meal.

Even if we were at a park, and I was sitting on the bench, she was uncomfortable sitting next to me and would much rather sit next to me on the ground. I never forced her to do it; and she felt it played a role in our relationship. To be honest with you, being her Dom spoiled the hell out of me, that I can't explain to this very day.

KNEELING

Art Imitating Real Life Page 131

After our breakup, I did not pursue this connection with anyone else because she held a unique place in my life. Just so you and I are clear, this is typically associated with BDSM, not with conventional relationships. Kneeling is acceptable in a setting that acknowledges the nature of the connection. Kneeling is allowed when the male enters the house or mentally prepares for the desired scene.

Kneeling is yet another technique for a submissive to demonstrate her Submissiveness and her commitment to her position in the relationship. This does not apply to long-distance or online relationships because that's unrealistic. I would not recommend this type of relationship because it is unreasonable and should be avoided; this is simply my protective mentality.

Being a black man and kneeling in front of me signifies something different. In a vanilla relationship, men are embarrassed when women kneel to their dominant partner. To reiterate what I previously stated, it is acceptable for a woman to kneel before her boyfriend in the correct environment, situation, and relationship. Am I saying you should kneel before your partner in public? Well that all depends on the type of relationship you two created when you first met each other, and don't have a problem with it, no matter what the environment is. Some people will read this and think, "I only kneel to the man above." If you truly embrace this philosophy, why would you kneel, period?

Before drafting this book, I met a woman walking in the gym parking lot from which I had recently walked out. I asked if she wanted to continue our amicable talk at the famous coffee shop across the street. It wasn't about sex or previous relationships; it was about life in general, and everything was going great. Given the intensity of our conversation, I felt compelled to demonstrate how different our personal lives were. So, I showed her a photo of a woman kneeling to me; this allowed me to know who I was dealing with quickly without wasting each other's time. She was disgusted and appeared to think that no "genuine" man would ever let a woman kneel in front of him.

Hell, I only showed her because she made me feel comfortable, not knowing she was horrified by it. I told myself that she was a closed-minded woman entitled to her opinion. It was easy to understand why because she had been divorced for over twenty years. You can't judge a book by its cover; our talk ended there. It took me years and three spouses to determine which personality type works best for me in a long-term relationship.

I have concluded that the kind of lady I need around me is someone open-minded, nonjudgmental, and who has experienced comparable life events. My attraction to B.D.S.M. stems from the types of women I want to surround myself with. I am willing to invest more of myself in this type of connection. My ideal location for that type of relationship would be inside my home dungeon filled with special equipment for my companion. Unless you have my permission, that one room in the house is off-limits.

Just imagine walking inside my home without being able to detect where it is located. Only like-minded men and women can freely express themselves without fear of condemnation. It would consist of blindfolds, wrist and ankle cuffs, floggers, nipple clamps, paddles, canes, vibrators, tape, collars, rope, a padding bench, a jail cell, an x-cross, a bed with four iron polls on each corner, and other unmentionable items. I can't emphasize this enough: first, establish trust to be respected when the safe word is used.

If anxiety comes into play, you should be able to trust your Dom, so it does not destroy your faith and submission. A man's top priority should be to please the woman first. Some men believe that it is all about getting their cock sucked. If they don't lick the pussy, it is indicative that they are not interested in their partner's orgasm." The reason they don't lick the pussy is because they don't care about their partner having an orgasm.

Additionally, foreplay extends beyond the confines of the bedroom. Foreplay occurs every waking moment you spend with one another. It could be a glance across the room, or a slap on the ass as you walk past, or a kiss on the neck. Even saying "thank you" might be considered foreplay. Over time, I have learned to pay attention and appreciate what my partner does for me. Most men take a woman's Submissiveness for granted and have unrealistic expectations, which leads to failure. Trusting me allows her to be vulnerable, knowing that I won't breach her trust, allowing her to give freely and enjoy the moment. In both films which I am certain you have read or heard about, there was a man who is both dominant and submissive and should have remained dominant.

They undermined his character; once he yielded, she no longer desired that connection with him, and the excitement subsided. She cherished their relationship, but he ruined it by succumbing to her demands. They had a fascinating topic to discuss, but they botched it.

I DECIDED TO LIST SOME OF MY MISCONCEPTION'S ABOUT B.D.S.M AND HERE THEY ARE!

A DOMINANT DON'T LOVE THEIR SUBMISSIVES /

A dominant can love their submissive while maintaining a D/s relationship. It is entirely possible to be both loving and dominant.

SUBMISSIVES ARE BISEXUAL
/

"Submissiveness is not dependent on sexual orientation. Not desiring a partner of a certain gender does not exclude someone from being submissive. Forced homosexuality can be consensual for some individuals."

SUBMISSIVES DO NOT HAVE LIMITS
/

"Submissives have boundaries, even if they say they don't. Everyone has limits, whether they admit it or not."

SUBMISSIVES ALLOW THEIR HUSBANDS TO ABUSE THEM
/

There are misconceptions about submissive wives allowing mistreatment. Many think it means allowing physical, mental, and verbal abuse.

SUBMISSIVES

/

Are nothing but doormats to men. They will do anything a man tells them. Submissives / have been abused by their fathers.

The one thing I have never understood is why people won't mind their business. I say this because there were times, she kneeled to me in public and white people would lose their fucking minds. I could see the disgusted look on their faces, and I did not give a damn either. I asked her one day why she wanted to kneel to me, and her reason was straightforward.

Lara believed black men were superior and all white women should kneel to black men. Her words, not mine, okay? Before you judge me for allowing her to kneel to me, you should be asking yourself,

"What's wrong with it?'

Why does what I do make you judge me of all people? Why can't this be acceptable in any lifestyle?

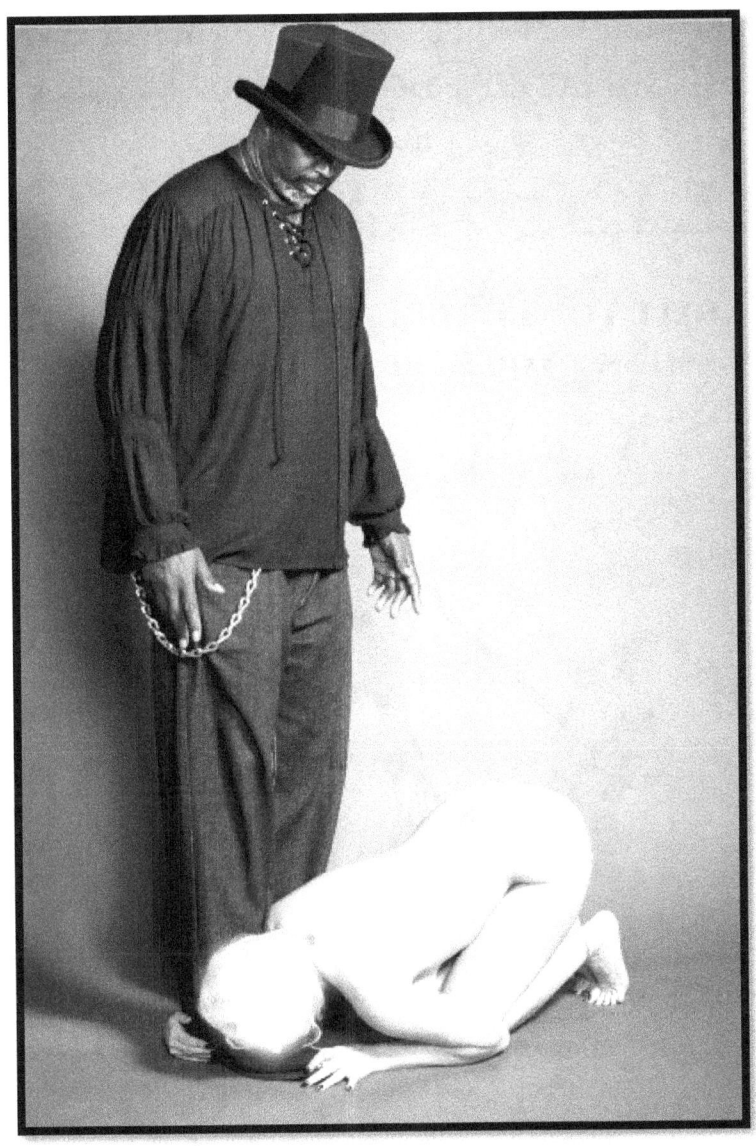

There are other chapters in this book that are far more disgusting than this unique relationship between consenting adults. In the proper dynamics, this is expected of a submissive in the BDSM lifestyle. There is one last thought I want to leave you with before you read this next chapter.

Most white men will never admit their desire to be,
"HUMILIATED & DONINATED", by a black
queen.

**KNELL YOU LITTLE FRAGILE WHITE BOY!!
DON'T YOU DARE LOOK UP AT ME!!**

YOU ARE NOT WORTHY OF THAT.

Glory Hole Days

READ WITH CAUTION

Here in Florida, there is a place called Fantasyland Adult Theater in Tampa, Florida.

From what I can recall, this place had different areas within the building for dirty magazines, X-rated videos, and an area for the title of this chapter: the "Glory Hole" area. Just so you have a visual, it is a large room with black-painted walls. In fact, once you enter the area, there is no information anywhere to be found saying "Glory Hole." Only horny, freaky, devious, kinky, perverse, perverted, twisted, and weird people would know of its existence. There was a website I used to search for couples to party with. When I say party (it is a code word for fucking), depending on how saying party is used in a sentence, I spoke to a couple online who planned to visit Fantasyland. I was excited, as I had never visited this place before and had heard so much positive feedback about it.

Yes, I was bold for driving two hours to meet this couple I never met in person, where the husband planned to allow strangers to sleep with his wife and, in some cases, his girlfriend. Do not get the wrong idea about women who enjoy participating in glory holes. Honestly, if she did not want to be there, she would not be. I am sure a vanilla person reading this right now saying how to your closed-minded self, how can she allow (wait, allow) you mean want strange men fucking her? I raised my hand from the far back last row in the classroom to answer that question, and my response would be because I love fucking, period.

You might say to yourself I like fucking too, but I don't need a bunch of strange men to do it with. If you said this, my response would be, look bitch mind your own business. She is an adult deciding what she wants to do with her body and who we are to judge. We drove up around the same time when I finally found the place. I was like a kid at an all-you-can-eat buffet as I stood around and waited outside for them to get out of the truck. When that did not happen, I decided to walk inside and wait for them.

Finally, they walked in and past me like Donald Trump walking past a journalist from CNN News.

I was crushed; they did not stop to say, "Nice to meet you finally." Glory holes are always an intriguing topic. Two strangers walk into separate, side-by-side, small rooms with closed doors. The wall features a five-inch-diameter hole, typically reaching the waist of an average-sized adult between 5'6" - 6'0".

If a man's cock has more girth than five inches, then this may be a problem. Nevertheless, if you are a dwarf, this may also present a problem. As I write this chapter section, a vision suddenly enters my mind, making me laugh. I visualized a male little person (I hope I am being politically correct here) looking through the glory hole instead of pulling down his pants and sticking his cock through it. Wait, I need a minute. LOL. Okay, I will say it. I had another idea: what if both sides of the glory hole room had little people in it? What on earth are they going to do?

The only thought that came to mind would be them looking directly into each other's eyes from both sides, and then say hello, and maybe shake hands and say, " NICE TO MEET YOU?" That is about all that can do, right? And that's only because I am assuming they are of a male and female. Seriously, I would pay to see that shit, "BIG TIME! Fuck it, I am going all in and say this. What if the man is around six feet, six inches tall like myself, and a female little person is on the other side?

Hopefully, my cock is not erect, so she can at least suck or lick me until my cock is hard. Otherwise, once I become fully erect again, there is no way she will be able to suck or lick my cock from above her head. Hell, she can't even get on her tippy toes to hang on it. On the other hand, I guess my cock could rest on top of her head, I suppose, right?... Or better yet, she could wait until I am soft again to suck or lick it. That is if I have not taken a "BLUE PILL" get my drift??

On 09/15/2024, another thought came to me, she could lube up her hands and then reach above her head and put her hands around my shaft and jack me off, right? Back to the original part of "Vanilla Sheets," Let me add a couple of missing sentences to this paragraph. The fact that I am 6'6" inches tall maybe I should warn her to put on goggles before I stuff my cock through the hole. If I ain't careful, I will accidentally poke her in the eye with the head of my cock. All right, all right, all right, enough. I will move on.

Back to the Glory Hole: One time, I was an observer. As an observer, you are among those interested in watching from a short distance away. A man put his cock through the hole in the wall, and there was someone on the other side. Yes, I was standing on the side, three feet away, like everyone else. I was waiting to see what was going to happen next. Keep in mind you are not on the side of the man putting his cock in the hole; you are on the side of the person who plans to do something with the cock in the hole. Got it? Remember that song by Grace Jones, "Pull Up to the Bumper"? I guess you can call this "Pull Up to the Glory Hole Baby" and stick your cock through the hole. Enough! Back to the Glory Hole: Before I experienced it firsthand, I had heard about it, and I must admit, after a couple of visits, I found it intriguing.

But I could never understand the fascination of going back daily. Do I still have your attention? As a male, imagine for a moment trying glory holes for the first time and not knowing who is on the other side. The head you received was so incredible that you wanted to go out on a date with that person.

You also wanted to know who was on the other side right after you nutted in their mouth. Since it was your first time, you did not realize you could not talk to them. Technically, you are supposed to leave after you busted a hot, fresh nut in their mouth, but not you, Mr. First Time. You decide to ask your neighbor, What's your name? They did not respond because they respected the rules of that area. You think they are being an asshole, but they are not. You then become angry and wait until you hear their door opening. What happened next jacked you up for the rest of your life. On the other side of your booth, there was a man after the door opened. What a trip, huh! And it was your wife's brother?

Fuck! All this time, you did not know that bitch ass mutha fucka got down like that. What would you say or do now? Hell, you can't even tell anyone what just happened to you. I could understand if you were the star of an X-rated movie and received hefty compensation for doing it. I assume you will be performing for free because you are reading this chapter, and compensation is unnecessary. You are a freaky-ass fucker.

Having this book is another reason you would perform for free. Never mind the fact that you are reading this chapter. So, who is the closet freak now? I suppose we would title the movie you played a starring role in, "My Brother-in-Law," part one. Because, more than likely, you are hoping your wife's brother will also star in the sequel. Glory holes can be enjoyable if everyone involved is familiar with one another. Like a group of your freaky-ass friends, all meet and go together.

No vanilla folks stay your ass at home and sit this one out. Reserve the entire room when your group finally decides to visit this place. This way, you won't have to worry about strangers trying to grab your ass, pussy, or get some free head. If I saw you all pull up simultaneously, I would make friends with everyone before you enter. Just saying. Anyway, I hope you took a damn shower before sticking your cock through the hole. No woman in her right state of mind would touch your stinky-ass cock.

This is particularly true if you don't adhere to the practice of circumcision. You may have lint around the penis head and no idea what else. Another thing to keep in mind is that if you are constantly worried about who is on the other side of your booth, it might be best to simply observe.

Request permission to enter the booth while one of your friends is inside and ensure that you maintain sufficient distance to engage in masturbation. Just make sure you are not one of those people who shoots cum all over the place. That will get you kicked out, and not only that, but you may also get your ass kicked. This type of sexual escape does not just apply to open-minded people. In fact, if you are sapiosexual, autosexual, demisexual, fluid, heterosexual, or monosexual, then at least try this once. If you are lesbian, gay, bisexual, or transgender, you may want to take part in the festivities as well. I suppose lesbians would enjoy this sexual activity also. As I am writing, I am trying to visualize, and the only vision that comes to mind is of two women, one on each side of the booth, with enormous, clits. LOL!

They both pull down their panties and stick their big ass clits through the hole. OMG! I am laughing so hard right now. This is additional information added on 09/15/2024, that is not in "VANILLA SHEETS" Another scene would involve using dildos on each other through the hole. You just imagined that didn't you? You don't have to admit it to me because it is our little secret. I can only assume those two women are going to either rub or suck each other's clit. I clearly remember saying the hole was only five inches in diameter.

I never mentioned width. We can just go ahead and assume it is at least two inches. To all of you down low or openly transgender folks, hopefully, that's enough width for you to stick your cocks through to the other side. Wait! I ain't assuming you all have narrow cocks either, nor do I personally know or care. Please forgive me, for I have sinned by talking about lesbians or transgender people in this book.

Now, if you have read this far into this chapter, it is time for me to address transgender people and cross-dressers again. You folks, wait, excuse me. I meant you ladies will have to decide who is fucking who when you visit the glory hole area. In other words, who's cock is long enough to go through the hole. Just make damn sure that decision is made before you people enter the booth, okay? If not, You Can Bet Your Bottom Dollar, the two of you will be arguing like a couple of bitches. Speaking of "Glory Holes" Back in 1998, Google says that George Michael made headlines for all the wrong reasons.

The singer was arrested for performing a lewd sexual act on a plainclothes undercover police officer in a public toilet in Los Angeles. I wonder what LEWD act he could be doing in a public restroom. There are only a couple of options, right? When I watched some of his videos, I would say he is a bottom, right? Or did you just say who the hell cares, right?

When it became public knowledge, I wondered what he was doing with the undercover officer? Did the undercover officer get his cock sucked first or did he penetrate George before he arrested him? What kind of evidence did he collect? So many unanswered questions again, right? Millennials won't know what I am talking about in this chapter. This is a good thing, though, for many reasons.... "Peace"!

Hair Pulling

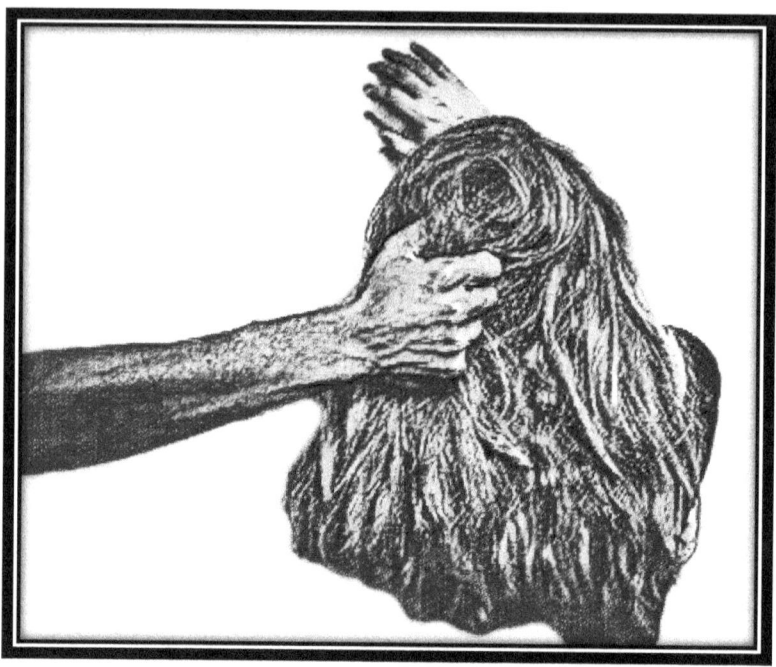

(From an instructional point of view)

In the audio version I have Royal reading this chapter. Keep that in mind while reading, please.

Before proceeding with the hair-pulling chapter, I request that you verify that the hair from her skull is her natural hair.

Just ask me, I should know, because my hair is so fucking nappy that I prefer to wear wigs or extensions. See, I told you. Cecil? Stay the hell out of my chapter you are letting me narrate please! Damn!! Alright Royal, go ahead. Thank you!

However, depending on the length and color of the hair, it is not natural for people of a particular ethnicity. Wait! what the hell are you insinuating here Cecil? WHAT THE FUCK ARE YOU TALKING ABOUT ROYAL? Never mind, asshole. I'll continue with your story Pay me no mind Royal; I'm just messing with you. Okay. Let me keep this shit one hundred.

I mean black women like myself wear hair extensions beyond the crack of our fucking ass, it is just as fake as a three-dollar bill with my face on it. If she pats her head sometimes like I do, this is another way to determine that she's wearing a wig, and it's hotter than a motherfucker under there.

Personally, when I see other bitches wearing their natural hair, I have always been envious of those fair skinned HOES! Royal!! Continue please. Okay! As Cecil wrote the last paragraph, I can't help but laugh when I see black women sporting a weave or extensions beyond a natural look. It is possible that people of all other ethnicities who have long hair also wear weaves or extensions, but the length and color of those bitches' hair are similar, making it difficult to tell.

We, I mean I am aware that some men enjoy pulling a woman by the hair while acting as if they own her. Wait a minute... Cecil! You know you have me as a Dominatrix in a chapter called "Under the Cover" right? Yea! I am aware of it, why?

You know damn well I ain't down with some cock sucka pulling my hair, right? Royal!! if you keep this shit up! I am going to have to continue with my own story, myself. Well, umm, I can't make any promises, so here goes.

What you are about to read or hear does not apply to Royal, period! Anyways, there are appropriate and inappropriate ways of grabbing a woman by the hair. Some egotistical assholes are so ignorant that they believe all it takes to turn ladies on is to simply grab them by the hair and pull. It is messed up to think so because that's far from the truth. If you are a male reading this chapter, please remember that I wrote this with you in mind. As a man, you should never pull a woman's hair before you have conversed with her about the things that she finds pleasing.

Talking with each other about the things that excite and irritate both of you is essential so there are no misunderstandings. This Hashtag MeToo movement is something you fellas should keep in mind when you think of pulling her by the hair. Do not pull close to her forehead at any time.

As you get closer to her forehead, you will stretch her neck back more, which is a potentially dangerous move. Pull the hair close to the skull and tug it slightly but firmly to give her the impression that you are in control. It is also important to pay close attention to the sounds she is making and her body language. If you make this mistake, you might as well assume she does not want to fuck you, as it won't only turn her off but also make her feel uncomfortable. Peace!

Head Honcho

M

ost women become defiant immediately upon hearing the term, "submissive."

I have come to the realization that the misinterpretation of the term "submissive" is a result of previous abusive relationships. I will reiterate it one last time to ensure that the woman in the rear of the room can hear me: being submissive does not make you a doormat.

You can only be treated that way if you consent to that behavior and don't advocate for yourself. Right now, I am not going to concentrate on that one!

One day, I decided to add I was dominant on a dating website. Most women who contacted me asked, "Does this imply that you must maintain complete control and the woman has no say in the relationship?" "Some women chose to assume I was insensitive to their needs and desires.". The true meaning of "submission" or "submissive" was only known to a few women who contacted me. Most of the women who were alpha females could not resist leaving negative comments on my profile.

I snicker while reading their messages, shaking my head in disbelief and leaving me stupid ass messages. Afterward, I realized that having that mentality wasn't totally a woman's fault. I blamed the men in her past relationships before meeting me.

I am depressed by the reality that a young girl must witness the distressing and traumatic sight of her mother enduring both verbal and physical abuse during her crucial formative years. "There is no doubt in my mind that it has an impact on their adult lives and the choices they make regarding the men they fuck and have babies with.

As I wrote in one of my chapters titled "My Gay Ass Cousin," I am familiar with the experience of growing up in an environment that's not conducive to healthy development. I know from personal experience. For instance, if you were to overhear your mother discussing the father's affair with another woman, that would serve as an example.

I don't know what the consequences of a father having an affair are will have on his children. As an adult, facing the reality of your upbringing with an untrustworthy parent could be even more distressing. On the other hand, I believe this will have irreversible long-term consequences for the girl or boy. As an illustration of this, one of my closest friends needs to have the feeling that she oversees every decision in the relationship that she is in.

For example, if you ever find yourself in the driver's seat of a vehicle with her. You should expect her to tell you when to stop, turn, and accelerate. I can bet that she experienced something in her previous relationships that caused her to feel like she did. Please read this entire chapter because I plan to take this story in a specific direction, so please be patient.

The following is an example that I can recall in absolute detail. After going to Crystal's apartment multiple times, I noticed she had Internet service from two internet providers. I might have been able to avoid catching it or act like I did not care. It is neither my place nor my money, so I chose not to ask about it and just observe. It would be reasonable to assume that I would keep my mouth shut. However, not caring for someone is not a trait that defines me.

I asked Crystal how long she had been paying for two different Internet service providers, and she said it had been for a little over a year. She said a little over a year without hesitation, and I thought, WTF, why? To be clear, that wasn't the only thought I had in mind. Naturally, I intended to say something about it to her; nevertheless, I decided not to say anything.

After several weeks, I asked how much she paid monthly for both Internet service providers. Again, she was unable to provide a reasonable answer that made sense. If she can't give the amount of both bills, then why is she continuing to pay for both services?

I convinced myself that she must be incredibly lazy or unconcerned about the situation. When she told me the amount, I could not help but scratch my head and wonder how much she could save if she canceled her subscription to just one of the Internet service providers. At that point, she had already paid for both internet providers for over a year. To give you a rough estimate, her monthly payment was $185.

Because I am perceptive, I requested that she turn off one of the Internet service providers when she had the opportunity. After a few weeks had passed, I inquired once again about whether she had removed one of the Internet service providers. I never asked her after that because she became upset almost immediately after I did. I could not break through that barrier to convince her otherwise because there was no way for me to accomplish it. I was looking out for her best interests.

Still, her previous experiences with men caused her to get defensive, as if I were attempting to push her to do something against her will. Even though I was correct in evaluating her circumstances, she would not allow me to assist her because of her past experiences with men.

She finally cut off one of the Internet providers three months later, saving almost fifty percent of the monthly bill of $185. It does not matter when she decides to act; what matters is that she did it all on her own.

This chapter targets the men reading it: if you value the person you are interacting with and understand their reluctance, given that the relationship is typically based on a past relationship, you should approach it cautiously and patiently to avoid drawing attention to yourself. In addition, having a traditional lady who understands the responsibilities men bear in a relationship is crucial. This chapter was boring, but I wanted to convey that not all men try to manipulate and control you.

We see things differently and may want to help. Thanks for reading this chapter and I hope you heard this message I was trying to convey.

Peace! Thanks for reading...I hope it wasn't too boring? I was just trying to make a point...

Her Story
Not Mine

From me to you:
This chapter gets real about suicide and the dark thoughts that some of us face. If you've ever been there — or if you're there right now — don't fight it alone.

**Please reach out. Call or text
988, or visit 988lifeline.org. I'm rooting for you.**

This chapter is a tough pill to swallow—and a rollercoaster of emotions. So do yourself a favor: find your nearest 7-Eleven, grab a Big Gulp, and get ready to force down this big fucking pill I'm about to pop in your mouth. Cool? **

Oh yeah—one last thing before we dive in:

Cecil has already warned you (more than once!) that he's got attention deficit disorder. So don't act surprised when shit gets a little... all over the place

Reader, there are about 4 characters in this chapter.

- o **John:** One of the narrators
- o **Earl:** Another narrator
- o **Candy** the main character in this story
- o **Cecil** is the main character in this story.
- o **Zack,** Candy's husband, and last Earl the neighbor across the street.

Taken from the audiobook.

So, if Cecil happens to lose you somewhere along the way—or if something feels off or out of order—just blame it on his A.D.D. and smile to yourself. He told you upfront. That's his disclaimer.

Earl Speaking: There was this one sweet, innocent girl named Candy. Born in Chicago, Illinois. Her mother drank herself unconsciously every single night after work. That was her routine. Come home, drink, pass out. And Candy? She grew up thinking that was normal. Now imagine that. A child thinks that blackout drinking is just what moms do.

Cecil gets it. He's lived through some of that. His father was an alcoholic too. So, this ain't a story from afar—it's one that hits close to home. And yet, he believes in something deeper:

That boys and girls absorb trauma differently.

Not better. Not worse. Just different.

But here's the hard truth: girls with an alcoholic parent are often more vulnerable to fucked up shit than boys. Cecil stands on that.

Let's argue it out for a second. When a girl's mother is passed out drunk—face down on the couch—is her risk the same as a boy's?

Nah. It's not.
We know there are child predators in this world. Right?

Now close your eyes—no seriously, just for a moment—and picture this:

You're Candy.

You're a little girl.

Your mama is out cold in the living room, and you're just there... a child... unsupervised.

What kind of neighborhood are you in? What's outside that front door? Who's got eyes on your house?

What if your mama doesn't wake up easily when she's drunk? What if something happens before she even opens her eyes?

What if there's a man in the neighborhood—one who suffers from Pedophilic Disorder?

How would Candy, a child, even begin to recognize that danger?

Would she know the difference between someone being "nice" and someone grooming her?

Probably not.
That's the part people don't like to say out loud—but needs to be said.

Because by the time that mama wakes up, it could already be too late.

Would you agree?

Let's keep it one hundred: somebody should've called child protective services. Somebody should've said something. Because that little girl deserved better.

And so do a lot of other kids just like her.

Or some kind of intervention to protect her and her sister. Yes—she has a sister.
My bad, I forgot to mention that earlier.

Instead of the mother getting help or the father stepping in, they did what some families do when they don't want to face the truth: they handed Candy and her sister off to yet another religious institution to be raised. That's what you're about to read—or listen to—depending on which version of this book you picked up.

Once Candy got old enough to comprehend life—and have real conversations with her father—he began to doubt whether Candy and her sister were even his daughters.

I don't know how old you are as you're reading this, but there's an old saying that goes a little something like this:

"Momma's baby, daddy's maybe."

Yeah. You remember that one?

There must've been moments—probably late at night—when he questioned where the hell she'd been after the bar closed. She'd come home twisted drunk.

And maybe, just maybe, he wondered if she'd slept with somebody from the bar and didn't even remember his name... or how she got there...

It's me Cecil again, I have doubts that my youngest son is mine. I won't address that in this chapter or any other chapter. I have my reasons, and I hope you understand there are some things you must keep buried deep in the ground, if you know what I mean. Candy's parents married twice, divorced, and realized they loved each other but could not live together. So many of us have been in this situation and should have gone our separate ways instead of making each other miserable. I was married three times and left in each of those cases. One potential reason for my difficulties in commitment could be related to personal identity and self-love. It is not necessarily that my past partners or relationships were flawed, but I struggled with self-acceptance, understanding, and identity.

My lack of self-awareness blocked my ability to engage in and commit to relationships fully.

Go ahead Earl is there something you want to add? Let us get deeper into Candy's life, shall we? Twelve years in Catholic school and four of those years were in all-girl Catholic high school, and we have heard how they put the fear of God in them, and they were going to hell if they broke the commandments.

I see you are in agreement with me, so go ahead Cecil. I won't add my opinion about being in that institutional environment like Candy and her sister.

Earl: Being told what to do, where you can and can't go, curfews, no boys, no drinking, no smoking, can't learn from your mistakes, tongue kiss, no sucking her first cock, no pussy licking by a male or female, no skinny dipping, no opinions of your own, everything is yes, mam, no mam, damn!!! Fuck no! I can't even imagine being in such a restrained environment like that, can you? Here is the kicker: can you imagine how naive Candy was after high school? Being hand-fed information from birth to adulthood must be confusing as hell.

Cecil: Now that I have given you some background let us put some hot sauce on the BBQ ribs for your brain. Now Candy is finally on her own and likes the first boy who shows her some interest. I am unsure if that is a mistake, but you should continue reading.

Earl: A 24-year-old bad boy named Zack was hanging out with his friends in a forbidden location called "The Woods." While out there, he made his move, and Candy lost her virginity while she lived with her parents.

Cecil: I just had a thought while writing this part of the chapter that came to mind. That was Candy's first introduction to sex, and you can just go ahead and wonder what the rest of this chapter is like with Zack as Candy's boyfriend.

Earl: Metaphorically speaking, as we prepare to descend from the peak of this rollercoaster, it is crucial to ensure your safety and comfort. If you are wearing a wig or hairpiece, please take a moment to remove it to avoid any potential disruption during the rest of this chapter.

Are you ready? Of course, she did not know anything about condoms or any type of protective prevention for becoming pregnant or diseases. You know damn well that Catholic school did not teach Candy any of this while being told everything related to sex is sinful. Honestly, they should dedicate a class regarding sex, right? Candy did not even know they called the split between her legs a pussy.

Cecil: I am sure the first time she saw a man's cock; she must have thought that was some kind of weird growth. I can also imagine Candy wondering why that weird growth grew whenever he was near her. I am sure she thought of many things at that age.

Earl: Off the subject: This is why so many women end up being abducted or manipulated into prostitution or tortured. Candy was seventeen years old, and Zack was twenty-four.

They were married three months before having their first child.

Cecil: This chapter will become engaging, and you are about to read what I mean, so I highly suggest you keep reading. Again, I just wanted you to have some context about Candy and Zack, that will all make sense later in the chapter, okay? I am sure there were many signs Candy should not have gotten involved with him.

Earl: Zack brainwashed and controlled her from the beginning of their relationship, and Candy was too naive to notice. Being in a Catholic school from damn near birth to high school, how in the world would she know what to look out for, right? This shit happens all the time to girls sent to Catholic schools, and those schools are not teaching anything about sex, boys, pregnancies, diseases, drugs, etc.

Cecil: I am surprised a pimp did not find her before meeting Zack and brainwashed her into being one of his bitches.

When I say she was lucky a pimp did not brainwash her, I mean

because she was young, naive, and ready, as we used to say when I used to be a pimp. Nevertheless, her new-found boyfriend Zack has some serious issues that she will soon discover. It became noticeable to Candy that Zack was fighting

his demons without knowing his background.

Earl: One evening while Candy's mom was drunk again on the couch, Zack, and Candy snook in the house, and he fucked Candy on a dirty-ass mattress that was in the basement. This behavior explains Zacks's mentality and tells you everything you need to know about him. She mentioned sex was always about him from the very moment they met. If you have been in or in this type of one-dimensional sex, please keep reading.

Cecil: In one of my chapters, I mentioned how some men can be very selfish, and Zack is another. Here is why I gave you so much information about her earlier. From the moment they met, Zack was a selfish, controlling fucker, no pun intended. This time, I won't put all the blame on Candy. You know why, right? Most of the blame should be on the Catholic school and her parents. Neither one of them did not teach her about contraceptives or sex.

Cecil: Candy mentioned how they would scare the holy ghost out of them regarding boys and sex. However, we know what happens when you try to tell someone not to open that door with the red X on it and fog coming from the bottom of the door. You can't help but become curious, right? Fuck it!, I know I would. That happened to Candy's curiosity when she graduated from Catholic high school.

John: Let us take a break for a second from talking about Candy and Zack, okay? Some systems are so messed up when it comes to institutional religion. Many girls grow up with the impression that sex carries a negative connotation. This perspective can shape their views and experiences in ways that are not always healthy or positive. And that is messed up. Would you agree? Please don't give this book a one-star review because Cecil is expressing his opinions.

Cecil: I am going continue talking about Candy and Zack and their life together before his tragic ending. She told me that sex from the moment they met and for over 40 years was about him only. Her needs were never of his concern, and he would just touch a few times and stick his cock in and bust a nut. Wait! Afterward, either go right to sleep or get out of bed to get on the computer. He also wasn't a touchy-feely kind of kid either. Zack was also a very jealous kid, which never changed; I will address this later in this chapter. I almost forgot that everything had to be on his way in every aspect of their lives together. There was no WE in their relationship.

Candy: Fox News was Zack's source of news. That also applied to voting Republican when me and my father were Democrats, as far back as I can possibly remember. I would do whatever Zack wanted, and that was voting against my heart.

Cecil: I wasn't surprised, because I have heard of this happening to women such as Candy and countless others.

Candy: Zack slowly became an alcoholic, and his favorite alcohol was Jack Daniels or Jim Beam on the Rocks. The difference between the two was that Jack Daniels made him angry, and he suddenly wanted to start a fight. A prime example would be the one time a couple with kids in the car pulled up next to us and looked over at the same time he did. While driving I stopped at a red light, that's when Zack jumped out of his car and started yelling and "SCREAMING! at the couple in the other car,

FOR ABSOLUTLY NO REASON! I was terrified and begged him to please get back into the car. It was a situation that I should not have been a part of. Having a mother who says never to leave your man and do what he tells you is also messed up. This is why I didn't say or do anything about it. It took Zack a few days to calm down from it. Honestly, this was another reason I did not know how to leave Zack and was scared to move away from him. If I had moved away, I would not have been introduced to all sorts of FUCKED UP SHIT, during our marriage. If you are wondering what kind of FUCKED-UP shit, I am talking about?

Then, here goes, liquor and coke for starters. I failed to mention that Zack had messed up parents, just like mine. Someone should have taught me what to look out for during my Catholic School days, right? But, since you are paying attention, how would I know the difference between what behavior is acceptable and what is not? When you have an answer, please make sure this does not happen to anyone else. I'll continue...

My father was hardly ever around because my mom was always drunk. It made sense for them to put me and my sister in a

Catholic school and not take responsibility for raising me and my sister. Thirty-eight years into my marriage, there were subtle signs that something was happening to my husband, and I couldn't put my finger on it. After several years of symptoms, he opted to undergo a series of medical tests. A P.E.T. scan revealed the presence of lung and colon cancer.

Additionally, I found out he also had thyroids. Zack was being hardheaded and refused all medical treatments that were suggested by our doctors, and friends. No matter how many times I tried to encourage him to get the treatment, he refused. Zack and I had a neighbor across the street, and we were close friends.

One evening, Zack told Ray the neighbor, that he was tired of thinking about cancer treatments. Zack also told Ray he was considering ending his life, and

Ray: Shut the fuck up with all that nonsense.

Candy: It's obvious Ray didn't take Zack seriously—and he should have. I'll explain later. I overheard the conversation between Ray and Zack, and I started to cry. So, I left the room to gather my thoughts because I couldn't believe what I had just heard.

Cecil: Close your eyes for a moment and just imagine hearing someone you love talking about ending their life. Stop and ask yourself—what would you do? Well? What is it?

Candy: So I took a moment to gather my thoughts and didn't say anything else to either one of them about it. On a different evening, just like before, I entered the room and overheard a chilling conversation between Zack and Ray.

Zack: Ray, I'll take care of her.

Candy: I'm curious about the private conversation you had with Zack.

Ray: That's between Zack and me—it's none of your business!

Cecil: Are you hanging in there? I hope you are, because I'm about to share some depressing information.

Candy: There was this one time when Zack came home early while I had a few neighbors over for Domino's. Zack walked in as usual and met everyone and was friendly and even flirted a little. Since all my friends are females, they soaked it up like lotion on a black man's ashy feet.

Right afterward, Zack walked over to Ray's house across the street until my friends left. Even then, Zack seemed to be okay, and I could not tell any difference than any other day when he came home early from work. After my friends left, Zack came home and started drinking Jim Beam, straight from the bottle. Shortly afterward, Zack, Ray, and I drove to our favorite local restaurant for pizza.

Zack invited another neighbor to come along, and he declined and told him, "You'll be sorry!" As soon as we walked into the restaurant, Zack accused the waiter of flirting with Me. ZACK! became belligerent and started arguing with the waiter about bringing his drink first. He continued being an asshole to the other patrons of the restaurant. Can you imagine how I felt? I became so embarrassed that I asked Ray to stop him.

Cecil: Hey, reader, have you ever seen a dog that barks at everything passing by the fence? That's what Zack was acting like to me, JUST SAYING.

Candy: That's how Zack was acting while walking out of the restaurant and arguing with anyone for no reason I could possibly think of. Ray had no choice but to intervene and grabbed Zack by the arm and led him out the door and over to our car. When Zack and I returned home, I decided to put away the leftovers from the restaurant and relax before doing anything else that evening. Suddenly, Zack wanted to walk over to another one of our neighbor's houses to play darts, but Zack continued drinking. This time, he is drinking "Crown Royal" while singing and dancing, which is the opposite of how he acted earlier.

Candy: Isn't it weird that his behavior changed so drastically just hours later? After dancing and drinking at the neighbor's house, we staggered out the door. Ray had to help hold up Zack so that we would make it back inside the house.

Cecil: "Hold on for a moment! You are about to dive into the fragmented memories that linger in Candy's mind. Following this, I will share Ray's account of the moment he discovered her in the bedroom, overwhelmed and paralyzed by shock."

Earl:

This is Candy's foggy memory of what happened next:

Candy: Finally, in the night, I took out my contacts and washed my face, and that's when I heard something like the pop of a champagne bottle. I became curious because that sound came from the bedroom. Before entering the bedroom, I had concerns and called out for Zack, who never responded. After several attempts to call his name, I slowly and cautiously walked toward the sound I heard, just seconds ago. What I ended up seeing changed my life and now yours forever if you are still reading. I stood in the doorway, SHOCKED and MOTIONLESS. My vision became blurry, and no words came from my mouth. My words quickly transformed into screams that resonated and went unheard by our neighbors.

Candy: I stood there in disbelief like ah stiff deer mantal on the wall, that Zack was on the floor with half of his face blown off while in a puddle of blood. Blood was dripping down the walls and dresser when I glanced up. To this day, I can only assume the reason Zack shot himself in the head is because he no longer wanted to deal with the fact he was slowly dying from Cancer. But!! That was not his choice to make without me.

Hey, it is me, Cecil, and I am unsure why he didn't think of his wife and kids, who loved him unconditionally.

Cecil: Back to Candy's foggy memory, of what happened:

Candy: I screamed, "NO!! NO!! NO! "Oh, my god, "What have you done?" "Why did you do this to me? "Oh my God! I immediately picked up my cellphone and tried to text our neighbor Ray from across the street. Frantically, in a desperate, wild, or frenzied way, I kept texting Ray because what I had witnessed didn't make sense at the moment.

Cecil: "Wait!!, are you thinking what I'm thinking? Why didn't she just pick up the phone and call Ray or run straight to his house? It seems fair to assume she wasn't thinking clearly at that moment, doesn't it?

Candy: Ray had not responded to my frantic text messages I sent him. In desperation, I finally sent another urgent text message that read 'HELP ME! It was only then that Ray stopped what he was doing and decided to come over. By the way, Ray did not need a key, as I had unconsciously left the front door unlocked.

Ray: This is my Account of What Happened that horrific evening:

Cecil: Ray cautiously pushed the door open and stepped inside her house, calling out for Candy urgently and loudly. His heart and mind were racing simultaneously with concerns from Candy's text messages. The air in the house felt thick with tension as he made his way towards the bedroom, where the shocking scene unfolded before him: Candy standing near Zack's lifeless body that was once her husband of 38 years. She was engulfed in her turmoil and shock while covered in blood that she did not even hear the door creak open before Ray entered; his sudden appearance frightened her from the shock she was in."

Ray: While I was standing behind Candy, I asked, have you called 911 yet?

Candy: "I didn't think to do it after I walked in and saw my husband lying here on the floor motionless while blood was making a puddle around his head."

Ray's Account of What Happened:

Candy: Ray said he found me in the bedroom, shaking like a leaf on a tree and crying hysterically.

Candy: He had to ask me again, "Did you call 911?" But before I could answer, Ray stepped up and called 911 himself. While he was on the phone... I screamed, "My husband is gone!"

Cecil: Ray immediately helped her up from the floor and guided her into the living room.

Ray: "STAY IN HERE. Don't move." His voice was firm.

Cecil: Candy kept trying to go back into the bedroom to be near Zack. The only thing that stopped her were Ray's final words—

Ray: "STAY IN HERE."

Candy: "I want to be with him!"
Ray: "That's not a good idea."

Cecil: He wouldn't let her back in. Each time Candy stood and tried to walk toward the bedroom, Ray physically stepped in front of her, blocking the path. When Candy asked again about being with Zack,

Ray replied, "Zack isn't with us anymore; he's gone."

Cecil: Ray walked back into the living room where Candy was. She was still crying hysterically, repeating over and over that she wanted to be with him.

Candy asked Ray, "Why would he do this to us?"

Cecil: Before the police arrived, several neighbors came by asking questions—even though it was none of their business. But that's how it is in a community like Candy and Zack's. Nothing happens without someone poking their nose in.

Shortly after the 911 call, the police and EMTs showed up. Ray gently asked Candy to come with him across the street to his house.

As the flashing lights from the ambulance and patrol cars lit up the street, the officers put up yellow police tape across Candy's driveway.

While the police were still on the scene, two detectives and two forensic investigators walked over to Ray's house to ask questions. Just like in the movies, they took photos of Candy's hands, feet, and nightshirt. One of the forensic techs even swabbed the inside of her mouth while apologizing the entire time. They were kind, actually. And that's the only part she remembers clearly.

The police cleared Candy of Zack's death by suicide.

Zack chose that evening to end his life while Candy was in the bathroom, and she did not know he had a gun in the house.

Candy later discovered that Zack had asked Ray for a gun or where to buy one. Ray did not take him seriously and should have. That was a cry for help, but Ray did not know better.

Ray's Account of What Happened:

Candy couldn't stop crying and shaking while sitting on the floor at Ray's house. Ray didn't understand why she wasn't sitting on the couch, but he didn't say anything. Instead, he walked over, stood her up, and hugged her for a while.

Candy kept repeating, "Why would he do this to us? Why? Why would he do this to me and your kids without saying bye?"

Cecil: When you're in shock like Candy was, you tend to do things that don't make sense. You just move on impulse. That's why she kept asking Ray to take her home. But of course, Ray wasn't about to let her go back alone—or be in that house by herself.

Eventually, Ray agreed to take her back so she could grab some clean clothes—but only because he was going with her. When Candy walked back into the room, she saw that the EMTs had moved her husband's body to the other side of the bed. That meant the blood was all around the bed... and still thick on the floor. Candy remembered walking out, going back to Ray's house, and falling asleep on the couch. After Candy wakes up, Ray is uncomfortable with Candy going back inside her home. Candy remembers arguing with Ray because she wanted to call and tell her kids what had happened.

Yes, again, Ray did not want Candy to return home until he called a service to clean the home back to normal. Candy's heart still has unresolved resentment toward Ray and has not told him. The memory of being denied a final farewell to Zack lingers painfully, casting a shadow over her thoughts. Candy feels it will haunt her forever since she did not get to say goodbye. I read this part of the chapter a few times, and I hope I did not repeat myself or lose you in the process. Peace!

Two years later after the death of her now deceased husband, she meets Me, Cecil. The Freaky Negga!

And I'm going to wrap this chapter up with a subtitle called "Me, and Mrs., Mrs., Candy and Cecil. Before you continue reading, reader. I did not make a typo when I typed "Me and Mrs. Mrs. Candy and Cecil. I am not sure what age you are reading this book but, remember that song by Billy Paul, "Me and Mrs. Jones? There is a part in his chorus that goes: Meeeeee annnnnd Mrs. Mrs. Jones, right?

Well, me and Mrs. Mrs. Candy and Cecil. Does it make sense now? I hope so, and now, let us continue. Oh, hell naw!! I am not going to leave you hanging like that. Candy and I met on a dating site, and our conversations were great. She knew how to converse online by leaving me lengthy messages, and I would do the same. I eventually asked for her cell number, and we stayed connected. At some point, things changed drastically from your basic vanilla conversation.

Let me explain, and you will read what I mean. There was this one evening while talking on our phones. Candy wanted to give me a little show with FaceTime after only a few conversations. I was with that but surprised because you can't always tell what the book is about until you start reading it, get my metaphor? In other words, what is on the outside may not necessarily be what's on the inside. She proceeded to ask me to tell her what to do next, which I liked! So, me being me, I asked her to remove her robe and bra. By the way, you, yes you! the reader!!: I ain't sure if you already don't like where this is going, so all I can say to you is... this is my muthafucking story, feel me?

She did whatever I asked of her and so much more. Before long, she had everything off; while I was watching on my cell phone, Candy was using her vibrator until she had an orgasm. I was like, this can't be even though I witnessed it. I was impressed with Candy's willingness to be sexually free. As I matured, I liked this method of getting to know someone by removing the barriers that won't allow us to be authentically ourselves. After the show she performed, we said good night. What Candy didn't realize is her show did not impress me, but her willingness to be sexually free was the turn-on, and, ladies and gentlemen, which had my attention. After her performance, I wanted to meet her.

If you are wondering how long we have known each other, that is none of your damn business. Okay, I will tell you, it was two weeks. Are you satisfied now? All up in my business, man, oh man!! I know I am a hypocrite, right? So, get over it.

Anyways, back to Candy and me. When we first met at a local bagel restaurant near her home, she was shy, and making eye contact with me was difficult. She was blushing and sitting sideways to distract herself from facing me directly. I found that interesting, and it told me everything I needed to know.

We had not talked about life experiences yet, but that came with time. We first met away from her home because she did not know me that well, nor did I know her. We both could have been serial killers. Our first face-to-face meeting went great, and we laughed about something not worth mentioning right now.

After 30 minutes of conversation, I could tell she wanted to invite me to her home. Since I respect myself, I did not rush or indicate that I wanted her to take me to her house. It would not have mattered if Candy changed her mind at the last minute because I am not a thirsty muthafucka like someone you may have known in your past. Explanation of thirsty for you vanilla folks: Urban Dictionary defines thirsty as "too eager to get something; desperate for sex."

Dear Caucasians, don't add THIRSTY to your vocabulary. Let's have something for once, will ya? Candy hinted with her eyes and body language that I could take the lead and say, "Let's go to your place." I followed her car closely, thinking this should be interesting. When we arrived at her home, she invited me in, and I sat on her couch. Fellas, here is a little secret about Cecil; he gave me space and that alone made me comfortable.

While I was there, I looked around, so that I could see exactly where her favorite place to sit is. Fellas!!! Do not sit there but close enough to have an intimate conversation. Always look directly into her eyes while she talks to you. Always Keep your damn hands to yourself; otherwise, you may make her uncomfortable. Wait to see if she offers you something to drink or eat; don't ask. Also, watch to see if she is comfortable within her environment.

If she paces a lot, it only means she is a little uncomfortable and questioning her decision to have you there. So chill and cautiously proceed with a light, non-sexual conversation. If it does not feel suitable for anything other than conversation, allow some more time for more conversation. Back to Candy and me.

Remember I told you how sex was with Zack, right? If you have been paying attention, you know where I am about to go. We laughed while sitting on the couch, there was some serious flirting with our eyes and bodies. I could tell Candy was ready to head towards the bedroom with the look and smile she allowed me to see. I also realized Candy is submissive just by the fact I said let us go into your bedroom. It would have made her uncomfortable if she had said what I said.

So, of course, I made the decision that turned into us being in bed naked. There was still no reason to rush because I had plenty of time to continue flirting with Candy. Besides, I am not going to tap her on the shoulder and stick my cock in her. There was a lot of foreplay and talking before any penetration took place. I found out that she must stimulate her clitoris for an orgasm.

That's easy to find out by watching her play with herself while I was licking her stomach. She asked if she could use her vibrator while I was doing that, and I said, "Of course." I never had a problem with a woman using her toys while we were having sex. It just adds to the fun of it. There is so much I can say about our sexual adventure, but I feel I have said enough.

If that is okay with you, I want to share one more thing about Candy. Sometimes, she would ask if she could touch me while watching television. When it came time for Candy to ask me a question, instead of asking, she would say, "Can I ask you a question?" Candy had many triggers I had to pay close attention to.

Remember now, a drunk mother and abandonment father raised Candy, then quickly sent her to Catholic School, until she met her deceased husband, Zack. (rest in peace).Bad boy selfish Zack, controlled every aspect of her life while they were together. And because of that, she does not know how to make independent decisions without being told what to do and when to do it.

I have lived many different lives and when I come across someone like Candy, I must handle her like the most delicate flower that only grows once every other year. Last, it is not Zack's fault either how he spoke to Candy and fuck her. The blame is on the woman he met before he met Candy and Zack's mother and father.

He sort of had the same background as Candy except for Catholic School. In a lot of ways, all our lives are parallel to one another, aren't they? Ladies, you must establish an identity before becoming serious with any man or woman.

Otherwise, something could happen to that person, and you must find out who you are, and it won't be easy. Peace!

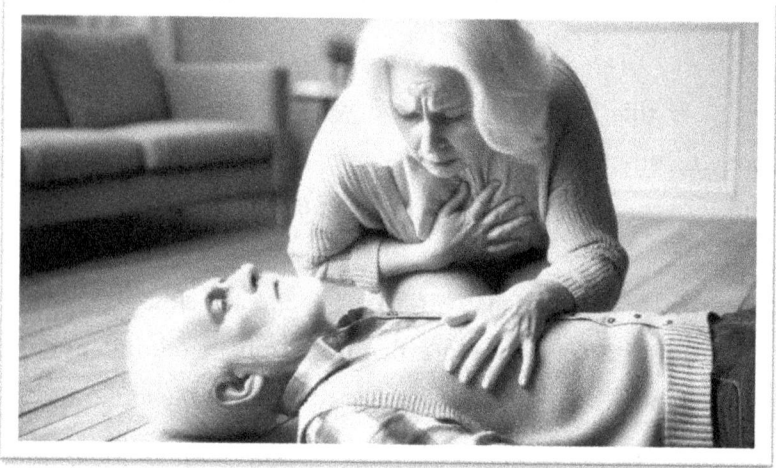

If you or someone you know has been molested, raped or have suicidal thoughts and is scared to talk about it, you can find me on most social media platforms if you just need someone to talk to...

I Shaved Her

This is straight from the Audio version of this book.

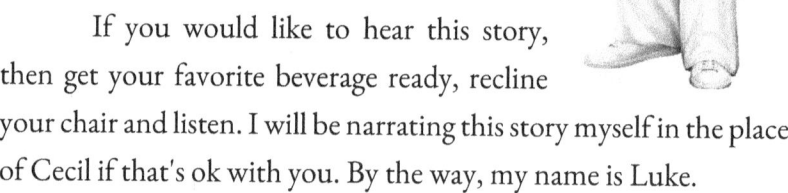

L adies and Gentlemen, this chapter is called " I Shaved Her". It's a true story how Cecil shaved another man's wife pussy, while he was watching from the living room.

If you would like to hear this story, then get your favorite beverage ready, recline your chair and listen. I will be narrating this story myself in the place of Cecil if that's ok with you. By the way, my name is Luke.

It always surprises me how many couples are in existence, and the husbands have not shaved their wives' pussies. I bet as a woman reading this, you just said to yourself, mine has not since we have been married. With one of my wives, I never had to shave her because she was damn skilled at it herself.

There was this one couple I knew that lived in Florida, with whom I had stayed in touch after my divorce, who invited me to their home on occasion. Ashley and George were good friends of mine during and after my Tampa Florida swing party days. By the way, their fictitious last name will be Mr. and Mrs. Insurance, for identifying purposes only.

I'm not mentioning their real names because, well, honestly, to keep them from suing my, wait!! you say it Cecil..."BLACK ASS" One evening while visiting them, Ashley walked towards the bathroom and announced she needed to take a shower. Immediately, naughty thoughts came into my mind like a wolf in a lamb disguise.

If you can imagine that for a moment, then you might as well include how difficult it was to keep from howling. I thought to myself either Ashley is hinting to me to fuck her or something just as interesting. I say this because there was no reason for her to announce it, right? In fact, I had already had a sexual encounter with Ashley at some of the swing parties we attended.

So, as a good Samaritan, I knew I could offer to shave her pussy because, her husband was sitting on the couch watching television with the remote in his hand. Obviously, the thought never entered his mind. I wish you could have seen the look on Ashley's face when I sprung that question on her. She was just as surprised as her husband was and enthusiastically said; yes! I would like that very much Cecil, you have no idea how difficult it is to shave between my ass cheeks, and especially from the bottom of my vaginal opening and asshole.

To date, I have been the only man who has offered and actually shaved her. What blew my mind was, her husband, of thirty plus years, had never offered," Go figure! Out of curiosity, I will ask my partner how she shaves those stubborn hairs and from what I was told it's not an easy task.

Anyway, Ashley's husband seemed surprised and confused by my offer. Not sure why, and can only assume George said to himself, WHAT THE FUCK!! While she was showering, I rubbed my palms together like I was a mad scientist creating Frankenstein in my Laboratory beneath my home. Occasionally, for some reason I would look over at her husband to see if he was uncomfortable. I did not want her husband to see me acting like an 18-year-old in a prostitute business in Vegas. Honestly, he looked jealous that he did not think of it himself, and that wasn't my problem.

Eventually, Ashley told me: I have everything ready for you to walk in and take care of me. I knew it was showtime!! When I walked towards the sensual lite bedroom, I hid my excited facial expression. She had a towel underneath her ass, check one. Shaving cream, check two. Her favorite shaver and a bowl of warm water, on the nightstand, check three and four. Watching Ashley prepare everything for me to walk in was impossible not to be as hard as a grape-flavored frozen Popsicle from the seventies. If you are younger than 45 years old, you won't know what the fuck I am talking about.

That's okay. Just use your favorite search engine and look it up!! Anyway, standing above her while she held her legs back on the bed was as tempting as not looking under the table when she said "I'm not wearing panties. Get my metaphor? First, I got on my knees and faced her naked body, then dipped my fingertips into the bowl of warm water Sue provided. Secondly, I held my fingers above her pussy so that the warm water dropped from my fingertips onto her stomach and pussy.

Naturally, I continued this procedure until the water I had applied completely saturated her pussy and ran between her legs. It is always fun to watch her jump, startled by the water that eventually drops down onto her body. Because it's so funny when she says, "Cecil." You are teasing me! Then, I would follow up with a Barry White voice saying, "I got this." Do not say another word, young lady. This is when being obedient and submissive is necessary. Ladies, don't be triggered by how I wrote that, okay?

Calm down!! My method is only understood by someone confident in themselves. This allows me to lead and set the mood in my head. Understood? No, Seriously, do you? I sure did not see anyone doing this in my family or anywhere else that I can remember.

Like most things I do and say, it just came to me. I picked up the can of shaving cream from the floor next to me and put some in the palm of my hand. Ashley's confidence and trust in me will allow her and me to relax and enjoy the shaving experience I had planned. Next up, I placed the palm of my hand over her pussy opening, either on the right or left side. This precise placement will prevent me from cutting her pussy's lips, clit, as well as shaving cream, from entering her pussy.

After shaving both sides, I proceeded to shave the area barely inside her lips. I would pull back the right or left sides of the lips to shave visible hair. Before I move on to the next step, I like to use my finger to feel if there are any rough areas I might have missed. My method would be to feel up, down, and side to side.

If there were some rough areas I missed, I would shave that area again until it is as smooth as a baby's booty, my mom used to say. The good ol' days. Once I have completed all these steps, there is one more area that needs shaving, and that's between her ass cheeks. In a firm voice, I told her to bend over doggie style and pull your cheeks apart.

This will also allow me to shave any visible hair I did not see or could get to while she was on her back with her legs pulled back. If you are trying this in the privacy of your home, make sure it is comfortable and quiet. Sudden noises are the last thing you want to happen while shaving her kitty cat, which could potentially land her in the emergency room.

There is nothing more seductive than a woman lying on her back at the edge of the bed with her legs pulled back with her own hands on her thighs, allowing me to shave her pussy. If I were to start a business, my clients would be women who required my exclusive services for shaving their pussy's while their husbands watched.

This reminds me of that old lollipop commercial on TV, where the kid would ask the owl how many licks it takes to reach the center of the lollipop. Some of you all may be too young to remember that commercial when the owl takes the lollipop from the kid, licks it twice, bites it, and says, "One." That's precisely what happens to me after a couple of strokes with the shaver. I want to lick the pussy. Peace!

In DaSwing of Thangs

SWINGING FROM MY PERSPECTIVE

I can still vividly recall sitting in front of the internet and pondering what it would be like to re-register on a swing club website.

As I looked at photographs of people having sexual encounters and switching wives, I found myself wishing I could be a part of the action. I was intrigued by the entire scenario. As someone who has always been straightforward and truthful, when one of my spouses spotted me using the computer and inquired about what I was doing, I responded by saying that I was contemplating joining up for a swinging website.

You can't imagine how excited I was when she asked me whether I was signing up as a single person or a couple. Oh, yes, without a doubt! I registered us as a couple and thought to myself, "Winner! Within a month of creating a profile for us as a couple, we began receiving emails inviting us to meet other couples of the same gender. It is not as enjoyable as you believe it to be. We need to have chemistry with the person we are interested in, and they must reciprocate our interest. Fucking is not always the focus of a relationship. The woman may be attractive while the husband is not, or the husband is attractive while the wife is not. Both scenarios are possible. During our time in Tampa, we attended swing parties and met new people who shared our mentality. Some of these individuals were hardworking and successful.

There were a few racists within the group; nevertheless, they respectfully handled themselves, assuming that there was such a thing as a polite racist. Despite greeting each other, they did not want to be with an African American or other minority. To my relief, I did not witness a significant amount of such behavior during the parties we attended. I never encountered a black couple during all the parties we attended.

This is a fact. Aside from the famous couple we all know, are there any other black swingers out there?"

However, on the other hand, what the hell did I care? If I were a fly flying above a bowl of rice representing white people, I would be wondering when to land. When it came to black men, white wives who were interested in black men or a black man could fuck me anytime I was available.

Regardless of whether they are racist, many white women fantasize about a black man anyway, and you know there is some truth to what I just said. Unfortunately, racist white men are unable to change their minds anytime soon, seems like.

This was Updated on May 2, 2024, and is not in "Vanilla Sheets". If you are a white male reading this right now, please understand that white women have always been naturally curious about black men, a fact that dates to slavery. The only way you can stop this curiosity is by deleting it, which is already happening in our society today.

Besides, I am not in the mood to address that right at this moment. Anyway, let us get to the important aspect of this chapter: Ladies: If you close your eyes and I am fucking you, can you honestly tell if it is a white man, or a black? I am implying that if white or black man have the same size cock or not.

Either way, at most of the swing parties I could bring most of the women out of their comfort zones; they would squirt and do things with me that they had had not done with their husbands.

They later informed me that whatever they did with me benefited their husbands. Some of these women were not even interested in anal until they tried it with me. Afterward, their husbands would inform me that, despite being with their wives for over thirty years, they had never developed a love for anal penetration.

They were always curious about the strategies I used to help their wives relax and enjoy anal. Previously, their wives had informed them that it wasn't possible. After that, the husbands had complete freedom to sleep with their wives whenever they felt like it, and they thoroughly enjoyed it. I have even received compliments from spouses who thanked me for making their wives comfortable. It is uncomfortable when a spouse approaches me and says, "My wife wants to fuck you." Do not laugh at my statement; there have been times when the husband asked me to have sex with his wife, even though I did not find her attractive. It is impossible to avoid situations while remaining polite.

I am relieved the spouse could not read my mind or analyze my facial expressions. In a few instances, this resulted in my removal from the party. When my wife asks me to have sex, I don't find it appealing. I suppose I should have sex with her regardless of the circumstances. It makes me question whether white individuals believe that I would have sex with any white woman because I am black, mainly because white men tend to avoid her. That's my cue to avoid interacting with her. My guess is that it started when I Googled "sex" and saw something about swinging on the first page. I wondered,

"What does swinging have to do with sex?" This was over thirty years ago, and swinging has a lot to do with sex. A few swinging sites piqued my interest, so I had to investigate further. I felt compelled to take a closer look.

As I perused these websites, I knew I loved what I saw and did not hesitate to join a handful of them. I won't say which sites they were, but please be cautious; not all swinging websites are authentic. Some bots are responding to your messages. If you are interested in swinging, there are a few sites worth investing in.

You are welcome to contact me to determine which websites I believe are legitimate. I joined several sites and looked at a few couple's profiles and photographs. I knew right away that I had found my new home. Looking at one of the profiles, I thought to myself, "Looks like this guy had a lot of fun while getting his cock sucked by one woman while eating another woman's pussy."

I imagined he was eating his wife's pussy while she licked another pussy.

I thought, "DAMN!"

To me, this was superior to porn because actual people were having sex. I met couples by placing my profile on some of the swinger websites. The next thing I know, I am talking to a few couples and meeting the husband first, then the wife. We would have sexual encounters on occasion, but it was always a bust because I wasn't interested in the wife.

I am starting to understand why white males dislike black men. Most notable sports figures are black, and we have that on lock.

Can you guess what else we have on lock? Black men fucking white women, and there is nothing that a racist white man can do to prevent it except, mind their own damn business, when they see it. Because when I see an attractive black woman with a white man. I mind my own damn business. If a white woman has previously fucked a black man, they may be hesitant to do so again, in fear of with others may think.

Btw, if you are a white racist man or woman reading this part and pissed off, keep in mind that it is well-documented that white racist police officers handcuff black men before beating them with their batons or shooting them in the back.

I can't think of one justifiable reason to intimidate, beat, or shoot an unarmed handcuff nigga can you? Could that be the reason there is so much pint up ager towards a Black strong and intelligent Alpha Male? Is it payback? Oh, and one thing before you pass around the offering comes around. Not all black men have big cocks, just putting it out there, I meant in here.

If any of what I have said triggered, please speak to a therapist as soon as possible.

Sorry, my ADD got the better of me.

Returning to the swinger websites, I signed up for one, and although I did not find much success, I enjoyed browsing the pictures. I saw one guy having a blast. It just looked like everybody was having fun. I finally said, Fuck it.

To be honest, it is not always about having sex; it is about the relationships and friendships built between people of the same mindset. I began frequenting Trapeze in Fort Lauderdale, but I consistently went alone. It was weird doing something like that by myself. I have been to several nudist resorts in the Tampa area, one called Caliente, and another called Paradise Lakes Resort. During one of these visits, a black man and his girlfriend approached me. He said, "My girlfriend would love to dance with you. I danced with her, but that was it. It wasn't until many years later that I ran into them again. At first, I could not figure out why they looked so familiar. Then it dawned on me:

They were the couple I had met years earlier at the Caliente nightclub on the resort's premises. Because I was so new to the lifestyle at that time, I did not realize that I was supposed to get acquainted with this guy's girlfriend while dancing and then proceed to fuck her. The black man had arranged it, and I did not know what to do. Indeed, I found her attractive, but I should have been more flirtatious. If she had liked what she saw and heard, we would have been in a sexual relationship.

They resided in Paradise Lakes, so her and I could have exited the nightclub and started fucking shortly afterwards. I had no idea I could have gotten some pussy that night. Had I known, I would have become familiar with the lifestyle and visited the area more frequently to find other potential partners. Update: Following the exposure of his scandal in the Tampa area, that mutha-fucka committed suicide. That's another story I am not wanting to write about right now and I hope you are okay with it. Thanks!

In the Tampa area, only a few blacks participate in a swinging lifestyle. They are typically black men offering themselves to white women or couples. This practice is not considered taboo. I am telling you; swinging can be fun. If you are two very open-minded (sexual) people, secure in your relationship, and take your time, it can be a fantastic experience. I say this next part with complete sincerity: try swinging if your relationship is secure. If you are a single male, there is a specific process to follow that I have learned over the years.

When a couple is interested in you, most single males assume that a couple might be interested in fucking them. Even if you are a single white or black male and the husband wants to watch you fuck his wife, there are ways to go about it. To ensure they will choose you for their fantasy and feel safe, take specific steps from the start.

As I said before, I am willing to answer any questions you might have. After running into that couple from before, I went back to the nightclub a few more times. However, it made me a bit uncomfortable, as it reminded me of buzzards hanging around on a tree branch, waiting to fuck and eat something.

That's how I began my journey into the world of swinging. My ads would say, "Single black male available for fun," which paid off with couples contacting me. Update: Given the current divisions in our country, it is not a good time for a black male to put himself in danger.

I would like to share some additional information with you. Some years ago, I was talking to this one lady, and she mentioned she was bisexual and had been that way since high school. She was unaware that those feelings had remained with her. None of her boyfriends or friends knew of her desire to be with women. What I could never understand was how a woman would get involved with a man, knowing she has strong feelings about having sex with women. A woman should never be involved with a man without sharing her feelings. I felt sorry for her when she told me she tried to talk to her boyfriend about being with another woman at the time.

Unfortunately, he became jealous and insecure, and she never brought it up again until she met me. In that same conversation, she mentioned that she stopped thinking about it. I understood why she had stopped thinking about it, but I wasn't inclined to pursue the matter further.

Many of you are reading this book and reflecting on your thoughts. I still feel this way, but I am hesitant to discuss it or bring it to the attention of the person I am involved with. And I will say this to all of you: It is a damn shame you are not comfortable sharing your honest feelings with your partner.

Updated, My Little Secret, added on 05/02/2024: I failed to add this to the first book called "Vanilla Sheets" Remember when I said I had a secret I wanted to share but had not told anyone? This is it. I understand it is improper to fall in love with someone else's wife.

Yet, there are instances when a connection can be so strong that it can trap you into uncontrollable desires and unresolved emotions. Let me explain. After attending a few parties in the Tampa area, we met Jessie and Debra, who resided at the Caliente Club and Resort, a community nudist resort in Land O'Lakes, Florida.

This place is amazing. I had a great time during my last visit and found the people friendly. The cleanliness, food, and scenery resemble being on an exotic island, accompanied by your favorite non-alcoholic beverage.

Personally, I don't consume alcohol. The nightclub is terrific and should be experienced at least once. I am not receiving any payment for providing or promoting this business. I am bringing it up because it is a space where individuals can freely express themselves without fear of judgment.

Okay, enough about that. Let us get back to Jessie and Debra.

After seeing them at a few parties, we finally introduced ourselves and became friends shortly afterward. They were a nice and attractive couple to have a conversation with. Debra was stunning, with long blond hair and mesmerizing eyes. Her body was flawless, (in my opinion) with a slight tan.

At some point, Jessie asked one of my wives if she would like to play with him, and of course, one of my wives said yes. They must have had a great time together because it was an hour or so before they came out of the room they were in. One of my wives was smiling from ear to ear, and I can assume she was glad she found someone to have a good time with. After Jessie and one of my wives partied a few more times, Jessie informed one of my wives that Debra was interested in meeting me. He also mentioned that I should introduce myself to his wife at the next party. I knew I could introduce myself to Debra because one of my wives told me what Jessie told her afterwards...

Note: I keep referring to one of my wives because I am trying to tell a story without specifying which one was with me at the time. So, that's precisely what I did at the next party. I walked over, said hello, and hugged her slightly above the waist. I wasn't overly enthusiastic, but I was courteous and respectful to avoid any misunderstandings.

Without knowing if she has been with a black man before, I must be careful when it is the first time. I want you, the reader, to understand that I never make assumptions and am always cautious and respectful.

Since everyone at the party is white and I am uncertain about their experiences with a black man, I must exercise caution. At first, it was difficult to talk to her because I wasn't paying attention and was preoccupied with gazing into her eyes, which reminded me of the 1960s x-ray glasses.

You may or may not remember the glasses, depending on your age. Talking to her was always interesting if I was paying attention. Debra's sexy submissive demeanor left me wondering how I am going to contain my thirst for her. At every party we met at, she and I would sit down and have an intimate conversation, which made us more comfortable. This lady had my full attention more than any other woman I met at the parties. Allow me to clarify a point that you might not fully grasp. I may have said this before, but I don't care how many women are interested in me at a party or in a vanilla atmosphere; I must have a connection that's not always sexual.

Additionally, I require eye contact, body language, interaction, and a mutual conversation (i.e., it is not just her or me doing all the talking), as well as a sense of humor, before engaging in sexual activity with any woman, especially at a swing party. After getting to know Debra, she had all these qualities. Looking back, it is amusing that one of my wives often asked, "Guess who's here," as if I wasn't already aware of their presence.

I was always happy when I saw their car parked out front or near the house we were visiting.

To give you a sense of excitement, imagine a dog seeing its owner returning home from Iraq after years of deployment, get my drift? One of my wives knew I had a great time with her because she shared the exact same personality as one of my wives. That personality is submissive and sensual, with a sprinkle of kink.

Finding someone with that personality at one of those parties is challenging, and it takes some time to establish a connection.

Now, let us get down to the essential details of this story without the need for a refreshing drink to wash it down. I asked her to join me in one of the bedrooms within this eight-bedroom house hosted by our friend in Tampa. Upon entering, every mattress was occupied, suggesting a party atmosphere, except for one mattress on the floor. This mattress, located on the right side of the bed and out of sight, seemed placed explicitly for her and me to play on. I selected that mattress as we undressed, sat down, and initiated our passionate kiss. Oh, and I usually don't kiss at parties unless it is with one of my wives or someone or someone I have played with before, because I consider kissing intimate.

However, with Debra, there was something different that I can't explain. When she and I were together, it felt like time passed quickly, and everyone dissolved into thin air. That evening, we were having such a great time that suddenly, she passionately said, "She loved me," without any concern to anyone who heard her say it. I was shocked at that moment, unaware that she harbored such profound affection for me. I felt the same way and had not considered discussing it with anyone. It caught me off guard because I wanted to ensure no one heard her say it.

It is forbidden to fall in love with someone else's spouse and not let it distract you. Please understand that no matter the sexual connection you have with someone at a party, you absolutely must refrain from falling in love with them. Marriages end in divorce due to feelings for another couple's spouse.

Hell, I remember people were playing just above us. I knew they did not hear what she said on the bed nearby. Otherwise, that could have started rumors we were not ready for. I tried to keep my feelings towards her in check. Still, it was difficult because of our genuine, authentic, and organic connection. Before she said she loved me, we looked for one another every time we saw each other. All I had to do was smile, and I understood exactly what that meant. Even without Anal, my experience with her was unbelievable.

At the party's conclusion, I suggested that we temporarily disengage from our sexual relationship because others were observing our connection, which is not conducive to a positive outcome. That's precisely how rumors begin, fabricating stories instead of focusing on the actual events.

Not long after that, we stopped playing altogether, and sadly, everything changed. Honestly, exercise caution. Avoid falling in love with someone else's spouse; if you do, they won't welcome your return, as they can't trust you. I mentioned to one of my wives that Debra said she loved me, and she did not seem pleased. I had to be honest with her and wanted her to know how I felt about it, too. So, am I a hypocrite? Peace.

Just Keeps Happening

READ WITH AN EMPTY STOMACH. YOU HAVE BEEN WARNED.

I **am not trying to destroy people's families or anything else, so I am not dropping real names in this chapter.**

I was also married when I met another married woman named Lisa. During her husband's absence, I frequently visited her home and fucked her in the same bed that she shared with her husband. I worked the morning shift during the week, which made it easy to meet her. She was a schoolteacher and lived forty-five minutes from where I lived in Ocoee Florida.

Anyway, what I discovered about fucking Lisa was that she would accidentally shit on the bed. For instance, I granted her an exception, as it only occurred during an orgasm. When it happened, she would always apologize and feel embarrassed about it...

However, I understand that unfortunate events do occur occasionally while fucking. It simply meant that her orgasm was so pleasurable that she was unable to prevent shit unexpectedly coming out of her ass. After experiencing it for the first time, she became self-conscious, so I had to reassure her that it wasn't a big deal. It took some time for her to relax after experiencing shitting and climaxing at the same time.

Shit never bothered me, as anyone who has read "Chocolate Starfish" can testify to that. Lisa once again urinated and shitted in her bed, following another orgasm; however, I refrained from commenting on the accident.

While Lisa was blindfolded, I removed the shit that was on the bed. Pardon me for what I am about to say next. I am certainly glad I found it before I passed out from sex, if you know what I mean. Could you imagine tossing and turning while sleeping and waking up with shit all over you?

So, when I found it, I picked it up with my fingers (ewww!!) and quickly placed it inside some tissue paper on the nightstand. Then I got out and put it underneath the bed, hoping Lisa would not see it. Immediately after I removed the blindfolds, she walked into the bathroom, suddenly turned around, and asked, "Why is that napkin on the floor under the bed?"

I must have looked stunned and wasn't sure what to say. She knew it wasn't there earlier before we started fucking, so I had to come clean about it. She asked because I forgot to put it far enough under the bed so she would not see it. But I did not want to put it too far under the bed; otherwise, I would not be able to reach it.

Lisa said, "Cecil, please tell me what's under the bed." I swear it was white when I placed it under the bed. Now it is turning brown gradually. Do you have a visual?

I hesitated and said, "Well, it happened." She apologized again, saying she was sorry. I was trying to conceal the situation so she would not apologize again. I said, "Look, shut up with all that; I told you that when 'Shit Just Keep Happening,' I take it as a badge of honor that you had a good orgasm." Lisa became comfortable enough to have an orgasm, knowing she could not stop the inevitable. We laughed about it. If this happens to you, ladies, your partner should understand. This is particularly true for individuals over fifty years of age. Peace!

Massage Envious

DDuring my dating life, my go-to method consisted of asking the woman I was dating if she would like to get a massage.

Massages are quite sensual, and because I am not a trained professional, I can cross some boundaries when it comes to sensuality. Nine times out of ten, when I offer to give them a massage, and it is our first-time meeting, they are under the impression that I want to sleep with them. That is far from the truth.

On the other hand, there is greater satisfaction in putting your faith in me, unwinding, and knowing that I don't require anything in return. I tailored the initial massage offer to meet their needs. Wait a damn minute; don't get it twisted. If I see a chance, this will be a wezafucking opportunity.

Usually, I start by exposing her privates while she is lying on her stomach in a posture that is completely bare. I am sure she is expecting me to immediately massage her cheeks. This is what she is thinking. Rather than focusing on her posterior region, I massage her thighs, calves, feet, and shoulders before moving on to the next part of her body on my list of priorities. As I massage her lower back, I use my fingernails to apply gentle pressure to her back, starting at her neck and going just above her ass.

I do this while massaging her lower back. As I complete this task, I meticulously pay special attention to her body language. Most of the time, I can notice indications that she prefers softer or harder massages and if that is the case, I pay more attention to her desires and whispers. I want you to know that I am cautious about this method because she may have an organism. If it is her first time having an orgasm with a massage, it could be very embarrassing for her.

Nothing is more satisfying than massaging one ass cheek at a time, making the ass the last area to receive attention. When I take the ass-cheeks apart, I can see all that the man above her gave her down there. Wait, let me add this right now before I forget. If she has an ass like some of these black women I see on IG, I may need a break afterward, if you know what I mean? In other words, to be more graphic, some back women's asses are so fat and juicy, I will need to take a break.

Since the creation of my first book, let me go ahead and add this now. Most white women don't have any ass, and there is only a crack back there if you know what I mean. That only means when they day face down, I don't have to part their asses to see their pussy. Take it from me: I know what I am talking about. Anyway, let us continue. In other words, it is a well-known fact that I find massaging a woman's body incredibly seductive. Plus, at my age, I need time to allow me to become aroused, and massaging helps this out a lot. Also, being sixty-something, this method makes me concentrate on them. I am sure that your partner or you may experience feelings of vulnerability in that situation, as I am fully aware of her vulnerability and mine. I completely understand what she is going through, and she is putting her trust in me so as not to surprise her with something we have never discussed or done before. After giving a slow and steady massage to the first hip, I move on to the other hip and continue the process. The next stage is to massage the inner thighs and the area that is as close to the pussy lips as you can on both sides of the body. This is a perfect time to tease the hell out of her.

Given that her legs are currently only a few centimeters apart, I will only lightly brush against the pussy, refraining from direct contact. By this point, you can see that I am already getting her all worked up and wet, and I am fully aware of what I am doing! Are you asking yourself, how do I know if she is wet? Come on now, are you serious? You can clearly see it between her pussy lips, or it is oozing out between her thighs. It is a good idea, not to mention you can tell she is excited.

Following that, I give her instructions, or depending on the relationship, I tell her to turn over so that I can massage the front of her leg and the areas of her inner thighs. I would like to once again emphasize that I massage the sides of the pussy from the front but never actually touch it. Because I worked on her thighs while she was lying on her back, I no longer feel responsible for doing so.

The second concern I have is her stomach, which can be a source of insecurity for some women. Putting her at ease is my main objective, and there is no reason for her to be nervous about anything. I made sure that she is comfortable.

There are certain signs a woman will show when she is uncomfortable with her stomach. First, she won't make eye contact with me while her stomach is exposed. Another way I can tell is by watching her place her arms in front of her stomach. Both ways or one of them tell me everything I need to know before I proceed to massage her. It is up to me to make her comfortable with the body that the man above gave her. Especially if she bore children and has stretch marks or has had surgeries. I may have mentioned something like this in another chapter. While I am observing her breathing, I proceed to rub her lips in a manner that is both leisurely and soft at the same time. I start approaching her breasts and nipples to gauge her sexual arousal, knowing that it will become evident.

Whenever I needed to warm the oil or lotion, I used my hands or blew warm breath on the oil. I would use this method consistently. Apply gentle pressure to her breasts, one breast at a time. As soon as it is time to move on to the nipples, move circularly around the nipple without contacting the nipple's tip. To what end? Considering that she is making assumptions about what I will do next, I might as well throw her off my scent just to be safe. I laughed aloud as I was writing this part of the chapter. Not only that, but the anticipation causes her to get much wetter than she already was.

Finally, clitoral massaging was performed in that specific order. I am aware that massaging a naked woman under the light of a candle can also be sensual. This has never been one of my favorite ways to massage a woman, considering I am a very visual creature and the lighter the betta.

Alternative sexy experience is when a woman trusts you to remove her clothes in front of you and give them to you. This is a really tempting experience. Suppose you are in the appropriate position when she ascends onto the massage table or bed. In that case, you may even catch a glimpse of her opened pussy from behind.

Assuming you are a visual person like me, in the correct position, you could potentially catch a glimpse of her ass and open pussy lips opening. In addition, if she wants to tease, she will approach the massage table or bed slowly while wearing a smile on her face. Furthermore, purchasing the lotion in advance should be as exciting if a man is interested in massaging.

Peace!

Must Be The Dog N Me

T he contents I am about to share may be offensive, but it is important to remember that Cecil was only nine to ten years old.

Please don't hold this against him; if you do, that makes you judgmental. Given my HO/ISH nature, you should read this chapter with an empty stomach.

Are you sure you want to continue??

By the way, in the audio version there are two narrators of this chapter.

Cecil wishes to prepare you for the remainder of this chapter one final time. On May 5, 2024, events in his life compelled him to dive deeper into secret files in his mind than he could have imagined. After careful consideration, he understood that this phase in his life had also reduced the long-term repercussions of Cecil's sexual abuse. Right? By the way, you cannot hold Cecil responsible for reading this chapter, okay? While growing up, Cecil's dachshund would walk around with his tail straight up towards the ceiling, exposing his butthole.

One day, Cecil's dachshund was walking past him, and a thought came to his little distorted brain, that you may or will find disgusting. As his dog was minding its own business he reached down and picked up his dog from the living room floor. If you ever meet him in person, DO NOT ASK, what the hell he was thinking at that age. As he rewrites this chapter, he's embarrassed to continue. But it is too late now because it is already in the first version of his first published book called **"Vanilla Sheets."** Not all children have these twisted ideas going through their minds you know, but he sure in the fuck did. To this day, he is still asking himself why. Slow down, and don't rush ahead to know where this is going. There were no books available relating to beastiality back then.

Also, he never met or talked to anyone performing it or knew of it. Hell, there has never been a discussion about it with family or close friends either! I am asking the universe why me? Am I cursed? Will Cecil be accepted in heaven after telling this true story? Or will he be going straight to hell with no boarding pass? No response yet, so we shall see.

As of 12/15/2024 Still no response. While his dog was in his lap, Cecil unbuttoned his pants with his right hand and held his dog still with his left. Cecil's dog didn't know what the hell was happening. Cecil then took out his cock and attempted to stick the head in the dog's ass. He wanted to see if would slide into his dog's ass without any lubrication; and of course it didn't. Cecil is fucking lucky that he wasn't trying to force things because more than likely, he would have injured his cock.

It seems to me he had no concerns for his dog's ass, right? I am confident that his dachshund was saying, "What the hell is this nigga trying to do to me? Why this muthafucka has me pinned down?" As the dog swung his head around to look directly at Cecil, the expression on his dog face and eyes, made Cecil know he was doing something messed up. Since Cecil's cock didn't go in, he removed him from out of his lap and put him back on the floor. To this day, Cecil asks himself why he did it, except to say that at the time, he was willing to put his cock anywhere he thought it felt good.

Some men say, "A hole is a hole," and you and I both know that's not a fact, especially in this case. I am certainly glad as a narrator of this messed up story, that Cecil's cock did not go into that dog's ass; otherwise, he would have become one of those messed up individuals who fucks dogs, chickens, pigs, horses, and farm animals. You do understand that this type of garbage exists on the internet, and there is nothing wrong with individuals who engage in it privately.

Notice I wrote "PRIVATELY!" Which means that if you are reading this right now, you are not alone. Okay? I am just saying! There are numerous messed up situations that exist that someone like Cecil will unknowingly or innocently get into. I understand that many people may share and discuss this story, and Cecil doesn't care if someone tries to portray him as a twisted, messed up curious child. Despite his lack of knowledge about girls, back then. Cecil is simply being honest, unlike most people.

It is a reality that there are individuals who engage in beastiality or far worse than fucking animals. Let's you and I have some fun with the following question that Cecil's about to ask: Which question can you digest? Do your neighbor fuck animals, or does he kidnap, molest, or rape children? Instead of responding with none of the above, please select one.

What Cecil learned from this chapter before publishing it, he considered whether he wanted to include it again, because he contemplated this decision for several days, and it wasn't an easy one. He was worried about who would judge him because he knew this was coming from a place of forgiveness for something he had experienced as an inquisitive, innocent child.

For some strange reason, Cecil found everything on that website fascinating. Some of it made him want to masturbate while watching it. Reflecting, Cecil's unsure where those thoughts came from or why. He gave up. You can diagnose Cecil in your mind. Btw, this was a major for him to include this for you to read. He will explain why in a chapter called: "Backstabbing Friends".

There is nothing you could tell yourself or Cecil. that's worse than this chapter.

Peace!

My Gay Azz Cousin

I'm aware that there are going to be a significant number of people like you who will express their disapproval of my misdemeanors.

The characters in this chapter are:

- Leon – Also known as **(L)** the **molester.**
- Cecil – Also known as **(C) the victim**
- David – Also known as **(D) the narrator**
- Momma – Also known as **(M)**

Str8 From The Audiobook

(C) When I openly share my life and experiences in this book, I am also cognizant of the potential judgment I may face. Before you continue reading, I want to clarify that I don't identify with any of the following categories.

*Pansexual, *bisexual, *gay, *allosexual, *Androsexual, *Aromantic, *Cupiosexual, *Gray Sexual, *Heterochromatic, *Skoliosexual, *Sexually Favorable, *omnisexual, or *Gynesexual.

David: I will explain at the end of this chapter, so please relax, and continue listening. I could identify as any of the following: *straight, *sapiosexual, *Autosexual, *demisexual, *heterosexual, *Monosexual, and this does not require a *plain old sexual orientation. I could also be a combination of these things. After listening to this chapter, about my interaction with my gay ass cousin, I am sure that you will either choose one of the previously mentioned statements or assume that several of them apply to me. There is an old saying that has been around for a long time, which goes something like this. If you can't stand the heat, get out of the kitchen, because I am about to share some of my honest feelings.

In that case, you may want to stop listening to this audiobook immediately, before it's too late. But! I eagerly anticipate you are going to listen anyway, so let us begin. When I was around fourteen or fifteen years old, I lived with my mother, Beatrice Hicks. In addition, we had a cousin named Leon, who was around thirty-three years old, and an openly gay man staying with us. However, I still don't remember how or why that happened.

I apologize for not providing specific dates and times for why he was living with us, and I ask that you forgive me. In summary, during our time together, Leon sexually assaulted me. When I say molested, I don't mean physical or unwanted penetration; instead, it refers to the fact that, at the age of fourteen, I experienced inappropriate touching and child exploitation. I was unaware how any of what he was doing would affect the rest of my life. Leon liked me, and I thought those were his ways of expressing his feelings toward me. Given that I was only fourteen years old, one would assume that I should have known that something was inappropriate and not what it seemed.

I am not sure how you learned about sex. Still, as a young man, my father wasn't around because he died from heart failure right after I graduated from Gompers Junior High School in San Diego, California. Back then, there was no such thing as the #METOO movement or child welfare agencies in black neighborhoods. As a result, I don't recall my father teaching me about sex before he passed away. As mentioned in another chapter, the only thing I remember about my father is that he had affairs and told me about them.

Nevertheless, the only encounters I can recall were with men who were dating my mom, married men having affairs at my house, or neighbors and bullies in the neighborhood who were a lot older than me. However, a young man named Dan lived in San Diego. One morning, while Dan was sucking my cock, his grandmother almost caught us in the act.

Reflecting back, neither he nor I would have been considered gay or bisexual back in the day; I would say I was more curious than anything. I understand the title of this chapter, "My Gay Ass Cousin." So, let us get back to it, shall we? Now I am fifteen years old, and one evening, my gay ass cousin Leon decided to abruptly walk into my bedroom and ask if I wanted to fuck him. Just pause momentarily, close your eyes, and picture me answering that question at my age.

I am confident you can't imagine the impact on my mental development. Nevertheless, I was confused and did not know what to say or think about his question. Honestly, I had never heard that word used in that context before. So, following his example, I said yes. What was I thinking at fourteen years old and have never been in a romantic relationship with a girl yet, and now I am receiving requests to use my cock for purposes beyond masturbation.

If you recall, I recently became aware of masturbation, and now I am engaging in sexual activities with my cock with a male. Seriously? I was unsure where to place my cock and other details. I remember watching him unzipping and pulling down his pants while my momma was in the living room watching her favorite television show, "Young and the Restless." This slick child molester knew what he wanted from an innocent kid in his room, minding his own business. Leon got on my bed; knees pressed into the sheets. Then he did something that's been burned into my memory ever since. He reached behind himself and spread his ass open inviting me to look.

I know that sounds wild, but it's exactly what happened.

And just so you know? I've never even seen my own asshole. But there I was... face to face with his.

He looked back at me over his shoulder and smiled—like this twisted look of permission. Like, "You know what to do." And I didn't.

I asked him, "What am I supposed to do now?"
And this boy—my cousin—he said, with no hesitation:
(L) "Put that hard dick in my ass."

Yeah... those exact words.

(D) He must've noticed the bulge in my pants, which I hadn't even realized was there. And before you judge me for that, understand this—I've questioned that moment for years. I still don't know why my body reacted like that. I've asked myself if it was trauma, confusion, adrenaline, fear, arousal, shame... or all of it tangled together in a knot too tight to pull apart.

I unzipped my pants. I pulled them down. I knelt behind him. And that's where my memory starts to blur. Not because I forgot... but because my mind won't let me remember everything clearly. Maybe I'm blocking it out. Maybe I'm trying to protect myself. Or maybe I was scared of what the full truth might reveal. My gay Ass cousin Leon must have liked pain because he did not bring lubrication with him into my bedroom.

All he did was spit in his hand, rub some on my shaft, and rub the rest around his asshole. If you've never experienced molestation or heard someone spitting in general, it can be a triggering sound if you ever hear it again. Once the spit wore off, I wasn't enjoying fucking him in the ass.

Without the spit it was stretching the skin on my shaft, and it was excruciatingly painful! After being confused and unsure what to do, I pulled out of his ass and pulled up my pants and left my bedroom. On a completely different evening, Leon must have been extremely horny, I suppose, because he opened my bedroom door just like before and walked in while I was minding my own business. As I mentioned, when his bitch ass opened my door again, especially without knocking, I knew what his intentions were without exchanging words. Here is the thing: I did not cum the first time while fucking him only because I was uncomfortable and uncertain about what I was doing. He asked me if I had shot my load in his ass, and I said no. At that point, he suggested that we could try again later.

I wasn't sure if there would be a next time. To be honest with you, I am surprised that my cousin did not physically assault and abuse me for his sexual gratification. Anyway, I have always felt that when something is not fair, I want to make it right. My momma was like that, too, so when Leon told me it was his turn to fuck me, I held my head down, looked at the floor, and said OKAY. It was as though I had no other option in that circumstance. I unzipped, pulled down my pants, and got on the bed, just like he did when he asked me to fuck him. I then bent over as he instructed.

Suddenly, Leon thrust his cock into me, causing excruciating pain. It wasn't like he had a cock larger than me and actually, we were the same size. He did not even spit on it before inserting it in my ass. I screamed " GET OFF ME" and issued a firm directive to him to vacate my bedroom immediately.

When I yelled, "Get the hell out," my mother must have noticed something was wrong with my voice. She immediately raised her voice and asked if I was okay. I wasn't sure what to say or think at that moment. I lied to her, not realizing how it would affect me afterward. Something about what happened did not seem natural or pleasurable. As I write this part of the chapter, I am sure that this is the reason I enjoy anal sex, as I am the giver, not the taker, or, in other words, I am a top, not a bottom. After telling Leon to get the hell out of my bedroom, I needed a moment of clarity. After some time had passed, his ongoing sexual advancements increased, so I decided to take him up on some of his whispers in my ear.

He whispered that he wanted to suck my cock. I wasn't sure what that involved, but the way he talked about it sounded like something I wanted to experience. After ongoing whispers and subtle advancements, it was time to find out what it meant to have my cock sucked. One evening, late at night, I sneaked into his room as he had instructed. After everything he had done and attempted to do sexually, Leon told me that sucking my cock would be more pleasurable, and he promised that I did not have to reciprocate. Now this mutha fucka has my attention because, to this day, 04/07/2025, I have not, excuse me allow me to repeat that,

I HAVE NOT!! sucked a man's cock since my conception. Well, wait just a second; there better be a gun to my head; that's an entirely different situation. And I am going to wrap up this paragraph by saying: "that mother fucker might as well pull the trigger".

(C) Anyway, my mom must've had damn near super-hearing to catch me sneaking out of my room at night. Didn't matter how soft I tiptoed—fast, slow, on my toes like a damn ninja—she'd still catch me.

(M) "What are you doing?"

(C) I'd lie without hesitation. "Just going to the bathroom," I'd say.

(M) "Yeah, okay," she'd shoot back, all sarcastic-like—like she knew I was full of shit but didn't want to deal with it at that moment.

(D) There was one night I remember more than the rest. I crept into the hallway, stood there faking like I was opening the bathroom door—making sure it clicked shut behind me. Then I rushed down to my cousin's room.

He was already there, lying on his side near the edge of the bed... mouth open. Waiting.

I remember three other occasions when I attempted to sneak out of my bedroom while thinking my mom was asleep. I was so desperate for him to suck my cock that I was willing to reveal the truth, as he was exceptionally skilled at it. Wait a damn minute, listener. Where do you think you are going?

I don't want you to stop listening to my homosexual cousin Leon just yet. So go use the bathroom if you must, or drink whatever you need to continue reading this lengthy chapter. As time progressed, I came to understand that Leon had additional techniques he wanted to demonstrate, as he was aware that I would never consent to him penetrating my ass once more. Is he putting me in that situation again, not even with the tip?

He cautiously inquired whether it would be possible to suck my cock rather than fuck my ass. For an unknown reason, I granted him one final opportunity. Like going into a gas station where I pull up to the pump, take the hose, and stick it in the gas hole, all I had to do was pull up close to the edge of the bed, drop my draws, and get my cock sucked until I came in his mouth.

Then I pulled up my pants, tiptoed back into the bathroom, and faked, feeling like I was flushing the toilet. Every time I tried to slip out of my bedroom to have my cock sucked, my mom used her hearing and supersonic powers and yet again asked, what are you doing? I asked myself, "Why does what I am doing matter?" You would think she must have had a clue, right? Aside from that, I was too embarrassed to admit what I was doing anyway.

I knew that if I said no to Leon, who convinced me that I would enjoy what he does with his mouth, he might ask me to fuck him again. Leon said all I had to do was walk in, drop my pants, watch him suck my cock, and leave. There was no possible way to avoid him in a nine hundred-square-foot, three-bedroom, one-bath house. Here we are again, just trying to survive a child molester in our home, and it wasn't easy. Do you believe me? I swear, every time I walked into his room to have my cock sucked, I ended up in his mouth. And, just so you know, he never swallowed my fresh, hot, milky looking cum because he would spit it into an empty can that was next to his bed.

Man, the noises he would make while sucking on my cock were addicting, like sucking on a popsicle from the ice cream truck that came around in your neighborhood. I am unsure how old you are, listener; do you remember those days? With no intentions of leaving anything out of this chapter, here is another memory of my flaming gay ass cousin Leon, which leads me to believe that molestation has altered my behavior as an adult.

One day, I was playing basketball at Ocean View Hills Park in Southeast San Diego. Leon, my gay cousin, approached the park to greet me. However, I was aware that his intention wasn't to greet me. All my gay azz cousin Leon had to do was make that cock-suck slurping sound like a man with a snake flute, and I would have an erection. At the time, I was embarrassed to be associated with my gay ass cousin because he and I had never been seen together publicly.

Back then, I understood engaging in such interactions anywhere I lived at wasn't a good idea, as it could lead to unwanted attention or worse. When I was twenty-three, it was finally time to move from my mom's house into my first apartment. At that time, I was a momma's boy because I never had a place to live on my own terms. However, I was thrilled to discover a bedroom on the third floor. This place was also cool because you had to use the intercom to reach me.

Just a few days after I moved in, my gay cousin Leon unexpectedly sent me a message on my cell phone. After saying hello, I desperately tried not to listen to the sound Leon was making with his mouth. As I mentioned earlier, please don't act as if you don't know what I'm talking about. I eventually told Leon to come over to my apartment and suck my cock; it did not take more than 15 minutes, and my intercom buzzed to let him in. As he walked in, I wasted no time, taking off my pants and underwear and throwing them on the couch. Leon did not waste time and reminded me of James Brown by dropping to the floor like he performed the splits.

I was already hard as a brick; he started sucking my cock and playing with my balls. I remember vividly standing above him, looking down, and looking at him like the submissive bottom bitch Leon was. He did something a little different this time, and damn, it felt good. He held my ball sacks with one hand and used the other on my shaft, all while moving his head back and forth. I must honestly say I came so fucking hard I almost passed out; my knees were weak, and I was sweaty like I had just completed a marathon.

I leaned over and pushed Leon's head away from my cock, like I wasn't satisfied. He stood in front of me as if he wanted to kiss, so I slapped the cum right out of his mouth. What is messed up? I released myself into his mouth, and he spit my fresh, hot cum all over the floor. He cried right after I slapped him in the face, walked out the door, and did not look back. At that moment, I knew it was the last time I would ever see him. Being with him all the time, I could have easily ended up like my gay azz cousin Leon.

1 UPDATED THIS AGAIN ON 5/9/2024.

.

There is nothing wrong with the path you chose for your life to be happy, okay? Here are a few situations in which manipulation would have been easy: Why is it that I was able to cum in my cousin's mouth, but since then, I am unable to do the same with women? Most of the women in my life, either by marriage or date, have asked me to cum in their mouths.

Throughout the years, I have had some exceptional BJs; however, none have been able to replicate my cousin's sucking style and technique. Trust me. Damn, I hate the memories I have of my cousin because they still evoke vivid visions that I can't seem to erase. As I type this, I see my cousin on his knees, making a slurping sound, moving his head back and forth, and using the palm of his hand to manipulate the shaft of my cock. It is impossible to replicate the actions of all three unless you are Leon, my gay cousin. Right now, I am filled with sadness, yearning for protection from my cousin's molestation.

He stole some impressionable years of my life and made me who I am today. It is too late now. I am still confused at times and question my own behavior. There were times when I tried to reenact that experience with my cousin and strange men in my late teens. Nothing came close to what that molesting azz nigga Leon did to me. As a woman reading this chapter, majority of black men won't be this open about something so messed up. For him to share his soul, you better not criticize or judge him for something he may not have known was wrong.

This is particularly true if it involves a family member or someone he trusted. For him to talk about it comfortably, you must make him feel safe from it ever happening again, even if you don't completely understand it. It is embarrassing, and more than likely, the trauma is buried deep inside him. So, if he does tell you about his molestation, embrace and hug him. At 9:57 a.m.

I added this for you to read or listen to, OKAY? I woke up with a revelation that I want to share with you. This is also the reason I stand up for those who face bullying, and I comprehend why Lil Nas X disclosed his sexual orientation following his rise to prominence. I understand why so many are afraid to express themselves. I am astounded that I did not end up with my wrist bent, holding a drink with my pinky finger erect, and being outright gay. Leon was so good at sucking my cock every time I was alone with him; I could have quickly become addicted to wanting my cock sucked by a bunch of strange men all the time. I would have been a selfish lover if I had been gay.

Okay, I will inform you immediately that if I were gay, I would have to be the top. Fuck being a bottom. No pun is intended. I am sure someone is listening to this right now and wondering, "Why do I like to fuck women in the ass but didn't like it when I fucked my cousin?"

First, I was underage; secondly, I was curious; and most importantly, my cousin's ass was extremely hairy! Every time I went in and out of his hairy asshole, my shaft rubbed against the hair. Do not laugh! This ain't funny; it hurts. On 04/20/2025 I just had another thought I would like to share. Recently, I realized when someone I'm fucking has hair around their asshole; it's another trigger reminding me of my cousin. Seriously, this happened fifty-one years ago, ain't that some messed up memories that I can't shake, no matter what I do. That's the end of my Gay Ass Cousin Leon chapter.

UPDATE: I realized I had a lot more to say than when this was originally written. I woke up the morning of July 17, 2022, and had a revelation about a male, well-known black actor.

Most of the revelations in this book & audiobook compelled me to speak up about them. This actor, who was a football player, made the unprecedented decision to publicly address allegations of another man groping him. I feel comfortable mentioning this subject, and we are all entitled to our opinions, so here's mine. I feel confident that this male actor gave subtle, and even intentional, signs that it was okay for his agent to grope him (allegedly).

How is it possible for a former American football player tolerating another man groping his cock and balls? Yes, you read that correctly. ALLOWED! There is absolutely no way that another man could grab my cock and balls, and I would not have said or done something about it immediately. Listen up before you criticize me! I was a child when I was molested not a grown ass mother Ex football player and actor when it happened! Big difference, am I right?

Let me repeat myself again, another way!

By no means was I an adult. Let us analyze his allegations, shall we? He was a muscular football player, and this was surrounded by peers his age and size. I wonder, while showering if he looks over his shoulder and drops the soap intentionally.

Just saying. Let us follow his career, where he convincingly played a manly man until his favorite song came on while sitting in the car in "Vanilla Girls." Just before that scene, his manliness was questionable. Hell, if anyone knows questionable behavior, it is me, without a doubt, right?

Nevertheless, I am correct in my assessment of this individual. In any case, he discussed the childhood trauma he experienced, prompting me to suspect a deeper narrative beyond his public disclosures.

As I watch television, his mannerisms are questionable. Hey man, you know who you are, and it is okay if your sexual orientation differs from the persona, you show us.

Yep, you read it correctly. So, go ahead and criticize me for my criticism.

ADDITIONAL INFORMATION I FAILED TO MENTION:

To be honest with you, writing this chapter was incredibly challenging. And let me explain why, as a black man being molested, it is hard to admit, and in most cases, many of us are scared to speak up and talk about it. There is nothing wrong with coming forward and telling the truth, no matter who believes you. But I chose not to hide behind the tragedy and allowed myself to try to heal. I don't regret writing this chapter for a variety of reasons.

Every time I talk about this topic, tears well up in my eyes as I acknowledge that molestation derailed my journey. There are many paths a child could take without trauma. Because of trauma, the decisions I made today have changed my life forever. For a while, my therapist did not even know any of this information, and I am not sure why. As I mentioned earlier, my promiscuity may have been because of this trauma. Someone asked me, is this why I like anal sex? I am not sure why I like anal sex, but it might play a significant role. This could also explain why adopting a swinging lifestyle became so easy after this chapter.

Even now, I frequently contemplate what my life might have been like if I had not experienced molestation. Even though I only added this on 2/23/24, I still feel guilty.

At times, I struggle to cope with the overwhelming feelings of shame, guilt, pain, and a strong desire to isolate myself from the outside world. That's why watching gay porn with my ex-girlfriend was never an issue. Most heterosexual men would find the idea repulsive, but it did not bother me.

Again, my experiences have shaped me into the open-minded, non-judgmental person I am today. I also believe that this trauma has changed the nature of my relationships with people in general. Sometimes, I question the decisions I make, and sometimes, I ask about the relationships I have had. Anyone reading this today who has experienced molestation you're not alone.

It affects your relationships with your children, your family, and even yourself. But I am here to tell you that even at 65, it is not an easy decision to finally face it. I may be stating the obvious, but I simply can't tolerate having my cock sucked by any female if it is not done with passion. Many women tried for over thirty minutes and demonstrated a high skill level. When sucked properly, it always brings me pleasure, but my Gay Ass Cousin's exceptional sucking skills spoiled me. Ain't that a bitch!

THIS SECTION PROVIDES A GENERAL, UNEDUCATED EXPLANATION OF THE DIFFERENT TYPES OF SEXUALITY.

PSEUDOSEXUAL:

Sexual orientations encompass persons who experience attraction towards individuals of any gender or sex category. Gender is not a determining factor in sexual or romantic attraction, which is a trait usually connected with those who have this propensity. Some people prefer one of these labels over the other despite their similarities.

BISEXUAL:

Bisexuality is the condition of feeling attracted to both individuals of one's own gender and individuals of other genders or to individuals regardless of their gender.

GAY:

People who identify as gay typically have a primary sexual attraction to individuals of the same gender.

ALLOSEXUAL:

This individual typically feels a strong sexual attraction toward others. Furthermore, they may also tend to engage in sexual intercourse with a partner.

Individuals who align with this sexual orientation may also align with another sexual orientation, such as homosexuality, lesbianism, or bisexuality.

ANDROSEXUAL:

Regardless of their assigned gender at birth, people who identify as androsexual are attracted to men, namely those who exhibit masculine traits or characteristics.

CUPIOSEXUALITY:

This term refers to those who experience a lack of sexual attraction yet have a strong desire to engage in sexual activities or pursue sexual relationships.

SPECTRASEXUAL:

Individuals are romantically and sexually attracted to a wide range of sexes, genders, and gender identities. However, it is crucial to understand that "spectrality" does not apply to all Spectrasexual.

SEXUALLY INDIFFERENT:

A sexually indifferent individual is someone who lacks significant emotions or interest in anything related to sexuality or sexual behavior.

AUTOSEXUALS:

May experience sexual attraction toward both other people and themselves at the same time.

SEXUALLY FAVORABLE:

When an individual is sexually favorable, it indicates that they have positive views about engaging in sexual behavior under specific circumstances.

SKLEPTOSEXUAL:

Individuals who identify as sapiosexual typically only find attraction in those who don't fit into the traditional binary gender categories.

A DEMISEXUAL:

A demisexual individual typically develops a sexual attraction towards someone only after establishing a strong emotional bond with them over time. It is conceivable that specific individuals who identify as demisexual may exhibit either a complete lack of interest or simply a minimal interest in sexual behavior.

SPECTRALISTS:

Individuals who experience romantic and sexual attraction towards multiple sexes, genders, and gender identities, although not necessarily all of them, exist.

MONOSEXUALITY:

Refers to the range of sexual orientations in which individuals experience romantic or sexual attraction exclusively towards one gender. This word encompasses all these sexual orientations. This group of sexual orientations encompasses both heterosexuality and homosexuality, as well as lesbian orientation. Intimate relationship. There is potential for people who identify with this orientation to also identify with another orientation. The experience of romantic attraction can be unique and individualized.

AROMANTIC:

An aromantic individual may lack the experience of romantic attraction towards any one person. They lack the desire to pursue the sexual attraction they experience. For example, someone may not have a romantic attraction towards others. Yet, they may still sense sexual desire towards specific individuals they come across.

My Momma
Beatrice Hicks

I would like to personally thank Anderson-Ragsdale Mortuary at 5050 Federal Blvd., San Diego, CA 92102, for the cremation of my mother Beatrice Hicks on June 25, 1998.

They managed my mother's burial with class and professionalism. In fact, during a critical period in my life, they dealt with the specifics flawlessly. I was a momma's boy, and I am fighting not to cry while writing this chapter.

So please bear with me while I tell you a little about her. Most of us will say the same thing about our mother: she was the kindest, most giving mother you could ever want, not just because she was mine.

She would give you her last dollar rather than leave you without food if you were in need. I knew this was true because I witnessed her always lending money to my cousin. This dishonest mother fucker never paid back the money he borrowed, for as far back as I could remember. Every time I shut my eyes; I can't help but reflect back when my cousin would mischievously grin and requests $20 from my mother. My mother would ask him, "when will you pay it back?" She had to be fully aware that he was dishonest. On a side note, I don't borrow money from anyone because of my cousin's constant dishonesty and betrayal, which I find unacceptable.

And it is also why I don't like loaning or giving someone money unless it is an emergency. Anyway, I could see the joy on her face even as I typed this. I saw her grayish hair, gorgeous brown eyes, dimples, and a smile I will never forget.

As of July 29, 2024, no one can cook like my mother, and many ladies have tried but can't replicate it. Despite being a sensitive and kind individual who has married three times, I have never made them feel they could not match my mother's cooking. If you are one of my three wives reading this chapter, you can grin since your cuisine is never compared to my mother's, and I never admitted it. My mother made the tastiest banana Nilla pudding, and to this day, only one place can match it.

There is a restaurant in Georgia called: The Cupboard in Dillard Georgia has been and still is the one and only place that comes close to my mother's recipe. In fact, as soon as I tasted the first tablespoon of banana pudding, I immediately thought of my mother because it was so amazing. Would you like to know how good it was?

It was so good that I tried to figure out how to mail it to me the next day while keeping it cold and preserving its texture and flavor. Are you thinking the same thing I am? It must have been an exceptionally delicious banana pudding, and indeed it was.

I swear, if I was just released from prison after 30 years and had a choice between my wife and kids I have not seen since being incarcerated or one teaspoon of this banana pudding, this might take me a few days to decide, just saying! So, back to my mother. She faced numerous challenges from my father, and she was aware that he was cheating on her. He also struggled with alcoholism, as I have previously mentioned in another chapter. I am glad I did not follow in my father's footsteps and became an alcoholic. I am sharing a brief story about her to highlight our close bond. Watching her battle with my father's alcohol addiction was so challenging to process as a child, and I felt utterly powerless.

Finally, I made a critical decision that I believed was correct. On Monday, July 17, 2022, I finally returned her ashes to the world. If you use a calculator or your fingers and toes to figure out how long I have had her ashes with me, it was 24 years and 2 months. As awful as I am remembering shit, I am surprised that I have had her ashes all those years. Consider this: I've carried my mother's ashes through three marriages, three divorces, and a Noah's Ark shipload of single women I fucked, licked, sucked on, and nutted in, as well as three used cars, including a Cadillac, Cutlass, Supreme, and Pontiac Bonneville, to name a few.

Additionally, I owned a brand-new, fully paid-off truck for seven years, spent sixteen years at my previous job as a janitor, invested in two unsuccessful businesses, lost one home, moved apartments three times, and engaged in many romantic relationships. So, carrying around her ashes for twenty-four years is a significant accomplishment.

Are you following what I am saying? Let me summarize everything before moving on to the next paragraph below this one. My mother was cremated, and I had her ashes with me from June 25, 1998, to July 17, 2022. I have visited many parks in the Orlando area, and there is one specifically that spoke to me to spread her ashes. I chose the park that spoke to me and could peacefully scatter her ashes. A revelation occurred just a week after I released her ashes on July 24. Before my mother died in 1998, there was and still is an angel following me.

    * I will elaborate more at the end of this chapter, okay? Here is one example of many: While in San Diego, I was on Interstate 805 heading to my girlfriend's house, who became my ex-wife later and before relocating to another state with one of my three ex-wives. What I said sounds confusing and useless, but I wanted to include it anyway. In other words, I was headed to my girlfriend's house when this happened, but by the time I left San Diego, it was with a different woman to whom I was married, if this makes sense.

    I am trying to remember where I came from, but I remember where I was going. So, there was no specific reason for me to stop and say hello to my mother while driving down Interstate 805. During the day, I contacted her at least once and asked if she needed anything from the store in case she ran out since my mother could not drive. While driving one day, a weird sensation came over me about five miles before I reached the exit, guiding me to my mother's place. The strange feeling intensified as I drove closer to the exit. I knew I did not need to use the restroom, and I wasn't hungry. I wanted to throw up two miles from the exit, and the feeling grew, forcing me to pull over for a few minutes.

    Believe it or not this still happens to me. I exited my car immediately and walked around it, wondering whether it was a dangerous odorless gas through the air conditioning. Not feeling any better, I returned to my car with all four windows rolled down. I could not understand why that strange feeling would not go away. Whatever that feeling was, it made me nauseous, so I took the exit towards my mother's house just in case it worsened. **Royal** cound not help herself and said: I bet you had gas from all those tacos you ate the night before. I just about had enough and said: Royal! Not now! Royal: Well then when? Cecil: I'll let you know, so step out for a minute! In fact, about a mile from her house, I began to feel a little better.

To this day, 09/12/2024, I am still dumbfounded and don't understand why I felt that way in the first place. Cecil! You are dragging this story out, WHY? Royal! I have one simple explanation for you. And, what's that? It's my muthafucken story to tell. Well, umm okay then, keep going. That strange feeling vanished as soon as I stopped questioning it. My mother lived thirty minutes from the freeway exits. Remember, I planned to call her once I arrived at my girlfriend's house. That's why I had no reason to visit my mother that day.

After I pulled into the driveway, stepped out of my car, and opened the door, I suddenly heard my mother calling my name in a way I had never heard before. She sounded far away and distressed, as if in the backyard, lying near the bathroom window I used to peep through. (I elaborate more about peeping through the bathroom window in a chapter called "The Bathroom Window") I knew something was strange since Mama wasn't watching her favorite television show, "The Young and the Restless." in her favorite chair by the front door. So now I am wondering what is going on.

And why is she screaming my name from behind the closed door leading into the hallway? So, I cautiously opened the door and poked my head around the corner, looking left and right. I asked, "Momma, where are you?" She said, "I'm in the bathroom." My initial response was that she must have shitted on herself and did not wish for me to enter the bathroom while she was in it. I checked her bedroom first to ensure she wasn't there. I looked inside my bedroom, and she wasn't there. I also checked the other bedroom, and she wasn't there either. She had not stopped screaming my name, which made me anxious, so I finally opened the bathroom door. When you are in shock, you may find it difficult to believe what you are witnessing.

In this case, I stood there in shock because my mother had slipped and fallen backward inside the bathtub. In a moment of uncertainty, I asked, "Momma, what the fuck happened? " Even then, my mother barked, "Okay, boy, don't talk like that." I am laughing as I write this, just so you know. Even then, as an adult, I had to apologize for my poor choice of words. I will explain if you are curious why I did not immediately remove my mother from the shower,.. just hang in there... (don't become impatient now.)

As far as I can remember, she has always been an enormous woman (I am being polite since she is my Momma). Wait! I ain't sure what enormous means. Um!! Oh! I think I know what that word means now. And what's that? You are basically calling your momma a, FAT BITCH!! Hell, no Royal I am not, by any means. Then why refer to her weight at all? Good point, but my reason will be mentioned later in this chapter. This is going to be the first time I apologize to you. Cecil, I am sorry and would you mind continuing with your story? Sure, thanks!

She gained weight as she grew older due to a lack of exercise and healthy nutrition. In other words, she was too heavy to lift out of the bathtub on my own. I needed to think quickly about what to do, and my neighbor immediately came to mind. So, I left her in the tub sideways and asked whether she was in pain or had banged her head when she slipped; she responded no and assured me she was okay. I ran over to my neighbor's house next door and thanked the universe that he was home. When I told him what had happened, he immediately walked with me to help. Unfortunately, my mother was butt naked, and I am sure she was mortified when my neighbor walked in with me. I had to reassure her that it was okay because I had no other way to get her big ass out (fuck it, I said it), at least not by myself.

Despite the situation's urgency, I had not saved enough money to hire an emergency crane service to drill a hole in the roof and hoist her big ass out of the bathtub. Another thing I know for sure is that if I had tried hauling her out of the bathtub by myself while she was sideways, I would not have been able to write this chapter. So, when my neighbor stepped in, he was startled to see her in that situation. We stood there, scratching our heads, trying to figure out how to help her get out of the bathtub together. It was like two minds trying to figure out Chinese mathematics together with a non-English-speaking teacher in China.

Have you already laughed? I experienced the same feeling as I was typing this chapter. My mother had been in the bathtub sideways for a while. She wasn't strong enough to pull herself alone because she had a larger upper torso and skinny legs. I am not trying to be funny, but she reminded me of an ostrich whenever I saw her in tight clothes. Why am I mentioning it? My neighbor and I knew that once we removed her from the bathtub, her ostrich-like legs would not hold her upright.

We both realized we could not keep her upright without shouting out timber like a tree was about to fall. Furthermore, we had not put anything on the floor or walls to cushion her fall. Now, it is time to attempt to get my mother out of the bathtub. My hand was on her left arm, while my neighbor had the right. Cecil! Yes, Royal what the hell is it NOW?!!! What made you think of, .. ostrich legs? Well, if my momma was still alive, you wouldn't be asking me that question. I asked because that was funny as HELL!!. SHIT!!,.. I almost peed on myself!! Wait!! are you laughing at my momma NOW? No Cecil I was not, Ok! Ok! Please continue. We counted down from three to one, like in the movie Lethal Weapon, which stars Mel Gibson and Danny Glover. Seriously, we slowly lifted her out at the count of three. Trust me, when I say this wasn't easy, but we completed it on our first try. Yes!!

We got Momma out of the bathtub, and she could stay upright without assistance. She stood before us in her birthday suit with no candles to blow out. Our neighbor quickly fled because he could tell my mother was uncomfortable and ashamed standing there naked. My neighbor, already in his fifties, was fragile and underweight, so I am surprised he and I could lift her out of the bathtub. All of that's irrelevant, right? He and I were able to lift her big ass out without the services of a crane, as I indicated previously.

Cecil!.. Yes, Momma. I decided to fly down to speak with you about this paragraph and say,.. I almost peed on everyone down here from heaven. You mother-fuckers would have thought it was raining all of the sudden. And it would have been piss!! Momma! You got jokes! So, it's ok baby, it's all good and continue. I really like what I hear and I know it's coming from love.

Momma, I miss you. I know you do baby, but you must continue with your story about me, okay? Thanks momma and you can fly in anytime. Cecil! yes momma, Continue please. If my neighbor and I could have picked one theme song to play while lifting my mother out of the bathtub, it would have been that song from Rocky, starring Sylvester Stallone and written by William Conti. When he left, I asked my mother how long she had been in that position, and she said at least two hours. I cried right there in front of her for a while.

Even under duress my mother took a second to console me. While creating the audio version of this chapter, "I miss her tremendously". She is an irreplaceable void in my life and I'm not sure if I was ever the same after you keep reading.While writing this chapter section, it was challenging to think that my mother had been in the bathtub for more than two hours without a phone nearby to dial 9-1-1. That had to be the universe doing everything possible to ensure I returned home that day.

Otherwise, I wasn't planning to go home until the next day. Who knows what would have occurred if I had not returned home? That had to be the reason I was feeling strange on the freeway. I indicated previously that an angel was following me, correct? Since then, that weird sensation has not returned. What other explanations is there for feeling that way while driving just a few miles from home? I told you a little about my mother to show how spiritually and emotionally close we were. Since that day, I have been paying attention whenever I sense something within myself. It has not failed me yet. It is the same reason I wrote this book: I felt obliged to share my story. This is not about glorifying my sexual activities or, shall we say, my free choice; rather, it is about sharing, learning, and inspiring others. I saved the most difficult aspect of this chapter for the end.

Before I go any further, I apologize for bouncing around all over the place in this section. If you were wondering what happened to my mom, here it is in detail, okay? One of my wives contacted me, urging me to return home promptly. As I arrived, I discovered she had our two sons in the car, and the ambulance had just closed the door with my mother inside. I am lucky one of my wives did not tell me what happened over the phone because I would have broken every law known to men just to get home.

She requested that I park my car and enter hers while we drove behind the ambulance. I remember asking what occurred, when, and why, but she had no answers. We parked and ran inside the emergency room, where the receptionist directed us to the appropriate room to await the doctor's arrival. I recall being terrified, impatient, and feeling like time had stopped. I also remember one of my spouses telling me to sit down because I was pacing like a caged lion, or so it felt. If it had been her father, I am confident she would not have sat down, and based on my knowledge of her, she would have been in the room with him instead.

I swear, it felt like hours had passed since we arrived. Finally, when I looked down the hallway where I knew my mother was, I noticed the doctor walking towards us. I want you to understand how I felt as I saw this doctor approaching me down the corridor, as if he were moving in slow motion. As I do every day, I observed his body language and facial expressions, and I did not like what I saw. He finally stopped staring at the documents in his hand and moved towards us. As you may recall, my mother and I shared a spiritual connection, so I sensed something terrible had happened. When he opened the door to the waiting area, he looked up and uttered something that would forever impact my life. At this point, even his words seemed slow and whisper-like.

When I finally regained consciousness, I heard him remark, "I'm sorry, but your mother suffered a terrible heart attack, and there was nothing we could do for her." I remember cursing at the doctor and yelling, "What the hell did you just say? " As he stepped away from me. For no apparent reason, one of my wives apologized. So, he repeated what he had said: Your mother died from a massive heart attack and did not survive. The doctor asked: Would you like to see her? But I declined because he also said to me: I did not remove the tubes from within her mouth. I was selfish, but I wanted to remember her without tubes, lying on a table with her eyes closed.

Does any of what I have stated make sense? Walking out of the emergency room, I was in a haze for a while. At this moment, I am closing my eyes to see if I have forgotten to mention anything, and I will conclude this chapter with a thought that occurred to me. After the shock of my mom's death subsided. I was able to dwell on what had upset her days before she died. Even though I can't remember where I was when Mom called, I remember not hesitating to see what was happening.

When I arrived, I had to calm her down, and she gave me the phone bill. I was stunned when I realized what had happened. Her phone bill was around $1200, whereas her previous bill was under $100. I immediately contacted Mom's phone provider, who provided me with confirmation of how much it had increased. After a few minutes, they had voice proof that my oldest son had called one of those 1-800 sex call centers. She was on a fixed income, so there was no way she could pay that bill, and that's why I believe she suffered a massive heart attack. Since it was my weekend with my boys, and I suppose I wanted someone to blame, I chose my oldest son who made the sex calls, and was only about ten years old.

I vividly remember looking down at him, pointing my fingers at his face, yelling and sobbing while blaming him for my mother's severe heart attack. I am optimistic that blaming him did not help. I won't explain my noncommutative connection with my sons in this book.

My Revelation: By the way, what you are about to read will tie everything together in this chapter, so stick with me, okay? On July 24, 2022, at about four a.m., I awoke from a deep crying sleep and gazed up at the ceiling. My pillow was drenched, and my bedding was damp. I lay there, wondering what the hell I was dreaming about since I could not fall back asleep.

I am wide awake, weeping, and trying to snap out of it. I was wondering whether I had had a nightmare; that's something I might recall easily. Whatever that feeling was, it caught me entirely off guard. I usually figure things out. I could not resolve the issue this time, which made me uncomfortable. I lay in bed for more than an hour, crying uncontrollably. I started interrogating myself as if I were an innocent black man minding my own business while being harassed by a white racist police officer.

The only thing I can attribute to this is that shortly before going to bed, I was thinking about all the women I had fucked, dated, married, or had one-night stands with. Consequently, and to my surprise, I realized that maintaining monogamy had proven to be a challenging aspect of my dating and marriage experiences. I am perplexed as to why I have never been faithful to the women I have encountered, and I even cheated on my first girlfriend in San Diego. While writing this chapter, I am trying to think back as far as I can remember: has there ever been a woman with whom I have been monogamous?

If I were my own psychiatrist, after months of therapy, I would finally have a diagnosis of why I woke up crying. I attribute this to my father's infidelity with my mother, as previously mentioned in one of my chapters, as well as my uncle and brother-in-law's infidelity with their spouses and girlfriends, which I will elaborate on now. I know this because I was with them when they lied and fucked around.

On numerous occasions, I witnessed every woman my uncle was associated with cry and beg me to set him straight. "They asked me if I knew how to talk to them and what to say." These women would occasionally pull me aside and drill me to tell them about his daily whereabouts. Can you believe those bitches asked me to spy on my uncle; ain't that a bitch? I paid the price when my uncle discovered I was reporting back to those women. It was unfair for those women to question me whether he was manipulating them or not. I did not notice the difference because what he did to those women seemed natural as far as I was concerned. I was constantly involved in everyone else's bullshit and nonsense. My brother-in-law cheated on his wife, and he told me about it.

He occasionally pulled me aside and bragged about his relationships with other women. His engaging stories always drew me in. He made an affair sound like something men would do naturally and without shame or guilt. Even though he was married to my aunt, he would frequently brag about all the ladies he fucked with. Upon reflection, it is a damn shame that they were unaware of the confusion and harm that their adultery would have on my life as an adult. In one of my chapters, I wrote about married couples who visited my house and engaged in adultery. They had scandalous affairs while pretending to be my mother's best friend. My most impactful years have been filled with dishonesty.

When I think about it, everything seemed entirely natural at the time, and I had no idea how much of an impact it would have on me later in life. I remembered this one woman I was dating, and everything was going well. While holding hands on the beach, she stopped and turned to face me. She then looked me straight in the eyes and asked if I had slept with anyone the night before. I hesitated to answer her inquiry because I did not understand how she knew. Her instincts about me must have prepared her for the response to her question. When I told her the truth and said yes, she cursed at me and struck my arm with her fist. I did not understand why she was upset with me. She became quiet and begged me to take her home in an angry, disappointed tone.

Even then, as angry as she was, I had always believed that honesty was the best policy. That honesty terminated our relationship immediately. I am not asking for forgiveness; I am only trying to convey why I am the way I am. That's one reason I am glad I did not follow in the footsteps of my brother-in-law and cousin. Well, I just lied. If I believed that lying would cause physical harm to someone, I would certainly do so.

As a child, I witnessed adults lying to me on numerous occasions, and in the same breath, they would say they loved me also. Someone who acts like me. And it is no surprise that I can relate to people going through something similar, but I don't understand why. Does this make me a hypocrite because I cheated during my marriages? I hope not because this happened before I found who I am today. On one unfaithful day, while one of my wives was at work at a university, I had two different women at our home, one of whom I had sex on our blue carpet. I was usually hornier while she was at work than when she was home.

I found myself jacking off a lot while watching porn, shooting cum all over our carpet, and never cleaning it up. One day, she asked me, "What are all those stains on the carpet?" I shrugged my shoulders as if I had swallowed the canary and answered, "I don't know." That was the appropriate answer, knowing I had masturbated all over the carpet. Watching porn made me sleepy by the time she got home to have sex with her. I became involved with another white woman named Becky, who lived 10 minutes from where I lived. Becky was the only person I fucked on our blue carpet while my wife was at work. Becky and I were together for a year of my marriage.She was a sweet woman with a bi-racial son.

(You know who you are). I don't recall how we met, but she was tall and had light brown hair. After fooling around behind my wife's back, Becky finally had the confidence to end our relationship. Becky met a nice man, and they married. The fascinating part is that she invited me to their wedding. I recall shaking her husband's hand and complimenting her as if she were a coworker, so he had no idea who I was. I am talking about other married couples who have cheated on their spouses or, should I say, their significant others.

To be politically correct, I have changed the term from spouses to significant other.Dear reader, to conclude this chapter, when you meet someone for the first time, you meet their representative, including you. Before judging someone, know who they were as a child. Be sure to check your closet before judging them. If nothing I have stated in this chapter has convinced you of why people behave the way they do, you should reflect on your childhood. When you do, I guarantee that it will appear unexpectedly.

Like me, you will struggle to understand why you react to or handle certain situations negatively. "Many explanations exist for our behavior." Why is the swinging lifestyle acceptable to those who participate and despised by those who don't? Why do some people find it okay to degrade someone? Why is being lied to so acceptable? If someone lied to you, why forgive them? Especially if it was more than once. You may be unaware of something in your background that makes lying acceptable.

Despite the current events in our country, people persist in believing the lies propagated to them, and there is a reason for this. Whoever prefers lies to the truth must have experienced something traumatic. With this mindset, you can only try to comprehend and sympathize with their point of view.

Who are you to judge them as a baby, a child, a teenager, a young adult, a middle-aged adult, or, most importantly, as myself? Update: Since my epiphany, I have spent some time alone reflecting on how to deal with the memories of my mother that I discovered. Understanding what I know now has been a challenging task for me. Some of my relationships have been incredible, and I wish I could turn back time. As a realist, I am prepared to push myself to do better.

My mother heavily influences all my actions and thoughts in this chapter. As of April 9, 2024, I still miss my mom. In many ways, I know I resemble my mother. I omitted the following information from the original book: Mama always taught me to respect everyone, including white people. My mother felt compelled to teach this lesson to me because of the treatment she received while growing up and working with white racist people.

An example of what she taught me would be seeing a white person while walking down the street and displaying my teeth to make them feel more comfortable. Ain't that some messed up shit to be taught by your mom, huh? Also, if a white person is approaching me, I should step aside. In other words, give them the right of way. But it was a way to ensure that I got home securely. Living in Mississippi, you had to watch your every move and what you said, or you may end up missing.

But she had no idea how timid that made me feel. I see grown black men behaving in this manner all the time, which worries me. Their mothers must have taught them the same thing. This is evident in today's movies and television shows, particularly in the roles they assign us. Do not get me wrong; my mother was doing what she thought was best at the time. It took me several years to realize how wounded I was. Sociologically, she was destroying the man I needed to become to survive.

My second wife was domineering in our relationship, which catalyzed my self-realization as a man. My mother's inability to deal with my father appears to have influenced me also. When I think about it, the way my father treated my mother disgusts me.

I still miss her to this day. In many ways, it equipped me with the intuition to identify instances of abuse.

If I could do it all over again, I would not let many of the events that were taking place inside my home continue. We reconnected with one of Mom's Facebook acquaintances. After a few talks, I remembered how she had disrespected my mother's home. Wait, I had a thought: Could this be the same reason I cheated on my first two wives? Is it possible, correct? Peace

My address then was: 4110 Hemlock Street San Diego California.

And I still have memories of this house that plague my thoughts today. While I am alone, I cry wondering whatever did, I say or do that made him want to do that to me? I used to sneak out from my bedroom across from my mom's bedroom to have my cousin suck my cock. When he was done, he would always spit the cum into the trashcan next to his bed.

Just imagine that sound for just one moment. Here let me help you, you know that sound you make when something is tickling your throat. Yes, that one. I am still traumatized when I hear that sound. I hope that helped. Also imagine hearing that sound as I am having sex. It is a distraction. I always had to apologize when my cock goes soft, and I would never admit why. I hate to lie but in this case it was necessary. I would take that moment to distract her by eating her pussy, works every single time.

By the way, pardon me if I have already mentioned this in a chapter called " My Gay Azz Cousin" As usual when I end a chapter what do I say? if you have been paying attention... Btw, I hope you get a chance to listen to the AudioBook. Cecil! have you looked up the house you sold for $68.000 back on Sep 30, 1998, and is now selling for over $500.000

Wait a minute! You mean to tell me my son sold my; I meant our house for only, $68,000! and 27 years later it's worth WHAT? It's worth over $500,000 ahh huh! Damn!! Cecil, what the hell, I meant heaven, were you thinking?

And even though I am up here in heaven I can still read your damn mind. So then, why did you sell it? Royal, leave me the hell alone, will ya! As I was about to say, Momma, I love you and all I can say is, I wasn't taught in school the value of property in any of the schools I attended.

You right baby, I am so sorry.

The schools you attended were created to keep you ignorant. Because, I can't remember you expressing what you learned in finance or business classes.

No generational wealth for you my son, and it's my fault. Momma, I be just fine without it, you'll see. By the way momma, yes, baby what is it?

There is this book I am working on that will change my life and others, you'll see. I know and I have faith in you. So, I am going back to heaven if that's okay with you?

Yes, it is momma, talk to you later.

My Shaft, U Damn Right

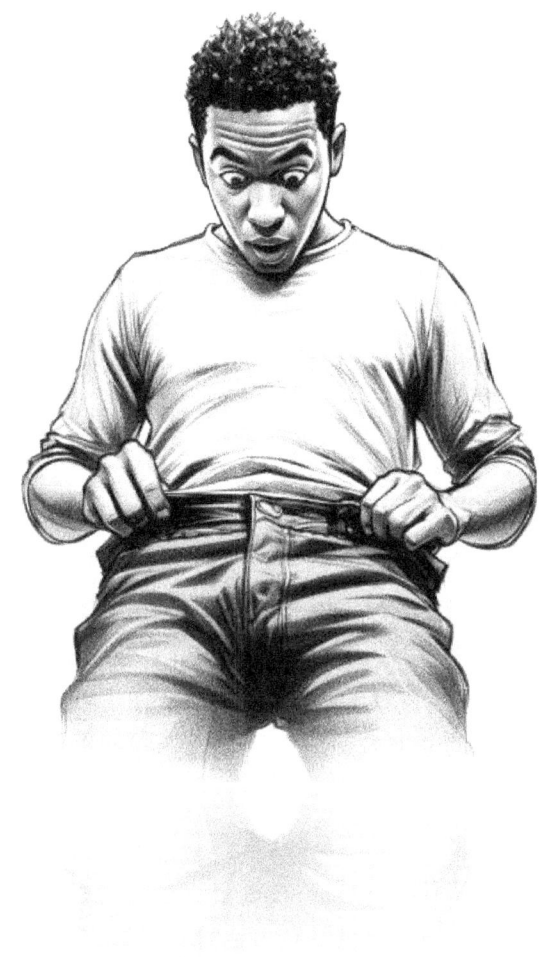

T hank you for a little bit of your time. Please continue reading. Let us get started, shall we?

I dislike women with hairy pussies for a variety of reasons and here is one of them. If there is any visible hair, I will refrain from engaging in sexual activity, such as licking, fingering, or massaging it.

I am willing to admit that I would not mind shaving the pussy, but only if she wants me to do any of the things that I described above, or possibly all of them. For example, when I meet someone on a dating website, I am patient and won't ask the question during the first conversation. Now, depending on how I feel about that person, I may wait for more before asking them about their pussy. I will be repeating this in a different way below, OKEY?

Please understand that whenever I repeat myself, it is just another way to get my message across to you.

I assume you have just asked yourself, "What is the question?" Are you familiar with a man asking this one? Have you shaved down there lately?

Remember that I did not ask this question in our first conversation. I try to gauge when it is appropriate to ask. Usually, it is never a good time to ask, but why should I waste my or their time if they have a hairy pussy? What I am about to say does not matter if you are male or female. If this is not talked about before fucking, this may be a deal breaker, right? Besides, some of these bitch's got pussies that look like they have Don King in a headlock. Did you laugh? I hope so because I did. If they say they have the Full Bush or Bikini Line and plan to keep it regardless of who they date, I might as well stop pursuing them.

I may be okay with a landing strip, but this won't stop me from moving forward. Having read what I have written up to this point, you are already aware that I prefer well-shaved pussy, or, to use the more appropriate term for it, the Brazilian. So, let us dive right in more, shall we? Why is my preference for a shaved pussy? After reading this chapter, hopefully, you will understand why that's my preference. There was this one sista I met on a dating site.

Before we met, we talked on the phone for hours before meeting each other. I considered myself a gentleman then and still do; otherwise, it would be the first question out of my mouth, even before saying hello. I am not someone who must talk about sex in the first conversation, but it would be nice at some point to have it. Like I said earlier, I would only inquire about their pussy if they gave me the impression that they were straightforward and uncomplicated, like myself. If that's not the case, I am extremely patient.

Typically, I enjoy engaging in an adult conversation about sex, and it is most enjoyable when the conversation is with a woman who shares my perspective. The last thing either one of us wants is to talk for weeks and find out that my preference is a "shaved pussy." Oh! A couple of weeks is too soon for you, isn't it? Well, we are not compatible and go our separate ways. Personally, I can't stand talking and texting without mentioning sex at some point. I know, damn it! I am repeating myself and changing it slightly, so please continue reading. Jackie and I must have talked for about a month before meeting in person. When we finally decided to meet, we only shared a kiss and did not discuss sex.

All I can say is that I wish we had discussed sex before our meeting, especially at the beginning of our conversations. That way, I could have averted the unfortunate situation I am sharing with you. Unlike a famous Porch Nigga, whom I have not personally met, he has an Afghan hound mustache over his upper lip. According to one of his televised shows, if a woman does what that motherfucker suggests, she should wait two to three months before fucking and asking questions, only to find out she does not like to shave her kitty cat. Fuck dat shit, and what a waste of our time. Here is why it should have been necessary at that time to have discussed the hair on the pussy. Before I fucked Jackie, one evening, while Jackie's roommate was working, she called and asked me to spend time with her, and of course, I said yes. Even though we talked about sex on the phone, it was going to be our first time together sexually, and we did not waste any time talking once I walked in. She had coco butter skin and a nice body.

She and I did not waste any time taking off our clothes. For starters, unlike most women I have met, there was no foreplay, kissing, sucking cock, or eating pussy. She got up on the bed and laid down on her back, waiting for me. Therefore, while she was lying on her back, I took advantage of the opportunity to position myself beneath her. Despite not using any lubrication, I reached down and proceeded to place the head of my cock in her pussy.

While I anticipated having a good time, I had my game face on. I hope you remember that we have not discussed sex or her hairy pussy and certainly have not brought up lubrication. To refresh your memory, when I mentioned my preference for baldness, I was referring to a shaved pussy. After a few strokes, I immediately felt something I had never felt. Based on the expression on my face, she found it difficult to comprehend why I wasn't fully engaged.

I tried as hard as possible to have fun, but I just could not, no matter how slow or fast I went. Keep reading; it is not for the reason you think it is. Her pussy was so hairy. (How hairy was it?) It looked like she had a black, nappy-headed Pekingese dog down there!! Suddenly, I felt a stinging sensation in my cock, which intensified into a burning sensation, prompting me to stop immediately. I lay next to her for a little while, and I apologized for going soft while I was inside her. I can honestly admit that I did not see her anymore after that.

She felt embarrassed for me, unaware that she was the root of the problem. So, I stood up and put my clothes on. In fact, I wasn't even aware that I was bleeding inside my underwear.

Here I am, sixty-plus years old, and to date, I have not yet felt anything like that. Let me explain what happened. The reason I could not continue fucking her was because my shaft kept going in and out of her hairy pussy, causing my cock to become extremely uncomfortable. I did not realize I was rubbing the shaft of my cock raw. In fact, the pain was so intense that I began to bleed. Let me break this down for you: exactly what happened?

The moment I penetrated her; my shaft was rubbing against her hair. To visualize this, imagine the hair on her pussy being long enough to travel both inside and out of her. That is why her hair felt like the abrasive side of a dish sponge against my shaft. Just before I left to return home, I asked if I could use her bathroom.

While in the bathroom, I had to pee and noticed more bleeding when I touched my cock. It was all because she had a hairy pussy. In the beginning, if she and I had had that adult conversation about her preference regarding hair in the pussy, what happened to me would not have happened.

Am I right or not? Those weeks of conversation have come to an end, and our first date is now a distant memory. I am sure there are guys out there who like hairy pussies, and this may not have happened to them. These days, if I discover a woman has a hairy pussy, I still avoid interacting with her.

UPDATED ON: 08/10/2024:

I am slick about asking now so they don't think I am too aggressive. If you are a man reading this chapter and like hairy pussies, make sure they shower before eating the pussy. Take a second to think about it, you nasty MOFO. There is sweat and urine mixed in that hairy pussy you can't smell. A woman without hair is more attractive, and if she has any pimples or other issues with her pussy, you can clearly see them because there is no hair to hide them. You may not like my opinion on hairy pussies, but guess what? IDGAF! Wait! Do not google it. It means I don't give a damn! I am sure some men like hair all down and between their cheeks; I am just not one of them.

Oh, and one last thing, spitting hair out of my mouth while I am eating the pussy is annoying and a deal-breaker. Wait just a second!! Suppose you have a hairy pussy and think that should not be a deal-breaker. In that case, I highly recommend eating another woman's pussy with hair all over the opening. Then get back to me about it, okay? Peace!

No Such Thang

THE CENTRAL PARK FIVE

I decided to make a modest contribution to this topic. I hope this resonates with you after finishing this chapter.

While I may not have a degree in this subject, what is a degree without years of experience? However, I can guarantee that these so-called therapists or psychiatrists have yet to have had some of the experiences and roles that I wrote about in this book. I can say this with absolute certainty.

Now, with that in mind, shall we proceed
with our discussion?

One thing that bothers me about certain women I have interacted with, whether in person or online, is their pursuit of the perfect partner who will support them unconditionally despite my belief that there is no such thang as the perfect man. For him to be the ideal man, there are too many variables. I have had the opportunity to meet and speak with women who are, in every conceivable way, industrious, honest, nurturing, loving, attractive, business-minded, strong, intelligent, and hardworking. When two people fall in love with one another, they give completely of themselves. Hey guys? You are correct in thinking this kind of woman is a unicorn and fussy as hell.

The woman I described just before this paragraph usually ends up falling in love with the following personality or behavior: thinks his shit doesn't stink; wears a wife beater tee-shirt, pants sagging, thirty-inch gold rims on his car while living with his momma; renting rims, loud music playing, saying. I'll pay you back next week, flashing money he should have paid you, too many baby mommas, doesn't pay child support, always asking where the hell are you, how come you have not texted me back, smelling like smoke, looking at his text messages while on a date with you, watches Pornhub in the bathroom, never cooks, never tips the server, wants his cock sucked without returning a favor, has already lied to you twice, (notice I said twice?

Goes straight to sleep, speaks in slang, is selfish, spends all day playing video games, expects you to pay for everything, isn't trying to find a job, is insecure with ED, deals drugs, is always high, uses the word "conversate" instead of "converse," is never optimistic about life, constantly blames the white man for his failures, is jealous, immature, wears fake gold teeth, and texts other bitches.

I should have started with that last one, right? We all know damn well that if a man disrespects his own mom, who gave him life, fed him, and changed his diaper, then why should he treat any woman, especially you, any differently? While writing this chapter, I realize that the women I previously described don't, I repeat, don't develop romantic affection for the following personalities: His appearance is geeky, he is respectful, he always compliments you, he asks how you are doing, he kisses you on the forehead, he says he hopes to see you again, he asks if he can see you tomorrow, he asks if I can call you tomorrow, he says I miss you, he does not assume that he is fucking on the first date, he is always courteous, he minds his own business, he respects your ideas, he listens to you, and he is inspired to improve his situation.

Ladies: Everything you want to know about a man will reveal itself by watching and listening to how he treats his mom, sisters, or other women. Do not be blinded by his good looks or his money. That's if you are considering him for a long-term relationship. Come on now, seriously!! I was talking to a friend, Sue, whom I had known for years since I worked as a cashier. Every time she shopped at my location, she came through my checkout. We constantly flirted with each other. This time, she was shopping; she did not know I was watching her from one aisle over.

My co-workers came over to me and said, "Damn, Bruh! Did you see the chick in the soup aisle?" I pretended I did not know her. Observing the co-worker's reactions when Sue entered the warehouse was hilarious. At the time, Sue's Asian husband was aware of me and was comfortable with our flirtatious behavior. Even though they divorced, she and I remained close friends. Given the nonsexual nature of our friendship, Sue felt confident in telling me that she had decided to venture beyond her comfort zone by flirting and fucking with black bad boys. She knew they were not relationship material and decided to switch it up. After several months, she stopped dating all together. If you are already familiar with the chapter, I apologize for what I am about to say. When Sue revealed her preference for black men, she liked fucking but also added that they were not relationship material.

It made me think back to the days of slavery movies. *Therefore, while it is acceptable to engage in sexual pleasure with niggas from their plantation but are not suitable for being inside Masta's house. If Masta were to catch us, you would lie and say I raped you. On the other hand, Masta would either hang us or beat us with a whip to make us suffer the consequences of our actions.

This method would also detour any other nigga from even looking at his wife. I was glad Sue could not read my mind now since it caused me to reflect on the past. So, she decided to date this nerdy-looking white man exclusively, even though she was still attracted to well-built black men. She never said the word "nigga" to me directly, so I must assume that's not her mentality, and I am not aware of every thought that passes through her mind. If you know what I mean, one only knows once it is time to choose sides. Continue reading as the situation improves, like in the song's lyrics. "I can see clearly now that the rain has gone."

RETURNING TO THE NARRATIVE:

On a particular day, I went to Sue's place of business to engage in a discussion, exactly like I do with my close friends. To illustrate my point, Sue shared with me that she transformed into a free spirit following her divorce, making up for the time she had lost during her marriage. Later, she decided to try something new and went out with a white boy who was a nerd. According to her, he was as straight as they come, which is the opposite of what Sue is accustomed to having sex with. His nerdiness made her question why she allowed him to get to know her.

Sue first told me that she wasn't attracted to him. Despite her determination to move on from her past, she found herself deeply infatuated with the nerdy white guy. That nerdy idiot hurt her heart; now it is time for everyone to learn about it. To a certain extent, none of the black guys she has played with never attempted to break her heart, unlike the nerdy white muthafucka.

This spineless POS's decision to return to his ex-wife and abandon her without any notice fucked up her emotional state of mind. How she spoke about him showed me that she fell deeply in love with this dipstick. "For months, Sue cried and concealed her deep-seated suspicions and refused to trust anyone due to undeniable circumstances he caused." Therefore, this incident teaches us that most women overlook the details.

I am convinced and confident she ignored several red flags because he was so different and white like her. The lesson here is to allow the man to feel comfortable and let them be themselves for three months after fucking them. This will let you determine what life would be like outside the bedroom. How do your friends treat you when they enjoy dinner with you? These days, most people don't commit time to getting to know one another. What surprises me about people over fifty years old is that you would think they would have more experience, right? I have heard that some men often request exclusivity immediately after their first fuck date. What is that all about? Before deciding to be exclusive, consider talking on the phone, texting, hanging out for a while, and deciding whether you share similar interests, such as watching television shows, working out, and listening to music.

The bottom line is that investing time in learning about all the aspects mentioned earlier is necessary. Women often enter committed relationships prematurely, failing to allocate sufficient time to fully understand their partner. Now, I feel obligated to mention that it can be challenging to find someone willing to engage in sexual activity on the first date or at least discover what we have in common, even if we agree or disagree.

It is not my intention to have months-long conversations only to realize we are sexually incompatible. Before I am too old, I would love to try a polyamorous relationship. When I say old, I mean I am in my seventies. I lowered my age since the conception of my first book, "Vanilla Sheets," because I feel a few more aches and pains than usual. My ideal romantic partnership would be with someone like this. Share an apartment with two bisexual ladies. Not only do we share a living space, but we also travel together, cook together, eat together, and sleep together simultaneously. In addition, we have sexual activities in my purple dungeon. Because this dungeon features a throne, I can unwind and observe the girls eating each other's asses and pussies.

Both activities are intriguing to me. For those interested in Only Fans, I would equip my dungeon with cameras to enhance their experience. I will tell you what: I already have two women, so I would never consider adding another unless she is famous and wants to join our family. If she is not famous, making anyone the third indicates my complete and absolute arrogance. Before the publication of this book, I had the opportunity to become involved in the life of someone who was experiencing a similar situation to mine. We had a unique connection, and I was the one who shattered it, even though she knew about my contact with another woman. Should I ever find myself in a situation comparable to the one I am currently in, I would make it a point to love each separately. Peace!

*I will elaborate more on the highlighted part below. The persistent issue of false allegations, particularly regarding Black men being accused of rape, has been consistently reinforced throughout our history. A century ago, white women embraced this allegation, and today, it continues to find support. It is imperative to understand that this allegation is deeply rooted in history to comprehend its prevalent influence on our society.

Groveland Four - Emmett Till - Scottsboro Boys - Exonerated Five - Christopher Coope - Pervis Payne - Patrick Lumumba - Brian Banks - The Central Park Five - Elias Clayton - Elmer Jackson - Isaac McGhie

Before you go on to another chapter, I want to you to consider how many black women have made allegations against white men? Go ahead; I will wait for your response. **Peace!**

... 911, what is your emergency?

...I'm scared, because there is an angry black man behind me, and I ...believe he is following me.

... Excuse me! Mam, did I hear you correctly? You are scared ...because the black man looks angry?

... Yes, that's exactly what I said.

... has the man threatened you.

... No! he has not.

... Why did you call 911?

... Because I know I can get away with it without being held ...accountable!!!

That is About White, Right?

Oh No
Not Again

BEFORE:

I am only going to give you one warning and this is it. If you can't tolerate a conversation discussing "crap", "poop", "excrement", "feces", or stool, then I highly suggest skipping this chapter.

Stolen from the audiobook:

The characters are Cecil. Royal and Shelly

Cecil: Royal, where did the hell you come from?

Royal: You wrote me in here, dickhead.

Cecil: Who the fuck are you calling a dickhead?

Royal: You, You and You! ... DICKHEAD!

Cecil: Royal, I am not going to entertain you right now.

Royal: That's probably a good idea. Go on!

Shelly: Cecil, who is Royal?

Cecil: That's one of my bitches, in another chapter.

Royal: There you go, calling women bitches again!!

Shelly: Cecil, is that true? You call women, BITCHES?

Cecil: Yes, it's true. But I don't mean the way it sounds in a degrading way. Anyway, why the hell am I explaining myself to a couple of characters I added to my book anyways!!

Royal: Yes Cecil, go ahead.
Cecil: What about you, Shelly?
Shelly: I agree with Royal, continue.

Shelly: I have a question: Are you a woman reading this right now? If that is the case, if this has ever happened to you, then this may be an embarrassing chapter to read, just saying! **Cecil:** Do you know what it is like when your partner knows you are about to cum, and they stop or change the position? It is messed up ain't it. That's why I am not about to tease you with a long, dragged out beginning of this chapter and just get right to it. I like women who have experienced rape or molestation for some strange, twisted reason.

Wait! "IF YOU ARE SHOCKED BY WHAT I JUST SAID", please continue reading this chapter; hopefully, you understand what I meant by that. My explanation is simple: they overcame trauma and became stronger and more independent. This is particularly true for those who have chosen to be sexual with a male again. Being with a man could quickly remind them of their trauma all over again. When a woman confidently shares her experience of rape or molestation, it does not grant anyone the right to manipulate or traumatize her once more.

Time out: If at any time anyone you are with does not have any compassion and understanding of this, please don't hope for a relationship with this muthafucka. That's why it is essential to ask a lot of questions before fucking and understand their past sexual experiences. Another white woman named Sunshine lived in Florida. I am sure it seems that I prefer fucking with white women, right?

Well, then draw your own conclusions if you like. That's why I said another white woman. At this point, I, don't, give, a, damn!!!! Seriously! Continuing: Sunshine had a horrific experience with a boy she trusted growing up.

Later in this chapter, I will give you more details about her awful experience. Sunshine's horrific experience robbed her of her innocence, leaving a lasting scar deep within her mind.

That experience may have influenced her tendency to be downright nasty-minded despite her shy, innocent demeanor. I had the opportunity to witness that side of her personality. Sometimes, I would take Cialis two hours before her arrival to ensure I did not disappoint myself or her. You want me to elaborate on why I needed Cialis, don't you? Okay, well, here goes: She likes pinching and playing with her own nipples while I am eating her pussy. That only means she enjoys what I am doing below her belly button. I would be able to tell that she is having a good time by looking up through her titties and observing her actions from also looking over the mound above her pussy.

While licking Sunshine's clit and pussy lips, I like to stick my fingers all up inside her, like I am a perverted gynecologist with an office in the alley near the dumpster. Do not ask me why I like doing that either; I don't know where that idea originated. I get off from manipulating Sunshine's pussy with my fingers; however, you may be wondering, "How many fingers do I have up in her?"

Her pussy hole could handle three lubed fingers at a time, for starters. Let me repeat this: "Three lubed fingers." If anyone plays with a pussy without lube is inexperienced. Obviously, she kept her eyes closed while engaging in play with her pussy, and I am grateful for that. Why? This is because it enables me to make that "OMG" face, just like Wendell Pierce did in the movie "Waiting to Exhale," Lela Rochon was staring up at him.

At this point, I am reaching for the lube, ready to start playing with her ass while I continue to eat her pussy. Sunshine's head moves from side to side as if possessed by the demon in a movie. I try to keep her there. With two fingers all up inside in Sunshine's pussy, and before I know it, I will have four fingers that extend to the first joint on my hand. Depending on my mood, I would alternate between inserting four fingers into Sunshine's ass and licking her pussy with my other hand. I am usually excited at this point, so I will shove a pillow under her ass.

As she tilts, I insert four well-lubricated fingers into her ass, reaching up to my knuckles. Do not laugh, but sometimes I wish I had a mining hat on so I could look up at her ass.

That's messed up, ain't it? Only like-minded people will be able to relate to what I just said. By sticking my fingers up her ass, I could determine whether Sunshine needed to use the restroom. Occasionally, I would use my fingers to extract shit that was there hiding, waiting to be pulled out or dropped in the toilet. Gross huh? Shhh!!!, don't tell anybody. I am not sure why the smell of shit does not bother me. I am sure no psychologist can explain it to me in a way that I would understand. I am fully aware that someone must have dropped me when I was a baby. They also never had me checked out to see if I was okay. Who else do you personally know behaves in such a manner as I do? I am not talking about people on the Internet, either.

Some of the porn I watch makes my book PG-rated. As previously mentioned, those individuals will find me relatable.

My bad, my ADD kicked in yet again!! "What happened with the shit I extracted from Sunshine's ass, right?" Well, I made sure I had a roll of toilet paper nearby to place the shit inside of it.

In fact, I had enough toilet paper to clean my fingers and between her ass cheeks, if needed. I always keep a new roll of TP around, just in case. Furthermore, why should I disturb her while she is in a possessed state and her eyes circling in her head? I thought to myself, "I'll just keep going and worry about the shit later" (no pun intended). After she calmed down, I finally disclosed what I did with the shit I pulled out of her ass later that evening, and she was appalled. However, she continued to return to her shitty self.

(Get it?) When I experimented with nipple clamps and flogging her, trust came into play again. Anyway, I am not going to explain what flogging is right now. For those who are unfamiliar with flogging, in the search bar of Google, type in "flogging BDSM" to satisfy your curiosity. I appreciated Sunshine's trust in me, and we need to have fun with one another.

Throughout this book, I will repeat... that trust is the key. I hope you are still reading this chapter; I want to share something else about Sunshine. I had known her for a while and realized she wasn't able to achieve an orgasm. This wasn't something I discovered right away but over time. You can't say my cock size contributed to that either, asshole. I can't believe that was one of your thoughts that popped into your head. Remember, engaging in foreplay or eating her pussy won't cause her to experience an orgasm. I had a good time with her, and she squirted all over my pillows and sheets.

But, yet again, no orgasm.

At times, I would simultaneously use four fingers in the pussy with my left hand, up to my second knuckle, and four fingers in her ass with my right hand, also up to my second knuckle. When I stopped, she would become lightheaded, and that's about it. As a woman reading this, was the lightheadedness her way of experiencing an orgasm? Could you relate to her in some way? Ladles, could you please describe what it is like to never experience an orgasm during a sexual encounter?

What does it feel like to masturbate without experiencing an orgasm, even though it feels good? After years of marriage, how does it feel to never experience an orgasm? Do you lie when a man asks if you had an orgasm after sex? Have you faked an orgasm with your husband? What happened emotionally?

Do you go from one relationship to another, searching for an orgasm? Do you feel inferior to a woman for not experiencing an orgasm? To be honest, I believe that after the rape, Sunshine compartmentalized her trauma and chose not to revisit it. Hold on a moment before I continue.

On July 8, 2022, around four a.m., I woke up to add this revelation: she may be unintentionally and unconsciously not wanting to experience an orgasm, in fear she is giving up the one last thing she has control over. If I were to use my gift to evaluate her, I would conclude that her fear of pleasure from any man stems from the rape she encountered. In either case, I am not, or claim to be, a psychologist or therapist with a degree in assessing a woman's state of mind. What has been your personal experience following a rape or molestation?

How did you overcome the feeling that you had something to do with it? Did you ever tell anyone? If you did, what was the response you received? I have always wanted answers to these questions, and I hope a woman will come forward and tell me her story one day. Apart from the women I have seen on television, I have not personally met any of them.

I have observed that women who have experienced rape often label themselves as defeated, ashamed, and unworthy of love. Some turn to drugs and alcohol to numb their memories. The cycle continues until they seek help.

After talking to this woman for a while, her story became fascinating because she began to realize what wasn't working and made some significant changes in her life....

This is an Update since, "Vanilla Sheets":
As of May 30, 2024,

It has been 9+ years since she drank alcohol, and I am proud of her accomplishments. I already mentioned that my father was an alcoholic, right? Anytime a person can get this monkey off their back, is a strong person. It is not easy, and it is a road worth traveling. If you are reading this right now and overcome being an alcoholic congratulations.

By the way, if she can do it, so can you!!

AFTER

Peep Show Booth

H ey, millennials. Have you ever been inside a peep show booth? I honestly believe that, depending on your age, the answer is, NO.

The only way you could know about peep shows is if your father told you or if you googled it. If you are over fifty, you may have heard of it or been inside one. Let us go down memory lane. "Like a Cave Man" (The J.C.B., 1972). Are you ready?

FIRST TIME:

There was one early morning, about 2 a.m. when I awoke hornier than a teenager on his first date with his girlfriend alone. Since I owned a car, I ventured into my first peep show booth in downtown San Diego, California. The main room was filled with vile publications of naked white women, like the bookstore I discussed in another chapter titled "Dirty Magazines," and it also featured a section for those over the age of eighteen.

I walked around the nasty magazine room, trying to muster the courage to enter the X-rated movie area. I could see into the room and spotted other men roaming about like zombies in heat. I mean that when you give a man too many options, he becomes disoriented and will seek a woman's advice on which one to buy. As a curious teen, I want to know why they had that lifeless, horny zombie expression on their faces. So, I walked to the rear of the room, into the X-rated video area.

When I entered the video room, I saw only X-rated videos of white chicks on the wall behind a glass case. Each video was assigned a reference number from one to fifty. This would allow me to select which video I wanted to watch from the ones assigned a number behind the glass case. While looking through the movies on the wall, I spotted a Mexican man going around with a mop bucket. I observed him for a while and could not figure out why this man required a mop bucket at a peep show.

After some time and a few more late-night trips, I finally understood why, and I was outraged that they had employed a Mexican to clean and mop the floors in each booth, after a man walked out. Cleaning up what, you just said to yourself, RIGHT!?

It was fresh hot cum from horny ass fuckers jacking off in the peep booths. After a few trips, it became clear why each booth smelled like pine sol: the faster the cum, made another room available.

SECOND TIME:

I could not enter the second time because the peep booths would only accept a certain number of people in that area. Therefore, I patiently waited until someone had vacated the area before entering. Only one booth was available, and it had my name on it (not really, just saying), so I strolled in and sat down.

Regrettably, I nearly slipped on some left-over cum on the floor, and the Mexican worker still had not cleaned it up. It is not like he is waiting around, watching everyone zipping up their pants while walking out of each booth. He is simply there to mop up any cum left behind on the floor. Here is a graphic, and I want you to close your eyes and imagine everything I am about to say.

As soon as I inserted a quarter into the slot, a light would flash to alert anyone attempting to enter that same booth that someone was already inside, which was insufficient to protect my privacy. Even though the light was flashing, someone tried to sneak in anyway. On my third visit, someone placed a chain across the door opening after I walked in, and the warning light was om above the door. I believe a law in San Diego prohibited the closing of doors. That's why people may stroll inside the booth without fear of intruding on someone's privacy. It does not matter if the person inside the booth is masturbating. LOL.

They also changed each peep booth into a maze, and when you tried to walk in after the newly created peep booth, you could not instantly see anyone sitting down on the inside. I felt better and safer walking in once they made the improvements, and since then, I have returned frequently. Somehow, this place must have known I was spending significant money watching peep shows. They must have been watching me since I inserted my first quarter into the slot.

After someone left, I stopped going into a peep booth because I disliked seeing cum on the floor and having to sit down.

The most distressing aspect is the possibility that I could have fallen on someone's hot, fresh cum. Over time, I would only enter a booth once the Mexican man with the Pine-Sol in his mop bucket had washed and cleaned it. Once inside the booth, I placed the chain across the entrance, and the warning light worked. Are you old enough to recall peep show booths? Before inserting my quarter into the slot, I often wondered who created this fantastic idea. It took me a while to understand that putting your quarter in the slot and seeing a few seconds of the video you chose from the wall generated more revenue than showing the complete movie.

That was a huge moneymaker back then. One quarter only bought you thirty seconds of video. Hell, it would have been cheaper to buy the fucking video (no pun intended) and watch it at home for far less. And you would not have to cope with a swarm of strange men like me watching me while I am watching them.

Are you curious if I jacked off while inside the peep booths? I certainly did, but I was always worried that someone would walk in on me.

Another time, I remember entering one of the readily available booths. I mistakenly believed the booth to be clean, only to find cum splattered all over the screen, floor, walls, and uncomfortable seats. I was like, "Dang!" This could not have been one person with so much cuming all over the place. It was worse than a crime scene or any television episode I had seen.

Nevertheless, I left that stall. and I tried another stall that did not have the warning notice or the yellow chain across the entrance. I jumped back because a motherfucker was waiting inside. This nasty mother fucker purposefully did not put up the chain, and I caught him jacking off.

That man acted as if I should join him in a circle jerk. I became enraged as he repeatedly intruded into my vision, bringing back memories of my cousin. I turned back and walked out; seconds later, the same man walked out, humiliated. As soon as he left, the Mexican man returned with his mop bucket. I felt sad for him because I never saw him wearing gloves or a mask.

THIRD TIME:

Another time, I went back to watch movies and jacked off like usual. But guess who was waiting for me when I stepped out of the booth? That's right—the Mexican man with his mop bucket, ready to walk in after me. I walked past him, embarrassed and humiliated. Consider this: You have heard the phrase "young, dumb, and full of cum," right? That's why the Mexican man waited for me to emerge. After a while, the owners and the Mexican man recognized my name, which wasn't too strange. Finally, they gave me free tokens. Damn!

FOURTH TIME:

The fourth time I returned to watch additional X-rated peep show films, I spotted someone I worked with, and we both laughed. We knew neither of us would ever say anything. After that, we simply smiled whenever we saw each other at work, knowing precisely what that meant. It meant neither of us could pull a girl; therefore, it was our secret cum release spot.

FIFTH AND FINAL TIME:

Oh, and I should have mentioned this earlier. Another time, which was also my last, I walked into one of the booths and sat in someone else's sperm, leaving stains on the back of my jeans. Imagine how I must have felt and looked, especially since it appeared as though I had farted it from my ass. If I saw someone walking out of a peep show booth with wet spots on the back of his pants, I would expect another man to walk out afterward with a smile. Think about what I just said for a minute. Alternatively, he might have had a sexual encounter before entering the booth.

Either way, it would not be a good look. I immediately went home, took a shower, and never came back. That's my peep booth story, and I am sticking to it. I just wanted to clarify that I wasn't trying to be disrespectful when referencing the Mexican man carrying the mop bucket.

During my time there, I never saw a single white person working in that position, and I am curious why that's the case. I am sure there is a clear-cut reason, right? Peace!

Hey, millennials.
Have you ever been inside a peep show booth? I honestly believe that, depending on your age, the answer is no.

Pimpin Ain't Ez

In San Diego Cali

On

May 13, 2024, Cecil updated the following chapter from "Vanilla Sheets."

Str8 From The Audiobook
There are only two characters:

Cecil – Main Character (C)
And The Narrator (N)

Cecil's thoughts and inspirations are now included here for you to read or listen to. Just to clarify, his pimping days occurred in his early twenties. Regarding his prior exploits, He is neither embarrassed nor regretful of any of his decisions, back then and even now. Furthermore, he has already assumed you are a European American reading this at the moment. Because, honestly, Cecil feels that black folks don't read or support this type of book. In that case, you may find this entire chapter boring and incomprehensible unless you are willing to be open-minded and allow Cecil to demonstrate the ongoing exploitation of Black folks from his perspective.

You should read this chapter with caution and a sympathetic mindset, as its language resonates with his personal pimping experiences. In addition, Cecil is confident you are reading this chapter to find black exploitation movies and shows. But, at the same time he is also aware Europeans may not necessarily want to watch anything with black folks in leading roles.

He is exposing every single movie and television show that has portrayed black folks negatively, both past and present. Honestly, nothing has changed, and in fact, the situation has worsened. So, don't expect Cecil to write something controversial and degrading relating to black folks. Europeans are accustomed to starring roles being given to Europeans, just ask, Viola Davis. Cecil's parents molded his personality into the person he is today.

To anyone who considers themselves holy, he also hopes you don't take this chapter personally, especially when it relates to European Americans and no matter their faith. By the way, if you happen to meet him anywhere, don't splash your fake cheap ass holy water from the tap, on him either. All because he expresses his opinions honestly and shares his unfiltered thoughts with you.

(C) Let us begin, shall we? There are several ways that non-Black production companies can easily disguise Pimpin' Black people. Here are some ways I see non-black production companies exploiting black men and women: To be honest, BET has been pimping us for decades, and there is no indication that this will change anytime soon.

The creators and producers of blaxploitation films were all white or Jewish men, to the best of my knowledge. Those thieves, widely acknowledged, profited handsomely from exploiting black performers. They only produced and distributed blaxploitation films, which are stereotypical depictions of black men and women.

Here is FACT number one: C.J., is a well-known rapper, who produces and directs stereotypical entertainment for profit, much like a Black Pied Piper of the twenty-first century.

I would like to elaborate on C. J.'s accomplishments in producing and directing blaxploitation television shows.

ALLOW ME TO ELABORATE, HIS SLAVE MASTERS MUST APPROVE ALL DECISIONS RELATED TO HIS IDEAS, INCLUDING:

Power: A drug lord named "Ghost" reports to his business manager, Simon Stern, a white man. In other words, Ghost is not the H.N.I.C. (head nigga in charge).

B.M.F. glorified drug traffickers as brothers, peddling narcotics and killing niggas once more.

Power Book II: Ghost: The teenage son of "Ghost," another drug dealer, has a bit of collard greens and a white cast as a side dish.

Raising Kanan is nothing more than leftover potato salad with raisins in it. Just the way white folks make theirs.

For Life: Just another so-called innocent man in prison trying to get out. Fact: After two seasons, no more episodes are available. In other words, CJ's white superiors concluded that the show did not depict anything negative enough.

You would think after an excellent movie classic like, The Shawshank Redemption, he would not follow it up with another series about a black man trying to escape a jail or prison. Feel free to agree or disagree with my opinions.

Here is fact number two:

Without a doubt, all the previously mentioned television shows portray black men and women in stereotypical roles. Are you curious about the things that I used to watch on television and drive-in theaters when I was younger? I will tell you a little later in this chapter okey? Many readers of this chapter's earlier version of "Vanilla Sheets" expressed dissatisfaction with this section.

So, before I go any further, let me explain why I am about to describe all the stereotyped movies and television episodes available to you if you are interested and want to see them. I presume you are searching for examples of blaxploitation films that white men have consistently produced and distributed. I would like to begin with one of my favorite films of all time from the blaxploitation genre.

AS A TEENAGER, I BECAME FAMILIAR WITH BLAXPLOITATION MOVIES IN THE THEATERS LISTED BELOW:

Super Fly (1972): Niggas as Pimps and Street Hustlers, directed by Gordon Parks Jr., a black man funded by a white entertainment company.

The Mack (1973): Michael Campus, White Producer.
** In reality, it is no accident that I became a pimp after watching blaxploitation films that taught me to embrace such behavior.

Petey Wheatstraw (1977): Cliff Roquemore, a black director funded by a white entertainment company.

That Man Bolt (1973): Henry Levin, David Lowell Rich—let us assume two white men.

Friday Foster (1975): Arthur Marks, a white producer, produced the title of this movie,

The Legend of Nigger Charley (1972): Martin Goldman (let us just assume he is white).

Black Caesar (1973): Larry Cohen, White Producer.

Willie Dynamite (1974): Gilbert Moses, black director, funded by a white entertainment company.

Coffy (1973) and Foxy Brown (1974) Jack Hill, a white producer, produced.

Dolemite (1973): D'Urville Martin, black director.

Across 110th Street (1972): Barry Shear and White Producer Melvin Van Peebles directed Sweet.

Sweetback's Baadasssss Song (1971), which received funding from a white entertainment company.

Which movies, actors, and actresses did you idolize and imitate? If you are not black, what message am I trying to convey to you? Producers and directors who were white and exploitative were aware of the long-term effects of making such films. They believed that only populations of African heritage could access the movie.

I COULD SEE THE POSITIONS OF LEADING BLACK, STRONG, MUSCULAR MALE PERFORMERS FADING AWAY, AND THEIR STRATEGY IS WORKING WELL.

We are now in the twenty-first century, and I can see what is happening. Just keep reading, and you will realize why there are fewer opportunities for positive black male entertainers. Recently, there has been an increase in the number of black men appearing on television dressed as women. In today's world, seeing a man dressed as a lady must be highly puzzling for a young black male. P-Valley, a popular blaxploitation series, portrays black people negatively.

In truth, it is the same entertainment corporation that C. Jackson employs to sell and produce his television series. Honestly P-Valley reminds me of To Wong Foo. Thank You for Everything! Wesley Snipes stars Julie Newmar. So, if you are open-minded, choose one and watch it.

Thank you, Dave Chappelle, for declining the producers' request to dress up as a lady. Even though another well-known black male actor declared he would not dress like a woman, I researched his name and found him dressed as one. Fame motivates people to commit heinous acts to gain fame. Have you seen the movie Day Shift, directed by J. J. Perry, starring Jamie Foxx, with a cameo appearance by Snoop Dogg?

I looked up the filmmaker, and I am not sure what ethnicity he is, but I am positive he is not black. While viewing the film, I am paying attention to how many black actors appear and their roles. I also watched how much time white producers gave black performers compared to white actors.

This movie receives two thumbs down and a soft cock. I counted fourteen non-black actors and five black actors in this stanky ass movie. Aside from Snoop, there may have been three runners-up in a potato sack race among those five black actors. In most situations, when writers and producers develop a role for a black actor, I take notes on the characters they play in big-budget films. This is particularly true when their name appears in the headline. This film did not disappoint my expectations of being another clever example of blaxploitation.

Why the hell am I using this word again? Because nonwhite writers, producers, and entertainment companies continued to exploit black performers for their financial advantage, Master Reed Hastings, a white man, provided the final clearance. I am sure most of you are accustomed to deception, so allow me to explain. Jamie Foxx portrayed a prominent black actor in a starring role. At the same time, Snoop appeared in a cameo role, primarily to draw in black viewers. You can't give a rap icon like Snoop a fifteen-minute role unless it is generating revenue for the movie. That movie irritated me so much that I had to leave and return later to finish it after I had calmed down.

Apart from the film's poor writing, what bothered me was why Peter Stormare's portrayal of Troy, a white man, required Jamie and Snoop to submit to him? If you watch this awful movie, you will see Snoop and Jamie imply they have a boss. Before Jamie walked into the office, I expected his boss to be a white man because that's how they subtly show who is in charge.

Finally, at a certain point in the movie, Jamie walked through the door of his boss's office, and as I had anticipated, his boss was a white man. And I be damned if I am right again. Then, to exacerbate the situation, Jamie had to plead with Troy, the White Man, to rejoin the force, which left me nauseous. In fact, he made me forget that he had ever appeared in Django. Jamie, if you are reading this movie review, why would you headline a movie and allow the writer, a white man, to use your name to beg for your job later in the film? The way the writer wrote the script; you might well have sucked his cock under the desk at which he was seated.

We, as black men, and women, are always relegated to supporting roles in most available films. That's my casual evaluation and perspective on the shows listed above. When I previously discussed the issue of guys dressing up as women, my criticism did not specifically target a prominent landowner in Southwest Georgia who also dresses up as a woman. The distinction is not due to necessity; other actors have worn dresses.

It is crucial to remember that the presence of black filmmakers in the past does not necessarily indicate that the financing came from a black entertainment corporation.

In other words, white-production corporations could also dictate the narrative. Do you understand what I mean? So, what exactly has changed? As you expected, not a damn thing! I would like to take this opportunity to express my gratitude to anyone reading this book who is not of African American heritage. Am I right that this book has been challenging to understand?

Even though only a handful of well-remunerated black performers feature in high-budget films, I intentionally stated this to convey the situation. White counterparts co-star with the remaining well-known black entertainers. This is particularly true for a movie or series that leaves a positive and lasting impression. The next time you browse your source of entertainment, consider looking for diverse characters in the films or television shows you enjoy the most. Consider the fact that white men and women have been in starring positions of authority for decades and then compare that to the fact that black men and women have been in leading roles. Monitor the available alternatives. You can email me your views to disprove what I said.

The editor wanted me to leave this out, what you are about to read. She feared I would face harsh criticism for incorporating this information into my book. We will see, right?

Okay, enough of the nonsense; I will now recount my experiences with Pimpin Ain't Easy. Please accept my apologies; I went off topic for a moment, right? But I am now back on track. When I finally encountered a pimp, he exuded an air of swag to which I could relate. He offered me sex with one of his prostitutes, but I wasn't interested. Besides, I had enough ladies without having to fuck any of his girls. Around the same time, I met a black girl named Natasha, and we began hanging around. During the day, she worked part-time as a cashier at the Thrifty Drug Store in San Diego.

After spending time together and fucking each other's brains out, she decided to come clean and tell me she was a prostitute by night. In other words, she was a hoe, which did not disturb me. I did not try to stop her because it was none of my damn business. I was okay with it because whatever Natasha felt she needed to do for cash was her main priority, not mine. Aside from that, who was I to criticize her anyway? That would have made me a hypocrite and judgmental. Natasha had a puzzled look on her face because I was more open-minded than her prior partners. I thought hanging out with a hoe was an interesting side hustle.

As I recall, it was more about getting to know her as she performed her hoeing and having her back if anything happened. I will never forget the day I needed a knife because a man was threatening to harm one of my bottom bitches. After all, he wanted some free pussy. I keep forgetting that a majority of you muthafucka's are white people reading this book. I am also certain that some of you Negro's, don't know what the hell I am talking about when, I call a hoe my... " BOTTOM BITCH".

Here is an explanation from Urban Dictionary that may help: Sitting atop the hierarchy of prostitutes serving a certain pimp is a bottom girl, a bottom woman or bottom bitch. Usually, the prostitute who has been with the pimp the longest and routinely makes the most money is a bottom girl. Being the bottom girl provides the prostitute authority over the other women employed for her pimp. Still, the bottom female also has a lot of duties.

Such as working the track in her pimp's stable, running interference for and collecting money from the pimp's other prostitutes, and looking after the pimp's affairs if the pimp was out of town, incarcerated, or otherwise unavailable". The P.I.M.P. teaching Manual also details the responsibilities of the bottom girl, including teaching and recruiting additional prostitutes as well as handling money. She also keeps her pimp's prostitutes in the game and gives them "pep talks," therefore interacting with them most of all. As you already know, I was close by to ensure her safety. There were moments when I drove alongside her, watching her stroll the streets of National City, California. She would give me the money, but I only spent a small portion of it myself.

Eventually, Natasha became my bottom bitch over time while I was fucking another girl named Jazz, who was my girlfriend. I made sure that Natasha met Jazz because Jazz said that she had always wanted to be a prostitute but did not know how to become one. Natasha took on the role of Jazz's hoe instructor, a transition that Jazz found easy due to her previous experience giving up the pussy for free. Jazz then expressed a desire to join my stable alongside Natasha. Now I am accountable for two bitches' safety throughout the evening while Natasha is hoeing on one block and Jazz on another.

One evening, I was driving along Market Street in San Diego with Natasha. Natasha checked in with me right before banging John (a client). Once she had finished fucking him, she simply waved to let me know she was okay and went back to work.

(N) Wait a minute. Yes, that's right, Cecil called it work, and if you are narrow-minded, he is certain you will not be able to relate.

(C) After months of living a double life, I began speaking with another woman named Tasha, who was desperate for money on occasion. Indians owned a local convenience store where I met Tasha. Just so you know, Indians and Arabs own and operate most convenience stores in black neighborhoods. They have been exploiting our ignorance for decades, and I don't blame them a bit. I digress. I introduced Tasha to Jazz, Natasha, and Babies, and the four quickly became close friends.

Since I was idolizing white-produced and marketed blaxploitation flicks, I bought a stereotypical 1976 Cadillac Seville. I spent about a thousand dollars customizing it, adding a massive chrome grill with the Bentley girl on it, a fifth wheel in the back, chrome "S" bars on the sides, and faux fur on the steering wheel. Everything the Blaxploitation Media showed us was excellent; it made me primed and ready like a wet pussy to start pimping. Unfortunately, I was the typical ignorant negro who drove a pimped-out car that alerted every police officer within a hundred-mile radius. A thought came to mind while writing this section of the chapter. Historically, police have been known to arrest black pimps like "Iceberg Slim." So, after all those years of pimping, why weren't the police officers after my black ass? I am sure it had a lot to do with the fact that I exclusively pimped out black girls.

I am confident that if I had been pimping white women or a white woman in San Diego, the police would have battered, arrested, or planted drugs in my car. Nothing about pimping (or me) was subtle back then. I have no regrets, and now that I vividly recall it, it has helped me understand and relate to women in my sixties. I am driving around the neighborhood in my caddy, accompanied by three or four bitches, and receiving praise from my neighbors.

All the neighbors knew I was pimping, but none of them said anything nasty about me or my mother. They knew I was a decent kid and did not say anything because it wasn't their business. While I was driving around downtown San Diego, the girls were walking around looking for Johns (clients).

There was a moment in the evening when I saw them talking to another girl, and I was unsure why. After about an hour, Natasha and Jazz gestured for me to pause so they could introduce her to me. I wasn't sure if she would fit in, so I trusted my bottom bitch. I asked the new hoe her name, and she responded, "Babies," which made me laugh. Babies was a large Mexican girl who groaned while walking. When she wore a dress, you could tell her thighs rubbed against each other, from her pussy down to her knees. She spoke fluent English, which I liked for one reason: more clients. Because she was bilingual, having her with us was to my advantage. After introducing herself, all four girls left and continued walking, looking for clients. I refer to men looking for prostitutes, johns, and sometimes clients because it is a way to keep their identity secret and show respect.

While I was driving around, the police stopped all four of my girls and issued them a 647b prostitution citation. Prostitution is a misdemeanor offense in San Diego that can result in up to six months in jail. Fortunately for me and them, the police officers did not arrest them. I sat back in the driver's seat and watched from inside my car, a block away. I remember feeling relieved I did not have to bail them out of jail.

That would have exposed me, and jail tends to make girls point out their pimps. I would not have been pleased about that. Moving on, my friend Ant, who also graduated from Abraham Lincoln High School in San Diego, called me a tennis shoe pimp. Every time I entered his neighborhood, he would refer to me as the "tennis shoe pimp." I had to make this assumption because I only wore sneakers, not the dress shoes typically worn by pimps. I wasn't the typically dressed pimp depicted in black exploitation films.

By this point, I had been pimping for several years, staying between my mother's house and a hotel with my hoes. While living with my mother, I stashed away $10,000 in a small metal container I had received from my hoes. Remember that this is my mom's house, and I thought stashing it in the container was perfect. One day after work, as usual, I strolled in and found my mother reclining in her favorite chair. I greeted Mama as I always do, but this time it was different because, I thought, she was holding the small container I had hidden. Seriously, to this day, I wonder how she discovered it.

Especially when I had the container on the top shelf, blending in with everything else around it. Nothing I could say, it is her house, and I am in trouble. It became clear that I needed to reveal where that money came from. In other words, I needed to prepare a weak and convincing explanation that I hoped she would accept. She asked me where I got the money. She knew that my day job did not pay enough to have that amount of money, and she was familiar with my spending habits. And, since all she could hear was crickets, she wondered why I had that money in the can rather than in her bank. I told her a short lie, which she accepted, but she still had a look of surprise on her face. She knew I had been out late with at least two girls, and she wasn't naive. She never called me a pimp, but she was still suspicious. She simply remarked, "Boy, something is going to happen to you; you must stop whatever you are doing." Prophecy.

One evening near Sunset Boulevard in Los Angeles, California, the police stopped me and my girls. They asked us about something they "thought" was going on. Regardless of how the police officers interrogated us, nobody ratted out the others, but they arrested me anyway. After forty-eight hours in custody, the police had no choice but to release me because no one testified against me or appeared in court. If any of the three girls had testified, a guilty verdict would have drastically changed the course of my life. I would have faced jail or prison time for my pimping behavior. Upon their release from jail, I contemplated taking a temporary break from the pimping game.

I was particularly aware that the police were closely observing me, and my mother did not raise me to be a pimp. It was time for me to decide what the safest path to take. The prophecy is in effect. Shortly after my release from jail and the realization that the other three hoes had left me, my bottom bitch was waiting just outside the gates. I gave her a big hug, and we drove back to San Diego, California. A month had passed, and I desperately needed money, as I had already spent the $10 grand on frivolous bullshit. No generational wealth here that's for damn sure.

Wait just a moment: Blaxploitation movies glorified cars, clothes, and jewelry, right? Watching Superfly as a teenager was my favorite movie of all time. So naturally, I wanted to become a street hustler or a pimp. As of July 7, 2024, I still struggle to let go of the past, which glorified that lifestyle. After reading this chapter, "I Got You Sucka," everything will make sense. Imagine how the money I earned from working a full-time job and pimping in the evenings could have significantly impacted my life. Regrettably, my parents did not instill in me the value of money, a concept I still struggle with today.

In addition, my parents could have invested my pimp money. Instead, I am writing about it here, which has the potential to be lucrative. Back to my broken azz: one evening, my bottom-bitch Natasha knew I needed money and asked if she could return to what she does best. I told her yes and showed my appreciation. She asked for my car keys and went to work.

Do not play stupid now because you know what this is. We stayed at a hotel in National City, California. While I was sleeping, Natasha returned to the hotel and did not want to wake me up. Before falling asleep, she left me $900 on the nightstand beside me. When I woke up and counted the money, I did not put it in my pocket; instead, I drove away. Instead, I simply glanced at her as she lay in bed, exhausted from the night's prostitution.

I left the money on the nightstand and never looked back. I also knew it would be wrong to abandon Natasha just because I didn't want to pimp her anymore. I only left while she was sleeping because I did not want her to talk me out of my decision. She would have asked me not to go if she had woken up.

And as much as I cared for her, I would have stayed. I wasn't happy, and I knew what was best for me. I got in my car, looked up at the room she was in, and drove away without looking back. I returned to my mother's house, where she sat in her favorite chair again. My mother was pleased to see me when I walked in the door, as evidenced by the big ass smile on her face.

Shortly after I entered my mom's house, I received a call from my girlfriend, whom I thought was sleeping. She inquired as to why I had abandoned her. Dammit. I explained why, but she could not understand why I had not taken the money from the nightstand. She was accustomed to me keeping the money for myself at the end of the night. I informed her that I had left the money for her and that I did not want her to be homeless.

I wanted to ensure she had enough money to live. I informed her that I no longer wanted to be associated with any money she earned going forward. I walked out on my own terms and never looked back. After I stopped pimping, I felt better about myself, but that did not stop me from becoming a cheap hoe by fucking a bunch of nice-ass bitches afterward.

Pimping kept me bound to those hoes, and I wanted to spread my seeds further than I had before. Before I knew it, I had a diverse range of hoes in my caddy: black, white, Mexican, old, fat, skinny, rich, nasty-breath, stuck-up, married, divorced, no shame in their game, big titties, small titties, whigger, redheaded, blondes, and bald chicks.

Can I have a dollar woman, a one-legged woman with no teeth, without a job, on welfare, homeless, and a woman who is drunk all the time? I was trying to make up for lost time. All of what I just said could have been summed up by saying, I was fucking women that showed any interest in me that had a hole. Well, that concludes my "Pimpin Ain't Easy" narrative. The prophecy was fulfilled.

WHAT I HAVE LEARNED FROM THIS CHAPTER:

Do not hate me for saying this, but as of March 6, 2024, all the major networks, social media, and distributors continue to misrepresent black people. Nevertheless, if their income originates from a European American source, entertainers and athletes are merely wealthy hoes. These agencies are not interested in positively promoting black people. What were your thoughts when you first saw the cover of this book?

Did you say I resembled a pimp? How did that concept enter your head? Growing up in high school, I knew all about pimping. In this chapter, I have previously listed all the movies I grew up viewing. On a brighter note, several of my dating strategies from the past are still in use today.

If you are wondering how this is possible, allow me to explain. It has dramatically enhanced my understanding of women, giving me a distinct advantage when interacting with them. I pay attention to their body language, facial expressions, hand gestures, eye contact, and the tone of their voices. I understand that most males don't notice subtleties like those described above. While living with three to four women at a time, I learned valuable lessons that I still apply today. I take pride in being nonjudgmental.

When someone makes a decision that contradicts my beliefs while reflecting on my pimping days, I am grateful to be alive and able to talk about it. Btw, I have never utilized my expertise or experiences to get pussy. (N) So, readers, was it a good or bad decision to add this information to this book? Will you judge me, or will you give me a pass? By the way, Cecil is looking forward to getting your feedback on this book or chapter.

JUST A FUCKING SECOND

THIS MUTHA FUCKING STORY AIN'T FAR FROM OVER.

On June 27th, 2025, I thought came to me to try to connect with one of my sons' mothers after more than thirty years. I tried Facebook, Instagram etc. and nothing. Even if she was or is on Facebook, I know damn well I would not be able to recognize her. I almost gave up and gave it one last final try, and it happened. For some fucking reason I could not go back to sleep around 3:00 AM. Of course, I got up and started working on this chapter when that idea came across my mind. A cell number appeared that gave me the impression it could be her. So, I texted the number and asked if she knew me and was her son named ADH (for privacy purposes only).

I also had to keep in mind that if it was her, she lived in the west coast area with a time difference of 3 hours. Suddenly, I could see someone was about to respond to my message and it was Natasha. We texted back and forth for a little while and I became flooded with memories I failed to mention in "Vanilla Sheets" I heard she was shot 34 times in the upper torso area and survived. From my understanding she was under an investigation for some time.

After collecting the evidence, they needed and rushed through front door of her apartment while she was laying down on the couch with a gun in her hand. Whatever her reason was for laying down on the couch with a gun in her hand, I never found out. No matter if she was on drugs or protecting herself while sleeping, you are going to use your gun in some kind of capacity, right? I imagine she suddenly heard a noise and raised her gun. That's when the officer lit her ass up like a Christmas tree!!

Honestly, this has happened to many times with someone being shot thinking they are being robbed. Can you Natasha survived and doing well for herself. I am aware I mentioned that I was flooded with memories, but I am going to stop right now and just let you imagine what her life was like as a child.

Pine Hills Florida

T here was this blonde lady named Jane that I had been seeing for a while; she lived in Clearwater, and at the time, I lived in Pine Hills, Florida.

There are only two charters in this chapter.

Cecil – Also known as **(C)**
Royal – Also known as **(R)**

(C) Sometimes, I would get in my car and drive halfway to meet her. Since it was a long drive for her to see me, she would pay for a hotel room halfway between us so we could have sex—I mean, fuck. And that's because she had young children living with her back then. One afternoon, she decided to drive the entire distance, not knowing what I had planned for her.

When she arrived, I was like a dog waiting in the window, wagging its tail. I am glad she did not see me opening my drapes as I wondered what took her so long to get out of her car. Having opened the shades numerous times, I decided it was time to calm down. Through my window, I watched her walk towards my front door; if I could have barked and wagged my tail like a dog, I would have. Jane wasn't expecting what I had in mind when she entered the door.

Once I closed the door and locked it, I immediately frisked her like a police officer. I passionately slammed Jane's back against the wall. After being with her three times, I could tell she wasn't expecting what I did to her. I used one of my hands to hold her arms above her head against the wall. Then she used the other arm to pull down her pants and panties. I told her to kick off her shoes while her arms were still in the air.

While she was taking off her shoes, I kissed her passionately. She loved every fucking second of it; no one had ever done that to her but me. As she is still pinned up against the wall, I started playing with her pussy before I fucked or, ate her. At that point, she was so fucking hot and ready you could blow in her ear, and she would cum.

Cecil: On a different morning, I remember driving to her place instead of her coming to mine. She lived in a beautiful, spacious home—and I was impressed. I'm saying all this because, hopefully, she'll read this book and remember me.

Just like she planned, I unlocked the door and walked in while she was still sleeping. That always scared me a little, because a lot of Black men haven't made it out of situations like that.

Royal: Wait a damn minute, Cecil...

Cecil: What's up, Royal?

Royal: What if someone else had broken in before you got there—and hurt her or worse?

Cecil: I feel you on that. I totally agree. But just listen to what I'm saying, okay?

Royal: Alright, I'm listening.

Cecil: Appreciate it.

So yeah, I'm a Black man walking into a white woman's home in a nice-ass neighborhood. That alone could've ended badly if anyone saw me or made assumptions.

Royal: You got that right.

Cecil: So, I'm standing over her while she's sleeping, pulling the covers back slowly like a damn prowler. There's something about watching a woman sleep naked with her legs slightly open... and seeing her pussy just barely parting. That shit always got me going. Most times, I'd jack off just watching her sleep. But this time, instead of nutting on the sheets, I held it in.

Royal: Whoa, whoa—hold up. Did you just say you usually jack off on her sheets?

Cecil: Yes. That's what I said.
Royal: Why the hell would you do that?

Cecil: Look, I'm just being honest. The only explanation I got—and maybe it makes sense to you or the readers it's how I get the quick nut outta the way. That way, when she wakes up, I can last longer.

Royal: Ohhh, okay. So that's what some of y'all be doing while we're asleep. Damn. Alright, carry on then.

Cecil: I crawled into bed next to her and started kissing the back of her neck. Jane went from snoring to grunting—that meant she was awake. I slipped my dick inside her, and after just a few strokes, I came. I was that damn excited.

But I wasn't done. I went down on her. She came so hard on my face that if she could squirt, she would've. That's just how our sexual chemistry was—intense. She was a petite blonde, wild when she let herself go.

And just like I said before, I'm not dropping full names in this book—but I'll say enough for the right people to recognize themselves. Anyway, that's my experience with Janc... in Clearwater.

WHAT HAVE I LEARNED FROM THIS CHAPTER?

Most white men and women who have chosen to date outside their race, especially when they are Black, don't have a clue how cautious and guarded we are. Let me ask you a question: Does white privilege exist? In the year 2024, it is disheartening that I still feel the need to bring up the topic of racism. To this day, Jane does not know why I always wanted to meet her at a hotel or home when we saw each other.

Interracial dating these days comes with so many unforeseen circumstances. Dear white folks, this is an excellent time to remember what I will say next. When you are driving anywhere, and a police officer is behind you, what are your first thoughts? Are you asking yourself why he or she is pulling you over? I can assure you that it is not our first thought. With so many white police officers on the force, it is difficult to determine who is racist and who is not. Once that flashing light comes on. Are they stopping me for something I haven't noticed?

Or is it because of the color of my skin? Those are the sort of things that you, as a white person, don't have to concern yourself with! I know I am assuming you are a white listener. If not, you know damn well what I am talking about, right?

Now, take a moment and imagine driving around with someone who has those concerns; it is highly uncomfortable. That level of discomfort is something you know nothing about until things change. I said all this to say, Jane, that's why we met somewhere other than your home. If she reads this part of the chapter, Peace!

Real Father & Life Lessons

T his segment is about my biological and adopted father, whom I should have mentioned in the book's first edition of, "Vanilla Sheets".

Please remember that as I refer to my mom and dad throughout this chapter, they are my aunt and Uncle. I will refer to this occasionally in case you have forgotten, been confused, or my ADD kicked in again. There is Dad, who is my uncle, and Mom, who is my aunt. Got me? Imagine being me, trying to write this to help you understand "my story".

Enough, let me "continue"! I don't remember my exact age, but if I were going to guess, it was between eight and twelve years old. I vividly remember chasing this kid, and this man stopped me suddenly and said, "Hey, you know who I am?" I looked up at him; I said, "No." He said, "Okay, well, nice to meet you." Then I ran off chasing the kid that I was after. I was later told by my father, who saw me being stopped by the guy, that he was my biological father.

My biological mother never spoke of him before me being stopped by him. She never mentioned his name, either. He must have been just a sperm donor. A mutha fucka who impregnated my mom and bounced right afterward.

Does this sound familiar to you, the reader? I am deeply sorry if what I said relates to your present life. Before he stopped me, my mom and dad could have said, "Hey, I need you to meet someone." Mom and Dad did not even have to say he was my father; they should have introduced me to him and allowed me to talk to him for a while. But that never happened. Years later, we attended a family reunion, and my cousins and I needed to pick up a barbecue pit.

Uncertain where and whose house we were going to, I have yet to say a word. The drive to this house was weird because my cousins kept looking at one another like they knew something I did not. While headed there, one of my cousins mentioned that the house we were headed to was, without a doubt, my biological father's house. Now it all makes sense why they looked so strange at each other, right? I asked him how they knew this.

All they could say was they heard stories of my bio mother giving birth to me, and soon afterward, my bio father left her stranded. Besides that, the house I mentioned was only a few miles away from where the family union was. That gave me time to collect the thoughts rushing through my head. I was overwhelmed with emotions and anxiety I can't explain as I write this for you to read.

Everyone knows everyone's business in a small town like Lural, Mississippi. I bet you could not have an affair without everyone knowing who is fucking who. That song by Aretha Franklin, "Who's Zooming Who," meant the same thing.

Nevertheless, once we arrived and walked towards the house, a girl around my age answered the door. She looked at the three of us, remembered why we were there, and said the BBQ pit was out back. Just before heading back to pick up the BBQ pit, one of my cousins told the girl who answered the door that I was her half-brother. She had the exact same look on her face as I had earlier.

She looked me up and down like a burnt Mexican churro with legs, arms, and eyes. While she was standing there with a stunned look on her face, I saw something that looked like a photo of him on a table next to a couch. I asked her if her father were in that photo and if I could walk over and see it, and she nodded yes. I walked over cautiously and nervously picked up the frame with a photo of my biological father. Back then, we did not have cell phones like we do now to record our interactions.

All I could do was stare at it for a few minutes, put it down, and walk away. Imagine being told you have a half-brother who suddenly shows up at your door. Even though she did not say anything, her facial expression told me everything. If it seems impossible to you how I can remember what you are reading, then ask yourself why you are doubting me; that's the real question. I was about eight years old, I wondered why my mom and dad called me to come out of my bedroom, saying get dressed. We are headed somewhere and put this on that we picked out for you. Not questioning their authority, I was Confused, I put it on and returned to my bedroom. My dad said, "Hey, you must answer questions like.

"Do I like living with us? And how do I feel about them?" And I am like, "This is weird that they are asking me this stuff." And yet I am putting on this nice outfit and everything. While I was in the back seat quietly, I still wanted to know where we were going. So, we met an attorney, and I was curious. At the same time, he welcomed us in to have a seat in his massive office overlooking downtown San Diego. I thought I was just there for a psychological check-up or something since I have been to a few of those before.

After sitting in the suggested chairs, the attorney started asking me questions. Still, I could not understand why, even though my parents had already prepared me. I answered his questions with a puzzled look, you know? The meeting and questions served as a crucial factor in the decision regarding my living arrangements with my adopted father and biological mother, who have functioned as an aunt and uncle since birth. My aunt/mom could not have children, so my biological mom gave me to my aunt/mom and uncle/dad. (quick note: my father and my bio mother were siblings) Did you just shake your head like I reminded you of this already?

That meeting was about adopting me and continuing to live with them forever. I know I am repeating myself to you a lot. I am not doing it because you are not going to understand my writing style. I do this because. I don't want to lose you, okay? Even today, being with other people's families has never been easy because I know nothing about family gatherings. Let me briefly share a true story about a woman I dated, Jackie, in the "Wrap Her Up" chapter regarding her family. If I am not mistaken, she has two sons with different fathers and two daughters by the same father.

They are all incredible people doing well for themselves in all aspects of life. They all get along and love one another, "something I am not used to seeing"! Here is the kicker, when holidays come around, they all come together in one house. Just imagine her two daughters, one happily married, with kids, and the other daughter with a brilliant child. The sons are also brilliant and are doing well for themselves, bringing girlfriends. Wait!! It gets better. The fathers of both daughters and sons are also inside the same home, getting along.

Holy shit!! No arguing and having a good time. Not to mention, they have always made me feel I was part of the family. Not once have I ever felt uncomfortable or awkward. They reminded me of Bruce Willis and Demi Moore's extended family, who were close.

This is why I get so angry seeing people that don't cherish and appreciate the moment they have with their families together and argue about petty shit and don't talk to one another. Jackie is a phenomenal mother and grandmother. Something I Never Admitted 2 Anyone Until Now! Starting with My Father/Uncle. If I were to reflect on my father/uncle, I would remember that growing up, he would always say to my mom, "Cecil and I are going here or there," and never went to any of those places he mentioned.

He would always make me wait in the car while he went inside a house that wasn't ours after waiting for about half an hour. Then he came out after straightening his clothes, fastening his belt, and combing his hair, and he would get me some ice cream.

This was an effective and inexpensive way to keep me from hitting a high note, like an OPRA singer with a stick up her or his ass. I looked forward to going out with him, knowing I would sit in the car and get ice cream afterward. So, that became the thing to do with my father and me. I did not realize that my father was using me as a pawn so that he could sleep with women. Ain't that a bitch!! I remember doing exactly what my father did to me with my oldest son. There was this one time I met a woman at her home and fucked her while I was married to my first wife. Like my father, I told my oldest son to wait in the car until I returned.

Afterward, I got back into my car and looked over at my son, and I felt like shit because I reflected on what my father did to me, and I never did it again. I think my father taking me on these secret getaways with him while he was messing around, made me realize, the apple did not fall too far from the "GOT DAMN, TREE!! How could my father look my mom in the eyes and say he loves her, but at the same time, he is messing around with different women that my mom knew nothing about.

My father also had a temper. One day, while I was sitting at the dinner table, he threw a plate at me. It came so close to my face that I blinked while the food on that plate was all over the wall beside me. Rest assured; I never looked his way again. Or what we said back in the day: "I didn't side-eye him again after that. I already mentioned what happened to him in the "Dear Momma" Chapter." Neither One of My Father's "Taught Me"! What I Am About To Tell "You"!

Here is what I can vividly remember, REGARDING my first "REAL, GIRLFRIEND"!! I think she had been sexual before me. She knew I had not slept with anyone before her because she had to tell me where my dick goes. Once she placed my cock inside her pussy it felt good—oh, it felt good. And I was like, "Oh man." I became addicted to her, sneaking in and out of her house every chance I got, in the cars, at the parks, sneaking in at my mom's house. She knew I liked her and wanted more once I fucked her.

I turned into to be a bit of a little hoe. I found older women more attractive. I would say when I was 19, 20 years old. I fucked women that were in their fifties, and they would take care of me. There was a time when I got this one white girl pregnant, this girl that liked me. Her sister gave her three hundred dollars to get an abortion. That was one moment that scared me to death. I did not know about condoms, something else my father never talked or taught me anything about. Here are "Random A.D.D. Thoughts" I am going to share with you, OKAY!

My Third Wife: I always try to be honest about my thoughts or feelings, never keeping a woman in the dark. It fucks with their heads, and they can't seem to trust anybody. I told my third wife the truth from the very beginning. I met her on a site called eHarmony. When I met her, I told her, "I am a bad boy. You look conservative, and I don't want to hurt or mislead you. She said to me that she appreciated me telling her the truth because her previous husbands all lied and cheated on her.

Of all the women that I had been fucking, she was the one I would end up falling in love with and marrying because she allowed me to be authentically me. After time had passed, I eventually stopped fucking all the women I had in my life at that moment. Hint: you can't change unless you want to or love yourself enough to change. My reason is simple: everyone else made me feel like I could not do whatever I wanted. T

he one thing you are not going to do is tell me what I can or can't do. I have always been that way. So, fuck it, I will say it. She was the most open-minded woman I had ever met. I remember showing her photos of me fucking other husband's wives.

I was unaware that showing her those photos was turning her on.

I vividly remember figuring out how to introduce the idea of swinging together. The only way I would find out the type of woman I was dealing with was to mention it. I remember talking to other women about swinging, and they all would say, "No, I am more than enough for a man." Bless those who don't cheat on their wives, such as LL Cool J, who has not been slinging cock and balls around without his wife knowledge. If you are asking yourself right now, how do I know?

Well!! Because he is famous, black, and the Godfather of hip-hop and if he had cheated, it would have been blasted all over the news and social media by now, right? I loved the chaos, being from one woman to the next.

The one thing about me is I never lied to any of them. I always answered the question honestly if they had any concerns or, whatever. It is the only way to be and let the woman decide whether they want to be with me, but to lie to them was never necessary. I did not learn this from anyone in my family. Btw, I don't have a clue what it must feel like, having a father that says, "he loves you."

Release in My Mouth

I had a polyamorous relationship with Jazmin, an attractive, thick black woman with big fucking titties.

OMG! This woman's titties were massive. We met on Tinder, and then, after a few conversations, we exchanged cell numbers. I enjoyed talking to her; she was laid-back, fun, and engaging.

She surprised me by sending me pictures of her pussy when we were just getting to know each other; she must have assumed I would find them interesting. In all honesty, the photos completely turned me off. As I gazed at the images, I could not help but think,

"WTF?" Oh, is that her pussy?

First, she was a plus-size woman who took photos of her pussy with hair on it. I don't find that attractive, especially the short, nappy hair. Wait, Muthafucka, before you criticize me for calling her pussy hair nappy, keep in mind that I don't like hair on, around, or near the pussy, okay? Also, don't we all have preferences?

Back to "Release in My Mouth." Even though I never requested the unattractive pussy photos, I was still compelled to pursue a relationship with her.

I am confident that she was perplexed by my response, as I did not react in the manner that most men would have when pussy photos were displayed on their phones. Eventually, she trusted her instincts and came over to my place. We sat down, and without wasting time, I said, "Look, I'm going to tell you something you should never do again." I did not use those exact words, but they were similar. "I wish you had not sent photos of your pussy to me."

Jazmin had a shocked expression on her face; she asked me why. "There is one simple reason, and it is because those photos did absolutely nothing for me. In all honesty, if you knew how many pussies I have fucked and licked over the past sixty-plus years, you would have known Betta. My primary interest is the person to whom the pussy belongs, as well as the content of your heart. I went on to say, "Please, never send photos of your naked body to any man unless they are someone you have met and trust. It makes you look desperate, and you are degrading yourself unnecessarily."

Her positive response to my advice piqued my interest. It was constructive criticism anyway; would you agree? When men take photos of their cocks and send them to strangers, it indicates a lack of confidence. Furthermore, women don't assume that sex with someone like this will be reciprocal, either. I will confess that I participated in such childish behavior during my early twenties.

Still, I eventually matured after realizing women were appalled by it. Immature men often send photos of their cocks to strangers as if they believe women have never seen one. They have forgotten that natural childbirth has been around for ages.

In other words, refrain from sending cock photos, especially if they are not the size of a baby's entire body. Aside from that, most women over forty have seen all shapes, sizes, and colors anyway. I have always felt women should report men who send uninvited cock photos of themselves to the authorities. Eventually, they would understand the situation and take appropriate action.

BACK TO MISS BIG BREAST, JAZMIN:

She wasn't only a hard worker but also incredibly sexy and fun. Oh, and she could squirt like a fountain. Being fucked in the backside while she was playing with her big titties was another thing that she enjoyed doing. I deeply regret sharing this story because she not only wanted me to be myself but also wanted to submit herself to me. Together, we went to an event in the Tampa area, and people consistently complimented us on how well we looked together. This was our experience.

I wore my preferred gothic outfit: a black top hat and biker boots. The garments worn by Jazmin were a black dress and a black corset. Being five feet nine inches tall made her stand out much more than she would have otherwise. I was grateful that her tall stature drew all the focus, taking the pressure off me. It was a welcome change! Because I am six feet tall, most people notice me and confuse me with basketball players.

My confession is that most people who ask this question are white. I will say that. It is not common for black people to inquire about the height of other people of white, Asian, or Latino descent.

We are not nosy people, and in most cases, we mind our own business. Jazmin was the most open-minded black woman I had ever encountered. Before her, I assumed that only white women were eccentric and open-minded, especially since they knew I was fucking other women while we were together. And damn, when I licked her pussy, she was the only woman I had ever known to squirt in my mouth while I was licking all over her pussy.

I am referring to all areas of my nose, face, and beard. Her pussy would become sloppy and silky wet. I had never seen a woman squirt in such a way. Usually, women cum leaks from her pussy and drips down into her asshole while I am eating her pussy. I would always pay attention to her when she was ready to go. When she was ready, she would squirt a small amount into my mouth.

As soon as she squirted a small amount into my mouth, I knew she was about to cum while rubbing against my face. Her pussy squirted so much that I had to stop a few times. I was afraid she would soak up my bed to the point where I would need another. Sometimes, while her eyes were closed, I would rub her squirt juices all over my bald head. I know, a nasty muthafucka, right? I had Jazmin on lock, and then I messed it up. As I have previously stated, most black women would never consider submitting themselves to a man. Most of you assume that Jazmin must have experienced abuse to even consider kneeling before me. If you're a black man reading this and believe Jazmin kneeling before me was inappropriate, so be it. And if you are a black woman, I am sure you are thinking the same thing. And I am sure you are also saying that a black woman should never kneel before anyone except

God, right? Whatever! If it is in the privacy of our own home, why should you care? Aside from that, she was the one who wanted to submit to me. However, I wasn't in the right frame of mind to accept her submission to me. Believe me, Jazmin kneeling before me is not something I take lightly. It is the purest form of respect a woman can show to a man who has proven himself worthy of her submission. She opened the car and restaurant doors for me. Yes, I said it; she opened the doors for her king!! Caring for a man, not just financially, is perfectly acceptable. I am sure if she told anyone in her family about our relationship, they would assume I was pimping her or she was my sugar momma.

I wanted the same treatment as the other white girl I was seeing at the time. Let me explain what went wrong and caused our relationship to unravel. I knew Jazmin was attending a school reunion and wanted her to have a good time. I had advised her to pursue a sexual encounter with a man in whom she was interested or who was also interested in her.

We had an open relationship, and I was there to improve her life, not to suppress it. I have no insecurities or jealousies. She attended the reunion, where she met a man who had previously shown interest in her, leading them to decide to have an intimate encounter. She described the encounter in detail. She mentioned that being with him made her feel as if she were fucking me and that she nearly made a mistake by calling him my name in the middle of the encounter.

That's how talented this guy was. I was laughing my ass off and wanted more information. I told Jazmin that I was interested in meeting this guy and having a sexual encounter with her. I hoped he had come to Florida to see her, and she arranged for him to call me. She attempted to set it up, but the bitch-ass fucker could not take it.

According to her, he and I had the same cock size, and both of us enjoyed incorporating toys into our play to enhance our interactions. He and I could have had a lot of fun with Jazmin, and she would have had a cock in all her holes. She and I were both disappointed, as she had never previously engaged in sexual intercourse with two individuals who were so similar.

Then, one day, I was on Facebook and noticed she had posted photos of herself and this guy having breakfast or lunch. This marked the end of our relationship, and I will explain why. I went with her to see her family and friends, who were all very friendly. We had a good time. Her family and friends knew about me, and then she posted photos with this other guy, making me appear foolish and gullible. This is the point at which I reached my limit. Jazmin's family and friends were unaware of our open relationship, so they were unlikely to understand and would assume she was messing around. I told her she could not take photos with another guy and post them on social media unless her family and friends knew of our open relationship. I can only imagine her family and friends seeing her social media posts and wondering who the guy was. If I ever went back to see her family, they would think, "I wonder if he knows about that guy, she was taking photos with."

And I am sure they would think I am some limp ass mutha fucker while she is out fucking someone else because they would not know what we agreed to. I was furious, and that ended our relationship. After that, I was never the same, and she knows who she is. Most women are attention whores who post everything on social media, including what you ate, drank, and who you slept with. Why? Peace

UPDATE:

After almost five years of not speaking to one another, I wanted to reconnect. I drove by where Jazmin used to live, and I would never see her car there. Since it had been a while, I decided to try Facebook, but I could not remember her last name to save my life. I tried every way possible to no avail. Eventually, I gave up trying because there were too many women on Facebook with her first name. One day, while not searching for Jazmin, her name appeared in my feed.

It had to be the universe looking out for me yet again. I was excited and decided to reach out to her with a message. I tried several times and was about to give up when suddenly she replied to one of my messages. I could tell she was cautious because of how she would respond back. This went on for a few weeks, and gradually, we would leave messages for one another. After a month or so had passed, we planned to meet at a famous restaurant near her. Seeing her again was great; she looked great and did not age. We laughed, had a great time, and discussed what had happened since we last saw each other.

Now, remember, it has only been less than a couple of months of reconnecting. She mentioned she sold her home. I remember her buying it, and now she is renting a house. She always had a great job and was secure with herself. Jazmin was driving a different car than I remember. Now let me cut to the chase as we say. Since Jazmin and I met, we have never borrowed or loaned one another money. Remember, I am going somewhere with all of this you can learn from. I could never imagine Jazmin asking for money, and one day she did. I was shocked at first and asked if it was an emergency. She said no and now I am puzzled. After I asked her a few questions, Jazmin said, "That's okay." As in, never mind, forget about it. I wanted to be sure we were on the same page. I asked if this was a loan or if you wanted me to give it to her. Jazmin responded, "I was hoping you would give it to me."

Right after her response, I had to think about it. This is what I thought to myself. Jazmin is asking me to give her $150 without repayment. You may be shocked and SYH right now that it was only $150, right? Let me explain this in detail if you are willing to read it. I would have loaned her that money, no questions asked, but give it away, oh, no! You need to know that I was on a limited income when she asked and was about to move out of my living situation soon. You must understand here: I prefer to only borrow, ask, or loan money if it will interfere with my livelihood. If that money is not paid back, there is a good chance it will destroy any relationship. Being on a limited income then, she drove an MB, sold her home, profited from the sale, and worked full-time while paying over $2000 monthly rent.

Yet she wanted me to give her my money, right? Am I venting a little? Yes, but at the same time, you don't always have to do what makes someone else happy. You should always think about your situation first before anyone else. I could have folded and given her that money, but what would I do if I needed it? After 5 years of searching for her, I ended it right afterward. She should have evaluated my living arrangements and situation before assuming I would give her that money.

That only means she was selfish, and I am glad she asked. Because if I were not on a limited income, she would have certain expectations. Everything happens for a reason, so pay attention to the signs. I am done venting now, thank you. I owe you some money for reading my vent, so put it on my tab. Peace!

AM I BEING PETTY, OR DO I HAVE A VALID POINT?

I will trust your judgement if I ever meet you. Sometimes I am just going through shit and don't have anyone to share it with. So, it is you.

Secrets In
San Diego Cali

I grew up on 4110 Hemlock Street in San Diego, California. Shorter people, feeling they had something to prove, bullied me throughout my childhood because of my height.

They could easily demonstrate their superiority over me, as I never retaliated, allowing the bullying to continue until I broke down in tears like a young schoolgirl. There was one fucker who would bully me every time he saw me anywhere. As I write this, more memories have surfaced since releasing the first book, "Vanilla Sheets," which I hope to share for the first time.

Check this out!! Just because this happened over fifty years ago does not mean shit!!" Before you dive deep into this chapter, I found something that triggered more memories.". So, may I continue?

One morning, I had a vision that reminded me of the point at which I no longer tolerated bullying. I recall walking to school on the same path every day, and as I looked up, he was approaching me. At first, I considered moving to the other side of the walkway, but then I heard a voice. This voice plainly instructed me to keep my head up.

So, I continued walking down the same side of the sidewalk he was on. Usually, when I see him, even if it is a block away, I go to the other side to avoid him altogether. The closer he got, the more nervous I became. I am not sure where my bravery came from, but I decided it was time to confront this fucker. This time, he moved over and headed directly towards me. If we keep walking toward each other, someone must move.

That day in my mind, I made it clear that I would not be the one to step aside, uttering in a stern voice, "Look, dude, I'm not backing down, and I'm not crossing the fucking street anymore, so leave me alone." The weirdest thing happened: as he looked up at me and then around to see whether anyone was watching him, he abruptly stopped and said, " Oh, it's like that, huh," I said, "Yes, it's like that" and just like that he stopped bullying me.

Because I stood up to him, we eventually became friends. As you read this, I am still applying the lessons I learned from that event to this day.

Wait! Before I go any further, I would like to express my gratitude for taking the time to read this book despite your hectic schedule. I feel better now that I have acknowledged you and your valuable time. Let us now move on to the more interesting parts of this chapter. I suppose you are wondering where my kinky and wicked sexual impulses came from. To be honest, I would say I was born deviant from the minute the obstetrician slapped my ass. Here is an example.

One day, I had an idea while playing with a soap bar, as boys do. I was a creative little fucker, and nothing has changed, just older and wiser, right? You should know if you have gotten this far into the book. Because my cock was stiff, I soaped my hands. What motivated me to decide to apply soap to my hands and massage the shaft of my cock? Since I had never done this, I was unsure what to expect. I just kept rubbing my shaft till some white liquid gushed out of the hole in my cock. I had no idea what it was, but it felt so damn good.

I thought, "Wow, what the hell was that?" I am standing in the bathroom shaking like a leaf on a tree, enjoying whatever sensation that was.

I waited a while before doing it again, and as with the previous time, more white stuff came out. I rapidly developed an addiction to jacking off regularly, as I was uninformed about girls and the proper placement of the white liquid at that juncture in my life. I started using my imagination to produce novel ways to jack off. I knew using my hand would work. So, I asked myself, "What else can I put my cock into so that I can shoot out some more of the white liquid stuff?"

Naturally, I produced another idea while going around a cemetery in the neighborhood. Please don't ask me what the hell was I thinking since my response will be, "How the hell would I know?" I already told you I must have been dropped on the floor when I was a baby, so you should expect this by now.

I am only guessing since I looked down several times while walking through the cemetery and noticed empty open cans to place flowers at the grave sites. As a creative child, I thought a different approach might be practical. Therefore, I decided to experiment with flower cans. I hope you understand what I mean.

The cans are full of dirt. I looked around to make sure no one was nearby, then pulled my jeans down to my knees in case I needed to draw them back up. Lying face down on the grass, I inserted my cock into the dirt can. When I realized that it wasn't producing the same results, I stood up quickly, pulled my pants up, and kept walking. After some time, I realized that something wasn't right. This is just a glimpse of my life, which many may not understand.

And for those who understand, I appreciate your allowing me to express myself. Am I taking a chance telling this fucked up shit? Yes, people will criticize and nearly crucify me, and that's good. I am sixty-five years old and have seen and done things most people keep to themselves.

Over the years, I have witnessed and heard about individuals in San Diego engaging in strange behaviors related to sex, often without the knowledge of their own families. Please brace yourself for what I am about to say next. One woman confided in me about allowing her dog to fuck and cum in her, while another expressed a desire for her dog to lick her pussy. For some strange reason, this piqued my interest. I asked, "How did you get the dog to lick your pussy?"

You may not want to believe what she said, but she used creamy peanut butter and spread it on her pussy like it was a slice of white toast straight out of the toaster. That response piqued my interest, prompting me to ask another question: "Why peanut butter?" She told me with a straight face, "Because dogs like peanut butter and prefer to lick it rather than bite or try to chew it." Well, I will be damned! That answer made sense to me, and I had no further questions for her. You thought I was messed up, huh?

There are a lot more messed up people on this earth than you care to imagine. Oh, heck no! I am not sure what it is about me, but people tend to tell me their darkest secrets (apart from murder). I maintain a poker face when strangers share their secrets. I am not surprised by what people like with so many options available, and I don't care. I comprehend that engaging in sexual intercourse with an animal is distressing enough; however, there are far more horrific experiences available on the Internet. That's all I will say. Therefore, you are not alone if you relate to what I wrote. You can pretend you have never met me or reached out and acknowledge me anonymously; it is okay.

Nobody needs to know about the messed- up crap you have been through and experienced. For fear of misinterpretation and criticism, some individuals, like me, may choose not to publicly acknowledge your closet freakishness. If anyone understands why, it is me. You should not give a damn because it is what made you who you are now. The same people who may judge you for buying and reading this book also read it quietly. I am prepared to face any criticism that comes my way. In fact, I expect it.

So, I will tell you right now: don't read the rest of this book if you find what you have read so far disturbing, if you have a weak stomach, or believe you won't go to heaven. I don't need you to throw holy water at me unexpectedly. This book is not for the fainthearted. My target audience is people with an open mind and acceptance of everyone's kinks. If you have read this far, I like you. Peace!

Selfish MoFo's

A lot of guys that I have talked to over the years have given me the impression that men are the most selfish fuckers I know. Always bragging about women sucking their cocks then leaving right afterwards.

NOTE: THERE ARE TWO CHARACTERS IN THIS CHAPTER, **CECIL** AND **ROYAL** FROM "UNDER THE COVER"

While telling me their stories, I always find it disturbing because, I'm saying to myself, YOU ARE A SELFISH PRICK!! Royal, have you ever sucked a man's cock, and he didn't want to eat your pussy?

Royal: Wait a second, ARE YOU KIDDING ME!! HELL TO THE FUCK NO!! That's why I ask over the phone do they eat pussy in our first conversation. Seriously?

Cecil: Yes Seriously!! Cecil, you knew the answer to that question before you asked, didn't you? **Cecil:** I damn sure did, so I will continue with my story, if you don't mind.

Royal: I didn't ask you to be in this chapter or paragraph anyways!!

Cecil: I know, but I wanted my reader to know.
Royal: Well, they know now, right?

Cecil: Yes, they sure do!

Royal: This is one of those chapters I may not be able to stay submissively quiet, Cecil!

Cecil: It's okay, I expected that. When it comes to sex, the focus is entirely on themselves. If you are a woman reading this chapter, I don't blame men for being selfish lovers; instead, I blame the women they fucked with in the past.

Royal: Damn, good point, continue!

Cecil: To be candid, I will state the following: If you are having sex with a man for the first time and he fails to spend sufficient time with you after you fucked him or he fucked you, it is your fault, not his.

Royal: Say it again so they can hear you in the back of the classroom.

Cecil: The whole paragraph?

Royal: No, this part: If you are having sex with a man for the first time and he fails to spend sufficient time with you after you fucked him or he fucked you, it is your fucking fault, not his.

Cecil: You funny!!
Royal: Why do you say that?

Cecil: Because you just repeated it yourself, so I don't have to.
Royal: You are right, so, go ahead...

Suppose that a man exhibits selfishness from the moment you suck his cock. In that case, it will reveal all the necessary information you need before sucking his cock again. You should not hesitate and tell that selfish prick should get the hell out and go home immediately (with tact, of course).

Royal: Damn!! Cecil, you are saying shit these young bitche's now days, need to hear. Oh! and, some old ass bitche's too.
Cecil: Thanks Royal, I appreciate you saying that. **Royal:** Not a problem, continue. I understand that some women are uncomfortable expressing themselves openly to their partners.

Royal: Fuck that shit! I ain't uncomfortable!

Cecil: There is a way to make yourself comfortable talking about sex with your potential partner.

Royal: Cecil? You are being way too polite on this subject.

Cecil: This needs to be done before having sex and not on the phone but in person. I am not talking about you Royal, Okay?

Royal: I know, thanks.

Cecil: Having a conversation about sex in person will allow you to watch his body language and eye contact. You should also be able to tell if he is listening or just hearing you. There is a significant difference between the two. Hearing you is going through one ear and out the other. Listening to you is hearing everything you say and caring enough to ask questions.

If he listened to every word you said, he would not exploit you, and you must be willing to be vulnerable. The right man feels drawn to a woman who shares this belief, and he recognizes she is prepared not to tolerate his bullshit. Any man who possesses physical attractiveness and maintains excellent physical health, he is accustomed to women wanting to fuck him.

Some women are insecure and will say to themselves, "Oh, this guy is attracted to me; and he likes me." Most women don't know their worth and think negatively about themselves. When a player pursues a woman with this belief, he knows she will put up with his bullshit. There are some women, after years of sexual and emotional neglect, who are brave enough to love themselves and leave him. Regardless of the quality and quantity of the sex or their physical attractiveness. Do not be naive while reading this; understanding good cock and tongue will make you tolerate more than you must. Ladies, here are some of the signs that you are dealing with a selfish man:

Every time he stops by to see you, he wants his cock sucked like I said earlier in this chapter, but you receive nothing in return; after he cums in your mouth

Royal: Just so you know Cecil, I don't swallow.
Cecil: Royal? That's more information, I didn't need to know.

Royal: Well, again, you are the one who keeps adding me in, so I will say what you are thinking.

Cecil: Then he either rolls over and goes to sleep or puts on his clothes to leave, not giving a damn if you had an orgasm. If you are paying attention, there are sure signs to watch out for before engaging in sexual activity with this mutha fucka. Here are some examples:

There is no foreplay, and most men honestly believe their cock is sufficient to make you happy, Here are some more: Sending you pictures of his cock; not bathing before sticking his stanky ass cock in you; a noticeable underarm odor that he doesn't apologize for when you bring it to his attention; jealousy when another man looks at you; never preparing dinner; licking your pussy just a few times before sticking his cock in; not using lube; and refraining from playing with your clitoris while eating your pussy. This list is longer than I am willing to share in this chapter. However, you get my drift.
Royal: There are a lot of guys out there with this mentality.

Royal continues: Especially if you are a woman over the age of fifty,

Cecil: I am sure you have dealt with at least one selfish lover in your life, right?

Royal: Honestly, I have not!

Cecil: Not you Royal, the reader or the person listening. How did you feel afterward? Did you express your dissatisfaction by speaking up, or did you wait until he was absent and masturbate? Know your worth, ladies! Oh, I just remembered that I need to add this.

Royal: Some of you ladies who have been married for a long time must remember one thing. If you were a virgin when you met your husband, and he wasn't shown, taught, or cared how to please you, I am sorry. Yes, me too It will be rough for you to know what it is like to be pleased by someone who cares enough about you.

Especially if he has always been a selfish fucker, I meant lover. There is a good chance you will be because you don't know any better. How he fucks from the very beginning will be familiar to you.

Before you know what hit ya, you are invested with your heart. You won't see the difference until you meet another man who, gives a damn about ya.

HOPEFULLY,

YOU WON'T GRAVITATE TOWARDS
ANOTHER SELFISH LOVER.
PEACE!

She Got the Wrong One

I Remember this girl named Mya; I took her to see a house band on our first date. When we arrived, she was thrilled by the location I chose.

For as long as I can remember, I have maintained a ballplayer attitude despite living on a Top-Ramen budget. Of course, you must leave a $10 tip for the parking attendant. The walk-in was always stunning, like walking on the red carpet. You would notice light candles on the tables when you enter through the door.

The host would approach with a grin on her face, and you would follow her to the table she had chosen for you. You take a seat and enjoy your surroundings while waiting for the band to begin playing modern jazz. This is the kind of location where you should wear name-brand attire. Within two minutes of settling there, a waiter approached our table and asked whether she and I needed anything to drink.

Before I could look up at the waiter and tell her not now, this bitch, Mya, ordered a double-iced tea with lemon. You know, I had to order. one merely to fit in. The server returned to my table and announced, "That will be forty-three dollars." I asked, "What?" I asked my date this same question: "What the hell did you order?" She looked down, giggled, and exclaimed, "Oh!" "I requested a double-iced tea with lemon." I told myself, "Bitch, you've messed me up."

After paying for the drinks, I told Mya I would return shortly. I had to act quickly, so I approached the server serving us the expensive beverages. I leaned over and said, "Do not return to our table," as I tipped her ten dollars. Tipping the waiter $10 seemed like a better option than my date ordering another round of double-iced tea with lemon, right? I may have been about twenty-three years old when this happened to me.

Even at 26, I possessed the foresight to evade a woman's manipulation tactics. I did not see Mya again; she mistook my wallet for Shaquille O'Neal's. I did not care about how fine that bitch was; she was never going to use me again after this final date. I don't blame Mya for assuming I had ballplayer money; ballplayers tend to treat bitches like her with undue disrespect.

That has never been my mindset; I had to struggle for anything I wanted. I understand what you are thinking.

Suppose I don't receive sixty-forty in a relationship where I am sixty and she is forty. In that case, I might receive seventy-thirty, depending on her level of niceness. Fuck that crap; I am done. Bitches can quickly locate men who are naive enough to pay everything upfront and have never fucked. I am going to repeat these three words: fuck that shit. I enjoy dating women, where I purchase movie tickets, and they reciprocate with snacks, or vice versa. I don't have an issue with that.

WHAT I'VE LEARNED FROM THIS CHAPTER:

Attractive women can easily attract thirsty ass mutha fuckers but not me. Even after this book's publication, I avoided meeting women in pubs or restaurants. Thirsty ass mutha suckers will do anything to hit it. A woman usually recognizes a sucker when she sees one. First, if a man is eager to meet, he is a sucker. I am about to admit something for the first time: I do not meet a woman at a restaurant for our initial meeting. My argument is simple, BITCH! I don't know you like that...

Or, if we do meet at a restaurant, I will immediately say we are going Dutch, correct? If she hesitates, it indicates that she mistakenly believed me to be one of those thirsty individuals. Here is something else I have discovered recently, despite knowing it for a long time. Black men often display their wealth or cars to gain attention. Any man with confidence should not have to resort to such behavior. But that's just my viewpoint; what do I know about it? Peace!

Should've Known Betta

Tori, another white woman, was more than willing to fuck me. Keep reading, and I will explain why.

After several phone conversations, this bitch I mean lady, showed no hesitation, and agreed to meet at my house within a few days. I was like, "Damn, I like this shit." Sometimes I just want to fuck and see what we have in common. Hey, you excuse me, reader of this chapter, I am a hypocrite when I call a woman a "Bitch so don't take it personally or think I always refer to women as bitches." Wait!! Let me add one more and is that "Don't get your panties all tied up in knots."

Now that we are on the same page let me proceed. I was risking everything because of pussy by inviting her to my home, right? You and I both know there are some crazy ass bitch's walking among us all. They appear normal until you say the word NO!! AnyHoo!!

Fucking on the first meeting makes it easier to get to know each other and hopefully does not leave anyone disappointed. My opinion, of course. The last thing I want to do is talk to someone for weeks, if not months, only to discover that we are not sexually compatible. Life is too short to spend time and energy with an incompatible partner, in and out of bed.

Fuck that trying to figure it out bullshit. Or, like some I knew said, it takes time to get to know one another. That's bullshit also. If it ain't at least a firecracker from the first time you fuck then there should not be a second time. I am saying it may not be fireworks and eyes rolling back of your head sex but come on now. I read in Steve H.'s book that women should wait at least six months before giving up pussy. I asked myself, "Who is this mofo giving advice, and why are women listening?" Seriously!! There is not a single solution for every situation. But who am I to judge? He made a lot of money by saying what women wanted to hear. This is what old-school players and pimps say to convince them when to listen to their bullshit.

BACK TO TORI:

She took pleasure in receiving slaps on her ass, having her hair pulled occasionally, and engaging in sexy conversations. If you fucked her properly and had a decent-sized cock, she would cum quickly. Her being multi-orgasmic was unbelievable for my ego. Of course, now that I am rewriting this book, a memory jumped into my head like a wrestler on top of the ropes.

When I initially met Tori, she mentioned she did not like her pussy licked or should I say, eaten. In all my *40 years of eating pussy I have only heard this a few times, and I am always surprised when I do. When a woman feels comfortable enough to express that she does not like it, I always find an excuse for her. What I mean by this is I say to myself, you must not have had someone that knows what the fuck they are doing.

Or cared enough about you to keep trying, or better yet, was just a selfish fucker. In either case, it is a damn shame, which is all I am saying. Before I continue with giving you the 411 about Tori, just know I love eating and fingering a woman's pussy that loves it, not just like it. Anyways, Not licking Tori's pussy meant I had less to do to get her excited, right? All I had to do was let her suck my cock, tug her hair slightly, say some naughty talk, and she would be ready to fuck.

Furthermore, and like I said earlier, she was multi-orgasmic. I constantly thank the universe for providing me with a decent-sized cock so that I could please some women. Notice I said some women? Tori was a plus-size woman, but I still enjoyed being with her. I said "but" because usually big women have big thighs and asses, I don't have a long enough cock to go inside the pussy, no matter the position.

Usually bent over the bed or a couch while holding their ass cheeks open, I found to be more suitable when you have 7 to 8 inches of cock. Just keeping it real with ya! Wait! Before you continue reading, I would like you to imagine what happened while I fucked Tori in the ass, and I hope you find this funny. Okay, let me proceed. Once, while Tori was blindfolded, I fucked her in the ass and pulled on her hair. She slouched slightly over the bed, one leg propped up and the other resting on the floor. As I was balls deep in her the ass, a large puddle of fluid began to drip from somewhere near her body beneath my feet. I was wondering what the hell was going on and was unsure where the puddle originated.

The puddle on the floor naturally distracted me. I did not want to stop fucking her, either. Eventually, the puddle started to go towards my dresser, and you know what happens when wood becomes wet, right? Especially when I did not know what kind of fluid it was. Now, it is up to me to decide what to do about it. Should I stop or continue fucking Tori in the ass? Eventually, I pulled my cock out of her ass just so we could clean up to continue. She is still blindfolded and does not know why I am taking a break. Since trust wasn't an issue, she did not inquire what I was doing.

After putting my cock back in her ass, I looked down at the floor. I shouted as the late great *Rudy Ray Moore would have said, "BIIATCH, do you realize you're squirting all over my floor while I'm in the ass again? Tori said, "No way! Are you kidding me?" I told her not to move so that I could put on my tennis shoes and avoid slipping. We laughed when I told her my tennis shoes did not save me from sliding in her squirt puddle. I wiped it from the floor and continued, but I wore a different pair of tennis shoes to stop myself from sliding this time. I was so turned on by her squirting all over the floor that I quickly unleashed my hot cum into her ass.

Of course, that was only after I had wiped another large pool of squirt from the floor. She also enjoyed being dominated and slightly degraded, which added to the fun. I would yell something like, "Bitch, get on your knees," and she would comply with a smile. Keep in mind that I always know when I can get away with calling a woman a "bitch," and they are the ones who turn me on the most. Just saying. Even when I called her a bitch and did nasty things she enjoyed, she was always in control.

In other words, Tori allows me to believe I am in control because it turns her on like a light bulb. She could have easily gotten up, put her clothes back on, and left, right? I knew I could say, "Get down on your fucking knees and suck my cock bitch!" It holds no significance until she fully embraces her desires. Bottom line: A woman is always in control.

Any man who believes that instructing a woman what to do is acceptable without regard for her desires is nothing more than a punk-ass bitch. I can't imagine a self-respecting woman succumbing to that nonsense without consent unless she had a gun aimed at her head or was attempting to avoid being beaten.

We must imprison that individual and subject him to physical abuse every evening for the duration of his sentence. Do not attempt to mend his wounds; instead, allow him to recuperate organically. Let me say this another way you may comprehend, enable the prisoner to fuck his ass until that fucker bleeds internally. Do not send his bitch ass to the hospital as an option either and just let him heal naturally. Get my drift? This method will have more of an impact on the rest of his sentence, you would think, right?

Nevertheless, I had to stop fucking Tori because she was a female version of who I used to be before I met her. She was having sex with several other guys while we were together. I did not mind, but she was overly eager for an exclusive relationship with me, even as she continued to fuck other men. After only a few dates and sex, she is quick to want an exclusive relationship if the man she is fucking mentions it.

She fails to understand that developing an exclusive relationship with someone requires time and patience. I don't necessarily blame her for this, considering the men Tori chooses to be in a relationship with. They were some broke-ass mother fuckers, jobless, self-hating men. She was easy prey for this type of man. I used to listen to some of her encounters, and I would say to her, "Where in the hell do you find these types of men? I also feel that abandonment or a lack of self-worth can make anyone needy and desperate.

These were just my observations. But who am I, right? Just another mutha fucka with an opinion, right? I digress. As previously mentioned, Tori was fucking an excessive number of men within a short period. That started me to think if she continues, she might just surpass Wilt Chamberlain's record within a year, just joking, but you understand where I am coming from, right?

I decided it would be best if she and I remained friends without benefits. I felt like I was waiting to get on the merry-go-round when just to fuck her. What does that mean right?

If you have been on this earth long enough you have either seen or rode on a merry-go-round. And when it's already full of kids on it you have to wit till either someone falls off or was tired of going around in circles. Hell, some kids even threw up the last supper they ate because of that damn ride. So, you jump and hang on not while not going anywhere. Remember that?

However, things did not always go as planned, so Tori contacted me some months later and asked if I wanted to see her for a little while. She caught me in a vulnerable state of mind because I was tired of masturbating a few times a day. I responded, "Okay, fuck it, come on over to my place". However, it is worth noting that she only contacted me as she was leaving Daytona Beach after fucking another man she barely knew. You would think I Should Have Known Betta, right? Tori called me several days later, concerned about some symptoms she was experiencing like AIDS after sex with a man in a sleazy hotel in Daytona.

As an instructor, you would think she would be smart enough to go to the doctor first, right? Nope! Instead, the bitch Googled her symptoms and diagnosed herself as having AIDS. Tori then made a conscious messed up decision to get into her car in a panic state of mind and drive back to Daytona to confront the man she had fucked in the sleazy motel before me. Tori had the nerve and boldly believed that Daytona man was the one who had infected her with AIDS. Isn't that calling the tea kettle black when Tori will fuck a man only after a few conversations, sometimes on the same day of the conversation?

Additionally, she did not seek medical confirmation for her diagnosis. I just wanted to let you know that I am not blaming Tori for her decisions; I am glad she called me while driving to meet with this guy to bring some unexpected news. Without even knowing him that well, there was no way she could read his reaction to her AIDS claim. Now wait just a damn second picture this: you just slept with someone, and they look you dead in the face and say, *"You gave me AIDS,"* when the truth is it could've been them all along. And then get this when you ask how they "know," they tell you they Googled it. She **Googled** it. You think I'm joking? No. I'm dead serious.

That man from Daytona could've beaten the hell out of her or made her disappear without a trace. I'm not exaggerating when I say I saved that woman's life—talked her into turning around and never going back to see him.

Sometimes the universe steps in hard, and that day, it did. She called me before she drove over there again, and I shut it down. For the record I got tested. Negative. No AIDS then, and not now. I plan on keeping it that way. But I learned something that day, and I swore to myself I'd never put myself in that kind of situation again with anybody.

I'm still AIDS-free. And yeah, I know what you're thinking, *"Damn, he's bold for telling this."* You're right. I am. I'm an open book—no pun intended—and I've got nothing to hide.

UPDATE:

It had been several years since I last communicated with Tori, and here is why. After her marriage, I had the presumption that I would never have another chance to speak with her. Every time Tori fell in love with a man, she immediately broke off communication with me. Tori does not take responsibility for her choices or reflect on her past.

At some point, of course, she started doing the same old shit over again while married to the ex-boyfriend. How do I know? Well, let me explain. When I was living with my girlfriend L, Tori called me. Obviously, when the phone rang, I answered it because I had nothing to hide. Remember when I said I was with my girlfriend L while in the same room as me? She continued by saying that she was with one of her female friends and referenced the idea of her coming to see me. I told her I no longer live alone but with my girlfriend.

She seemed surprised and became extremely apologetic, which was unnecessary. After some time had passed, I decided to end my relationship with my girlfriend, and several months later, I reached out to Tori again to reconnect.

Tori's mentality was something I had to take into consideration, even though I naturally desired to have another sexual encounter with her. When we saw each other on occasion, she asked about the possibility of us developing a romantic relationship at some point. I said I would give it some serious thought, and I only said that because I did not want to ruin the mood.

It was fortunate that she did not possess the power to read my thoughts since it would have been devastating. Eventually, after some time, I realized that I needed to be honest with Tori. One day, I contacted her by phone and told her, "You are sneaky." For some reason, she could not comprehend why I referred to her as sneaky. She had wanted to have sex with me while living with her husband, and she genuinely believed that I had forgotten about her past.

She stopped calling me when I confronted her with the truth, realizing I would never trust her. All these attempts to convey that your actions toward others will reverberate back to you, often in unexpected ways. *I said 40 years of eating pussy because I did not understand how pleasurable that's for a woman. In my twenties, I wasn't eating pussy and sure in the hell did not know how.

Before you go, Tori misdiagnosed herself as having Aids. **Rudy Ray Moore – Please listen to Rudy Ray Moore's: "Eat Out More Often" Album.**

See what I mean? Peace!

Smack Dat Azz

W hile in my late fifties, I realized that some women enjoy having their asses slapped, and not in a childlike manner either.

Mia was the first woman who asked me to slap her ass, was terrifying, and that's an understatement. To be honest, the young lady was experiencing some mental instability, I think. My mother raised me to be a respectable young man, and any form of slapping resulted in the use of a belt as punishment. So, you can only imagine how confused and hesitant I was to provide the ass slap she craved without disappointing her. For a moment, close your eyes and try to guess the expression I had on my face when she was upset. Could you see the look on my face that said,

"What the hell?" Are you smiling?

In addition, it is my intention to fulfill rather than disappointment. I must admit, I was a little hesitant when I gave Mia the first slap on the ass. As I was writing this section, I could not help but laugh aloud when she looked over her shoulder and said, "Nigga, please!" Seriously!! Is that all you got. During that precise moment, I realized there was no going back. Without further ado, I proceeded to slap Mia's ass until my hand became numb.

Seriously, I could feel my heart beating in my hand; it was so numb. Her eyes were staring up at the ceiling, and all I could see were the whites of her eyes. I am going to admit listening to her moan with pleasure and only seeing the whites of her eyes was crazy, if you know what I mean.

You might wonder how I could see the whites of her eyes if I were behind her. The simple answer is that I had a mirror on the wall. So there! She expressed her gratitude to me, then slowly turned around and faced me with tears in her eyes. I tried to reassure her that it was okay, although she appeared embarrassed to express herself to me. Through experimentation, I discovered that slapping that ass harder makes them cum more easily.

I understand that a woman who enjoys spanking describes the sensation as indescribable, claiming it transports them to a specific location within their own mind. I call that her subspace, which means there is a psychological subspace, which is fundamentally a moment in submissive play during which her mind undergoes a transition unlike any normal feeling. To clarify this concept, visualize a sub is "messed out of her mind." The primary difference is that psychological subspace can be entered without engaging in sexual intercourse.

When this happens, she releases epinephrine and endorphins, according to my uneducated knowledge of it. The experience when she enters her subspace results from her body's release.

She experiences a light mental sluggishness, and her thoughts are exclusively on her man. It is so easy to substitute the safe word when they should not. I have always found it puzzling that most women struggle to articulate the pleasure they derive from receiving a slap on the ass. Out of all the women I have slept with, only a handful have fully understood why they love the sensation.

Each time I performed this, I had to apply ice to the palms of my hands because, most of the time, I felt more pain than they did. Also, for some reason that I don't fully understand, I find it attractive to look at a nice, freshly slapped ass If we ever meet again, I would appreciate it if you did not ask me why. Since the only response I will give you is, "I don't know," I won't elaborate further. Peace!

Snow Bunny Delight

Any man who has had sex with multiple women in his life should understand that they are like unicorns. And trust should be important to you.

The characters in this chapter are:

Author's Note (Real Quick):

Alright, listen—before you start asking, "Why the hell does this dude keep putting letters in parentheses like it's a damn algebra book?"—let me explain.

Those little codes like (C), (R), (S)?
Yeah, they're not secret government ops. That's just me letting you know who's talking.

(C) = Cecil (that's me—clearly)

(R) = Royal (mouth slicker than motor oil)

(S) = Susie (cool, calm, sometimes too honest)

and whoever else jumps in will get a letter too.

I ain't writing a play, and I'm not about to throw in "he said/she said" every five seconds. So instead, I give you these quick labels like a group chat with drama. It's clean, it's clear, and it keeps your ass from getting confused.
You're welcome.

Alright, now let's get back to the juicy stuff.

(C)There is no reason to believe that what pleases one woman will please others. Every woman on earth has a unique sexuality, which takes time and patience to uncover. Not all women, despite their uniqueness, enjoy the sensation of choking during sexual encounters. Suppose you lack experience before placing your hands around a woman's throat. In that case, there is a significant risk that you may choke her unconsciously. I have never assumed that all women enjoy rough sex. Here are my twelve favorite questions I have asked before having plain old vanilla sex, and guys should, too.

What was sex like with your past partner? • Do you enjoy experimenting with toys? • Do you play with yourself? • Can you cum vaginally? • Can you cum from anal? • Does an orgasm require stimulation of your clitoris? • How do you feel about rough sex? • Have you ever been slapped in general, and where? Do you like it? • Have you ever been choked? • What kind of relationship do you have with your father? • When and with whom did you discover that you enjoyed choking? • Can you cum without being choked?

These are critical questions to consider before having sex with a unicorn. This is especially true if you plan to engage in sexual activity in the future. The purpose of asking questions is to mask the real question. First, you should not ask, **"Do you enjoy choking?"** Ladies, I can only imagine what would immediately go through your mind and the questions you would ask even if you enjoyed it.

(C) The first thing out of your mouth should be:

(S) Why the fuck are you asking me that question?

(C) Even if you don't express yourself this way, it should still be a question you ask. Being choked or choking someone should not be taken lightly by either one of you. Do not attempt choking until she or he is comfortable, and trust has been established from what I have said more than once. Otherwise, you risk traumatizing her. Some women, especially Lara, enjoy being choked during sex. Rough play compelled me to grab her by the throat and choke her while she was masturbating.

She trusted me enough to know I was conscious of what I was doing for her and my own safety. While my gig ass hands were around her throat, I noticed her face turning a little red and knew she was okay. If her face turned into a dark reddish tone, I would relax my grasp around her throat and listen to her breathing. As I expected, I watched her face darken like a Northern Cardinal red after a few minutes. I held her throat long enough to make her feel powerless, and Lara understood what I was doing. I choked Lara as she masturbated with a vibrator on her clit.

The combination must have sent her through the roof because her eyes rolled to the back of her head, and she froze for three seconds. I was inches from her face and witnessed the metamorphosis as it occurred, just like in Part One of The Exorcist with Linda Blair.

Have you seen this movie? Holy molly, huh? Her hand released the vibrator and dropped it between her legs, which surprised me. She gazed at the ceiling, under the influence of the devil. Like the priest in The Exorcist, I thought of splashing some holy water on her, but I didn't have any available, to help her snap out of it. She calmly looked into my eyes and asked me:

(S)what "just happened?

(C)I described what happened in detail, and she responded,

(S)"Do it again."

(R) Okay I have to ask, where in the hell do you meet these women?
(C) Online why?

(R)I was just curious, that's all.

(C)Lara messed my head up with that question. I empathically responded, Oh, hell no! Obviously, she is not looking at this from my perspective. What if I mistakenly deleted her, and the police showed up? As an older black man and Lara in her early thirties, while living near Maimi, I would have struggled to explain what happened while choking a young, white, blond-haired female in her thirties with kids. Only a black jury, judge, and prosecutor I paid under the table could save my black ass in that situation.

In fact, the officers who showed up would also have to be black, trust my narrative, and lie on the report, claiming she was choked by someone who left the scene before they arrived. We all know, and it is documented, that they lie in police reports, so this would not be any different in my case. So that they would acquit me of Class A Felony and just say to themselves, she had it coming.

The jury would deliberate for two hours and acquitted me of all counts. The juror was asked why deliberation lasted only two hours; one of the juries would have had to stand up and state she got what she deserved for fucking a black man, and this case was dismissed. It was a unanimous decision. I have not done it since then.

I am not going to jail or prison for this, and I must worry about a well-known singer while I am there. A Different Scene with Lara: Another time, Lara slept in my apartment while I was at work. As I was leaving work, I wanted to know whether Lara was awake or asleep. There is nothing sweeter than strolling in and finding her sleeping in my bed.

I moved towards the door, discreetly inserted the key, and opened it. Lara must have heard the front door open and close. Walking down the hall, I heard her returning to my bed and pretending to snore. So, I stood in the doorway smiling, staring at her half-naked body, ass up and face down. The sheets were on the floor because she rushed back into my bed.

She knew I was watching her in the doorway because she arched her back and gently spread her legs, revealing her freshly shaven pussy. While standing in the doorway, I was fantasizing about all the horrible things I could do to her. I kicked off my shoes, pulled off my socks, and everything else. When I finished taking off my clothes, I grabbed the covers off her and forcefully planted the palm of my hand in the center of her back.

I instructed her in a firm, controlling tone, "Don't move till I cum." I pinned her down in one of my favorite positions, spit on my cock, and stuck it into her ass. I shot my load of hot cum in her ass in five minutes while she was pretending to be asleep with her face and cum running out of her sweet white ass. She enjoyed rough sex occasionally and I did not mind offering it.

She felt compelled to lie unnecessarily if you are wondering why our relationship ended. You have read enough about me to know I am nonjudgmental, correct? Nothing she could have done or said would have changed my feelings towards her. Regardless, I won't tolerate being lied to. Peace!!

WHAT I LEARNED FROM THIS CHAPTER:

As of 2024, I had never attempted or even considered sexually choking any woman. I have not even joked about putting my hand or hands around a woman's throat. Whoever contemplates undertaking this type of play must exercise extreme caution, as I was fortunate that nothing happened to her. Consider what could have happened if I had called 911. A white girl succumbed to choking, leaving no witnesses or video evidence. It would have been a terrible situation if I had to explain what had happened to the police officers.

UPDATE: 05/28/2024 AT 11:23 AM.

Freaky White Girl Lara, as I knew her, is no longer with us. Her faith now guides her on a path that's different than mine. As I understand it, Lara no longer talks about her past life. It can be challenging to communicate with someone whose personality has drastically changed. In fact, Lara no longer considers sex or participation in any activity relating to sex. I will conclude by stating that her life experiences have shaped the beliefs she holds today.

And honestly, all that matters is that she is content living her life in the way she believes works best for her. How I feel and what I think is meaningless. I have been brutally honest with you thus far, and if you met her, you would agree that she has drastically changed her life from the inside out. To be honest, you may not recognize Lara. In fact, her attire has changed dramatically, giving me the impression that she does not want anyone's attention and simply wants to blend in. Because when I initially met her, she wore revealing clothing that would show her fantastic body. That's my update. Peace!!

The Black Fluffer

I am venting my frustrations in this chapter, so feel free to follow along or skip ahead because, I am hoping who I am talking about reads this chapter.

By no means am I homophobic because you may already think I am anyways, right? There was a person I used to work with, and I won't disclose his position or name within this well-known company because mentioning it is not worth the trouble. From the moment I met, "MR. FLUFFER"!!, I immediately assumed he was gay, due to his unique walking and talking style, and his bent wrist, and his lisp.

There were moments when he would sing while working, and most of us around him would all look at each other and smile.

You know, that look of acknowledgment saying, "Yeah, he is." As we all know, this mutha fucker is gay, as a kite in the sky with a long tied on tail on it. I just wanted to give you a visual, if that was, okay? I would like to clarify that I have never had an issue with gay men or women; instead, it is this individual that I am discussing in this chapter. You will undoubtedly recognize this person I am referring to. Anyone familiar with me knows who the fuck I am talking about. Bitch ass! I am sure that after reading this chapter, you may even think I am gay or bisexual.

At this stage of my life, I don't give ah damn what you or anyone else thinks. I have already told you that I am venting and suffering from ADD (attention deficit disorder), and I might as well add old age to the mix. I identify as sexual, which means I am open to any activity that involves women and sometimes men, especially if they enjoy sucking and swallowing my cock.

To be clear, I have had no interaction with a male in forty-plus years. A woman who knows what the fuck to do with her mouth works for me. To put it bluntly, if there was an adult movie being filmed in Altamonte Spring, I would stop production and make this bent wrist mutha fucka I am talking about in this chapter suck my cock and!! replace the original white fluffer before filming.

I like this because it will excite his partner to watch us. I never had an issue with a guy sucking on my cock, especially in this situation. I once worked with Mr. Fluffer as my manager, and I will admit that there were times when I imagined him on his knees, sucking my BLUE PILL-taken black cock. You may need to understand why I said, "BLUE PILL- taken black cock," and it is because I want to make sure, he sucks my fucking cock for a while, and I won't go soft.

Did that help explain exactly what I meant by that? I am sure it did because you smiled, right? And while Mr. Fluffer is on his knees, I will tell him to open his fucking mouth and make sure his tongue is at the bottom.

Occasionally, I would slap him on the side of his face and insert a mini-ball gag into his mouth. How much more degrading could I be towards this fucker?

KEEP READING!

Not only would I slap his face and press his lips against my hairy, unshaven pelvis, but I would also place my hand on the back of his head. This act would be a form of retaliation for his deceitful actions against me, specifically when he lied and cost me my job. My lack of trust in him and most people stems from an unfortunate incident at work. I always enjoyed watching the upper management exclude him from meetings and walks within the building.

He would follow the managers around like a puppy dog without a leash, but he would stay close enough if Masta wanted something; all they had to do was snap their fingers. After all, they knew he was nothing more than a lap dog. Yes, I am talking about you, and you know who the hell you are. Every time I see Mr. Fluffer, I still crave for him to be on his knees, sucking my cock. After a few minutes of him sucking and licking my hairy ass balls and tossing my salad, I would release some hot, fresh cum in his mouth. As I am looking down at him, I will slap his face and say, you are a good little bitch. Now swallow. Afterward, I pull up my zipper and walk out the door, leaving him on his knees, pissed off. Of course, after he calms down, he will text me later to ask when he can come by to do it all over again. Damn it! Then I woke up angry; like I said earlier, I imagined it.

Yes right!! I am merely stating this to protect myself if Mr. Fluffer happens to read this chapter. In case you did not know what the hell a fluffer is, read below. Peace!

THIS IS THE FULL DEFINITION OF A FLUFFER:

Individuals of a particular age may find amusement in my reference, as in the 1950s, a 'fluffer' is usually a male who is responsible for maintaining male actors in an aroused state throughout a shoot. It is logical, considering that shoots may extend for several hours. The individuals on set may be male or female and are typically attired. A fluffer is often designated for guys alone. Fluffers exist within the modern adult film industry.

Numerous adult video performers assert that they are a complete fabrication (or male dream). Some assert that a fluffer may be present during a gangbang-style shot, where numerous guys must be prepared at a moment's notice. In conclusion, a fluffer can be executed through oral means, accompanied by physical or visual stimulation.

The A List

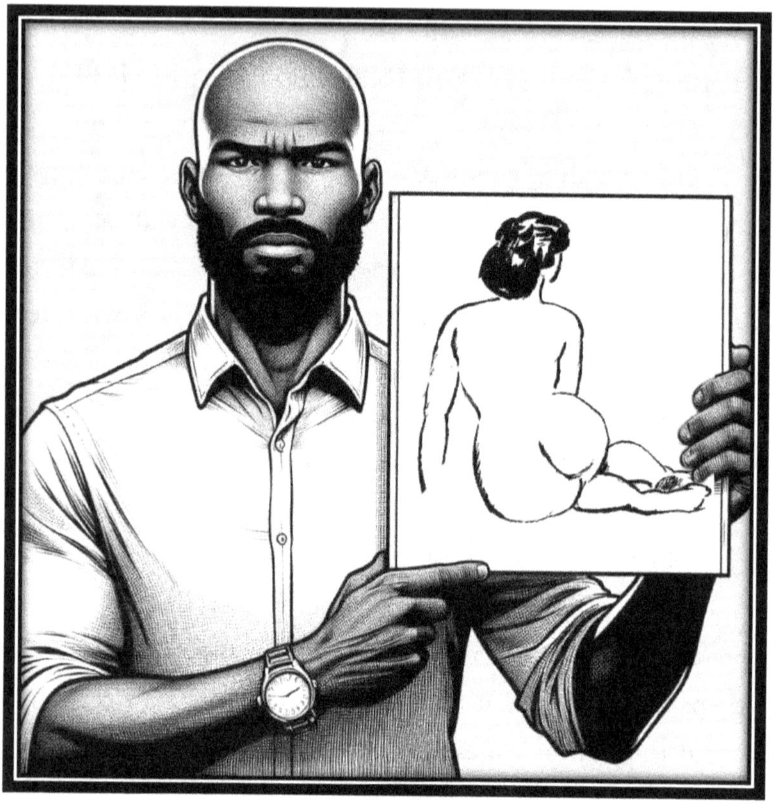

D

iving right into what needs to be said first.

To be clear, if a guy persists in fucking a woman anally, even after she has refused, it is rape, no matter how you look at it. No means, no period. Too many times, I hear women putting their trust in a man and end up being betrayed. Either forcefully or by shoving their cock in the woman's ass without permission or a warning.

Below is how I feel about a person being forced or coerced into anal sex. (being politically correct)

Whoever does this to another person does not deserve to be with a person (P-Di--y) ever again. In fact, like the Monopoly game, just send that asshole straight to prison without bail so he can get his ass repeatedly raped. Just so he can know what it is like when he says no to Bubba and gets fucked in his ass forcefully with no lube or spit on his cock. I will openly admit right now that I would like to watch something like that.

Just imagine visiting a prison and being in the audience to watch a convicted child molester, abductor, physical abuser, or human trafficker being treated like the crime they committed. Yeah, I said it, and I stand by it. On the lighter side, I am turned off when a woman tells me she has not tried something before and has already decided that she is unwilling to try or consider it.

A suitable example would be anal sex. For some women, their upbringing or school ministry forbids anal sex. Alternatively, they may have endured a terrible encounter with some impatient asshole whose cock was too thick or big and did not use lubricant to prepare her. At this point, do you agree with me, and have you experienced anything similar? I am so sorry, ok?

Before I say what, I am about to say. Guys who love anal sex will know precisely what I am talking about. When she is in the doggy-style position, her asshole is staring at me. I swear it is challenging to stay focused fucking her pussy when there is another hole so close to the one my cock is in.

When I have been with someone who has already made it clear it is a one-way exit, I must not look down just so I am not distracted.

In fact, I won't assume I can sneak my thumb in her ass, either. For the hell of it, let us just say I tried anyway; from that point on, she will be uncomfortable and tense up. Plus, I have lost her trust and the opportunity to change her mind, and believe me, I don't want to blow my chance over a lack of patience.

The best response a woman can give me when discussing anal sex is that she is never tried it and would like to. I am confident she has been asked does she likes anal at least once, regardless of age. "Building trust is crucial when initially forming meaningful connections with someone."

Unfortunately, for most men, it is a numbers game. How many can they fucked? I am no saint; I used to be one of those guys years ago, but after I realized how comfortable a woman becomes by taking my time, I earned their trust.

Listen up, men; if you don't care about who you are fucking, then don't fuck them. Not once have I put my cock in a woman's ass, pussy, or mouth I did not have chemistry with. Men who choose to rush and fail to prepare the woman for anal sex set a negative example for any man who follows behind them. I will try to convince the woman that I am confident and different from the last man they fucked. That is why it is crucial for me again to get to know the woman first. Hopefully, she will relax and hopefully trust me.

I don't usually care how long it takes to fuck, as I want the person comfortable enough to want to fuck me.

LET ME JUST PUT THIS OUT THERE:

I don't date women who are not into anal sex. Personally, I lose interest in regular sex when anal is not an option. Like I said earlier, when she is in the doggie-style position, I am looking directly at her asshole. Just imagine you looking over your shoulder, not realizing you are staring at me while I am looking at your asshole and sweating not to poke it. Did you smile? If you dated me without having anal sex, I am sure you just had an aha moment, right? Real talk. Peace!

The Bathroom Window

Depending on what chapters you started reading, let me brief you on my childhood, okay?

Cecil: Also known as **(C)**

Bev: Also known as **(B)**

Samuel: Also known as **(S)**

(C) This is something I forgot to mention in the chapter called "Bio Father" I just wanted to let you know at this very second while typing this for you to listen to, I started crying. Yes, real men "cry". I am crying because I wish I could have met my biological father before he passed away. I have many unanswered questions about my height, lack of hair, and medical condition, because I was born with a heart murmur. Stop!! Do not Google or Bing it because I will explain it now and save you time.

HEART MURMUR EXPLAINED:

When your heart beats, it pumps blood through a series of open and closed valves to allow the blood to flow in the right direction. As the valves close, they create two distinct sounds, commonly described as "lub" and "dub." However, if the sound of blood flowing through the heart produces a whooshing or swishing noise, it is known as a heart murmur.

This indicates that the blood is not flowing smoothly across the heart valves, suggesting a potential heart function issue. It is important to note that heart murmurs can also be present in individuals without any underlying heart problems, known as "innocent," heart murmurs. Here it is 10/18/2024 it still scares me sometime when my heart beats quickly then eventually calm down.

I will say oh no, is it my time to go? If by chance you are asking yourself, what the hell does my heart murmur has to do with this chapter? My answer is really simple, absolutely nothing but more information about me, that's all. Anyway, let us return to the reason why I called this the " Bathroom Window", shall we? I used to sneak out of my mom's house and into the backyard, only to look through the bathroom window. Even as I write this chapter, I am dumbfounded about where the idea originated.

Anyway, my motivation for sneaking out of the house and peering through the bathroom window is that I enjoy seeing people use our bathroom while urinating or shitting. You don't realize how difficult it is not to laugh while someone is taking a shit. They would make these crazy faces, enlarge their eyes, and then take a long breath, which piqued my interest even more. Being constipated recently helped me understand why they were making that straining face. The expression resembled that of someone blowing a trumpet. People were using our bathroom while having sex gets my cock hard even to this day. What haunts me is that this act also turned me into who I am today, older and confused.

Let me explain how I discovered what was going on in our bathroom. I made damn sure the bathroom window was open with the shades pulled back whenever we had grown-ups as guests. And I would sit at the dining room table, pretending to be playing cards. After a few minutes, one would announce that they needed to use the restroom, which was usually female, and their partner would promptly accompany her into the bathroom.

After watching this behavior numerous times, I became inquisitive. I wondered why they had to use the restroom at the same time. So, out of curiosity, I put two and two together.

One evening, the cheating couple I wrote about in "Dear Momma Chapter" returned to my mother's house. I was at the dining room table this time, playing cards as usual. I patiently waited for **one of them to say,**

(S)"I need to use the bathroom," I knew it was time to make my move. I got up, sneaked out of the back door, entered the backyard, and kneeled by the bathroom window. My intention was to observe the individuals in the bathroom and their activities. It did not matter which one said,

(B)"I'm going to use the bathroom,"

(C)because the person who said it knew they needed to go, and the other would soon follow suit. Upon reflection, I realized that the woman typically initiated the conversation because it was at her friend's house, who also happened to be my mother. The woman would walk in and close the door, leaving it unlocked.

She would then close the toilet lid, sit, and wait for the door to reopen. The man would walk inside, close the door behind him, and lock it. Remember that I am still watching everything from the bathroom window, unsure what will happen next.

At one point, I wondered whether they intended to discuss what they were doing in my mom's bathroom while she was present, but that wasn't the case. While the female sat down, the male stood before her, staring down.

Next, the female would glance up at the man before lowering her eyes to his crotch. I am confident they did not go into my mom's bathroom just to talk, but something else is about to happen.

She unzipped his pants and reached inside, pulling out something that resembled an elephant trunk. If I had only been kneeling and listening, I would have wondered what was happening in my mom's bathroom. His elephant trunk wasn't hard while she massaged it with the lotion she placed in her hands. It was apparent that he enjoyed having her rub his elephant trunk.

The minute he became aroused, she wiped the lotion off and placed it in her mouth. Reflecting again, I wonder how she got that into her mouth with the girth he had.

Anyway, she did not do that for long because he was making some kind of noise, and I was wondering why, not knowing if he was having a heart attack or what. A friend of mine died from a heart attack, so I was familiar with the look on his face. The woman sitting on the toilet did not look concerned, so I did not either.

She kept on sucking on it until he was forced to put his hand on the wall behind her to keep from falling. Suddenly, some white liquid from his trunk splattered all over her face, and all she could do was smile and stare at him.

To give you an idea of how amazing she must have been at sucking on his trunk, his eyes rolled back in his head, like Linda Blair in The Exorcist. In fact, he was mumbling things I had never heard before as if Satan had entered his body. Soon after the white fluid gushed from his trunk, he bent over and kissed her. The white goo that remained on her face after he kissed her made me want to vomit. When this happened, I had not even masturbated yet, so I wasn't sure what the white goo was that shot out of his trunk.

(S)Cecil?

(C)Yes, what's up?

(S)Let me narrate some of this story.

(C)Well, then go ahead. I need to take a deuce anyway.

(S)That's way too much information for me and the listener.

(C)Well?

(S) Alright! So, he stood back, said thank you, and tucked his trunk into his pants. He opened the door, walked out, and returned to the living room. The woman was still sitting there, wiping her face with a napkin from her purse.

Immediately, she reached into her purse, took out some lipstick, and reapplied it to her lips. She stood up, wiped her chin, and looked in the mirror before opening the door and walking out. Wait! That bitch is straight up NASTY! She didn't brush her teeth or use her mouth wash! Sorry listener, I'll continue. All She had to was do was look into the medicine cabinet!

(C)I digress! But you are absolutely right! So, continue.

(S) After I, meaning Cecil... stood there and watched everything, it was time for me to slowly return to the living room. I sat down and began playing cards, pretending I did not watch them have sex. Here is a thought I would like to add: it is not a couple having sex if only the male is getting his cock sucked. My opinion. I already mentioned this in a chapter called "Selfish Mofos.

"The couple glanced at each other and me as if they knew something but were not saying anything. If either one of them is still alive today or happens to listen to this section of the chapter, they will know who the hell they are without saying their names.

(C) Now is the moment to reveal a secret I have kept hidden from everyone until 10/04/2024. I am back and thanks!

(S) Thank you, and I'll talk to you later.

(C) One of my sisters piqued my interest, and she wasn't aware of it. She and I were playing a game one day before she mentioned she needed to go to the restroom. Are you asking yourself,

(B) Cecil, no you did not, did you?

(C)I am going to answer that question by saying yes, I did. I quickly stood up and walked around to the bathroom window. We lived in a quiet neighborhood, so I had to exercise caution when wandering around this time due to the dried leaves on the ground. And, with the bathroom window open as usual, I did not want her to hear me. I saw that the light was on, and the window was still open, so I slowly moved closer. I be damned, I stepped on a dry leaf as I approached the window, creating a loud cracking noise. She looked towards the window and almost caught me.

Before I ducked down, I knew she had heard something, so I remained in that position for two or three minutes. When I finally thought it was safe to look through the bathroom window again, I stood up and realized she had closed it and the shower curtain. As you know, I was tremendously upset but relieved that I had not been seen. That was the last time I attempted it, and this is the first and last time I will discuss this story. Peace!

NOT

AH

FUCKING

THANG!

The German Lady

I t's up to you, the reader, to decide if this is the most repulsive thing you have ever heard of someone doing, unfazed by feces, during a sexual encounter.

READ WITH AN EMPTY STOMACH. YOU HAVE BEEN WARNED.

Excuse me, but sometimes, I tend to jump straight to the exciting part. Please wait while I explain how I first met Susanne, The German Lady. Thanks for your patience. Most women I have met—past and present—were found online. To bring this up, when I was living in San Diego, I had the opportunity to meet a white woman named Susanne, who was originally from Germany. I asked her about her dating preferences, and she told me she exclusively dated black men. She elaborated a bit more by stating that black men treated her so much better than white men.

Here it is, March 10, 2024: I continue to see and hear about this from time to time, and it never ceases to amaze me why white men don't treat their women better. Wait, mutha fuckas, before you say anything about black men, keep in mind this is what I hear all the time from white women that have either dated or spoken to casually, Okey? I thought Susanne was vague, so I asked her if she could be more specific as to why she felt that way.

She hesitated, looked away, then looked back at me and smiled. I said, "I'm curious why you feel that way about white men when you're white as a 100-watt lightbulb yourself." I don't know where the hell that came from when I said it, but we laughed hysterically. She looked at me dead in the eyes. I wasn't expecting this answer. She said, "They fuck me better." I had a look of shock on my face. She asked me what was wrong. All I could say was, "Don't be shy now; continue."

The conversation continued with Susanne saying, "Okay, Cecil, it's like this: Black men fuck me with greater passion than white men." I prefer rough sex with a little bit of passion mixed in. I urged her to clarify her desire for rough sex. She stated, "I enjoyed the sensation of hands wrapped around my throat firmly, restraints, and a slap on my ass during the sex." Susanne expressed her preference openly and honestly and appreciated it.

At that moment, my ears pricked up, like a dog's reaction to a dog whistle; in other words, I focused on what else she was about to explain.

Additionally, she stated, "I am uncomfortable when a man with whom I am about to fuck asks me about my preferences." I hope he will fuck me with absolute authority by sticking his cock in any hole he desires without regard for my input. Wait!! Suppose you are a woman reading what I just wrote and like being treated like this. In that case, it is perfectly okay with the right man who understands your darkest, twisted secret.

Side note: Do not keep this burning desire to yourself; share it with your potential partner.

Otherwise, you are denying yourself the pleasure you are desperately wanting, right? Here is my last side note: You will be looked at as if you are crazy, but don't let that stop you from expressing your desires. It is not your fault he is not relatable. Susanne continued by saying, "It makes me uncomfortable when white males ask me what I want from them sexually, and that's something that typically happens with white men."

"I appreciate a confident man who knows precisely what he wants from me," Susanne continued. "I like a man who says what he wants and doesn't give me a choice. When I say, "Take me," I don't mean to rape me; instead, I want to simply submit and do whatever commands that are expected.

That's why, when it comes to black men, I am immediately turned on and aware of my role based on how they treat me when we initially meet one another. I was completely stunned by what she said next.

Additionally, Susanne said: I find that being around black men makes me feel completely submissive, as I dislike being in charge in the "bedroom". No doubt I have added another fuck friend to the stable of women I know already. It is not like I don't already have enough fuck friends, right Susanne called one day and wanted me to come over and fuck her, as I always do.

Given that I was already in my vehicle, her call came at the most convenient time. Reversing my direction, I made my way to her residence. The situation was different this time since she had already had a few drinks, and it was just two o'clock in the afternoon Eastern time. I was able to recognize the change in her speech because she was slurring her words when she said, "Come on in."

Okay, I will admit that occasionally, I like women who have had a few drinks. Because it lowers their inhibitions completely, enabling them to engage in sexual activity that they would shy away from without extensive conversation. This time, when I walked in, she was already nude, her panties on the carpet floor, and ready to be fucked.

I had not even shut and locked the door before she turned around and headed towards the bedroom. The moment she was near her bed, I placed one of my hands firmly against her back and pushed her down onto the bed, exactly where I wanted her. I needed to remove my clothes immediately because I did not want to waste time.

After removing my clothes, I stepped closer to the bed. The only thing that was going through my mind was fucking her; therefore, I did not want to offer her a kiss, talking, or being all lovey-dovey, if you know what I mean. I was playing with her pussy while she was sucking my cock, and then I pulled my cock out of her mouth and flipped her over like a cooked pancake so that she was face down and ass up.

Susanne had a nightstand beside the bed, and my favorite lube was inside. I quickly applied some of it to my cock's shaft. It was evident that I was going to fuck her in the ass, and she did not say anything. When I was ready, I positioned my cock and slid it into her ass. Because it felt incredible, I decided against cumming immediately. I kept putting my cock in and out of her ass repeatedly. While looking down at her asshole, I realized there was shit on my cock, fingers, hands, and sheets. You would think that would have stopped me, right? Bishop Bullwinkle's song, "Hell 2 Dah Naww Naww Naww," comes to mind.

The fact that I was having so much fun fucking her in her ass made it impossible for me to leave the bedroom, regardless of the shit that was all over the damn place. My mind then produced an idea: Why don't I use her sheets and blankets to clean off the shaft of my cock? I am very nasty and creative sometimes, so keep reading, and you will understand what I mean by that.

Grabbing a handful of her sheets in my hand, I continued to use them to clean off the shit from my cock till it was clean. If you happen to be wondering why, it is because every time I pulled my cock out of Susanne's ass, there was shit on my shaft and even my damn balls. I assume you are not eating anything right now, are you? I repeat, there was shit everywhere, but I made sure there was none where I was fucking her. When I finally shot a load of hot cum in her ass, I was wondering why she was motionless and wasn't saying anything the entire time. Let me explain how the universe looks out for me.

Right now, I will give you a visual so you can understand exactly where I am going with this. Susanne must have fallen asleep at some point because I was completely unaware that she had fallen asleep while I was fucking her in the ass. I must assume the midday alcohol she consumed knocked her out. For some reason unknown to me then, I decided to take my clothing to the bathroom with me, which was a good decision. And here is why...Before leaving the bedroom, I looked at Susanne, who was snoring like a freight train with shit all over her ass and sheets. Consequently, I made my way straight into her bathroom. Her house's layout allowed me to walk directly from the bedroom door into her bathroom, just a few steps away. There was absolutely no reason to look around the corner into the living room because her daughter was still at school, so I thought.

While I was in the bathroom washing up from having messy anal sex with Suzanne, I wasn't aware her fifteen-year-old daughter was sitting on the couch in the living room. I can't express my concerns about what was going through her mind. I am confident I can't understand her daughter's facial expression either. But I can say, "Thank goodness I walked out of that bathroom fully clothed. Remember how I mentioned that the universe is always looking out for me?

That's why I took my clothes to the bathroom instead of washing up and returning to the bedroom. Anyway, when I realized she was in the living room just before I was about to leave, I could not help but look away out of embarrassment.

As I walked past her, I could see the disgust and anger on her face while her mother still sleeping with her face down and her ass up. The door to the bedroom was wide open, and there was shit everywhere. As for me, I will end this chapter called "The German Lady," or unfortunate circumstance after another, whichever you prefer. Peace!

What Did I Learn from This?
"Shit Is Grainy"

(Going In and Out Without Cleaning Up Will Scratch Your Shaft)

It took me a month before considering having sex again... In fact, I had scabs on my cock for about another month afterwards. So, ladies if you wouldn't mind taking a shit before having anal sex and just know this could easily happen to your partner. It's something I would not wish upon anyone. That's why my preference is the pussy on most occasions.

Do you blame me?

The Intoxicated Neighbor

My mother, Beatrice Hicks, who I discussed in the chapter "Dear Momma, Beatrice Hicks," would attend a sewing class in the neighborhood every Tuesday, like clockwork, because that was her regular routine.

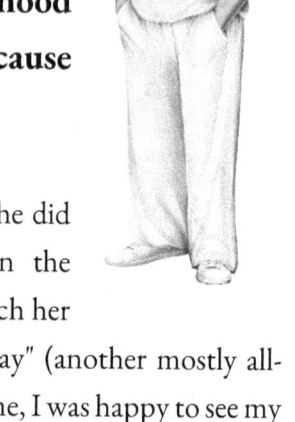

Before she discovered sewing, all she did was wake up in the morning, turn on the television, sit in her favorite chair, and watch her favorite show, "Young and Restless," all day" (another mostly all-white cast) before cooking dinner. Believe me, I was happy to see my mom get out of the house occasionally.

After my dad passed away, she became a hermit. While my mother was attending sewing classes, I realized I could be by myself and do whatever I pleased. To be honest, all I did most of the time was masturbate and watch whatever I wanted on television. I am willing to bet that, for a moment, you, the reader, believed I was alluding to drugs or women.

Am I right? For two months someone would pick up Mama and take her to sewing classes on Tuesdays. I am briefing you for a specific reason: the universe operates in mysterious ways. By now, you, the reader, will understand what I will reveal next.

Therefore, the universe also knew ahead of time to prevent something devious from happening. Here is why I say this, one evening, momma decided to skip sewing class because she wasn't feeling well, even though there were no symptoms of illness. The telephone rang while I was sitting in the living room, and Mom answered it. Her designated pick-up person informed her that she could no longer pick her up for sewing classes. When the person on the phone asked how she was feeling, Mom said: I'm not feeling well this evening for some reason, okay?

So, the timing was perfect. Shortly after hanging up the phone, our doorbell rang, the only night my mom wasn't feeling well. We both knew it wasn't the person she hung the phone with, which made us hesitant to respond.

If only you could have seen my mother and me pretending to be alone while our fingers were on our lips. Someone knocked again, but this time, it was a little louder.

Because I am the man in the house, I eventually said in a firm voice, "Who is it? I could not understand the person's words through the tightly closed, locked door. I asked again without looking out the window, "WHO IS IT!!

Well, damn, it was Shameka, our neighbor, who rang the doorbell. She has never knocked on our door so late for anything for as long as we have known her. I wanted to ensure my mom was okay with me opening the door at that hour of the night.

I wish you could have seen my mom shrugging her shoulder as if she were not sure what to do. My mom was no help with what to do in this situation, so I finally opened the door. I discovered my neighbor drunk as hell, like a fat man who hadn't bathed in two months, had a gut hanging five inches over his belt, mullet hair, was scratching his ass with his left hand, and was wearing a wife-beater T-shirt at an all-you-can-drink local bar in the neighborhood.

She was slurring her words while trying to open our front door, indicating how drunk this bitch was.

I wish you could have seen her stumbling around our house and holding our chairs to avoid falling after I let her in. I thank the universe that our neighbor weighed about 110 pounds while soaking wet.

With her stumbling around, the house would have looked like a crime scene after a burglary. Shameka was so drunk my mom had to help her get back home. Otherwise, I would have assisted her home rather than with my mom. By the way, This is my first time telling this story.

KEEP READING:

I am about to admit something embarrassing. Please remember that I was around seventeen years old when this happened. I will honestly admit that if I had been home alone when our neighbor knocked on our door, I would have absolutely wanted to see her naked.

That same evening, while stumbling around in our home, she looked directly at me and said she wasn't wearing panties or a bra. I am not sure why she blurted it out but imagine being a seventeen-year-old molested boy and having an intoxicated M.I.L.F. tell you something like that.

Remember what I said earlier, something about the universe?

WELL!!!

The universe knew ahead of time that my black ass would not have been able to contain myself, ... if I had been alone with an intoxicated woman with no bra and panties on, while drunk as a skunk in the middle of the jungle!! Considering the chaos I witnessed at my mom's house, I am sure that I would have tongue-kissed her, and she would have regurgitated in my mouth due to how drunk she was.

I would have sent the woman home with saliva dripping down her leg as if a huge, great Dane had licked her pussy. The adults in my family told me that a woman can become pregnant by licking a woman's pussy. After hearing this, the only thought that crossed my mind was that I hoped my actions would not result in her becoming pregnant. Also, imagine being next door, hoping her stomach does not grow.

Because I would have had to confess what I had done, and the adults would have laughed at me. I also would have been confessing something I did not have to.

And if the police had been involved, they obviously would have had evidence still leaking out of her pussy. Honestly!! Do you think at the age I was when this happened, I would have known she needed to shower or be cleaned up before the investigators and the medical professionals arrived? If they had shown up, all they would have had to do was turn off the lights, scan her clothes with a black light, then cotton-swab her entire body!!

I know for a fact, they would have discovered enough evidence against me because, my saliva would have been all over her clothes, hair, top lip, and asshole, and, maybe even her toes, fuck it!! I most certainly would have gone to jail if my mom were not home that evening, RIGHT?? Like I have said in a different chapter, I know an angel is watching over me, especially in this situation.

AS OF 09/02/2024,

I continue to feel aroused when I am around a drunk ass woman for an unknown reason. Wait, there is one reason now that I can think of, and that is because a drunken woman is more vulnerable than a sober woman. Besides, they won't remember what happened anyway. Peace!

The Mall

Starring Raven

W hat I am about to tell you happened over 40 years ago with a girl named Raven. The only way I could remember this may have been from Lion's Mane, which I have been taking.

(Audiobook Version)
Characters in this chapter are:

Raven – main person throughout
Cecil – main person throughout
Joyce (housekeeper)

Cecil: This all relates to me being perverted for a long time. When I was around 20 years old, I messaged a girl from the "Reader" magazine dating section in San Diego, California. We messaged each other for a couple of weeks and then decided to meet somewhere she felt comfortable. Back then, the dating section of The Reader, a local magazine, did not feature photos alongside their profiles. When meeting someone, you base it on the information in their bio, then eventually call and talk to them. Have you ever spoken to someone on the phone for the first time, and their voice sounded seductive and sexy?

The first time I called one of the profiles I was interested in, I hung up because I thought I messed up and dialed one of those nine hundred numbers, for a sex chat by mistake. WAIT! Just a moment, don't you dare say to yourself, how hard up for sex do you have to be to call one of those nine hundred numbers, huh? Just for the sake of answering that question you are pondering in your head, the answer is, I have never called one, period!!

So, I immediately called back, and the same voice that had answered the first time responded again. While embarrassed, I apologized and asked if my number had appeared when I called seconds prior.

Raven: yes. I recognized the number that appeared again, and that's why I picked up the phone both times you called.

Cecil: I apologized because I thought I had called the wrong number the first time.

Raven: Don't worry about it, I hear that all the time and it's okay.

Cecil: She laughed and accepted my apology, and I continued to get to know her. Her personality over the phone was unique, with some hidden darkness, because she had a carefree attitude and a twisted sense of humor. This woman and I had much in common, more than most girls my age, and the fact that she also grew up in a dysfunctional family made her relatable. When I heard her name in a personal dating message, I asked, which parent chose Raven as her name?

Raven: It was my mother.

Raven also mentioned: Joyce, our housekeeper, eventually provided the information I desperately needed and told me why my mother chose to name me Raven. Cecil, you have to understand there were no secrets in our home and Joyce witnessed everything that transpired between my parents. And that was just before my father packed up and left. Raven's voice trembled as she recounted the housekeeper's story, revealing a deep sadness.

Joyce, the housekeeper, told Raven: Your father, Larry, left your mother while she was nine months pregnant and right after her water broke. Just before that happened, I could not understand why your father was taking his clothes out of the dresser and closet and packing his suitcases.

Joyce: I watched Larry curiously, putting the packed suitcases near the bedroom door while your mom was cooking dinner downstairs. Shortly afterward, I watched your father walk downstairs while hiding the suitcases in the downstairs closet before entering the kitchen.

Joyce: Larry looked directly at me, covered his lips with one finger to signal hush, and said, "Don't tell my wife anything right now because it's a surprise. As we walked towards the kitchen, your mom, Jayla, suddenly placed her hand on her stomach, and a liquid ran down her leg and onto the floor. I didn't know what to do or say about what I just witnessed.

All I could remember was standing there shocked while Larry ran back up the stairs to the bedroom. As your mother screamed in fear for Larry, Larry ran back down the stairs with another small suitcase he had packed.

Cecil: Joyce and Jayla (the mom), watched in disbelief as Larry walked out the door without saying goodbye.

Joyce said: That asshole did not even turn around just before he closed the door.

Cecil: Joyce called 911 while she watched Jayla scream in pain while they waited for the ambulance. I must give flowers to any woman who had their child naturally. Just saying!

Just before the ambulance arrived, her mom heard a loud pecking noise from outside the living room window, and a Raven was looking directly at her. It was as if the Raven was comforting them during a scary moment in their lives.

As I Reflect, it was evident to Jayla that she should call her unborn daughter Raven. Personally, her story brought me to tears and drew me in like nothing I had heard before. Did you just say, aww? Raven told me that her mother died on a table right after she gave birth.

She spoke most of the time, and I listened intently to everything she had to say. Additionally, she mentioned growing up in five different foster homes while being passed around like a blunt by the men who would visit occasionally.

Raven witnessed more than I care to write about in this chapter. As a young girl, she was exposed to really hard stuff that boys won't experience. By the way, if any or some of what I write about in this chapter has happened to you, I want to apologize. Because I understand exactly what you are going through, "TRUST ME" As you are aware, I harbor my own personal demons, and I have not allowed those demons to derail me from drafting this book. This is my way of taking my life back.

PLEASE CONTINUE.

Most of the men who visited the foster home she lived in were recovering addicts or alcoholics. Those same men would insist she had a few drinks with them, not knowing what drinking alcohol would do to her mental state of mind. Let us just put it this way: they kept insisting she drink with them until she passed out. Over the years, she remembers passing out a few times and waking up naked and disoriented. Does this remind you of someone, and what has been happening lately?

In some instances, Raven wakes up in houses with more than a few people standing over her, masturbating, while looking down at her face and unclothed body. Unfortunately, there were times she could not take a shit because it was so painful. After hearing one horrific story after another, I asked her to stop. I did not ask her to stop because I did not want to listen, but only because I could hear her mood change drastically.

Raven: Thanks for allowing Cecil to discuss this sad story with you.

Cecil: Nevertheless, before calling someone crazy or insane and having no idea what that person has been through, this story should remind you that it could happen to anyone. I personally have no idea what it is like to grow up in a foster home and never see your parents again. As she grew older, some of her so-called friends and family members from her foster homes molested her, making her story relatable. I am sorry that this is a tragic part of the story, but it indicates how people become who they are sometimes.

I recognized that Raven had encountered considerable difficulties, and I was committed to not adding to her struggles or trauma. Our countless conversations over the following months pulled me closer to her. She also mentioned she feared men and decided to take a chance with me. I felt honored and humbled; she trusted me enough to admit any of it. I hope you have remembered that Raven and I have not met and only conversed on the phone. Finally, Raven wanted to meet, and I was excited. Raven had a full-time job and a house in a nice, upscale neighborhood. When I decided to pick her up, I did not want to go inside because I wanted her to trust me. She was stunningly unique when she came out the door, with cocoa brown skin and an Afro pick with the Black Power sign in her hair.

I was extremely fortunate, given that we had never exchanged photos or any other means of knowing each other's appearance. When she opened my door and started to sit down, I saw the laced underwear she had on, and I acted as if I didn't see them. I think she did it on purpose and I wasn't sure and did not mention it.

While driving, I sensed something unsettling about her that I couldn't quite pinpoint at that moment. Months of conversation, she failed to mention something that messed my head up in a good way. She told me that she is a nudist and an exhibitionist and typically does not wear clothes unless it is necessary. Because I did not know what a nudist or an exhibitionist was at the time, I used Yahoo to search for what it meant while I was waiting for the light to turn green. Once I understood the meaning of both terms, my curiosity grew even more.

And when you combine being a nudist and an exhibitionist, it makes me feel like I hit the jackpot. After sharing so much about herself with me,

Raven stopped and asked me: What about YOUR fantasies, Cecil?

Cecil: I must have turned purple and embarrassed to answer her question, fearing she would not want to talk to me anymore. She asked me several times before I felt comfortable suggesting a better idea. I asked if she wanted to go to the mall with me, and she agreed it was okay. I wanted to take her somewhere I knew other people would be so she would not feel uncomfortable.

As Raven was walking next to me, she noticed that I kept looking up at the stairs that would take people to the second level. I was unaware that I was acting that way, and she knew why I was doing it. After a few times of watching women walk up the stairs, she smiled as if she understood what my kink was. She was able to understand my kink because she's an exhibitionist herself. After an hour of being together,

Raven: looked over at me and said: Take me home and pick me up later this evening.

Cecil: After an hour, I said to myself, "Damn!!, what just happened?" All sorts of thoughts raced through my mind, leading me to believe I messed up and pushed her away. Before she opened the door,

Raven gave me a big hug and said: Pick me up later this evening around seven o-clock and don't be late, because I have a surprise for you.

Cecil: I can assume that was a good sign, right? Just before evening, she called and asked me to take her to one of Orlando's busiest malls, which had stairs on a Saturday. I hung up the phone and picked her up five minutes before seven.

Was I excited? Of course I was, what do you think?? I still didn't know what she had in mind and wasn't planning to ask, either!! Wait!! I did, sort of had an idea, but I did not want to assume anything because, as you know or have heard, assuming can make an ass out of you and me.

While she walked towards my car, it seemed as if she was walking in slow motion. Her attire was entirely different than when I picked her up earlier. She wore a cute little black dress with lace around the bottom and no underwear. Suppose you are wondering how I knew she had no underwear on. In that case, while I was looking through the front windshield, she purposefully dropped her keys in front of my car, allowing me to see exactly what she wanted me to see.

Are you aware of how sexy it is to pretend neither one of us know what the other is thinking? These days, we might refer to this as role-playing, but in the past, it was simply known as teasing. While on the way to the mall, we had a great time getting to know one another. While driving, I was sure that neither of us wanted to talk about our past experiences relating to our family, especially while having a good time together. After an hour's drive, we finally arrived at the mall. It was busier than usual, so I had to park far away. I chose not to get out of the car immediately because I asked if Raven was considering performing an exhibition act for me.

Raven: I am as excited about this as you are because no one has ever asked me, nor have I ever done this before for anyone.

Cecil: Considering everything I mentioned earlier in this chapter I had some reassurances; and started walking towards the mall. As the cars passed, searching for a parking spot, I occasionally glanced around and noticed people staring at her. One car nearly collided with the vehicle in front of him due to the driver not paying attention.

Watching her walk towards my car made me burst out laughing. Just before the door opened to the mall, I asked her to face me, and she reassured me with a smile and

Raven: I'm definitely ready.

Cecil: When the door to the mall automatically opened, I asked her to walk ahead of me and pretended I did not know her.

Raven: Time out for a moment. I need you to understand what it is like to walk ahead of Cecil. Imagine us as a married couple that has been together for over 10 years, could not have children, and gave up trying. And after years of disappointment, arguments, crying, sleepless nights, and failed fertility tests, the results finally show I am pregnant. We prayed for a healthy child, and we were told our child is healthy during our visit to the pediatrician's office.

Cecil: I hope you can imagine how excited I was that I found someone who understood me completely and wanted to fulfill my imagination. I wanted her to walk ahead of me because it allowed me to watch her hips move. And since we were role-playing, I had to stay far behind her while watching people's reactions.

The intriguing part was that other women also observed her and whispered among themselves. Even then, I had confidence in my relationship with her, and it did not bother me that other people were looking at her.

I am unsure why someone checking out my girlfriend did not faze me, and I have never been a jealous person. At the time, my attitude was that if you were courteous and not disrespectful, you could check her out as much as you wanted, knowing that I was the one who was fucking her.

It is a compliment when someone looks at your significant other, or at least that's how you should always feel. She knew that I was a safe distance behind her to bend over, so I took watched to ensure that nothing inappropriate happened.

Nevertheless, it was turning me on. The stairs were ahead of us, and people sat on benches at the bottom. It was the perfect time for her to walk up the stairs in that dress I mentioned earlier with no underwear. As she proceeded up the stairs, I was patiently waiting and watching others who were nearby. I suppose I wasn't the only individual, or more accurately, a pervert, who eagerly awaited the arrival of women walking up the stairs. Whenever a woman walks up the stairs wearing a dress, others try to avoid looking up. It always made me laugh. Everyone around the stairs started looking up as she approached the first level. A few people happened to look up and start talking among themselves in shock, as they could clearly see her kitty cat up close. Some people would glance down, immediately avert their gaze, and blush.

Raven seemed to have done this before; she never looked down to see who was looking, which surprised me. When she reached the second level, a crowd of young men and women stared up at her. Most people who looked up at her were white men, while walking with their wives or girlfriends.

In all honesty, it did nothing for me to watch someone I know walking up the stairs; it was more about watching others watching her walk up the stairs.

Eventually, I walked up to the second floor to walk with her while she waited, and we continued to the other side of the mall so that she could walk down the stairs. A walked ahead of her again, down the stairs, and waited at the bottom. People must have been talking about her before she started walking down the stairs, as the same group of men that were on the opposite side when she was walking up was now waiting for her to come down.

Raven: It was liberating for me to be with someone who wasn't jealous. You helped me to overcome my fears, and I'll use you as an example of what it means to be someone's soulmate. Try this at least once if you are in a relationship with someone who is adventurous. And especially if you have been together for a while and need to spice things up. Just select a weekend, choose a mall, explore the area, and then decide together. What Raven said is important because you are doing something together. In addition, choose a mall more than an hour away to avoid running into someone you know. I am sure you don't want your family, friends, and especially coworkers to know all your business—or, should I say, see all your business?

Update: I heard from her again on Facebook, and she told me she was now married with three grandkids. It was a pleasure to reconnect with her, and she informed me that my influence had transformed her life, and that it played a major role in meeting her husband. She wrote to me again and said that she and her husband have five kids together. It was good to hear from her again; she also changed my life. And that was the last time I heard from her. Peace!

The Moaner from the Club

I used to love going to this one place in Altamonte Springs, Florida, called the Why Not Lounge before it closed.

I recently checked the ratings on Google, which, despite being closed, had many one-to-three-star ratings. I should have anticipated its closure, as the Why Not Lounge was a hole in the wall. Despite the inadequate service and cleanliness issues, I loved going there regardless. I can't even begin to reminisce about the amount of PUSSY I had pulled out of there.

Honestly, it wasn't a lot of women because I was shy; in other words, I lacked confidence back then. On Wednesday nights, they had a comedy, which is fun to watch.

The bands they brought in always played a variety of music to dance to. **On 10/06/2024** I am rewriting this book and chapter, I will add this part you are about to read, okay? I was as tall as an oak tree and lacked confidence when the place appeared to be packed with honey's all over the place and most of them were attractive. If one of the ladies walked over to me, I would stutter and would not look them directly in the eyes. In many ways, I am glad I did not have the confidence; otherwise, I would have more than a couple of kids, if you know what I mean. I am not sure if you know this unless you have been there. Why Not was a well-known place to find someone to have sex with the first night.

Now that I have taken you on a nostalgic journey let us revisit the reasons behind the title of this chapter, "The Moaner." One evening, I was in Why Not Lounge with my girlfriend Rachel, and there was a white woman on the other side of the bar boldly staring at me while I was on the dancefloor. She was staring at me intently, so I responded in return with a nod of my head and a smile.

Another song came on, and Rachel and I remained on the dancefloor, and that was when The Moaner decided to dance also. The Moaner was only a few couples away from Racheal and me this time. The Moaner's stares were intense, like she was fucking me with eyes if that makes sense. Do you know how complicated it is trying to be respectful while being flirted with?

Let me just say it was challenging to maintain my composure and not have to explain myself. While Rachel was at my side watching people on the dance floor and waiting for a song we liked. Occasionally, I would make it known I saw her with a smile and a head nod. That evening ends with my girlfriend leaving together. Three weeks later, I decided to head out to a club called Backstage Billiards International Drive, located inside a hotel.

That evening, Rachel was at work. As I sat at the bar, glancing around the room, I saw the same woman staring at me from the Why Not Lounge. I could not believe she was here alone, like myself. She must have seen the surprised look on my face that I was downplaying. When I finally realized it was her, I looked back in her direction, and she was gone. I thought I missed my opportunity or that someone looked like her.

The next thing I knew, she tapped my shoulder, wanting to sit, beside me. She boldly introduced herself to me; I usually don't like aggressive women. I offered her a seat next to mine, and we spent the rest of the evening getting to know each other before leaving to have breakfast. After breakfast, Lillia (the Moaner) followed me to my car to chill a bit longer. Women always have an idea if they want to fuck a man or not. Allow me to say this another way: Women always know if a man she meets is fuckable or not.

I was trying to be politically correct suddenly. Go figure! It is us men who are not sure if he is fucking or not. So, while sitting in my car with Lillia, I broke all the rules and asked her to spend the night with me. She did not break her rule of not having sex on the first date, which she had set for herself, never mind the fact I was ready to have sex with her right then and there.

See what I just said? The first date, although not our first, marked our first meeting without Rachel accompanying me. We met a few more times after that, and the next thing you know, we were having incredible sex together. However, each time we had sex, the sound she made, I found slightly distracting while my dipstick was in her. Of course, over time, I learned how to adjust to her moaning; I knew she must be having fun with me, and I must be doing something right. Whenever I have been with someone who expresses pleasure in their own way (i.e., moan, scream, giggle, laugh) when they cum, I have learned to adjust my reaction. It is unfair of me to tell these women to stop, shut up, or even ask why they make a particular sound.

Any guy who expresses his negative thoughts on how a woman should express herself will make her uncomfortable the next time they meet. In fact, they should allow her to be herself. Also, if he mentions how she cums, she will shy away from cumming like that in the future. She will also be afraid to relax and enjoy herself thoroughly. I would never make a woman feel that she can't be herself, no matter how she cums. Of course, some women are so loud that they require me to cover their mouths with duct tape, and I am cool with that if she is. Honestly, there have been times I had to do just that because they were so loud.

That's what happens when you live in cheaply made apartments or condominiums. Sometimes, I.D.G.A.F. and will allow them to scream if necessary. Thankfully, my neighbors could distinguish between fucking and a situation that requires police intervention. I can't imagine the police conducting a wellness check.

I would have to explain to the police, "I'm just over here fucking and eating her pussy, and she was screaming and cumming." It would not be a good idea to say to the police, "If you don't believe me, allow me to eat and fuck your wife." Right? I am certain that's not going to fly over their heads without wanting to make sure I don't make it to the precinct. I can't always keep my hand over their mouth; I have other things to do with my hands and fingers that they will enjoy far more, so out comes the tape. A small piece works like a charm; they can cum and scream all they want. All I hear is "mmm" or "MMM"; it works incredibly well.

They can still be themselves and enjoy everything fully, knowing how loud they are.

My relationship with the loud Moaner Lillia lasted for a couple of years. When we first fucked, she wasn't into anal, but over time, she trusted me. I had made her comfortable enough, and she had really enjoyed it. She really was good for me as a person. Still, as usual, I fucked that relationship up because I had so many women I was trying to juggle at the same time. It really was ridiculous.

I saw six women, but only so many days in a week. Even though I was dating Rachel, I could maintain that many at once because I would space them out; I would see three or four women a week and slip in one more, depending on what was happening. I will repeat this: Read "My Gay Ass Cousin" and "Dear Momma." to understand why I was cheating on Rachel. After my divorce from one of my wives, I did not have my shit together. At one point, Lillia said something to me on the phone that set me off, and I retaliated by trying to make her feel like shit. Of course, after that episode, it was over and beyond reasonable recovery. I was frustrated and took it out on her. I really messed it up.

By then, it was too fucking late to take it all back—way too late. Years later, I still miss her. She was tall, too. I am six foot six, and she was around five foot eleven, a subtle change from the type of woman I usually sleep with. She was incredibly receptive to my advances. I still love her and regret the words I said, I am not perfect. I should have treated her with more respect because she had been there when I was at my lowest point. If I had not been an asshole, we could have remained friends, even nonsexual friends. I would have been okay with that.

If she happens to read this, I would like her to know that I think of her often, and I am so deeply sorry for the outcome of our friendship. Side Note: if someone has always been there for you in your darkest days, check your attitude before you mess it up. Peace!

The Pene

D iving right into the chapter with no chaser.

Some of you have asked, if I have ever felt jealous of another man having sex with either my girlfriend or one of my ex-wives while living a swinging lifestyle. There was only one time when I might have been envious. One of my wives had sex with two guys at the same time, and when she came out of the bedroom her knees were weak and shaking. I knew both men she had sex with were skilled when it comes to satisfying a woman. She could have chosen one of the men, which would have been fun, but she chose both.

Damn! I can't imagine how that felt for her, but I could tell it was a positive experience. One guy was in her pussy, while the other was in her ass. She enjoyed anal sex anyway, so the only way I could replicate it would be to reach around her back with a dildo and insert it into her ass and my cock into her kitty cat.

So, going back to my previous statement about being jealous, I decided to let go and remind myself that it was just sex and that she loved me. I never felt jealous again. Even if another man could make her squirt, I would tell them, "Damn, you are good," and give him a high five. Once you get past the idea that it is just sex, it can be rewarding for both of you, which you vanilla folks! would not understand. At my previous place of employment, men would inquire about my ability to observe men fucking my wife.

Usually, I respond by saying that my wife was already fucking and sucking men before we met. And if we divorce, she will eventually fuck someone else. So why not fuck someone while I am watching her and making sure, she is, okay? Sometimes, I don't need to be in the same room as her husband. This is when trust comes into full effect.

Anyone she chooses to be with, I know, won't harm her, and I am okay with that. I usually leave so she can enjoy herself and engage in an after-sex conversation or something similar. In most cases, it comes down to sex and friendship. So, it has never been an issue for me to watch my partner with another man because I am open-minded enough to let her have fun.

Why should I care if her heart belongs to me?

As I said before, it is just sex. My coworkers used to ask me, "Are you afraid your wife will leave you for another man who fucks her better?" Sometimes, people don't realize they are insulting me due to their own insecurity in the bedroom.

If one of my wives left me for another man because her sexual experience was different, our relationship would already be messed up. Seeing one of my wives having fun with someone does not bother me. In fact, I enjoy hearing about it on the way home from Tampa Florida. There was one guy with a small cock, my wife mentioned, half the size of mine, I recall being curious about how his small cock satisfied her, and I am seven and one-fourth inches (yes, I am claiming every inch), so there is no shame in my game.

Ladies, trust me, most men measure their cock but won't admit it. Men who don't measure their cock are those who already know they are larger than the average size that Google says. Yes, I even googled it, and it stated that five inches is average. One of my ex-wives told me she had the most fun with someone who knew how to use it. He also licked her pussy the way she preferred and performed various other positions she found pleasurable. She assured me that she would play with him more than once, and as Kevin Hart would say, "NO HOMO."

There are so many guys out there who believe that it all depends on the size of their cock, which is false. If you watch porn and the man has a significant tool, you will see that the pussy holds only half of the cock. When he pulls out, only half of her pussy juice covers the guy's shaft, leaving the other half dry. A woman's pussy can only hold a limited amount of cock; if the man is careless, he could easily harm her.

In any case, the distance between the pussy's lips and the pussy's back wall is only five to seven inches. I completely understand why some women desire or need a giant cock because they want their back wall pounded. There is this one internet porn star that can take a 14-inch dildo up her ass, and that's always interesting to jack off watching. I will repeat this; don't you dare judge me!! Now continue. They told me it sometimes hurt but felt so good. I understand their desires, but it won't come from me. If the woman I am with wants her back wall pounded, I will put a fist or a long-ass dildo up there. I understand that introducing toys, massage oils, and vibrators into the bedroom can be intimidating for some guys. Hell no, not me. I appreciate being asked if she could use them while I am fucking her; it aligns with my understanding of what pleases her. You will have a good time if she brings toys into the bed. I don't understand why toys intimidate men. To me, it only adds to the fun. Peace!

Thirty Clues

L ook, y'all, I won't waste your time with a long, drawn-out story about this chapter. So, let's jump out of the airplane without a parachute. For your information, I have a white man narrating parts of this chapter.

The characters in this chapter are:

Stright from the Audiobook

- Cecil Also known as: **(C)**
- Royal Also known as: **(R)**
- THE BITCH also known as: **(TB)**
- Narrator Also known as: **(N)**

(N) For your information, I have a white man narrating parts of this chapter. There is a specific group of people who tend to believe statements made by white individuals. That old-fashioned slavery mentality is still alive and thriving. Just keeping it real! Anyway, narrator, go ahead.

So, Cecil told me that you are reading this chapter because you are searching for a room to rent on Facebook, and it sounds like a good idea, right? Choosing the right environment and knowing what to expect is essential while in your search. Cecil tried twice and made some major mistakes along the way. He will explain the best way he can for the reason later in this chapter.

Wait, just a second Cecil, I have a question.

(C) Go Ahead!

(R) While you were searching for a room for rent, what was the ethnicity of those people?

(C) Mainly white people, why?

(R) Well, I guess people who look like you don't want a little extra money by renting out a room in their houses.

(C) I would have to agree because I must have met about 10 homeowners and messaged 20 different ads were all white folks like yourself! So, out of thirty there was one negro, and he wasn't born in united states and was from Africa. Anyway, continue narrating. Hold on a second! Did you say people who look like me?

(R) Yes, that is what I said!

(C) It's a good thing I already constructed this chapter with you in it. Anyway, continue narrating this chapter. Because I don't like your attitude.

(R) Personally Cecil, I don't give a damn if you don't like my attitude. So, I'll just continue reading your story and I would like it if you don't include me anywhere else in this book. I would appreciate it!

(C) Advantages of renting a room:

(R) Renting a room includes your room and sometimes utilities with Wi-Fi—usually between $600 and $900 a month—while sharing a bathroom. That's damn good when you are on a budget.

If you are lucky enough to find one without sharing a bathroom, it usually costs you between $850 and $975 monthly, including utilities. Furthermore, some come ready to move in with your bed and dresser. Whoever you rent from should have space to store your food in the fridge/freezer and dry goods in the cabinets. You may also have access to supplies such as pots and pans.

Common space should also be accessible in the living room and kitchen. It includes a pool and a backyard with a patio if they have one. In most cases, you have access to a washer and dryer. It is like having your home but sharing it with another person. That's if they mind their own damn business. The disadvantages include the possibility of living with someone who holds opposing political views, a situation Cecil experienced. This does not leave room for polite conversation and could lead to a horrible situation like his, which he explains shortly. Talk on the phone first and ask the questions Cecil has provided below one through thirty. Be absolutely certain you are a good fit for one another.

Because Cecil's experience renting a room for the first time was truly terrifying! It was like a scene straight out of Elm Street, Misery, 28 Days Later, The Shining, The Thing, Halloween part 1, and 2, Rosemary's Baby, The Thing, and that Classic Psycho movie all wrapped up in her five-foot two-inch white blonde-haired body! The Devil would not even try to reincarnate this BITCH if she was sent to hell!

I honestly feel she was and still is Linda Blair, from THE Exorcist in disguise, with vomiting coming from her mouth and smelling like a dozen year old boiled rotten eggs. Nevertheless, for years Cecil had lived alone, this time around, he wanted to save some money instead of renting an entire apartment.

Something made him look into renting a room in the Facebook Marketplace section. There were many places to choose from, and Cecil was overwhelmed, considering he had never done this sort of thing before.

So, listen carefully, otherwise he tried to warn you.

1) Ask if they have an area to park your vehicle (if you have a car)

2) Is it street parking or in a designated parking area?

3) Does that available room have separate air conditioning? (this is a crucial question because if it gets too cold or hot in your room, you should be able to control it)

4) If your room does not have air conditioning, what temperature is the thermostat normally set at during cold and hot weather?

5) Where can you store your food, and where is your space in the fridge and freezer?

6) Do you have access to the kitchen?

7) Will you be sharing a bathroom or have your own?

(C) Just a second. Sure, go ahead.

(N) While searching for a room on Facebook or anywhere else, that does not specify if you are sharing or do you have your own bathroom, please ask. Having your own bathroom should be your main concern. Because what if you decided to use the bathroom late at night and didn't turn on the lights? Then sit down on something unfamiliar to you. After turning on the lights, you discover it's one of the following:

(N) **shit, vomit, piss or all three!!**

(C) Now what are you going to say or do about it?

(N) I am certain you would be mad as a mother fucker, right?

(C) So, make sure you ask before you sign that lease Narrator?

(N) Yes, what's up now??

(C) Say mother fucker again for me.

(N) Umm, why?

(C) Because I am used to hearing mutha fucka, not mother fucker that's all. My bad!! Continue if you wouldn't mind.

8) Do they have access to the Internet?

9) Can you have a guest over? Are there overnight stays for the guests you invite?

10) How often do they have guests over? And if they are like the song by: Eddie Murphy, then this question is very important. Do they like having parties all the time? ..(Get it?)

11) Do you have storage access to the garage?

12) Do they have pets? If so, are they kept indoors or outdoors? Some of these mother fuckers that do not look like me have more than three got damn pets in their damn house. Wouldn't you want to know that shit before signing a lease?

13) What happens if you need to break the lease?

14) Laundry: What is the laundry situation? How often do you have access to that area?

15) Have they rented the room before? Because if it's their first time, there is a good chance they will be all up in your damn business every other day with some bullshit!!

16) Are you allowed to smoke natural herbs in the unit?

17) Do they have any health issues you should know about, and if so, what is it?

18) Is it a month-to-month or is there an extended period to rent the space?

19) What happens if you can't pay the rent? Are there any fees you should expect to pay?

(N) The questions above can save your life and your freedom. right Cecil?

(C) You got that right, continue because you are on a roll.

(N) The rooms he looked at were from $500 to $1000, including utilities and a parking space. This decision became apparent after Cecil read the advertisements and available photos. Cecil left messages with the ones he was interested in. Some called back, but most did not, which made him question his decision. Could you please explain why there is an ad for a room if there is no follow-up or acknowledgment of his messages? Cecil, if you wouldn't mind telling the rest of this story. I may come in a little later, but obviously, that's your call.

(C) I was desperate to leave my girlfriend's house at the time, and I won't talk about that in this chapter. Only one out of eight seemed interested in having me rent their room. It was a white woman who lived in Ocoee, and I am not about to mention her real name, so I'll call her Jane for now, hold on a second, I am being way to nice calling her Jane!

Let me think about this for a second. The Bitch, that works, as far as I am concerned! Why am I calling her the bitch? That's what you are asking yourself, I bet. Keep listening, and you may or may not understand why. She was calm when we chatted on the phone and texted each other. No alarm has gone off in my head so far. I decided not to ask the questions I mentioned earlier and was finally on my way to meet her at home the next day. When I arrived, the house was smaller than I imagined.

It was also one of those much older homes in an older area of Ocoee. Yes, that Ocoee, you heard or read about how racist it was and still is in some areas. I wasn't paying attention to the clutter when I entered the house. I sat on the couch for a few minutes, and she immediately started talking about politics. This was precisely the type of politics I was determined to avoid discussing with her. She kept trying, and I repeatedly told her that I don't discuss politics.

(N) That should have been your first clue not to sign the lease she had already started.

(C) I would strongly agree with you, but I asked her to show me around her place and the room she was renting.

(N) First, she showed you the kitchen,

(C) which was small but not a big deal.

I looked in her cabinets; they were full of food from back to front and up to the top.

(N) All the cabinets were overflowing, and there was no room for your food, RIGHT?

(C) Nope!! Was not. Continue!

(N) Cecil, that was your second clue. If you knew of the information you gave earlier, I definitely would have turned around and walked out. So, I can assume your dumb ass, still considered living there. I tell you what, I'm going to stick around for the rest of this chapter, so continue.

(C) I was curious and asked if anyone was staying with her, and she said no. I asked because DaBitch was only about 110 pounds (ca. 50 kg), with four bricks in her back pockets, and she had enough food to feed all the homeless in the downtown Orlando area.

(R) Are you exaggerating?

(C) NOPE!

(N) That was your third clue. She then proceeded to show me the room she was renting to me and the way she had it laid out.

(N) I bet you didn't consider how small it was, did you?

(C) But what you don't understand is, desperation will make you ignore all your instincts. I signed the lease and left there, hoping I had made a good decision.

(N) Who she supported should have been the decisive factor,

(C) right?

(N) Well, then tell everyone who she supported! Let me just say this, if we both vote Republican in 2024, then it would have been a good idea. That's all I will say about that because you get my drift. Now, it is time to pay the portion of the rent, considering it was December 20th, 2023. Avoid paying rent in cash to ensure a secure transaction record. I knew and paid with an app straight from my bank. This way, I have a digital record of the transaction, including the date and time I paid her.

(N) This is a good idea,
(C) so I will continue doing it. My first ex-wife taught me a valuable lesson: never pay in cash and always include a note in the note section of your payment.
(N) As you were moving in, you started to realize that room was too small for your big ass, so, what did you do??
(C) I asked her to move a few items out of the room because I needed more space.

As I moved my belongings into the rented room, I noticed that the items I had previously mentioned were still present. She said she had nowhere to put it, so it had to stay.

(N) That was your fourth clue.

(C) Fuck! I took the appropriate action and came up with a plan to get rid of the unwanted furniture. Holy craps: the closet wasn't large enough for all my clothes to fit without cramming them.

(N) Cecil, you knew you had made a big mistake,

(C) but I was hanging in there.

Here is when it all started to change for the worse and how the BITCH, got her name. She thought the small fridge in my rented room would be enough for me.

The rented room had a small motel-style fridge. I hope that clarifies. I bought food every couple of days, mostly sandwich-making food. Fuck that shit. I had to confront THE BITCH about the lack of room for my food in the small motel fridge. She looked frustrated when I said I needed room in the kitchen fridge.

(N) That was the fifth clue. I don't understand why she thought there would be enough fridge space for me or anyone else. I asked her why she thought the fridge would be enough for me, and **THE BITCH said**: it was enough for me when I lived in that room!

(C) The Bitch weighs about as much as a full-grown Chihuahua, compared to the three hundred I weigh.

Being as polite as I could be, I said I needed some space in her already fucking stuffed-ass fridge. She moved some items around the fridge and gave me one shelf. I felt defeated when she thought that was enough.

(N) Ok, I'll say it. She's a B.I.T.C.H., I didn't want to call another WHITE WOMAN the B-WORD!

(C) If you are going to come in and out of this chapter, then you better call her the BITCH, otherwise stay the out of the rest of this chapter.

(N) All right, Cecil, I thoroughly understand, so, continue.

(C) I waited a while before I asked again for more space in the main fridge. I said, I don't want you to go out of your way to make space for my food, fridge, and cabinets, so I plan to move soon. She became frustrated again, and I made myself feel like I was begging for too much— sixth clue. I finally got enough balls to say I needed my fridge. OMG!!! It was like I asked her to move a fucking mountain lion out of the bathroom, blocking the toilet.

She finally bought one and placed it in the garage. I was temporarily happy because I knew it would come with an attitude. I went to Costco and bought about four hundred dollars of food. I was excited.

(N) Don't you have **more Clues you didn't pay attention to?**

(C) She occasionally said something that made me curious about how she knew what was in my room. Next, **The Bitch said,** "You need to buy drainage filters for the sink and bathtub."

(C) After less than a month, she gave me something to sign, stating I would clean the bathtub and sink once a month.

(N) Wait!! It gets better.

(C) Next, I received a text message saying:

(TB) Don't use the trashcan near the kitchen.

(C) After that text message, I bought one.

(N) You are listening to where this is headed, right?

(R) That was your seventh and eighth clue.

(C) Being messed over by my first wife taught me how to manage myself in this situation. One day near Christmas, I was frustrated with all the shit inside the house. I vented my frustration; that question unleashed her inner Bitch. She started yelling and screaming at me like I was one of her fucking slaves named Buck Johnson.

I was calm as a cucumber and just stared at her as she screamed at the top of her voice directly at me. All I could do was remember what my mom taught me. Just walk away, and that's precisely what I did.

As I started walking down the hallway toward my rented room, **The Bitch got mad at me and said, "DON'T YOU WALK AWAY FROM ME!!"**

(N) Might as well say, nine through the nineteen clues.

(C) Exactly!! Before I could open the door, I could see her silhouette at the end of the hallway, still yelling at me. I shut the door and could still hear her yelling to herself,

(N) "clue twenty.

(C) I blame myself because if I had done my research, I would not have had to deal with what you are listening to.

(N) Oh, You ain't done yet. There is so much more to come.

(C) Next, The Bitch installed a security camera and directed it towards my car. She did me a favor because now she can't claim I stole something,

(N) right?

(C) She claimed it was protection for my car, and I thought to myself, "No bitch that's to watch me come and go.

(R) Now, we are at clue twenty-one.

(C) Remember me mentioning the fridge in the garage? Just imagine walking with two full bags of groceries through the front door, through the living room, through the kitchen, just to get to the fridge in the garage. When I opened the garage door, **The Bitch told me: "DON'T" use the garage door**

(C) when my car was only a few feet from where I was parked outside.

(N) The twenty-second clue, right?

(C) I failed to mention earlier that she thought I was parking too close to the driveway and wanted me closer to the bushes so she could get in and out of the garage,

(N) the twenty-third clue.

(R) Cecil wants you to be able to relate what he went through, that's all.

(C) When I realized this bitch was getting on my damn nerves, I texted her this: We are no longer communicating verbally. After she spoke to me and nitpicked, I wanted a paper trail to who said what and when. Smart right?

(R) Damn sure was, Cecil.

(C) That message did not stop her from trying anyway. I would walk past her even though I heard her. I did this a few times, and she would text me what she wanted to say. Fuck that shit. I am not taking any chances.

(N) Clue twenty- four.

(C) There was another time I was using her water filter in the kitchen, and **this bitch** said: **if you are going to use the water filter, you are going to have to buy some!!**

(C) She said it loud enough for me to hear while she was in the living room. I did not acknowledge her and went back into my room.

(C) Fuck I am at clue twenty-five now. I am winding down this chapter to say this. I started looking for storage places to get the hell away from The Bitch. I gradually moved items from my tiny, rented room to my storage space. Over time, I only had a small desk, a TV, and a few clothes.

(R) Oh, wait!! Continue reading.

(C) *Remember when I mentioned she knew I had something in my room to warm it up?

(N) Yes, I remember you saying that earlier.

(C) I had to use my heat dish because it was so damn cold in her house, and she had the audacity to hint how the electricity bill had increased since I had been there.

(R) Isn't that included??

(C) Damn sure is! Plus, I never asked how much her average electric bill was. Another mistake. If I had done that, I would know precisely how much it had increased.

(N) Clue twenty-six.

(C) I knew something wasn't making sense when **The BITCH said:** you must have something in your room to cause the bill to increase.

(C) That's when I decided to get the camera from Amazon called the ring, in my room. I pointed the muthafucka right at the door.

While visiting my girlfriend at the time, I happened to look at my cell phone, and I saw a notification that this bitch was looking around in my room with a flashlight.

(R) Cecil?
(C) Yes, Royal.
(R) You refer to her as, BITCH A LOT, in this chapter.

But, listening to some of what you went through, FUCK! I DON'T blame you, what's so ever! Thanks Royal, and I will bring you back in, if I happen to need you, okay? Not a problem. WTF!!! Without permission, no warning, no call, no nothing. What if I had a blowup doll full of old cum oozing from her ass and pussy, in my rented room and did not want her to see it? I mean seriously!! This ain't funny!!

(R) Clue twenty-seven.

(C) At this point, I did not have much in my room and was ready to get the hell away from her before I don't remember what my mom taught me. Once I found another place to move to, I gave this bitch my thirty-day notice to vacate. I laughed because she told me to give her the keys, and I did not because I had not moved out yet.

(N) Clue twenty-eight.

(C) I am finally ready to move completely out with what I have left. She looked up as I walked past her and asked,

(TB) " Are you moving?? I said nothing and kept on heading out the front door. I asked the neighbor across the street to watch me as I loaded up my car just in case this bitch got stupid. She had something else to say as I opened the door without texting me. **The Bitch** had the nerve to say, " **I am going to sue you.**"

(C) I am not kidding you. I walked right past her and continued loading up my car.

(N) Clue twenty-nine.

(C) Now, all I had left was to clean up the bathroom and clear out the fridge. I started cleaning my rented room first. Next was the fridge, and I wasn't about to walk through the kitchen door, the kitchen, or the living room just to put my refrigerated items in my car just outside the garage door. Guess what I did? Yes, you guessed it, I opened the fucking garage door anyways, even though I was told not to for some unknown reason, other than being a controlling bitch.

(N) Clue thirty, The last and final one. While loading up the last few things, I saw a text on my cell phone saying,

(TB) "Don't use my garage door."

(C) At that moment, I did not give a damn and was about to walk towards the garage kitchen switch to close the garage door. Suddenly, she entered the kitchen doorway, screaming

(TB)" I told you not to use my garage door!"

(C) angrily, and she slammed her hand against the door opener and closed it.

I was behind her slightly while she was walking down the hallway towards her bedroom still ranting, and suddenly, out of nowhere, I said: "Aw, shut up!!! the Bitch was about to enter her room, and after I said that she came storming towards me. I threw the keys on the floor and gave her the finger towards the security camera. Were you paying attention?

My move-in date was December 20th, 2022, and my departure date was February 12th, 2023. That was the longest two mutha fucking months, I have ever experienced in my entire teen and adult life. I will not be providing any further hints. It is over, and I learned enough to pass this one on to you, just in case you are considering the whole roommate thing.

(N) Hey reader!!

(C) Wait a minute more!! Remember me mentioning earlier that I learned a lot from one of my X-wives? This is going to be some straight up golden information I am about to drop on you, and you'd better take notes. When my first wife and I divorced while children were involved there was child support to be paid from me to her. Admitting, one of my sons was from another relationship. When we separated, I agreed to pay a certain amount of child support, no problem, no fuss.

(C) At the time I handed her a check each month paid to her directly. Back then I obviously had a checking account. I was not aware that having one would certainly save my ass from being high jacked. If you are now wondering how, then allow me to break this shit down for your ass, all right!! When we found out it was time to divorce one another it was a mutual decision, so I thought!

One morning while I was driving a forklift a man I had never met walked up to me and asked:

(N) are you Cecil Hicks?

(C) I thought maybe I had won the lotto or something but that wasn't the case. He then handed me an envelope and said: you have been served. I opened it in disbelief and sure enough it was divorcing papers. Something I assumed her, and I could have sat down and discussed the details.

Obviously, she said " FUCK THAT SHIT!! Weeks later, after finding an attorney to represent me, it was time to look over the divorce papers. So, when it came time to sign the divorce papers, I was wise enough to read over it. That's when I caught something fucked up, she tried to pass under the radar.

Come to find out she had the divorce papers drawn up as if I had never paid her one penny since our separation, which was a mutha fucking lie! I was pissed beyond words and had to figure out how to contest it. No help from mom or anyone in my so-called family, when this all happened. I was forced into figuring out on my own what to do.

Suddenly, I remembered that I wrote her a check for child support and in the memo section, I wrote See support, which is an abbreviation for child support. That abbreviation in the memo section saved my ass a huge amount of money, BIG TIME!!

Hey reader!! If I mentioned this in another chapter I would like to apologize. If I have not, there was a reason for adding it here. Another B- WORD trying to take advantage of a good honest man. I am done venting, and I appreciate you listening, seriously, take care. Peace!

Three Situations

In this light chapter, I am going to give you a different narrator that will give you a shot of liquor with no chaser.

I don't regret some situations without a storyline or build-up. If what I just said did not make sense to you, let me say it another way you may comprehend. If you like watching porn, do you watch the entire fake ass with dull acting, or do you scroll through just to get to the fucking and sucking? Well, this chapter passes by all the fluff and gets straight to the fucking and sucking, feel me?

FIRST SITUATION:

I remember this one chick—let us call her Latoya to keep her identity private— that I used to go to high school with. We stayed connected for a couple of years after we graduated. After years of chatting endlessly on our cell phones, she finally invited me to her house. We may have only talked for a few minutes before I told her to remove her pants and panties.

Before I continue, I want y'all to know I'm lucky to be alive while writing this memoir. In the past, I was careless about where I placed my cock or tongue. Also, keep in mind that for this woman I am writing about right now, I did not even ask if she washed her pussy before I had sex with her.

Therefore, I will now proceed to the next section. Reflecting: I was a nasty teenager. Sometimes, I pinch myself because I am surprised, I did not catch something that no medicine or shot could contain. I must have been eating that bitch's pussy thoroughly when suddenly I felt something wet inside my mouth, and I wasn't sure what the hell it was. I immediately took my mouth from her pussy and asked, "What the hell was that?" She looked embarrassed, said, "Oh, I'm so sorry," and got up from the couch.

Once she realized she had urinated in my mouth, she stood up from the sofa, ran into her bathroom, and proceeded to lock the bathroom door. I was cussing that bitch out and banging on the door. After a few seconds, I realized this fucking bitch wasn't coming out of the bathroom. I kept on repeating, "Why in the hell would you think it was okay to pee in my mouth?"

Seriously, think about it. Latoya had to know that was about to happen and did not warn me. I am going to be straight up with you; I have never asked or wanted this bitch to pee in my mouth. Remember me saying I am lucky to be alive? It also applies to what I will say next: the universe kept her alive that evening because that could have been disastrous. Have I ever urinated on a woman? Yes, as I mentioned in a previous chapter, I had urinated on my girlfriend's stomach, and she had requested that I do so. Had my upbringing been different, I could have dealt a severe blow to her. The thought of being imprisoned only to end up committing suicide or becoming someone else's bitch humbled me.

SECOND SITUATION

I had a crush on another girl from junior high school. Like Latoya in "First Situation," she invited me to her house. That sounds familiar, right? Wait ... Here it goes again; we talked for a few minutes, and she pulled off her panties without me asking.

Our conversations revolved around what she wanted to do to me and what I wanted to do to her. Before I rang her doorbell, we clearly understood what to expect. I ate that bitch's pussy until she came all over my face. I had her juices all around the top of my lips. In fact, I tried to be silly by grabbing my top lip and pulling it up towards my nose. I was acting as if I could curl my tongue upwards to taste her pussy.

While she was busting out laughing, I sat down on the bed and started pulling down my pants because it was time for her to suck my cock or something, right?

She tells me, "I'm not going to suck your cock or let you fuck me. "I stood up, looked at her directly, and said, "You know what?" You arc lucky as hell; my mom taught me to never do anything that could send me to prison. Honestly, if you ever do this again to another guy after he is eaten your pussy, and suddenly you play innocent, you could be dead, or he beats the hell out of you.

So, I am going to change into my clothes and leave. Please heed my advice and refrain from repeating this behavior. I rushed out the door, whispering a thank you to my mom for her wisdom.

THE THIRD AND FINAL SCENARIO:

When I turned twenty-one, I enjoyed dancing at Rasputin's Night Club in Point Loma, California. Imagine finally turning twenty-one, going to your first nightclub, and some older woman seeing a young boy toy and offering her number to me. Of course, I said yes and called her the next day.

This woman did not waste any time on my first visit to her place. She guided me towards her bedroom like. I was a newborn puppy, and she told me to remove my clothes. I was standing in her bedroom, completely naked, as she examined me as if I were a piece of fresh meat. She began removing her clothes, a move that left me feeling unimpressed.

Remember, I am twenty-one years old while she is fifty-two, and I am used to observing naked girls in my age range. Anyway, I was game to continue, and she started sucking my cock. Back then, I wasn't into eating pussy like I am now. I guess sucking my cock made her cum a few times. She immediately got up, turned around doggy-style, and placed her tits against the bed. I said that so you could have a visual; in other words, she was bent completely over, ass up.

Damn right, I did. I got behind her like a marching band, following a band leader with a stick in hand, and stuck my cock in her pussy. I was so into it that I wasn't paying attention to anything else. She loved what I was doing behind her, but suddenly, a foul odor came from somewhere.

It is hard to concentrate when something stank like fresh dog shit, especially when you don't know where it is coming from. Now don't get me twisted; I still got my cock in her pussy. Fuck that shit. While she is coughing, the smell intensifies. I am glad she could not see my face behind her.

She would have asked why if she had turned around and seen my face. When I finally looked down between my hands on her ass cheeks, I saw a cave where her asshole should have been. Her damn booty hole was wide open, and my cock had not been in there yet. Gauging by the size of her open asshole, my cock would not have touched the sides going in anyway. I don't have enough girth for that cave, and I was determined to keep fucking her pussy. However, between the cave and the stench, I could not continue. Let me give you another visual.

I looked everywhere but down, trying to prevent her stench from entering my nose. Sometimes, a man should know when to fold his cards. Even in 2024, it will remain the most repulsive smell ever. Obviously, that was a moment in time I will never forget. Since there is no word for stankiest, I am using it anyway. You understood, right? What have I learned from all three chapters?

All three situations could have easily ended badly, as I already mentioned. You might be familiar with someone who faced a similar situation and struggled to rationalize the act of physically attacking another person. Hearing some of the stories from my neighborhood also proved beneficial to me. Another reason I was able to avoid going to jail or prison was from watching a 1970s show on television titled Scared Straight. I must have watched every episode, and seeing those children around my age and crying gave me the inspiration I needed to avoid jail time.

My family taught me how to maintain my composure, which helped me avoid becoming a suspect in a crime. I know this chapter is called "Three Different Situations," but I met this one attractive black woman on a dating app; we will refer to her as.

FOURTH AND FINAL SITUATION

So here goes: Shay and I had an interesting conversation on the dating app. We had a lot in common before exchanging cell numbers. When we finally conversed, we did not lose our enthusiasm online, so we might as well plan to meet one another soon afterward. When we finally met, it went exceptionally well, and she confirmed that she felt the same way. The next time we met, she expressed a desire to drive down and see me, which I found impressive, considering she lived two and a half hours away.

Yes, I drove two and a half hours to see her for the first time. I made this decision because I was aware of her busy schedule.

We planned to meet on Saturday but did not discuss the time. Following our conversation that morning around 8:30, I assumed she would arrive at my address before 1-2 o'clock in the afternoon. Well, not only did she come later than expected, but she acted like it wasn't a big deal. Of course, you are thinking, what time did she finally show up? It wasn't until about 4:30; remember that we chatted at 8:30 that morning.

That's a significant delay even when you factor in the two-and-a-half-hour drive. She did not call me after she left her home, so I thought something happened to her. I had dinner later and wanted to take her to a park.

At some point, she finally called, but that wasn't until an hour on the road. If she had said she was leaving the house, I would have said stay your ass at home. She was an hour and a half away when she finally called me. At this point, I thought, "I'm not going to tell her to go home now," but I was furious. Whether you believe this should not have been a problem, I did.

Or am I being petty and inconsiderate? You might be thinking, "Oh my goodness!" She at least drove down to see me, right? After that, I can only say that we are two people with different life experiences that make us who we are.

What is petty to me may not be petty to you, and vice versa. My situation was unique because, as I mentioned in "Dear Momma," my mother had given me away at birth.

Sometimes shit creeps back into your memory unexpectedly. After this happened, I self-diagnosed myself, and that's my analysis. No, I have not!!! I have not spoken to a therapist about this yet. Anyway, back to the chapter. Here is the thing you must keep in mind: she had the day we planned to meet, which was earlier in the week, and from the moment we talked at 8:30 that morning, she wanted to visit me.

Considering it was around 4:30 when she arrived, it was too damn late for everything I had planned for us. She apologized because she could tell I was irritated and unsure what to say. I clarified that I was disappointed and decided to go out anyway. I forgot to mention this earlier; I was on time when I drove up to see her. However, even though it was later than expected and more people were out, our time together went well.

Our communication was also okay while getting to know one another. Now, let us dive into the essential details of this chapter. We decided to see each other again, and I wanted to drive up to see Shay at her home. I assumed she would be comfortable in her home with me. I was completely wrong because my visit did not go as planned. Going beyond what you have already read, here are some additional details about me. When I meet someone new, I am not interested in being anything less than a gentleman, including keeping my hands to myself and making the conversation interesting. I maintained eye contact during our conversation, refraining from looking at her or using my cell phone.

My drive took about 3 hours because of some traffic I encountered. Unlike her visit to me, I made it there in a considerable amount of time. It did not take long before I noticed something that immediately made me say, "WTF?" She opened the door and treated me like I was her Ex-husband, picking up the rest of my dirty clothes after our divorce. She did not even ask if I was tired and wanted something to drink. She continued talking on her cell briefly, which I found acceptable. Still, the initial greeting at the front door was disappointing.

After closing the door behind me, I told myself to go ahead and see her reaction. She eventually showed me her home, starting with the backyard and proceeding to the guest bedroom and garage. Because I wasn't planning to ask her about her master bedroom because I wasn't sure it was the right time. Walking into other parts of someone's house is one thing, but looking around in someone's bedroom is another.

She gave me the impression that she was comfortable and showed me her bedroom. Of course, I followed her and looked around. As I was about to walk out, I could not help but notice her extraordinarily long mirror on the wall. At that moment, an idea popped into my head: to be sensual without being overly aggressive. As she walked ahead, I extended my arms and placed my hands on each side of her shoulder to stop her. While I stood directly behind her, I asked her (not told) to face the mirror for me. At that moment, as I stood behind her and looked at her in the mirror, she did not seem anxious.

Wait just a moment before I tell you the rest of the story. When I am with a woman for the first time, I treat each woman differently, which is how it should be, right? Every woman is unique in every way and must not assume anything. So, given Miss Forth's situation, this would be the best thing to do. As I gently and cautiously touched her skin, I placed her right hand on the bedroom countertop with her left hand. I whispered, don't remove your hands from the countertop. I continued to touch her skin while she watched me in the mirror.

Remember that I am paying close attention to her breathing and body language. I must pay attention to everything so that I can proceed. If I notice she is anxious, I will stop and try again another time. I did not notice any anxiousness, so I continued touching her stomach. Then, suddenly, she removed her hands from the bathroom countertop, which surprised me. It surprised me because I asked her not to remove her hands from the countertop, and she removed them anyway. Therefore, I firmly urged her to return her hands to the countertop, but she did not comply.

I whispered again, "Place your hands back on the countertop," but she refused to comply. I am perplexed now because I did not feel I was doing anything that would cause rejection. I did not mention earlier that I had slightly pulled down her dress from the shoulder, did I? Anyway, I pulled her dress back up over her shoulders, turned around, and walked back into the living room. I only said something once we were in the living room, and she sat across from me.

I seriously thought we had a connection before I attempted to touch her. It was also based on our conversations over the weeks before my visit. If she had allowed me to continue, all I wanted to do was place my hands directly on her body and feel her skin. Surprisingly, I did not anticipate any sexual activity such as penetration; instead, my expectation was to explore each other sensually and seductively. Like the three prior situations, this one also had the potential for a disastrous outcome. I left after an hour, despite taking 3 hours to get there.

I felt uneasy even before driving to see Shay. This feeling intensified once I arrived. I wanted to confirm my feelings before deciding to stop seeing her. She later revealed to me, while I remained calm, that she was experiencing discomfort. I will conclude by reminding all the ladies reading this part of the chapter: You learn a lot about a man when he feels rejected. The fact that I walked out and drove back home was my way of saying goodbye rather than staying. Ladies, please be clear about your expectations. Peace!

Traumatized

I am conscious of the fact that all of us deal with traumatic situations that differ from one individual to the next.

Because most of you will bury it under your mattress, it is understandable that some of you may never bring it up again. This is a reasonable possibility. Some of you are either too ashamed, hesitant, or plain ol stubborn to seek a professional psychologist. Since the publication of "Vanilla Sheets", there are specific individuals, including myself, who continue to go through a significant amount of anxiety and denial.

Suppose the information I am sharing is found in a separate chapter. In that case, I ask that you kindly excuse me from mentioning it again. If you are reading this on a laptop or eBook, take a deep breath. I ain't taking a break naming all the triggers I can think of that has either, happened to me or you.

"Oh, and one more thing — I spaced each sentence out a bit so you don't feel overwhelmed. Cool? Alright, here we go..."

If you seriously think that you have overcome rape, molestation, mental and physically abused, sexual assault, unacceptable physical contact, attempts at penetrating your pussy, ass, or mouth without consent, inappropriate touching at work, unwanted sexually suggestive comments, forced sexual photography and pornography without consent, come home early and find out your partner is gay, isolated from friends and family, denied educational assistance based on one's race, denied to fulfill cultural and religious beliefs, can't express your personal opinions, invade your privacy with unwanted verbal assault, constantly bullied, you are too fat, you are too skinny, you ain't black enough, told you are stupid, too short, too tall, your pussy has an odor, unexpected pregnancy from a rapist, no concerns of your orgasm after they nutted, rolls over and goes to sleep after fucking you, pussy denial when you are married, your child witness you with another man or woman besides who they know is their mother or father, finding out someone has lied to you from the moment you married them, accidently finding out your partner has stolen all of your money and left the country, having to work again after retiring because of a lousy investment decision of your own or the firm you gave your money too, the person you love commits suicide in your home like Candy in a chapter called "Her Story Not Mine," threatened, name-calling and shaming, abandonment of any kind, deceived by your parents, handcuffed and beaten by a police officer,

BREATH Pease!! Or are you going to need a respirator?

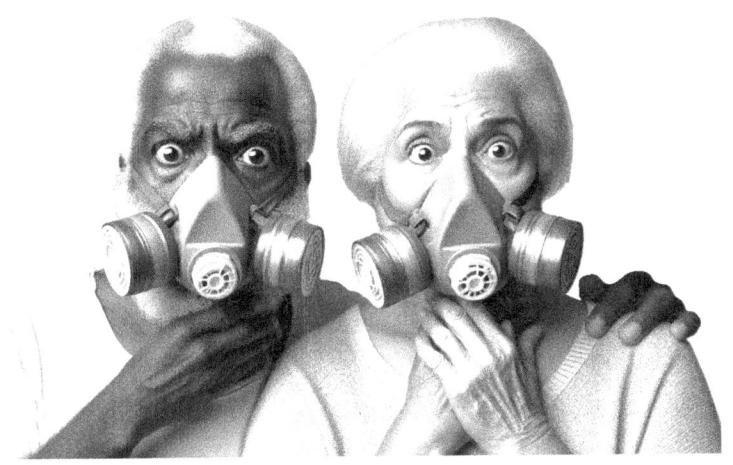

Followed and questioned because of your race, placed in handcuffs because someone lied, followed by people in the same neighborhood because they think you don't belong, saying go back to your country when they themselves are not from the country they actually live in, scammed financially, banking while black, refused entry to your own residence, your identity stolen, denied advancing within the company because of your race or religious beliefs, subpar repairs by a racist refers to you as "you people" or using an old reference to people of color as colored people, men now saying your body or choice, scared to vote for Kamala Harris because of your husbands beliefs, your nurse ignores your cry for help, your white patient you are assigned to does not want your assistance because of your race, someone of authority plants drugs in your car, your child's teacher speaks negatively to other teachers and you hear about it,

You are almost there, you got this!!

trusting your best friend inside your home and find out much later they stole something valuable from you, finding out the person you married is not their identity, telling the truth and no one believes you, you find out your home was under-appraised because of your race, racial tension, told you are never smart enough to think on your own, being called fat, black, white dumb bitch constantly, catfishing someone who fell in love, saying I love you and not meaning one word of it, Management ignores your ideas and uses it later for their own gain, and your ideas are never considered to advance within the company. Because you are of a different race, your employer has hired someone else to supervise you. This decision was made because you are of a different race. As the new supervisor, you must train them immediately, even though you have been on that job much longer.

There is a connection between trauma and every one of these symptoms. However, they may be minor or more noticeable. Every one of these symptoms is also connected to your relationships. Your life has been changed because of it, and no matter how hard you try to convince yourself otherwise, the fact remains that it has changed. It has no significance because it has impacted you, regardless of whether you can move on. Kindly pay attention to this.

Look muthafucka, I am very much aware I don't hold a master's degree and that I am not a clinical behavior expert for the reasons you are reading this. I can assure you that I can talk with self-assurance based on my experience and am responsible for making it acceptable. Do I have a complete understanding of this? Maybe or maybe not.

Even though you may be able to convince yourself otherwise at this very moment, this is the situation. It will be easier for you to claim that you have moved on from the circumstance if you first create a copy of yourself and then travel back in time to a period before the events mentioned above occurred. I want to emphasize once more that you need to investigate every single activity that your clone handled until the time when the trauma took place. A comparison between the two can be made to ascertain whether significant changes have occurred between the time in question and the present day.

Regardless of how long ago something took place, you have yet to acquire the ability to move on from whatever happened in your life. You have done nothing but trick yourself into thinking that everything is OK so that you can continue to waste away on the inside by remaining silent. This allows you to continue to waste away. Another point of view is that after the traumatic experience, every choice you make, regardless of whether it is a good or bad choice, is connected to what you went through. This is true regardless of whether the decision is negative or positive.

The traumatic experience will permanently alter the decisions you make in your relationships and how you connect with the people you care about, including your children. All these changes will be permanent.

My research has led me to believe that hypnosis is the only way to successfully eliminate it entirely. If you have made it this far and are still dealing with the aftermath, please be aware that you are not the only one dealing with it.

I am still recovering from the profound and impossible impact that the recent election had on me. I was so furious that I began cursing out loud, and there was no need to visit the hospital's emergency room. even though I was so overwhelmed with emotion. The fact that I had already predetermined that white women would vote against another woman, just blew my fucking mind.

It has been determined that European Americans have chosen to hate over the growth of the economy. If you have not had any of the experiences I mentioned above, I would like to question the location on this planet where you were born. What are the chances that you are a human being? I am just joking around!

No, but seriously? Peace!

Unanswered Goodbye

Some doors you walk through for fun. Some doors you slam shut. This one? It opened wide and ended in silence. Brace yourself, because this story doesn't leave with a smile.

Part One: The Open Door

To me, this is one of the saddest stories I've ever told. I almost didn't include it in this book, but my conscience wouldn't let me leave it out. So here it is—unfiltered.

I met a woman online—let's call her **Y&R**. Some of you reading this may know exactly who I'm talking about. If you're her son and this hits home, then yes—I'm talking about your mother. We connected on Match.com, sent messages back and forth, and eventually decided to meet.

From the jump, our conversations were easy. She was sharp, funny, and we had a lot in common. We hugged after that first meeting, promised to stay in touch, and we did. For a while, everything seemed normal. But over time, little things started to show.

I noticed she slurred her words now and then. At first, I brushed it off—figured maybe she had a few drinks. But months later, it became clear there was something darker at play. I didn't press; I just observed. And what I saw shook me. Now let's talk about the sexual part of our relationship—before we get to the disturbing part. Sex with her was wild. She was open-minded, down for almost anything, and if she'd been drinking, she'd get even more experimental. There were nights she'd call me and say:

"I'll leave the front door open. You don't even have to take your pants off. Do what you want, I'll already be in position. Then leave without saying a word."

Did I take her up on that? You damn right I did. I walked in, did what I came to do, walked out without a word, and sat in my car laughing, shaking my head. *Only in America.*

But not every moment was something to laugh about. One night, during an encounter from behind, things went sideways—literally. I pulled away, and blood poured out of her in a way I'd never seen in my life. It scared the hell out of me. I may not be the biggest guy, but I guess I went deep enough to hit something that caused damage. We rushed her to the hospital.

After that, doggie style was off the table for me. I was paranoid it would happen again, but she insisted it was a freak accident. And she was right—I've never seen that happen with any woman before or after her. Just her. Period.

I'm not here to rehash measurements or repeat what I've already said about myself elsewhere in this book. If you missed that part, that's on you. What matters here is this: Y&R wasn't just another hookup story. Behind all the wildness was pain, darkness, and self-destruction that I couldn't fix, no matter how much I wanted to.

Part Two: Who Knows

All of this—everything you're about to read—still happened within that first month. Can you believe it?

It started with those texts. One day I'm driving, a message pops up: *"I'm in the position you like. Stop by."* Lucky for me, I was at a red light when I read it. Wherever I was headed didn't matter anymore. I spun the wheel and drove straight to her place.

Door unlocked, just like before. She was already bent over, waiting in position. I did what I came to do, left without saying a word, sat in my car, and laughed. Shook my head like,

Only in America. Only here could a Black man walk in on a white woman wide open, do his thing, walk out without a word, and drive off.

That routine went on for weeks. And I had no complaints. She only lived twenty minutes away, which made it way too easy. Convenience has a way of making you ignore the red flags.

One night though, convenience got complicated. A friend was giving me a ride home, and when we pulled up, Y&R was already parked outside my place, standing by my car. My stomach dropped. I'd never had one woman waiting while I was with another. My friend noticed my nerves and asked what was wrong. I told her straight up,

"I know that woman. This could get messy."

She had my back, but when I walked over, it wasn't drama waiting for me—it was disaster. Y&R was gone. Drunk, high, or both, worse than I'd ever seen her. She slurred, stumbled, tried to apologize when she realized I wasn't alone. Then she got in her car and drove off.

I'll be honest: I stood there sick with worry. She was so out of it, I half expected to see her on the news the next morning in a crash report. But somehow, she made it home. I never should've let her drive, but I froze. First time I'd ever been in that position, and I handled it wrong. I own that.

But her demons didn't stop there. She argued all the time, about everything. Me? I don't argue. I talk it out, then I move on. But she kept pushing. Neighbors got involved once, knocking on the door just to make sure nobody was dying. That's when I realized I was in deep with something toxic. Walking out, slamming doors, speeding off from her house—it wasn't me, but that's who I was becoming with her.

And then came the pictures. Out of nowhere, another text, another photo: her bent over, spreading herself open, finger pointing like an arrow to the center. The invitation was clear. Did I go? Not this time. I was on my way to something more important, but don't think I didn't consider it. I did.

Eventually, I tried to peel back the layers. I asked about her childhood, and what she told me broke something inside me. The kind of trauma she lived through...I won't repeat it here. Too dark. Too heavy. But it explained everything—the drinking, the drugs, the rage, the recklessness. She wasn't just chasing a high, she was trying to erase memories that wouldn't let her live.

Being around that started to mess with my own head. I knew I had to stop seeing her. But weak moments are dangerous, and in one of mine, I let her back in. She came over higher than ever, stumbling through the door. I tried to keep it going, but I couldn't. I told her, *"Put your clothes on and leave."* And she did. That was the last straw for me.

After that, I ignored her texts, her emails, her calls. She tried knocking on my door unannounced, but I wouldn't answer. I didn't want to see her like that anymore. Too close to my father—drunk, high, unpredictable. I couldn't relive that childhood all over again.

Weeks turned to months. One month became two. Two became three. By the fourth, I thought I was finally free.

Then the phone rang. A stranger's voice asked, *"Are you Cecil?"*

I said yes, cautiously. They said, *"We have some of your belongings here. A folder. Notes. Looks personal."*

Confused, I asked why they were calling on her behalf. There was silence. Whispering in the background. Finally the voice came back, low, hesitant:

"She's not alive anymore."
I froze. "What do you mean, not alive?"

Another long pause. Then the words that cut like glass: *"She committed suicide. Left a note by her bed."*

I didn't believe them. Googled her name. And there it was—her memorial.

Six months earlier, she was leaving her door open for me. Six months later, she was gone.

Sometimes I wonder if things would've ended differently had I kept seeing her. If I'd stayed, if I'd answered, if I'd gone back one more time—would she still be alive?

But the truth is, that answer isn't mine to hold.
Who knows.

My Reflection

I didn't write this chapter to shock you with wild nights or to have you shaking your head at the mess I got into. I wrote it because this is life. Sometimes you laugh in the car on the way home, thinking you hit the jackpot. Sometimes you're staring out the window months later, realizing the person you laughed with isn't even here anymore.

I couldn't save her, and truth is, I wasn't supposed to. What I learned is that pain wears disguises—sometimes it looks like a smile, sometimes it looks like an open door. And if you're not careful, you'll mistake someone's wounds for your own second chance.

This isn't just her story. It's mine too. It's me admitting I didn't have it all figured out, that I made choices out of lust, out of ego, out of habit. And maybe it's yours too, if you've ever been with somebody who was broken in ways you couldn't fix.

So when I say *"Who knows,"* it ain't just a question. It's the reminder that some answers never come, and the only thing left is the story itself.

I kept living. She didn't. That's the line we never crossed together.

That's the line we never crossed together.

Under The Cover

irst, before you listen to this chapter, go ahead and think of Cecil as a Nasty, Perverted, Kinky, Open-Minded, Bizarre, Unconventional minded muthafucka from the 70s sitting on a gold throne.

Adam: And since he is the author of this book, it seems appropriate that he has surrounded himself by a bunch of bitches on his left, and one black one on his right. And last and most importantly, the author of this book.

Cecil: Here are the characters and their roles within this chapter. I am doing this now because I don't want to confuse you because of my attention deficit disorder better known as A.D.D. and don't want you to scratch your head as to who is who. Now, let's get started, shall we?

Adam: Damn Cecil!!
Cecil: WHAT NOW!!

Adam: What Cecil is trying to say is, don't get confused or frustrated while listening to this chapter.

The characters in this chapter are:

Adam: will be my white Narrator and is also a friend of mine who will appear from time to time. Or when he needs to take a pee break or choke the chicken, if, y'all know, what I mean.
Cecil: SHUT UP!!
Adam: My bad!

My name is Eden: And I am one of the main characters and also the wife of James Lucas.

Hello, my name is James: I am also One of the main characters and the husband of Eden Lucas.

Scarlett: And pardon me, my name is I am the Eden's big sister.

Cecil: Wait a mutha-fucking minute!! Who is this fine ass BITCH?

Royal: Look Negga, I know you didn't just call me a BITCH!! Have we met each other somewhere before?

Cecil: Prior to this face-to-face, I would have to say, No!!

Royal: That's exactly what I thought. Well, then I don't mind being called a bitch and ain't looking for a sugar daddy! Excuse me!! Why the fuck am I last? Anyway, my name is Royal: And I am Scarlett's best friend during the day and secretly a Black Queen Dominatrix at night.

Adam: So, if there are any ministers listening to the audio book, who need to repent, you know where to find her.

Cecil: By the way, Royal, I did not add you last because you are black. Just setting the record straight!

Royal: Well, then I appreciate that coming from you. And what's your name, Mr. BIG chocolate!!

Cecil: To all you MOFO's here, including you Miss Royal, they call me Mr. Cecil Hicks, and the author and creator of "Bloody Finger".

Royal: Well okay then that's all you need to say.

Cecil: All right moving right along,... now that we have all introduced ourselves to the mutha-fuckas who's listening to this audio book, Adam, you are up, so go ahead.

Adam: This remix has more details and forgotten stages of Cecil's life as a child to become who that motherfucker is today. By the way, if you have a moment, make sure no one interrupts you during this chapter, okay?

It's time for Cecil to take you down memory lane, and the only question I have for you is, are you relaxing in your favorite chair while you are reading this chapter? What beverage are you going to sip on and what time is it? I asked the time, because if it's too late you know your old ass will fall asleep with this book in your hand. I am going to offer my suggestion, and you can take it or leave it, go take a nap, especially if you're over fifty years of age. You and I both know, you will not remember where you left off if you don't use a page marker. Hey Cecil!

Yeah!! What's up.
Adam: Go ahead with your story, okay.

Cecil: Alright here we go. Many years ago, I made a white man by the name of James, kneel before me while his wife's sister named Scarlett was standing next to Eden, pouring a shot of Hennessy into my glass. If You were paying attention there is a black woman by the name of Royal, on my right side with a leash in her hand. She is the epitome of black excellence if I ever met one, and does not take shit from anyone, especially if they are white trying to disrespect her. I will disclose more about Royal later in this chapter. Here is the reason. Royal is on the right side of the throne.

Adam: History states a lady walking on the right side originated in the Middle Ages when knights wore their swords on the left side of their bodies, allowing their right arm and hand to respond quickly to protect their lady and himself from evil or danger.

Now that you understand why Royal was on Cecil's right side of the throne, he will now share some of his favorite sexual adventures of all times with you, and I hope you find them interesting. In fact, this is not an entanglement, as someone famous once said at a red table married to a famous actor and rapper.

All of his sexual adventures were with white, kinky ass mutha-fuckas around his age and, on rare occasions, much older. So, relax in your favorite chair, your legs up and recline, and be ready to masturbate with your favorite lube or vibrator, whatever your preference is.

Now that I slapped you in the face with a warning like Will Smith did to Chris Rock, buckle up bitches, and let us go for a little ride with Cecil, shall we?

Cecil: Let me tell you about this white couple, Mr. and Mrs. Lucas, commonly known as Eden and James, lived in Miami. They resided on the fifteenth floor of a condo that overlooked Miami Beach. You can see for miles in whichever direction you look. Those stupid seagulls were always landing on their lookout rail and pooping on their patio because they were so high in the air. To be honest, visiting their terrace at night was always an incredible experience. Being around them made me feel uneasy because of my own insecurities.

When I met them, however, they were generous with both their time and money. I mentioned their money, so let us take a short recess to explain why I mentioned it.

When I first spoke to them on the phone and realized how far away, they were from where I resided, they offered to always compensate me for visiting them. I hope that explains it. Usually, one would associate their lifestyle with individuals who prioritize their own lives over others, like the black characters acting as slaves in Dino De Laurentis and Richard Fleischer's 1975 film Mandingo. (check out that movie when you get a chance)

In other words, people who usually live in places like Mr. and Mrs. Lucas feel they substantially better than black and Puerto Rican people. I have been to parties where the majority of the mutha-fuckas there were white or should I say, European. I am swearing because every time I was around them, they tried to talk to me as if I weren't intelligent enough to hold a conversation with them. Since I am rewriting this chapter anyways, I might as well add this fucked up memory to the mix.

There was this party I was at and yet again a majority of the mutha-fuckas that was there were white, asked me where is the drink trey? It wasn't that I had on butler like clothes from slavery, fuck that shit!! One more example I have for you is, this one European woman actually thought it was okay to kick me in my ass with her fucking shoe!! I turned around and in a firm mutha-fucking voice I said: DON"T YOU EVER DO THAT AGAIN and I DON"T GIVE A FUCK WHO YOU ARE AND WHO YOU KNOW!!! That bitch had the audacity to look surprised that I even said something!!

Cecil: Anyways, I digress!!

Adam: If you are a black person reading this chapter, don't you dare say, " THAT"S WHAT Cecil GETS"!!

Cecil: Anyway, back to Eden and James. "This couple didn't give me that impression they were SNOOTY. I felt comfortable enough to continue and I asked them where they met each other and who flirted with who first? While relaxing with them, I could tell this couple was clearly in love, as seen by their body language whenever they narrated their story. Judging by

Eden's body language, I could tell that she was going to lead the conversation, which I found interesting.

Eden: When we originally met at our friend's birthday party, I certainly did not have any physical attraction or common interests with James. Plus, it was during the summer, and he wore turtleneck sweaters with long sleeves regardless of the temperature outside or indoors, which I found peculiar to say the least! And because I wasn't interested in him, I did not ask why. James also had a mullet hairstyle and enjoyed listening to Billy Ray Cyrus' song "Achy Breaky Heart." "I passionately emphasized how I hated that song whenever I heard it.

I swear that combination of James's hairstyle and his taste for music was a deal-breaker right out the gate like a fake rabbit at a dog race chase. I also overheard that muthafucka saying "nigger" on occasion among his white friends, and I wasn't impressed, but disgusted! I am so sorry Cecil, when he would use that word "nigger" with emphasis on the R, all I had to do was give him a look of disgust!!

Cecil: Well, right after Eden said that James looked down and was embarrassed to make eye contact with me. He promptly looked in my direction and apologized, which was unnecessary. Again, there was no eye contact. "Driven by his insecurities, James made up in his mind, that he didn't like Eden because he convinced himself she was out of his league." He knew Eden's independence and dominance in her workplace and social life, so James automatically expected she would not date or speak with him.

He questioned whether he could manage the attention Eden was receiving from other men. James had seen her in several coffee shops around town but was too afraid to approach her. I can assume that James met her ex-boyfriend at some point because of how James spoke about him.

Adam: What's up with that, man?

Cecil: Well, for starters he drove a blue and white Maserati and was famous all over the world. Fuck!! You can count all of my friends on one hand with four fingers down already. I did not know or realize that none of this made a difference in who Eden chooses to fuck at the time. I finally accepted and understood their attraction to each other despite their considerable age differences. I am ready to finally share their unique story with you on how they became husband and wife. Wait! I meant "wife and husband," which is correct, considering I can clearly tell who is the dominant one.

Adam: Here are some of my notes on How Eden and James Met:

Eden: I was jogging one morning when I saw a man sitting on a park bench just ahead of me. I never seen him before despite running that same trail numerous times. I was determining whether to turn back or continue. Fortunately, other joggers were around, so I felt secure enough to pass him without recognizing who he was.

James: I looked up and recognized Eden but was too shy to say hello. James mentioned that there was a moment when he considered jogging beside her and revealing his identity. James knew Eden exercised regularly around the same time and path every morning because it was his favorite park also.

Cecil: On a different morning, he sat on a different bench further away from the path she jogged on, but when he saw her jogging, he chose the bench that was closer to the path she jogged on.

Anyway, when Eden saw the same man get up and moved closer to her jogging path, then sat down on the park bench and looked in her direction. She wasn't sure what was happening and wasn't going to take any chances. She reached into her pocket and placed a taser in her hand just in case.

Eden: I eventually remembered who he was, so I stopped and asked James: "Do you remember me from the birthday party you and I attended?"

James nodded his head in agreement. Eden found it particularly strange that James refused to establish eye contact while she was attempting to communicate with him. Their encounter lasted several weeks until

Eden asked James: would you like to meet for drinks instead of stalking me?

Cecil: After a few dates, Eden became more aware of his mannerisms. She thought it was interesting that he continued to look down when she spoke directly to him. One evening, Eden walked towards James, elevated his chin, looked James in the eyes, and made eye contact. James's behavior clearly turned her on, and she knew precisely how to manage him and what he required. She was once the co-founder of a business most people are familiar with, so she is used to dealing with men on all levels. The rest is history.

Cecil: They would call me three to five times monthly to visit or spend the night. This continued for over six months, as that was their way of getting more acquainted with me. They initially discovered me on a website called, The Cage, for likeminded people who like BDSM. That prompted them to take a few extra precautions to protect their identity. After three months, I began to sense an energy that made me cautious.

The most bizarre thing I noticed immediately was that he wore long-sleeved shirts inside their home at 80 degrees. Also, during the first couple of months, there were moments when I noticed something peculiar about their communication with one another.

It became apparent after our first face-to-face meeting after three or four lengthy conversations. According to my observations, Mrs. Lucas (Eden) would force Mr. Lucas (James) to stand up and face her directly, after which she would slap him severely for saying "nigga." Watching Eden slap James publicly and privately helped me understand the dynamics of their relationship.

Every time James said anything demeaning, Eden would apologize on his behalf, then slap the hell out of him. After the first time Eden slapped James, why wouldn't he stop, right? Being around James for the first few months was uncomfortable due to his frequent use of racial epithets. I could find no indications that he and his wife were closet racists.

You may have asked yourself, "What does a closet racist mean?" Well....They are no different from those who express themselves openly but have chosen to hide their racist ideology and remain as racist as ever.

Thanks Adam, no problem. Carry on...

Remember, James never referred to me as a nigger, either directly or indirectly, as he understood that doing so would ruin our opportunity to get to know each other. The peculiar thing is that each time Eden slapped James, she would glance at me with a devious wink. Indeed, their arrangement is different from most vanilla relationships.

I was intrigued by Edens' way of getting James's attention. With a straight face she would slap James across his face right in front of me. At one point, Eden slapped James's face so hard that her hand left an indentation on his face. I was relieved that no one was present when she did this.

From my understanding, he deserved it and would immediately look down at Eden's shoes, while rubbing his face. Right afterward, he would turn around, embarrassed, and walk away like a little bitch with his tail between his legs. Wait! When she slapped James that was a trigger for me. My father had to look down at the sidewalk also, but the difference was, when white folks were walking towards him. Honestly, I am glad I did not have to endure any of that shit while growing up in the South.

With the mentality I have as you are listening to this, I guess someone's going to have to move over, and I'm damn certain it ain't going to be me. Unless I see them making the effort to slightly move over. Oops, I did it again. Sorry, back to the story. Damn! I might as well have told him to stand in the corner on one leg with a dunce cap on his head. Before Eden met James, I was surprised he did not express his negativity towards other ethnic groups verbally.

When I first met them, I was cautiously watching their behavior and trying to fully understand their sexual arrangement. Since I have been involved in the BDSM community long enough, I know that some husbands will get on their knees and submit to their wives. Based on my observations, I could not definitively determine whether James was a switch or not. Oh, pardon me; let

Adam quickly explain what switch means. I need to take a break for a moment, and I'll be right back. Adam, go ahead.

Adam: Thanks Cecil, I'll try to explain it the best way I can. Here is a simple reference: A switch is someone who can take on either the dominant or submissive role, depending on their preferences and the dynamics of the sexual encounter. The desire for dominance or submission does not have to be evenly split; some switches may mostly prefer one role while occasionally exploring the other. Just so you know, James is not a switch.

If you want to learn more about "switch," Google it. I have no time right now to go into complete details, okay? That's why it was initially unusual, considering James' behavior when he wasn't around Eden or Cecil. They are a unique couple in the way they speak to one another.

Cecil: Okay! I am back and I hope Adam satisfied your curiosity, did he? It is not something I am accustomed to seeing in my household. My dad was the alpha in our family, even though he was drunk most of the time. He still behaved as if he were the head of the household with Mom and me. I could not understand why Eden would suggest treating James like a submissive. She looked at me occasionally, hinting that I should treat him no differently than she did. Now and then, Eden would clue me in by secretly texting me while I was in their living room. James was nearby while I texted Eden back.

This was my way of acknowledging the text I had received without James knowing about our conversation. There was no need to act on it right away; this would require time to figure out the level of trust and love they had for one another. Eden looked over at me again and smiled; she knew to give me space and time to study their sexual arrangement. Not to mention, in the months

I had known James and Eden, his wife and I never discussed or mentioned cuckold or sexual humiliation.

At that time, I was knowledgeable of cuckold relationships and knew my assessment was precisely correct. After twenty minutes of receiving Eden's text, I decided to have an intimate and private conversation with them together. Oh shit!! My bad! You don't know what a cuckold is, right? Here is a straightforward explanation from the Urban Dictionary:

Cecil: Adam, tell them what's up!

Adam: A man who finds amusement in watching his girlfriend or wife fucking another man. In most cases, this usually takes place at a hotel. motel or holiday inn ... you know the song, and on rare occasions at their home. Cecil, not me, has been in unique situations, and it's always been at their homes. That has always been their preference. By openly discussing their kinks, Cecil would analyze their relationship. James and Eden knew he was nonjudgmental and open-minded, which made it easier for them to express themselves. They could talk freely about their desires, experiences, and expectations. Cecil had similar cuckold encounters with other couples before meeting James and Eden.

Many of the couples he has met were on adult websites. After reviewing some of the couple's profiles and engaging in three or more conversations, they typically request a face-to-face meeting, which is how Cecil met James and Eden.

The difference is that trust was already in place with James and Eden, which made our conversation intriguing and unusual, to say the least. Let us take a break to explain my method of meeting cuckold couples online. While visiting couples, I assessed their body language, eye contact, posture, demeanor, and overall comfort level to understand why they selected me to be a part of their fantasies. In addition, I evaluate their mentality and maturity toward others living within their truth. My metaphor is, we all tend to hide our sexual desires behind closed curtains.

And while we prepare ourselves for the curtains to open, we are clinching our fists because we expect rejection and humiliation by people who we shouldn't give a damn about. And it is a shame that we can't live out our truth while freely expressing ourselves. We should be the same person behind the scenes when the curtains open. I mentioned everything above to emphasize that women and most couples tend to shy away from interacting with each other.

My insight comes from the universe when evaluating a couple's mannerisms and body language.

Adam: Let's go back to my friends James and Eden in Miami. **Cecil:** While trying to understand their relationship, Eden intentionally left James and me alone in the living room. Eden must have known that whenever I was alone with him, he would become subservient to me if that made any sense. I could not understand why James became that way, considering we were in our late forties. It was so subtle initially how James acted when we were alone, even when watching football. I would watch him change his mentality and become subservient to me. Honestly, we played basketball and pool and watched football on Sundays.

I could not help but wonder why a man would desire to submit himself to another. While writing this chapter, the only way to make sense of his behavior is to say that he had a top-bunker prison mentality.

Adam: Just in case you were born in a small racist town like, Cullman County, Alabama, allow me to explain what "top bunk" means. In most jails or prisons, the top bunk is considered discourteous because it is usually seen as the least desired sleeping arrangement. Most of the time, the top bunk is associated with a lower status or being a newcomer, making it more challenging to protect oneself from unwanted attention. This may explain why Cecil has not ever been to prison.

Cecil: I'm sorry, my ADD kicked in again, didn't it? So, let us get back to the chapter. James and Eden consistently reassured me that their accommodations were exceptional, due to James' masterful catering skills. Every few minutes, he asked me if I needed anything. This puzzled me, as I am self-reliant and find self-care effortless. It became apparent to me that James would get upset whenever I said "no" and became frustrated.

Can you believe that a grown man could have such a pouty face? I knew what to do on the next visit to get James' attention. Just like before, Eden left us alone in the living room, and right away, I told him to cook chicken wings (you know damn well, we black people like chicken wings). Without hesitation, this mofo entered his kitchen and put on Eden's apron and hair net. Then he looked at me with a smile, which made me a little uncomfortable, but knowing why he was smiling made it okay. While I was relaxing in the living room and waiting for my chicken wings, James looked around in his refrigerator for my favorite drink he had bought earlier. Are you smiling and in disbelief right now? Let me guess why. You are saying to yourself.

Adam: No Fucking Way!!
Cecil: Right?

Adam: Is it considered role reversal in the purest sense when, a nigga can instruct a white man on how to behave himself in his own home?

Cecil: Wait! I am trying to think of one major movie or series that features a white man serving a negro. Well, I am confident that there is not a single major movie or series where a white man serves us. On the other hand, google that shit and let me know what you find.

Adam: Side note: You won't find one fucking show, movie, or series of a white serving a black man or woman. What is up with that?

Cecil: While I sat directly across from James, Eden texted me to make James get up from the couch and make him my servant. Otherwise, I would have needed something to use as a reference to know what to do next. At first, I was a little uncomfortable allowing James to serve me dinner first, before his wife. The last time I remember a white man serving me was at a fancy restaurant in downtown Tampa. Florida.

The difference was that I did not have to tip James a damn dollar. Don King once said, "Only in America." Can you envision such a scenario? Here are my observations as to why James was comfortable being subservient to me. James consistently expressed a desire to cover any and all dinners cost and gratuity.

PLUS! Allow him to order last, when it's time to order food. Here is an A.D.D. moment again: James was still walking around wearing long-sleeved shirts, and I had not asked why yet, but I was curious. By the way, if you are curious like I am, keep listening. Every time we were hanging out together, James gave me the impression that he was intimidated by me which always made me feel uncomfortable, but when he did cover the cost of dinner and the gratuity, that was him going beyond the call of duty to make me happy.

Adam: Hey Cecil, do me a favor?

Cecil: Sure, and what's that Adam?

Adam: Tell them to Close their eyes for a moment and imagine being in your shoes for a few minutes. Now imagine you are six feet, six inches tall, with a shaved head, and people describing you as intimidating. And because they have made themselves feel insecure, they meaning white people, want you to show your fucking teeth, like you are that big ass nigga on social media dancing all the time.

Cecil: Which one?

Adam: I ain't saying his name!

Cecil: WHY NOT!

Adam: Because I don't want a defamation lawsuit filed against you.

Cecil: I appreciate you looking out for me.

Adam: Not a problem, I got you. By the way Cecil, your ADD kicked in again and you need to continue on with your chapter, okay?

Cecil: Damn you are right. Where did I leave off at?

Adam: Let me go back through my notes, just a second. Oh! You were talking about James made you feel uncomfortable...

Cecil: Oh Yea!! That's right. James was treating me like a chick he just met on Tinder, trying to impress her on the first date. Fuck! James should pull out my chair while he is at it. It took time to adjust to James' subtle on-and-off subservient behavior towards me. He acted like a friend, but he changed his persona around me. Another ADD moment: Most white men I have met in person call me Sir. I can't even remember once in my adult life that a black man called me Sir. I can assume we don't have respect for one another. right?

This is merely an expression of respect, not anything more. Are you asking yourself, "What's wrong with James's nurturing personality?" Nothing! That's not what this is about, trust me. There is a significant difference between nurturing and being subservient. James had an ulterior motive I was unaware of when he first contacted me on a B.D.S.M. site. Aside from that, I won't explain the differences to you, vanilla folks' what's the difference is right now.

To clarify, I am not referring to white people when I use the term "vanilla." Let me repeat, I am not referring to white people. I am saying that vanilla people are predictable, unexciting, and have a routine that's boring as hell in the bedroom. Ladies, this does not apply to you if you are the dominant one in the bedroom. In addition, if you are the dominant one in the relationship with someone who lacks confidence, you will find yourself constantly explaining how to please you and asking questions about your preferred positions.

Here are some examples: Adam, go ahead. Baby doll, would you like to roll over on your back now, please!! Or you are about to cum, and he stops and asks: Are you okay, Oh! here are a few more: Hey honey, can I play with your titties?
Another one is: Would you mind rolling over on your back, please! baby doll. While I am on a roll, here is the last one before I continue: I know you don't like anal, but I wouldn't mind paying for it.

Adam: That's what vanilla means in Cecil's world. Now that we have broken that shit down for you let us get back into "Under the Cover."

Cecil: I asked Adam about James' behavior, but he didn't have an answer that resonated with me. He and my friends joked about it, but I did not think it was funny. They made innuendos about him wanting to fuck me, even though I was sure that wasn't the case. I gave them the middle finger and walked away. Finally, I said, Fuck it. I set aside my independence and curiosity when James called me to hang out with him to watch a football game.

I chilled and allowed James to accommodate me this time. For clarity and setting the record straight, James and I have never experienced a sexual attraction for one another, only Eden and I, period!! Oh, wait! I have not mentioned what James's kink is, right?

Well then, I might as well share it with you now and it involves him watching me fuck his wife Eden in the bed they sleep on. Trust me when I say, I leave my DNA all over their sheets after I leave there. He would sometimes masturbate while standing next to his wife while I was licking her clit on their bed. Some people may label it as voyeurism, which is acceptable if it serves to rationalize his actions. Call it whatever you want that will help make this relatable for you. Of course, I never objected, as there was a psychological reason behind it. To be clear, every time James sleeps in his own bed, he can reminisce about Eden fucking me in it.

Adam: Hey reader! Don't you dare say NO WAY! It is James's kink, not yours, so keep your judgment to yourself. Cecil!

Cecil: Yea what's up?

Adam: Who the hell was that that said "no way?

Cecil: Oh! that's Royal all up in our business.

Adam: When is she umm...

Cecil: Adam, stay focused! I will allow her to speak a little later in this chapter.

Royal: Wait Nigga!! Did I overhear you say, you will allow me to speak later in this chapter?

Cecil: Yes, I said it!!

Royal: It's a good thing you are the author of this book! Because I would tell you to kiss my mutha-fucking ass!! I ain't saying another word, I am out of here. See you later,

Adam: Go-ahead Cecil, continue.

Cecil: For a specific reason, I purposefully and intentionally chose not to reveal this tantalizing detail earlier in this chapter. I wanted to keep you guessing about the nature of my relationship with James and Eden. Did it work? I hope so. Now, let us continue. Oh, I have messed up your brain now, haven't I? Are you asking yourself, "Does this shit really exist?" Indeed, it does exist, which is why you are still listening to this chapter.

One morning, I decided to spice things up from what I usually do with James. This time, James was subservient to both his wife and me. I told James to take off his pajamas and put on his wife's pink apron in the kitchen. Again, as a vanilla person, you will not understand my reason for making James wear that pink apron. It's another form of humiliation, and he appreciated it coming from me.

Royal: Speaking of humiliation, have you noticed how many black alpha males have been told to wear dresses lately?

Cecil: Yep! I sure have and, I am not about to roll call their asses to the front of the class either!

Royal: That's probably a good idea, so go ahead with the rest of the chapter.

Cecil: Thanks for interrupting again.

Royal: Go on, continue.

Cecil: To be clear, I would tell him what to do, and it was simple but effective. This is another grown-ass man I spoke to, but I was also aware of his kinks, so I had to be convincing in my tone of voice. While James was making us breakfast in bed, Eden told me: "Don't be nice to James under any circumstances this morning." And when breakfast is close to done and ready, I want you to yell out, "What the hell, bitch! Where is our breakfast?

And you better have everything we asked for." I got the memo, and smiled to myself, this is going better than I could ever imagine. While James was preparing breakfast, I said: WHAT THE FUCK, BITCH! WHERE IS OUR BREAKFAST? Eden was next to me laughing hysterically and so loudly, that I had to put my big ass hand over her entire face to shut her up.

After calming Eden down from laughing I said: And you better have EVERYTHING WE asked for." I also made him repeat out loud what we ordered, like he was our cook, food server, greeter at the door and valet parker. Remember, I am a Black male or (whatever you as a white person want to call me), acting as if I owned James as my white slave in his own home. Eden smiled and thanked me for knowing what he needed and how to express it. Minutes before James walked in, I had this big cheese-eating grin on my face.

James: What are you smiling about, SIR?

Well, honestly. "During slavery, lying in bed with a white woman would have resulted in immediate lynching. Mentioning this made Eden appreciate our arrangement and friendship. By this time, James walked in with our breakfast, with one of his hands under the tray, just like a waiter at the breakfast pancake restaurant. You could see the steam coming from the food. Surprisingly, he knew the protocol and served my breakfast first, waiting until I had everything I needed. After that, James served Eden.

I said, "Good boy, let us enjoy our breakfast, you little pervert, now take your little dick ass back into the living room, where you belong. "And stay there until I ring this bell on the nightstand." I was genuinely surprised by what I had asked James to do in front of his wife.

Reader, don't hate! This white boy skipped out of his bedroom like a college co-ed girl. Months of watching and listening to Eden humiliating James paid off.

Later that evening, while alone in the living room with James, I told him to get up from the couch and make me a drink; he failed the task intentionally. As a result, I made him walk towards me and stop because I wanted him within an arm's distance. As he stood before me, I slapped the right side of his face with the back of my hand, like Eden had done many times before.

He deliberately disobeyed me because he wanted to be punished, which is precisely why I did it. Once I became part of their lifestyle, he knew his refusal to fulfill my desires would result in me slapping him with the back of my hand. Btw did you know slapping a man is more degrading than hitting him with a closed fist? This will be the last time I mention this. But that's why a well-known rapper, actor, father, and husband opted for this method of expressing his anger instead of using his fist. Eden texted me while James was soaking and throwing a tantrum, and Eden texted me while she was in the bathroom.

Eden's Text Message: Would you please humiliate James in the living room while he's throwing a tantrum??

"Yes, not a problem."

Eden also texted her sister saying: Do you and Royal want to stop by, and do ya'll want to come over to watch my husband be humiliated? Eden's sister Scarlett texted back with a response saying, "Hell yeah!" Scarlett texted back asking:

Under the Cover, Part Two.

Scarlett: Who is doing the humiliation? Eden: texted back: "By some good-looking black man we met online, and... he is in our living room right now." Scarlett sent laughing emojis and a thumbs up, saying we are not that far away.

I was surprised James wasn't curious about what his wife was up to. While I was sitting in the living room near James, it was apparent Eden, and I was texting one another. You know that sound your cell phone makes once you receive and send a text messages, right? It seemed to not matter to James; because he trusted us enough to know we must have been up to something interesting. When the doorbell sounded, Eden walked over to the door with a mischievous smile and opened it. Scarlett, her twin sister, walked in first. She was an attractive white chick with dark blonde hair, a black dress, and silver shoes. Scarlett must have been at least five feet six in height, carrying a 2011 Hermès Black Matte Alligator Birkin 30 P.V.D. purse over her shoulder.

Don't tell her it's a knock off from China. Scarlett reached into her purse and pulled out a single malt bottle of Macallan – Anniversary Malt 1928 it' a 50-year-old Whisky I have never seen or tasted.

No sooner than three to four steps through the door, Eden and Scarlett were talking and hugging one another, and while that was going on, I googled the names of her Macallan Anniversary Malt and the Hermès purse.

"Fuck that! I wanted to know. Whoever is listening to this right now, you can go ahead and call me a NOSEY MUTHAFUCKER, RIGHT NOW, to yourself! They ain't no shame in my game!! I am sure you would agree; those two items, the liquor she and her purse, looked expensive. I had never seen anything like this before among all the liquor stores in the hood.

That liquor she brought is not even on the top shelf at a black nightclub. I am certain when it's delivered it's in an armored truck with two guards and guns drawn and ready.

Let us not compare this liquor to what women in the hood carry in their purses either.

FYI, Macallan Malt is worth $32,3999.99 a bottle...Mutha-Fuck!! RIGHT?

Fuck it, I will say it: flea markets are usually in the hood or near trailer parks, and you know damn well that purse that Scarlett came in with would be Chinese knockoffs. Do not get upset at me for speaking the truth; y'all know I am right. I could not believe it.

What the hell! It made me wonder what Scarlett did for a living—buying something that was damn expensive to drink.

Never mind the purse's price. Nevertheless, I had to pretend it did not matter as if I had been around people with more expensive tastes before. The only distinguishable difference between Eden and her sister was that Scarlett had dark blonde hair with silver shoes and a silky short black dress, whereas Eden had red hair with a white blouse and a shorter black skirt with white knee-high boots; she looked like a seductive high school teacher with the glasses she had on. Damn! For this evening, both had big ass titties and plenty of cleavage. Shortly after, Scarlet's best friend walked in. She was a stunning five-foot-seven Sista with a natural, red-tinted afro and red up-to-the-knee boots.

Royal confidently walked in, with arrogance oozing through the pores of her dark chocolate skin. It was undeniable that Royal had a beautiful smile and body that turned me on. Royal also arrived with an expensive Hermes Fjord BIRKIN 30 Rouge

H handbag worth over $18,000. Remember, I had time to research this while they ran their mouths.

This purse is also a knock off from China and I ain't telling her either. She wore porous red satin pants, over-the-knee red leather boots with black buckles, and black gloves. I am still determining where Royal bought her tight-fitting BDSM-styled corset; googling the embroidery, it was also expensive. I closely observed Royal's every move, like a dog patiently waiting for someone to leap over the fence and come close enough for me to bite them. When Royal first walked in, I thought, "I'm not saying she's a gold digger, but she ain't messin' around with a broke-ass black man." And while I was drooling over how attractive Royal was, the three whispered amongst themselves. While trying to listen to their conversation, I could only assume Royal and Scarlett were curious why there was a throne in the middle of the living room, just like I was.

As I asked what they were whispering about, they suddenly huddled up and turned their backs towards me. I can ignore women when they behave in such a manner. I am confident the three of them were whispering about what to do with me and the throne in the middle of the living room.

Finally, I strolled towards the living room, stopped, looked over my shoulder at Royal, and gestured towards the throne. I could not help but ask her,

"What's your plan for this throne?" Royal raised her right finger near her juicy, natural lips and asked me to hush. I can't believe that bitch raised her finger at me first of all and secondly, it's a good thing she's fine as hell!!! So, yes, I gave her a pass for the one evening. She would not tell me why the throne was in the living room.

Eventually, Eden, Scarlett, and Royal said it was for me. It was scary that they said it at the exact same time. They asked if I was willing to explore whatever they had whispered about. Many thoughts ran through my head, but I knew they would not ask me to do anything that would jeopardize my purpose of being there.

So, with a big ass grin on my face, I agreed. James and Eden just wanted to fulfill one of their fantasies with someone they trusted, and they would not sell their privacy to the highest bidder. So, I sat on the throne, waiting patiently for whatever the ladies had planned for me. At this moment, Royal walked in my direction, then leaned over and said, All of the sudden Royal looked at James and said "It's restitution time for, this white boy. Are you ready?"

Cecil: I paused for a few minutes because I had never met a black girl from the valley, until now. You have no idea how tough it was not to burst out laughing while she's telling James what to do. Personally, I could not take her seriously, that is, if I liked being dominated with a voice like hers.

Damn!! I am going to have to put on my poker face every time Royal says anything to James. I digress! I said, "Of course I am." I knew what she meant, and it made me hornier than a teenager sitting across from a woman with her legs slightly open, wearing a miniskirt with no panties. I sat down with my back against the throne, got comfortable, and waited. In fact, I was ready for whatever the ladies had in mind while James stood before us with a puzzled look.

The moment she whispered in my ear earlier, I was confident she knew exactly how to direct this scene without my assistance. I liked how Royal directed the twins to stand left of me while on the throne; her directness was on point. She had to walk over and point where she wanted the twins to stand on my left side. The reason why Royal had to point and verbalize it was because Scarlett and Eden were about to stand on the wrong side of me. Royal wanted to be on my right side while James kneeled in front of me, waiting for the command from Royal, like a good obedient white boy.

At that moment, the twins and I were waiting for whatever Royal had in mind. I asked Eden to pour me another shot of liquor. Of course, she wasn't paying attention and spilled it. I gave Eden a specific look, and she knew what to do. She leaned over and licked my fingers clean. Royal reached into her Chinese knock-off expensive handbag and retrieved a gold dog leash with a leather spiked collar attached.

Since you were not present as a listener, allow me to describe the collar. It was custom-made exclusively for James because it had gold spikes on the outside of the collar. To get James' immediate attention every once in a while, she would yank on the leash. I knew what would happen next, but Eden and Scarlett did not... I smiled because I knew Royal had been in this situation before being with us.

Her black book she carried around was composed of powerful white submissive men, just like James, whom she had dominated or should I say, had a mutual agreement with over the years. With her demeanor, Royal knew what to say and do to get our attention. She turned around and stopped James from just standing around looking confused and made him stand in front of her. Honestly, how she spoke to James in a firm voice, TURNED ME ON, well sort of! Even though she sounded like an interracial woman with a Valley girl drawl, I like the tone she used to express her demands to James.

Royal: "Come here, you little white bitch, and stand here, and don't you fucking move until I say so.

James: "Yes, ma'am."

With his head down, Royal pulled up Scarlett's dress past her waist and told James:

Royal: "You nasty little white bitch, now lean forward and lick Scarlett's asshole."

Cecil: Eden looked shocked that Royal told James to lick Scarlett's asshole. Shit! I could not believe that they had taken this to a "WHOLE NEW "FREAK LEVEL! I knew this because Eden did not even try to stop it from happening. Royal's insight was spot on, yet again. Of course, James licked Scarlett's asshole cleaner than a wash towel straight from the dryer and then stood straight up and looked head down at the feet of Royal. Royal looked directly at James and said:

Royal: Turn around, while I put this dog collar around your FUCKING NECK.

Cecil: Then she yanked on the leash, just for the FUCK OF IT! That was the only way Royal was going to get Jame's attention. Right afterwards,

Royal said to James: Stand directly in front of me like a good little cockles white bitch, and don't you dare move, UNDERSTOOD? James - nodded his head.

Royal said it a little louder this time, "I CAN"T HEAR YOU"

James nodded again, but this time he knew what to say...

James: Yes Ma'am, I understand!

Cecil: Royal, will consistently refer to James as a "little white bitch" throughout this chapter for a specific reason. And that's because white folks are comfortable calling us niggers these days. So, Royal is flipping the script and reversing "MAKE AMERICA GREAT AGAIN"!

When James intentionally ignored Royal, she knew how to get his attention. Royal grabbed the dog leash and yanked on it, forcing James to drop to the floor on his knees like James Brown, while making a choking and gagging sound. While on his knees Royal yanked on the collar again and said: who are you looking up at? and you better look down, BITCH!

Cecil: While James looked down, Royal reached into her purse and pulled something resembling a dog biscuit. It was meant for James to eat it. So, Royal extended her arm and opened her hand. Of course, James had to eat it from the palm of her hand like a good boy.

After eating it, James said, "Thank you, Mistress Royal." Royal's commanding valley voice forced James to wait for the next command. She must have been a "TAKE CHARGE KINDA GIRL" while in her mom's womb, RIGHT? Royal and I gazed down at James, who was kneeling like a crying Karen being arrested and taken to jail for lying. While Royal and I were staring down at James, Royal had one finger in front of her lips, expressing her desire for James not to say anything, until asked. As James waited for the next command, I looked at Royal with a devious smile.

I told James: pull down Eden's dress before me and wait for the next command. Just as James was about to pull down Eden's dress,

Royal STOP! I want Eden to bend over in front of you then lean over and place her hands directly on the throne's arms. I am preparing James for what's about to happen next because Eden expressed her unhappiness in the bedroom. As James was about to pull down Eden's dress, Scarlett decided she wanted to be a part of the scene.

Royal and I, ... told Scarlett to take off Eden's dress and panties.

Scarlett was excited and knew exactly what to do next, and that's what she did. She pulled down Eden's panties and lifted her dress over her sister's head until Eden was in her birthday suit and said: Royal, what do you want me to do with my sister's dress? Royal did not respond to for some reason and just rolled her eyes. The way Eden and Scarlett giggled showed Royal and I, that they had never done that before.

One of James' fantasies is to put on a chrome Chastity cock cage, and watch Eden have sex with me, like a H.N.I.C. (google it)

Wait!! If you had to look up what H.N.I.C. means, then, you are not black, like Joe Biden said on the "Breakfast Club interview... Just saying!! Plus, at that moment, I took over and pulled down my pants. I looked down at my cock, and it was stiff as a bottle with soda still in it. I told Eden: "turn around and put your hands on James' shoulders to balance yourself". As I stood behind his wife, my stiff cock was ready for a fucking good time. Royal stood next to me and slowly added lubricant up and down my shaft as if she were trying to JACK ME OFF. While I was looking down at Royal lubricating my cock, it almost made me pop off a load before the fun started.

While James was still on his knees, my cock shaft was all lubed and ready. Scarlett made James use his right hand to guide my cock into Eden's pussy from the back. Damn, I almost shot a load of cum once the head of my cock was in her, because Eden was so attractive from the back. The expression on my face clearly convinced Royal I was going to cum in a few strokes. Royal looked directly at me and said: slow down, Cecil. I guess Royal had something specific in mind for it. And as soon as Royal said "Relax, Sir,"

I blasted a load of my fresh, hot cum into Eden's pussy and sat back down on the throne while my legs shaking like a leaf on a tree. Then, Royal yanked James's chain, ordered him to bend over and look down at the floor. Royal in a firm, commanding voice said, "Lick the cum off the floor that has leaked from Eden's pussy and down her leg. "Fuck!! That sounded incredibly seductive coming from Royal, didn't it?

Adam: It damn sure did, Cecil!

Cecil: Unexpectedly, ... Scarlett walked over and placed the palm of her hand on the back of James' head. She guided his head towards every drop of cum like guiding a dog's nose while punishing him for shitting in the house. Royal and Scarlett did not realize how late it was and started collecting the items they brought with them. Before Royal walked out the door, she yelled out one more command for James.

Royal: "Look, little white, small cock bitch; I want the floor to be as clean as it was before Cecil fucked your wife, and there better not be a single drop of cum anywhere." AND I DO MEAN ANYWHERE!

Cecil: And just before Scarlett walked out the door, she was looking for drops of cum that may have leaked out of my cock onto the throne seat. James missed a drop of cum that must have dropped off the arm of the throne.

Scarlett looked down at James and said: you missed this one, right here. Lick that up too.

Cecil: Once the floor was free of cum spots, Scarlett said: goodbye and Royal said: See y'all later, right? And closed the door behind both of them. Keep in mind that, as disgusting as that all sounded, James pre-came right in his pants. His fantasy dramatically altered the dynamics of our relationship, particularly between me and Eden.

When I first met them, I did not understand why Eden wanted to watch her husband be subservient to me, but it became more apparent as time passed.

In fact, I learned more about their lifestyle than any other couple I had ever met before. You must remember that I have been living this lifestyle for a while. I made up an excuse not to see them for a while to allow them to reconnect and hit the reset button. Sometimes, couples should hit the reset button and reconnect if they feel out of sync. Years had passed, so I decided to call them.

From the sound of Eden's voice, I could tell she was pleased to hear my voice, and I was relieved that they had not forgotten about me. The universe must have brought us back together, as our connection was undeniable. While on the phone with Eden, James was listening, so he interrupted and asked, "Are you doing anything this weekend?

He requested that I come over and spend the night with them. Without hesitation, I selected a few pairs of pants and shirts, hopped into my car, and drove to their condominium by the ocean. As soon as I walked in the door, I gave Eden a big hug and a kiss. When Eden turned around, I gently slapped her on the ass while James watched. That's when that that kinky ass bitch said: That's all you got??? Maybe you can smack my ass little harder later on this evening, right? See what I mean?

James, extended his hand for a handshake, smiled, and said: "I am glad you called; it's good to see you."

The universe works in mysterious ways. I forgot to mention that Eden texted me seconds before I arrived, and said: I was happy to hear from you again. And they were ready for whatever kinky shit I had in mind this time around. So, I walked in and sat down in James' favorite chair, just as I had done before, while James began to prepare dinner.

He would only be content if I were happy, and his wife also became my servant. In other words, when I visit them, they become my servants, and no one else holds the same importance as me.

After dinner, James wanted to massage my feet while Eden was present. Just like at an Asian nail salon, he had everything ready and sat down on his little pink stool. James leaned over, placed one of my feet in his lap, and started massaging. Yes, that's correct. I am degrading him once again, well actually, he is degrading himself and he would not want it any other way. James massaged my feet with a lemon-revitalizing and moisturizing foot scrub.

I will admit I almost fell asleep because it felt so good. Afterward, I told James, take off Eden's panties in front of me slowly, and he did that with a cheese-eating grin on his face. The poem "Cheese-Eating Grin" is inspired by a poem about a cat with a cheese-eating grin after eating its best friend. You may not have heard that expression before, so, let's continue, shall we. Once Eden's panties were off, I told James to put her panties inside one of my pants pockets that were hanging on the chair. Eden understood why I wanted to take them home but remained silent. Even though this may not seem important to you, as the listener, it was for him to complete the task I gave him.

That evening, as a reward, I told him to put on his cock cage and a diaper, walk out of the bathroom, and model it for us.

Do not ask me why I knew he wanted to be in his favorite cock cage and diaper that evening; what matters is that he fulfilled both of my requests. There is one word that comes to mind: obedient.

Of course, it is James' unique kink, and I was rewarding him for putting it on and modeling it for us.

I then instructed him to gather our clothes from the floor, fold them, and hang them appropriately. Yet again, he completed that task too while smiling, like a fat family at an all-you-can-eat buffet.

I walked into the bathroom after the floor was clear, and the clothes were all on hangers. While looking into the bathroom mirror, I noticed the throne was still in the living room in the exact same spot as when I last saw them.

So, I asked James why the throne was still in the living room. James said: It is a continuous reminder of the fun we had when you were last here. I was happy to hear that because I missed that throne. Eden picked up her cell phone as the evening approached and started texting her sister Scarlett and her best friend Royal again; accept this time, she wanted them to sleep overnight.

I had been there one night before they arrived, and I thought to myself why not stay another night?

When the doorbell rang, naturally, I was happy to see Royal and Scarlett and this time they were dressed more laid-back, and Scarlett did not bring that expensive liquor.

Of course, Royal looked as delicious as ever, and I made that clear the moment we made eye contact. Usually, I don't feel attracted to a dominatrix. Still, there was something about Royal completely different from any Sista I had ever met. We all sat down on the couch, getting reacquainted, and discussed what happened after our last time together.

Scarlett said: I chose to disconnect towards men after I saw how James was afraid to share his kink with us.

Cecil: Scarlett was also afraid that most men will not allow themselves to be vulnerable with a woman and understand their kinks, especially if it was similar to James's kink. Royal decided to retire early from a corporation we are all familiar with after thirty years to become a dominatrix full-time. I looked out the window and wondered whose Bugatti was next to my car. Fuck! Judging from the custom-made necklace she wore around her neck, that car had to be hers.

Hey reader? I would like to deviate from the chapter for a moment and let me explain something hardly anyone talks about. Finding an attractive Black dominatrix is like trying to find one tiny diamond that is fifty feet deep in the Atlantic Ocean at night. She is rare, but she understands her role with the men who arrange to meet her. She is not flamboyant and must be reserved because it is not widely accepted today. White professional men who desire to be disciplined by a dominatrix, have an undeniably hidden thirst that is only shared between them.

As far as I am concerned, a licensed therapist or psychologist is not mentally qualified to manage such a task emotionally, and physically. Here is the thing: You will not find a Dominatrix on the back of your local paper anywhere.

This special type of service usually requires membership and is word of mouth only from a trusted individual or on websites that provide qualified new members.

To all the mothers, wives, grandmothers, and girlfriends listening to this right now: Some of you are already dominating men without even realizing the association.

Unconsciously, most white men in high paying positions, yearn for being submissive and desperately want to kneel and worship a strong domineering black woman.

He may find it challenging to ask, depending on his childhood upbringing.

Royal: Being a dominatrix is not about pleasing a man's twisted sexual desires but more about mind control.

What is fucked up is that any of you vanilla folks, out of ignorance, associate it with prostitution, and I am not sure where that comes from.

People who choose this lifestyle do so out of a desire to serve and worship their dominatrix. Another misconception is that the lifestyle is abusive or exploitative.

Hey, you listener!!, ... I'll be right back, I have to use the bathroom and let Adam take over for a little while, Okay? I know you like my deep voice but, like I said, I need to take a break and eat something. Adam, where are you?

Adam: I'm here.
Cecil: Go ahead....
Adam: Okay, I am back for a little while so let's continue. The reality is that the foundation of a lifestyle is communication, consent, and trust.

A professional dominatrix is a highly skilled person who puts the safety and well-being of their clients first.

The relationship is based on respect for each other and clear boundaries. All activities are consensual and agreed upon in advance.

Another common misconception is that the lifestyle focuses only on physical pain or humiliation. For some people, the lifestyle is about inflicting harm and perpetuating abuse. The reality is that the lifestyle encompasses many different activities and dynamics, ranging from role-playing, sensory deprivation, bondage, and discipline.

The goal is to explore power dynamics and fulfill consensual fantasies in an environment that's safe and controlled. Each session is exclusive to the submission and is based on their specific desires and boundaries. The overall goal is to provide a pleasurable and meaningful experience.

Adam Continues: Cecil deviated from the story for a little while, but his reason for doing so, was to clear up some misconceptions about the lifestyle for some of you, Vanilla Folks. Now, back to "Under the Cover" starring Cecil, Royal, Scarlett and Roy.

Cecil: Royal got up from the couch and sat next to me. I swear, Royal had on a dress that was about two inches below her pussy lips. Just before Royal was about to say something to James, I said just a second. Tell me about the background of the men who hire your unique services.

Royal smiled, looked around, and said, "Mostly white men in high-profile jobs and business owners." She also told me that a high-profile minister visited her; she chose not to tell me who it was for her safety and mine.

"Royal trusted her instincts to tell me about this one other client, and if I were to mention his name too in this audiobook, it would, blow your FUCKING mind.

I did not want to believe her at first, considering we all know who he is or have heard his name before.

Let me say this with all sincerity, he is so high up in the ministry also, and if I dare mention his name, I might as well go to the nearest police station and force them to lock me up.

I have seen this man in commercials and talk shows over the years and would not have ever guessed his private life. Oh, and by the way, I asked if she finally had an Asian client, and she nodded no. In disbelief, I said, "You mean to tell me you have not had one Latino client yet, either?" Royal responded, "Nope!

I would guess Latinos and Asians have their own kinky lifestyle, that I am unaware of. After ten minutes of reminiscing,

Royal suddenly stood up and told James, "Get up from the couch and walk towards me.

Cecil: When she stood up first, her big, juicy ass was three inches from my face. When I finally stopped staring at Royal's ass, James was standing directly in front of her, displaying a smile. We all knew what his smile meant, but we kept our poker faces. As James stood directly in front of Royal, she opened her purse and pulled out the gold dog leash with a gold spiked collar once more.

Then she reached back into her purse again, pulled out a long piece of rope, and placed it in James's left hand.

All of us but Royal were wondering what was up with the rope, considering she did not bring it the last time we were together.

Royal told James, turn around and spread your legs apart. WTF!!, I know, right? James was barefooted and was wearing blue jeans and a long-sleeved shirt.

Eden knew more about James' obsession with long-sleeved shirts than I did, so Royal did not inquire about it. I thought he must have had a severe skin condition and was scared I would judge him. When Royal told James, "remove your long-sleeved shirt", he became anxious and looked at Eden, me, and Scarlett.

Eden had a concerned look on her face and told Royal: - "James will not be taking off his long-sleeved shirt, at the moment".

Feeling concerned, I asked, "Is there something you'd like to share with me?" At this point, I raised my voice and asked Eden, "Why in hell is James reluctant to take off his shirt?" James looked at Eden one last time, and she nodded in approval for James to finally take off his shirt.

In fact, it wasn't due to any skin condition, contrary to what I and Scarlett had previously assumed. While his back was towards us, I could finally see why James never removed his shirt.

It was because there were Nazi symbols tattooed on the inside of both arms near his elbow. No wonder why this asshole wore long- sleeve shirts. You might wonder, "Would it have made a difference if I had known about this earlier?"

Well, it is too late in the chapter for you to ask me that question, and honestly, those tattoos looked fresh. It made sense that Royal had brought the rope earlier; she remembered James liked bondage and feeling helpless. Royal went into full dominatrix mode and told James to kneel in front of her. As I mentioned, Royal had a way of getting a man's attention with the tone of her voice.

While James was on his knees, she took the rope he was still holding in his hand and carefully and strategically tied him up with it. Eden quickly discovered that James had busted a load of cum in his pants. It took Royal about an hour to tie James up with the bondage rope she had in her purse. I was wondering why she required James to fold his arms, and now I understand.

His Nazi tattoos became visible when she decided to punish him for an unknown reason. Royal knew all along that James had those tattoos on his arms.

Royal recalled meeting Vivien, her partner in a different state, and fellow dominatrix to discuss James' tattoos during their meeting for lunch.

Vivien described her session with James in detail, mentioning his tattoos and how he shot a load of cum in his pants in the last session they had together. Vivien also mentioned that James had booked one weekly session for years before meeting Eden.

Once James married Eden, the sessions stopped because he feared she would find out and would not marry him.

Adam: Cecil's A.D.D. just kicked in again, didn't it? Back to the chapter.

Royal told James: stand up and turn around and kneel before Cecil and respect the fact that he is the H.N.I.C. which means: (head Negga in charge). Eden, Scarlett, and I laughed at James because there was a big, wet spot in front of his pants again. I stopped laughing because I knew Royal wanted a serious atmosphere to continue dominating James.

Therefore, I stood on the side of Royal, and just before his knees touched the floor, I asked him to stop and return to standing. That's when we all applauded him for overcoming his fear that black people were taking over the planet and allowing himself to fulfill his desire for humiliation by someone he trusted. Just a moment, I am going to take a break for a brief moment and let Adam the narrator take over, okay?

Cecil: Adam, go ahead:

Adam: Here is some background on James, who genuinely believed that black people were taking over this country he called the United States of America...

Cecil: Wait! Seriously?
Adam: Yep! may I continue?
Cecil: Yea, go ahead.
Adam continues: Cecil's friend was pissed off at him because they had gone to a football game together and Cecil refused to stand and sing the National Anthem. James leaned over and asked Cecil to stand and

Cecil said, FUCK THAT SHIT! while his arms were folded in protest. The people who were next to Cecil and James also looked upset that Cecil wasn't standing.

Cecil said: FUCK THAT SHIT again, so loudly that the white folks several rows in front and back started to voice their thoughts towards Cecil and James. Cecil told anyone who could clearly hear him: have you mutha fuckas ever read the words of that "SONG", WELL, HAVE YOU? It clearly says, "land of the free," which I am certain that excluded black people then, and today.

I see you are getting a little worked up while I am telling your story, should I continue?
Yea, Go ahead.

Cecil stood up again but this time on top of the seat and yelled out: "If I am free, why can't I walk, talk, drive, sit, stand or live WHEREVER THE FUCK I WANNA LIVE, HUH!! Also, why in the hell do this country still have "Sundown Towns"?

And why Colin Kaepernick a American Civil Rights spokesperson, banned from football? We all know the fucking answer to that question, RIGHT! It's because a WHITE MAN and those who agree with his opinions, didn't like the fact he kneeled during the National Anthem? As a matter of fact, this PEACE SIGN, big afro pick wearing, black panther party, ONLY IN AMERICA protesting mother fucker is better than half the mother fucken starting quarterbacks playing right now!

Go ahead, Adam!

Adam: James was aware that freedom did not extend to slaves also, and yet he expected Cecil to be sympathetic and share his ignorance. James must have overlooked that Cecil had to stand up and sing the National Anthem during his childhood, when he didn't know any better. His family, particularly his father, instilled these falsehoods in him as a child, dating back to his earliest memories.

That same day, James's drove to his favorite tattoo artist's parlor and had those Nazi symbols removed from the back of his left and right arms. James was overwhelmed by the guilt and shame he was carrying. Royal and Scarlett were always aware of his deep-seated yearning for humiliation.

Eden understood that James needed someone who understood his desires without passing judgment. In fact, trust played a significant part in why they chose Cecil initially. The fact that he's a nigger, oops my bad! I meant an African American or black, whatever!! He has lived many different lifestyles and was simply a bonus. He later discovered that for years in James' business, he would make sure not to advance black people within any of his companies unless he benefited in some way or another.

His justification was to solely appoint black individuals to positions with high turnover rates, a tactic he used to justify his perceived laziness in hiring practices. He also knew how to avoid discrimination lawsuits by utilizing his review practices effectively. The troubling part is that within all his companies, he would appoint a black male or female as a supervisor or manager to oversee the termination of black employees.

We are now in the 2000s, and it still happens today. Most of the promotions within James's companies were for white men between the ages of 27 and 35. This was due to their straightforward manipulation, enabling him to exploit his ignorance without resistance.

Well, that practice was as effective as the palm of my right hand, with a little lubricant added, and it consistently worked. Never mind that his entire family supported and approved of his hiring practices. James would smile at the faces of black employees but humiliate and demote them behind their backs. Black women who worked for James advanced faster and differently than the black men within his company. Cecil knew this because he decided to sit with him and watch his hiring, firing, and promotion practices. He must have thought Cecil was an Uncle Tom and even thought he would side with his practices.

His intentions were evident when he promoted black women at a higher rate than black men, despite the latter having more experience. He knew it would create a hostile environment, with jealousy and hatred causing division among the black employees. WOW!! And that concept worked like a charm. There were times when James and Cecil would sit back and watch the communication between black men and women and was amazed at how they did not see how, they were set up to stay divided and envious of each other, purposely. That approach remains effective even in 2025.

Nevertheless, James treats his family and employees in the same manner. James knew he needed to let go of that mindset, and his wife Eden understood this and was willing to support him through it. Before they met Cecil, they did not know of a way to heal him from his racist behavior. After that scene I mentioned earlier was over, they had a group hug, and Cecil will remember that moment for the rest of his life. Update: Since January 2022 when this was originally written, James' company has promoted one of his long-term black employees, named Hakeem, to management.

Many white employees voiced their concerns immediately after the announcement, despite their short tenure of three to five years with the company. Hakeem's work ethic spoke for itself. Indeed, Hakeem deserved a promotion back in 2017. James was perplexed as to why a few of his white employees found the promotion problematic. At that moment, James reassessed his familiarity with working with individuals who resembled him, in other words, were white people. He was unaware of widespread discrimination until he reflected on himself.

Adam: While Cecil was visiting James at his office, Cecil could clearly see there was tension you could cut with a butter knife. Before walking into his office, Cecil and James decided to go to the break room for some water. They noticed immediately that a few employees were whispering among themselves and looking over their shoulders like masked thieves in a jewelry store. They both thought that was suspicious behavior and remained quiet and watched them on a security camera. In fact, those employees should have realized there were microphones and cameras throughout the building, especially in the break room. Just as Cecil walked into James's office, he was asked to shut the door and close the blinds. Cecil's first thought was messed up and yours too, right?

Hey Cecil, would you mind telling the rest of this story, please!

Cecil: James wanted to show me some video footage of employees in the breakroom. Listen to what my own employees were saying in the breakroom about Hakeem."

I was shocked to hear they were plotting against Hakeem, and James held his head down in disbelief. Once James realized those secretive, spineless fuckers were planning to set up Hakeem to be fired, he separated them into different departments. Eventually, James could fire two of them for misconduct directly related to the plot they were pursuing. This woke friend of mine never realized how damaging his racist mentality was to his health and the people who loved him. James pulled me aside and said: I gotta tell you something profound but truthful. I never considered how detrimental my decisions could be to a generation of people. I also never personally experienced or dealt with this issue while growing up, so it was unfamiliar to me.

Before I started my business, my bosses, nurses, doctors, teachers, and principals were all white men and women. In fact, my friends were primarily white. I say "mostly" because I had one other Puerto Rican friend, and that's it!

As I previously mentioned, his parents were profoundly racist, and I am grateful that he did not instill this mentality in any of his children. However, reading "My Gay Ass Cousin" has taught me that indirect, subconscious exposure to hate does not require instruction. Whether subtle or blatant, you can tell what is happening in our country now.

Whites and Asians are comfortable expressing their ignorance and racial insensitivity. To wrap up this entire chapter, I decided it was best to never meet them again. We hugged and said our goodbyes, while I still had some of James's wife pussy juice on the shaft of my cock!! Oh! How did that happen you just ask yourself, right? Eden and I slipped into the bathroom for a few minutes, and I nutted all in her pussy, one last time.

Adam: Make This Make Sense:

James: It is interesting to note that a significant majority of black individuals in the United States of America accept being treated like third-class citizens. Unbelievably, you can find many YouTube videos that support this assertion.

Royal: Keep in mind that every time Cecil turn around, there is another damn Karen blaming black people for something and, of course, not minding her own damn business.

Adam: James and Cecil huddled up like a quarterback talking to his team and talked a bit more about James's past and concluded that these were some of the messed-up questions he and his white buddies would ask black people, instead of minding their own business.

Cecil: Here goes my list, READY?
James: Yep! Go for it...

Cecil: Number one on the list is: Do you live around here? And right after those questions comes: What's your name? Those two questions seem to be the go-to when you are in a white neighborhood. When I was an Uber driver, I heard that a lot because them white folks just could not mind their own business.

Coincidentally, if you are wondering how I managed the situation, let's say I ignored them. Otherwise, I would have played into their ignorance. James mentioned that a couple of months ago he walked up to a car parked across the street and asked a black family, "Why are you parked there? That's definitely another question I often ignore, preferring to roll up my windows with no response. That's precisely how I would have responded if James had asked me that question while in my car.

Adam: By the way, if you are not a Black person, I have a question for you. If someone you didn't know knocked on your car window and asked, what is your apartment number while in the parking garage, and do you have a key? What would you say or do? Seriously!! Oh! I forgot to mention, they are not even part of the security personnel either.

Cecil: Well? I'll wait for your answer whenever I meet you in person. Those questions irritate the fuck out of me, as though you are unaware of its implications. I was in an elevator when a white woman boldly asked me that question.

Naturally, I also chose to ignore her. I decided to save these two questions: I got a couple more for you. Is this your car? And where are you headed? In most cases, white police officers have asked me those two questions. Honestly, it is none of their business. What bothers me the most about the last two questions is that I can't slap the crap out of them for asking.

Just saying!! It is as if black people are required to display their freedom papers when they walk among white people. James was offended when I said this. Freedom papers explained:

During slavery, African Americans who were legally free were required to register with the county courts and obtain Certificates of Liberty. I can say confidently that some, not all, white folks want us to get on the horse and gallop back to the pre-civil rights era.

Back then it was against the law to teach black people how to read and write, ain't that a bitch! One thing I could never understand to this day is, even if we could read and write, what the hell were we going to be able to do with it, while being enslaved? Stop!! think about that for just a moment, before listening to this next paragraph...What is even more problematic is that, for unknown reasons, intelligent black people tend to intimidate white people. You and I both know there is some truth in what I just stated.

Otherwise, you wouldn't be all up in our damn business and watching every move. Ya'll either take, steal, or copy it, the profit from it. Don't get upset with me while listening to this because all I am trying to do is provoke some dialogue to talk about with you one day, I hope.

Royal: Honestly, black people don't care about white people's destination, origin, or identity, and you can understand why. It's none of our business motherfuckers, and we don't give a damn!

Adam: If you are white listening to this chapter, Cecil has a question for you.

Cecil: Why do white people alter their appearance to resemble black people?

Adam: Royal asked James that same question, and he gave her the finger and walked away. Does that sound about right? If you have a problem with what Cecil just said, challenge his opinions. He is always ready for a stimulating debate. Otherwise S.T.F.U.!!

What have I learned from writing this chapter?

I have encountered several couples like the one described in this chapter. One common interest I shared with all of them was that they, as white individuals, have a fondness for fucking black men. In contrast, I have a similar affinity for fucking married white women. You see, here is the thing about having sex with a married woman: This implies that I can have sex with a married woman in a way that I wouldn't necessarily have with a single woman.

In other words, NUT AND LEAVE. Often, the wife would call me just to say thank you for the excellent time, and her husband would eat her fresh, hot pussy afterward. I also learned that a strong, confident black man intimidates white men. Just ask the coach in Colorado. He has the confidence and career to go with a smile. He is the kind of man that young black kids should look up to.

I have always admired him for his ability to avoid the pitfalls of fame and celebrity. Another thing I have learned from experience is that I can intimidate weak-minded white men.

Honestly, I don't intend to intimidate weak-minded white men when I am out conducting my own business. What I am about to say right now will be controversial, and I am prepared for it to become a topic of discussion. There are white men among us who aspire to have a black, powerful Alpha male dominate them. They conceal this desire from others, fearing the judgment of their peers and the title they hold within their corporation. This audio version was very difficult to put together with different voices for each character. I tried not to confuse you, and I thought of every imaginable way to make it known who's talking. How did I do?

There are a lot of white man walking among us who romanticize about being dominated like this!!

Understanding Molested Vs Rape

Shelly Speaks: Before you dive into this chapter, I need to be upfront with you: I'm not a therapist, a psychologist, or any kind of licensed professional. What you're about to read comes straight from my life and the lives of others I've crossed paths with. This chapter deals with some painful, sensitive experiences — stuff that might trigger memories or feelings you've buried deep.

So please, proceed with caution.
Protect your peace as you go.

O ver the past 30 years, I have developed connections with approximately nine women, give or take, who have experienced molestation, rape, or in rare cases, both.

This audio version has several characters.

Cecil:

Narrator:

Royal:

Shelly

Cecil: Whether you are a newborn, a teenager, or an adult when it happens, this open non-healing wound will linger for the rest of your life. I should know, and I am an advocate for women's right to choose what they do with their own bodies and seek help to understand any trauma they have suffered. Unlike someone powerful in our country, they are taking away those rights that's been established since 1890.

By the way, listener, don't let my editing confuse you. Stay focused on my message not my errors. Remember, I did all the editing myself and it's not easy when there is more than one voice to carry the entire chapter. Please be patient. I would really appreciate it.

Narrator speaking: It can be challenging for a person who has experienced molestation to ask their partner to replicate the sexual experience without facing embarrassment or criticism. If you are confused and have questions, "What am I referring to?" allow me to elaborate. "Imagine this: When a predator or attacker behaves gently, nonviolently, it can be very confusing for us as adults.

Someone who says they love you can be misinterpreted when that behavior is replicated.

Personally, when I am with someone who has not had these experiences, I feel I will be misunderstood. Let me just say before you continue reading, trauma is a bitch! It will haunt you for the rest of your life. Your path has been altered, and your journey will be derailed. Discovering who you are will be challenging and complex if not dealt with professionally. Sorry for the interruption. Please continue.

Shelly: April 5, 2024, unlike "Vanilla Sheets", Cecil remembered this information, which he is willing to share since revising the first book and now the one you are currently listening to.

In retrospect, back in 2023, Cecil had a limited understanding of monogamy. It was during that time that he became acquainted with a woman online. Through their interactions, he uncovered new dimensions of his character that Cecil had previously kept hidden from others. His experience of molestation derailed his path that the universe had intended for him, since his conception.

And, regarding his relationships, that's another difficult pill to swallow because I have only seen him in love twice since we grew up together. I have discovered that when I connect with someone who has gone through similar experiences, like Cecil and I, we can support each other, particularly if we have endured molestation. Regarding kissing, we both realized we are no different than Julia Roberts in "The Lady in Red." What did either one of us know about kissing and penetration at 14–16 years old? As far as I recall, our parents did not kiss often, nor did our closest friends or families.

At the time, I knew Cecil wasn't into girls, so what is the connection between kissing and molestation? Everything, because it can be confusing, especially as a teenager, when an older male or female pretends to love you and treats you in ways you have never experienced before from your parents. Cecil likes to repeat himself so that you can hear and understand where he's coming from. Some of you are listening without understanding the author's intent, and you know who you are.

Narrator: Even though Cecil was still in high school, older women would flirt with him as he grew older and taller. Most of them were between 15 and 20 years older than he was. Upon reflection, even back then he was being molested in his teen years. Let us take a deeper plunge, shall we? Since he wasn't of legal age, let us consider the perspective from an older woman.

Cecil was around 5'9" in junior high and appears to have grown another seven inches over the summer. So, by the time he was out of high school, Cecil was the same height as he is now.

Naturally, Cecil attracted the attention of older women, who did not feel remorse for their association with a young, black, naive boy. Once again, older women were continuously molesting Cecil and clearly taking advantage of his adolescents. His subconscious mind did not fully understand why traditional sexual activity was ineffective. He needed a woman comfortable enough to take the lead without kissing.

This section of the chapter reminds him of the film Precious, where the mother treats her daughter like trash rather than kicking out the molesting coward she sleeps with or reporting his ass to the authorities. Having experienced deceit and abandonment from those claiming to love him, he struggled with trust issues during that period. As he previously mentioned, this was particularly true when a close family member or friend was involved.

He also never understood why the mother directs her anger towards her child instead of the man who is attacking her daughter. His experience has also shown that if a woman experiences molestation at a young age, she may misinterpret her love for sex and may not always understand what is happening. I hope my following words are clear. What if the girl grew up in a pleasant familial environment, and her mother was oblivious to her molestation? The husband or lover is the one who perpetrates the abuse. Let me explain this as best I can. I hope it makes sense.

What if the husband or boyfriend has experienced childhood assault and remains unaware of the long-term effect of it.

Furthermore, suppose that husband or boyfriend has been loved and cared for by a generational child molester. How can they know what is and is not acceptable?

I believe that detecting this type of molestation is challenging until the unsuspecting victim experiences the act, and only a trained specialist can recognize the warning signs. Let us return to what I am trying to convey:

Shelly: What if this generational child molester does it unknowingly, as he was raised by his father or his mother's partner? Nevertheless, he is now an adult, raising his daughter in the same setting where he grew up. It gets worse; he does this perversion with his daughter in a horrible, messed up, loving manner. In other words, he claims he loves her while she sits on his lap.

Additionally, he inappropriately tickles and caresses her when his wife is not around. This implies that he recognizes the inappropriateness of his actions, as it mirrors his father's treatment of him during his childhood. As they mature into adulthood, all of this can be very perplexing.

Therefore, when a woman tells a man that she wants to be choked and pushed against the wall, she might be trying to repeat the abuse she endured as a child from a family member or someone they trusted.

What are your personal feelings about what I have said? Please reach out to Cecil on social media, anytime, OKAY?

Cecil: I have dated women who have experienced rape and abuse, and I'm ashamed to admit that -- I find those women to be more intriguing.

Narrator: Shelly, you looked pissed off. Are you?

Shelly: Wait!! Excuse me!! What the hell are you talking about, Cecil?

Cecil: Well, if you had not interrupted me, I would have answered your question. Look! bitch, may I continue?

Shelly: Go ahead and continue, because I am certain this should be interesting, I hope!

Royal: Cecil!! No, you didn't call her a BITCH!!! I wasn't planning to say anything until, "under the cover" Fuck that shit now!! DO YOU REMEMBER that rapper Queen Latifah?

Cecil: Yea, WHAT ABOUT HER?

Royal: Well then, who you are calling a BITCH!!

Cecil: Alright, Understood, okay?

Royal: Yea, alright, continue on with whatever the fuck you were mumbling about.
Cecil: Fuck you Royal!!

Shelly: Thanks for having my back, Royal.
Royal: I got your back, always, okay?

Cecil: Are you two done, hissing? Just as I thought, I'll continue now.

Narrator: These are the types of women I unconsciously draw towards, especially if they have overcome tragedy and still enjoy sex. They are usually shy and will beg me in a subtle, indirect way to repeat the molestation. I have never viewed women as damaged property, and to be honest, I find it attractive when they disclose their experiences of molestation or sexual assault.

The trauma I experienced as a teenager continues to haunt me even in my sixties.

Later in this chapter, I will go into more detail about this. My deceased mother is still unaware of this. Yes, this book is therapeutic for me and, hopefully, for you. Aside from that, who has not had a rape roleplay fantasy? Anyone who condemns me for what I just said, make sure you are honest with yourself. Years later, I grew interested in being in a Dom/Sub relationship.

It is important to understand that some women desire both sexual and emotional dominance in their relationships. This applies to women of all ages, backgrounds, and income levels.

That's why the statement "Do whatever you want with me" from a woman is like waving a red flag in front of a bull!

Shelly: Does anyone have anything they would like to add before Cecil ends this chapter?

Royal: I'll let Royal rap this up. Royal, please go ahead. We are about to wrap up this chapter with this important information. We can't over emphasize the importance of discussing sex with your spouse (or potential partner) from the start. Cecil has no intention of sticking his cock anywhere until he has had a mature chat about his desires. And I'm not letting some hood Negga or red neck try to stick their cock up in me either!

It frustrates me and Cecil when we are attempting to establish a rapport with a fuck partner, and they are unwilling to discuss sex immediately. They assume we both want to fuck them, separately of course not the same chick, which is not the case. Mature adults should enjoy discussing the topic, and we understand that many women find it difficult to talk about sex.

Their upbringing or past experiences with rape or molestation are contributing factors, emphasizing the crucial importance of understanding everyone. Peace!

Shelly: And by the way, remember, **Royal:** RAPE or MOLESTATION is usually done by someone that says, ...

THEY LOVE YOU

Unfaithful Part One & Two

Before you read this chapter, read "Dear Momma, Beatrice Hicks, and My Gay Azz Cousin," which explains in detail why I am the way I am.

Btw: the audio version of this chapter is slightly different than the audiobook purposely!

That is only if you still want to read it. I am trying to downplay my mentality. Vaguely put. You may wonder why I say one of my wives. It is to protect their identity and which one of the three I am talking about. Yes! I have been married three times.

This chapter will be my first revelation. One of my wives may become angry with me after reading this chapter. In that case, I am not apologizing but acknowledging my unfaithfulness. This does not exonerate me of the ignorance you are about to read. Two out of my three ex-wives were not freaky at all. Sex with the two of them was just okay; the best I have had was with one out of my three ex-wives, which I won't mention her name either. Of the three ex-wives, I had an affair while she was at work with a white woman named Mya. Mya was a woman I met in a chat room on AOL. She did not live too far away and was also married. After we talked for a while in the chat room, we trusted each other enough to exchange cell numbers. After a few weeks, I picked her up in a shopping mall near my house.

Since all the houses in my neighborhood were approximately ten feet apart, I needed to figure out how to bring her into my home without anyone noticing. I knew we had nosy-ass neighbors who always looked out of their windows a lot. Occasionally, I drove around the neighborhood alone a few times a day just to see who would notice and say something to me.

While driving around the neighborhood several times during the day, I felt confident that no one could report or gossip about the affair I was planning. I went to the meeting spot we agreed on. She was there, just as planned, and she became nervous while I drove home. When I pulled into my neighborhood, I asked Maya to lean over as close to the floor as possible. Then I opened my garage door and drove in.

We conversed over the phone for several weeks, and I understood Mya's preferred communication style, which turned her on. Once the garage door closed, I wasted no time telling her to get the hell out of my car. I told her to go inside my home and immediately remove her clothes. Mya started with her shoes, pants, blouse, and panties and left the best for last, her big-ass bra. Once I unsnapped the final clip of her bra, her titties dropped and bounced around for a couple of minutes (just kidding) like two giant ass water balloons tied together. Her bra flew into the air like a helium balloon. I know I am exaggerating a little bit for the hell of it. I just wanted to make sure you had a visual, that is all. I remember her facing me so that I could visually see her big ass titties. And, while she was naked and vulnerable, I inspected her big ass titties.

Yes, I said taste because after sticking one or several fingers inside her pussy her and her cum was all over them, so I decided to lick them. Then I told Maya lay face down on top of the pillow I had on the carpet while I applied my favorite lube to the shaft of my cock. Then I fucked her in the ass until I felt like I had exploded. Maya did not want me to make **love** to her or fuck her like I cared about her; she could get that from her husband.

So, I decided to make her walk naked and blindfolded into my garage. I then told her to put her arms out in front while I tied a rope around her wrist. Then I instructed her to raise her arms above her head so I could secure them to the garage door brackets above with rope. Of course, she was nervous and excited because there was cum running from her pussy and down her legs. I flogged Maya a few times in places where her husband would not notice.

She told me they only fucked once a month, and that would give her plenty of time to heal from the bruises from being flogged. Aside from that, it was time to take her home. And just like when we came into the garage, it was time to pull out (no pun intended). So, I instructed her to lean down again. I opened the garage door and slowly drove out of my neighborhood, ensuring my nosy neighbors would not notice. I dropped her off near a bus stop in case anyone she knew saw her. We never saw each other again after that one time together.

PART 2

Before I continue with "Unfaithful Fuckers Part Two," I would like to pose a question to the women reading this chapter: why do you feel the need to associate with a man you can't trust? No one else on earth possesses the intuition that you women do. It never ceases to amaze me some women continue to tolerate his lies. Not only do I not blame men for lying, but I also blame women.

What exactly do I mean when right? If he is dishonest about trivial matters. I can only imagine what he will say to you when he is caught cheating. With that in mind, let us discuss my decision to label this chapter Unfaithful. When I was in my early forties, I worked with a man named JoJo in a warehouse in Florida. One day, I sent him a message asking if he would be interested in working for me on some deliveries. I operated a delivery service that delivered furniture from various local businesses.

While I was driving, his girlfriend would repeatedly call his cell phone every couple of minutes. While driving, I overheard him say, "I am with Cecil, and we are making some deliveries." It is not like he only said it once; it was at least five times in a row. This bullshit went on for an hour or so. This spineless muthafucka wanted me to tell her he was working for me.

Remember that I am the driver, and JoJo was in the passenger seat, so I could hear everything he told her. Even with his cell phone close to his ears, I could hear every word she was saying to him. I was irritated at his behavior. Instead of taking charge and promising to talk to her when he returned home, he was in the passenger seat, acting like a little bitch. Not bitch referring to a woman or girl, but he left his balls in her purse before he left home. Get my drift?

One other way to look at this. He was acting like a neutered female dog. That is Mo betta!! Some men like crazy ass bitches, but the one he was dating takes it to a whole new level of crazy. He would tell me stories like getting off work and his tires were cut, and by the time he returned home, his front door was scratched up. I remember another moment when she burned some of his clothes, like in the movie "Waiting to Exhale."

After some years had passed, I realized that he was a submissive doormat and must have liked being spoken to that way. That is based on how he dealt with his girlfriend at the time.

No male or female should tolerate verbal abuse of any kind. This is especially true when someone acts crazy, causing your cell phone to explode every few minutes. Anyone who does not believe you is telling the truth for the first time. There will be more times to come when they won't believe you. Depending on what they have experienced in their past relationships, it is them, not you; walk away. There was a reason she treated him like that.

He cheated on his girlfriend when they first met. It now makes sense why she was blowing up his cell phone every few seconds, right? She was concerned he would do to her what he did to the girl before her. I saved that information for last. Why am I telling you this story? It is because men are inclined to label a woman as "crazy" without providing the whole story. **Peace!**

THE END

See you in the next

Vanilla Vs Picante

THE CHARACTERS IN THIS CHAPTER ARE:

Cecil: - Also known as **(C)**

David: - Also Known as **(D)** With a southern voice Narrator

Matilda: - Also known as **(M)** A Soft-spoken female

Sassy A: Also known as **(S)** and also Royal in other chapters.

VB: Also known as **(V)** Believes in white privilege

Characters from the audiobook

Hey, it's me Cecil, you have read me telling you my story and now I am about to allow someone else to read it for me, if that's okay?

(C) My throat is a little dry and I just want to chill during this chapter. Maybe near the end, I'll have a few words to say. So, for right now, let me introduce you to "David". He's been a friend of mine for a while and knows all my darkest secrets. David, go ahead!

(D) Well aright then, here goes. As I have said before, it bothers me that a lot of single men don't take the time to get to know women before having sex. When I was participating in the swinging lifestyle, I came to this realization. The truth is that in a conventional lifestyle, you often find yourself assuming a person is not interested in sex. I am a grown-ass man and too damn old to play head games to see if we are compatible sexually.

Additionally, I don't want to spend weeks trying to get to know someone only to discover we are not sexually compatible. Swinging is an excellent option for sexually inclined individuals, such as me, because it eliminates any unnecessary conversation that may lead to leaving the party with blue balls. There is no way you can tell me that at a vanilla nightclub or private party, you will find someone you can vibe with, especially if you are a single black male.

Participating in the swinging lifestyle is all about experiencing someone or something different. That's why a black couple, a single black man or woman, is ideal for a swing party around a bunch of white freaky ass mutha fuckas. Let us face it— white people can indulge in slavery fantasies in this setting. Did you at least smile when I said that? In fact, they may not realize their attraction from what I observed and that white swingers find themselves drawn to individuals with dark skin tones. Oh! They better keep those slavery thoughts to themselves. If they share it, they may end up in crutches. Or I am going to jail. And trust me, I completely understand the attraction of reversed slavery. I also like white women for the same reason.

That's why a tanned white woman does not personally appeal to me in the swinging lifestyle. Suppose I am lusting for a darker complexion. In that case, I will engage in sexual relations with black women, who are available in a variety of skin tones without tan lines. Sorry for rambling a bit, but when a thought comes into my head, I must share it with you, okay? I have always been a person who wants to know the woman before having sex, even in a vanilla environment. I also have never walked into a swinger's party like a black outlaw with three fully loaded six-shooters, assuming I am having sex. I mentioned that I have three fully loaded six shooters and one of them will be in the back belt just in case they decide to take the other two.

It is my backup, lol. I am mixing fiction with actual events, but isn't this more interesting? The atmosphere must suit me; if not, I will return home. I also like getting to know the husband first, which means asking him about his family, work, etc., and marriage to his wife. I do this because he is the gatekeeper and nothing sexual is happening unless he approves.

So, while talking to the couple at a private party, I stand by the husband's side and try to have a genuine conversation to understand his mindset. Please keep this in mind. I already know his wife wants to fuck me because of her body language and eye contact. Conversing with the husband or boyfriend helps me to determine whether to proceed or leave. (black people say con--va--satan). When they say it I laugh to myself. In most cases, the wife has already informed the husband that she wants to fuck me.

What she is doing is seeking her husband's approval, which I always completely understand. There was only one time when the husband was unfriendly towards me, anticipating his wife would feel uncomfortable because of his insecurities. If this happens, I won't attempt to party with the wife after our conversation.

In all cases, if the husband disapproves, nothing happens between the wife and me. Here is a real-life scenario of how I approach couples: I survey the room and wait to see if one of the wives at the party makes eye contact with me. When I receive eye contact and a smile from more than one of the wives, I eventually walk over and introduce myself, one at a time.

Sometimes, the woman is aggressive, and I shy away from that personality. Straight and aggressive women remind me of one of my ex-wives. Aside from that, aggressive women only care about themselves, and I am not down with that personality. I can always detect if a woman has a dominant personality.

Furthermore, I find it uncomfortable to receive sexual instructions. Imagine her pushing my big ass down onto the bed and telling me what to do while she is trying to fuck me! In most cases, I won't be hard enough to fuck her anyway, and now I must justify my limp cock. You can tell that I have been in this situation before, right? Trust me, having to explain a limp cock can be uncomfortable. One final thing I want to mention about aggressive women is their tendency to slap or try to stick fingers up my ass, which is another reason I won't date, party with, or marry aggressive women.

In other words, that's a Hell no to the no, no, no. Just saying. By getting to know the couple first, I am ensuring we are compatible and determining if there's attraction. This makes the swinging lifestyle great; it removes all our barriers. During this time, you share a common interest and engage in sexual conversation with multiple likeminded people.

When both partners share their sexual fantasies and are open-minded, the experience becomes truly remarkable. Vanilla folks often lack understanding of the lifestyle and have never indulged. Then have the nerve to speak negatively about it. I try to emphasize that it is simply about having sex with like-minded individuals, nothing more, nothing less. It's a well-known fact that some individuals separate or divorce after participating, primarily due to a lack of honesty in their relationship or trust issues before participating.

To me, it is all about enhancing the relationship between two people. Couples can still have sex with other people, but when it is over, it is over, and you two come back together again. There are alternative lifestyles that work for some people, and those individuals understand them. I have always found comfort in sitting around, enjoying a few drinks, and engaging in meaningful conversations about various topics. These conversations don't always have to be about sex. Did you happen to catch I said a few drinks?

(C) Honestly, because I don't like being intoxicated, it reminds me too much of my father. Rest in peace.

(D) If I make just one connection with one woman, I will ask if she wants to get together at the next party. I should have said this at the beginning of the chapter, so I will say it now. If you are a black male reading this chapter, and you are at a swinging event, nightclub, or private party where most of the women are white, please refrain from asking them if they have ever dated or fucked a black man. I can testify to their distaste for the question, as they often reveal it to me immediately following the inquiry and during our ongoing conversation. Introduce yourself and let your mannerisms speak for themselves.

Flirt a little, but not too much, because that makes you creepy in her eyes. Also, don't be all touchy-feely when you first meet, and keep a safe distance, just in case she may have had a horrific experience with a black man or a man in general. Stand back, watch for the clues, and always be respectful. Writing this chapter has confirmed what I already know. Suppose you consider yourself an experimental sexual person living in a vanilla world.

In that case, finding the right partner to explore that part of you will be challenging. This is why, in terms of lifestyle, you can experiment with individuals you feel a strong connection with. And once you find him or her, you will see them again at the next party. By the way, the chapter "In the Swing of Things" contains a secret I have not revealed to anyone within the lifestyle community, until now. You may have or may still need to listen to that chapter.

That's all I will say now until you have heard it. I am exposing myself and another couple in a way that may spark some dialogue between them, and I am not willing to discuss this with them outside of this audiobook.

Someone recently crossed my mind, and I thought it would be beneficial to share it with you. I recently met a lady, J, who I will only refer to by her first initials so that she can identify herself if she happens to read this book. I met J and her boyfriend at a swinger party at my friend's home in Tampa, Florida.

I immediately felt a sexual connection with J when I looked at her; she just had a freaky look, if you know what I mean. I said to myself, I may not be fucking her tonight, but hopefully sooner than later. The few times we saw each other at different parties, we did not have sex, but we continued to talk whenever we had the chance. Sometimes, I would attend a party and find myself unable to connect with any of the women to have sex with.

When that happens, I will occasionally chill and converse with a few of my friends. After a few months of seeing each other at my friend's home in Tampa, we finally had sex, and it was fun. She made it clear when we first met that she loves to suck and fuck, but no anal sex. J and her boyfriend had an agreement before attending the party. He must had known I wanted to fuck that bitch in the ass, damit! Anyway, I was okay with it because I understood their relationship's dynamics. So, around the fifth party J became comfortable around me.

Her boyfriend kept hinting for me to fuck her every chance he got since the first meeting J. Excuse me for a second, following me may be difficult because I know I'm all over the place. I will continue discussing J. Eventually, she asked me to participate in an activity unlike any party I had ever attended. One evening, J asked me to follow her as I passed by the bedroom with mattresses scattered across the floor.

At first, I wondered why she was whispering—and what the hell her intentions were. I also couldn't help but notice how she kept glancing around, which dialed up my paranoia.

Honestly, the only way I can describe it is like watching a woman holding her boyfriend's phone up to his face for facial recognition—while he's half asleep. Shady as hell.

(C) "Time out, David. I want to explain this part coming up, okay?"

(D) "Go right ahead!"

(C) "If you're a white woman reading this right now, you've got to understand where my head was at with J's suspicious behavior. It's a documented fact that white women are still out here falsely accusing innocent Black men. So yeah, I was hesitant to take another step toward that bathroom.

And I know what some of y'all are thinking—'Man, you're being too cautious.' RIGHT?

Well, let me remind you—it's been proven over and over: a white woman can call the cops on an innocent Black man and ruin his entire life."

(C) "Okay, I'm done. Go ahead, David."

(D) Jay whispered, (M) "Follow me to the bathroom."

(C) And that caught me completely off guard.

I followed her, cautious as hell, looking around like a teenager who just saw someone drop a wad of cash on the floor and walk away.

She whispered again, softer this time.

(M) "I'm gonna wait until everybody's out of the bathroom."

(C) At that point, my mind went straight to, "Does she want me to shower with her—or do something... more interesting?"

When the last woman walked out of the bathroom after *** douching, Jay grabbed my hand, and we slipped inside immediately.
Right after I walked in behind her, she closed the door. I was hesitant but not scared. And it became crystal clear why she locked it.
She said softly, (M) "Look, I need you to pee in my mouth."
I froze. like a parakeet, I repeated her exact words:
(C) "You want me to pee in your mouth?"
She nodded, calm as hell.

(M) "Yes... and I've wanted you to do that for some time."

(C) "I can't believe I'm telling y'all this."

(D) "Alright, continue."

With a confused look on my face, I said,

(C) "Well... alright then."

She took off her clothes, stepped into the shower, and kneeled submissively in the bathtub—arms behind her back, mouth wide open, waiting.

Now, if you've ever watched porn, you'll notice the dudes are usually at least semi-hard when they're peeing in a woman's mouth. I assumed that's how it worked.

Turns out, I was wrong.

J didn't care if I was hard or not. She just wanted me to pee in her mouth—assuming I was just as wild as she was.

(V) Picture it: a Black man standing over a white woman kneeling in a bathtub, mouth wide open... waiting for me to let it go.

(D) "Umm... Cecil?"

(C) "Yeah, what's up?"

(D) "Tell that mother sucka who just spoke to stay the f out of my chapter—I'm narrating!"

(C) "Oh, I got you! Hey!! Get the f*** outta here!"

(V) "What did I do? I thought my white privilege card gave me full access to your audiobook!"

(C) "No, it doesn't."

(C) "Okay, David, he's gone."

(D) "Thanks again!"

(C) "Not a problem!"

(D) Here is the thing: I have seen it on pornos, experienced it unexpectedly from a girl in one of my chapters titled "3 Similar Situations," and peed on my ex-girlfriend's stomach while she was in the closet. Now, a once-in-a-lifetime opportunity presents itself to me, and I could not pee in her mouth, even if she were on fire. As I write this part of the chapter, I am frustrated. I tried and tried, and she kept waiting and waiting. You should have seen my cheeks; I looked like Dizzy Gillespie's twin brother.

(D) Nothing came out of my cock, and I was disappointed. She said,

(M)"That's okay; it happens to most people who have never tried it."

(C) She was correct; I had never pissed in a woman's mouth before. I was disappointed that I could not piss in her mouth, as she would have been the first to do so. Well, I thought I was freaky as hell to even try it. What do you think? What is particularly problematic about this situation is that as soon as she exited the bathroom, I felt the urge to pee. The fact that you attempted to piss in that woman's mouth is something we must discuss later,

(S) you are just straight up nasty, Cecil!

(C) I know, right!

(D) By then, my inability to pee earlier had become a source of frustration. There is nothing sexier than a woman on her knees, with her mouth open, waiting for me to cum in it, not piss. Her boyfriend must have done that with her a few times. I have seen it in videos, but it does not turn me on.

I had the opportunity to piss in J's mouth after she expressed interest, but I was unable to do so. Life goes on, and I am okay with not being asked to try that again. So that's my "To Pee or Not to Pee" story. Just before you go, I have a few more words for your ear, okay?

(S) Cecil, where in the hell did you find this proper speaking nerd?? He almost made my pussy dry up! He might as well say:
(VB) "Pardon Me, Do You Have Any Grey Poupon?"

(S) Yes, I know I got jokes!

(C) Royal?

(S) Yes, what's up?

(C)You need to start being around educated folks. Because those ghetto ass mother fuckers you be hanging with got your way of thinking all messed up!

(S) Well, maybe you are right.

(C) Okay!! I am back to finish the rest of this chapter and thanks, DAVID!

(D) NO PROBLEM! And Take care Cecil. Oh, and by the way, fuck you ROYAL!!

(S) Fuck you too,

(C) alright, alright enough! Besides, Royal I need you to stick around for a few more paragraphs.

(S) I am right here and waiting, just let me know.

Now, let us discuss the various ways in which two people can agree to participate in the swinging lifestyle:

GRIN AND BEAR IT:

(C) The title says it all, right? Simple: if I am not attracted to the husband's wife or girlfriend and my partner is attracted to her husband or boyfriend. Neither one of us is taking one for the team just to have sex with them. Under no circumstances is it fair to indulge unless you both like them physically and on a conversational level. Before getting into the lifestyle, it is a beneficial idea to discuss some way of communicating to each other that you are not interested in having sex with the other couple's partner. Consider using hand signals, specific phrases, or even a wink. I used it with one of my wives on many different occasions.

Anything is better than nothing to convey to each other you are not interested in continuing. It would also help if you knew your partner's taste should you decide to continue. Sometimes, my partner did not like how he spoke to her, or the vibe did not feel right; this often led to the signals I mentioned earlier.

I just remembered something today on 04/20/2024 that's off the subject. We once attended a party where the only guests were elderly individuals. When I say old, they should take a tablespoon of Geritol every hour, if you know what I mean. Seriously, they should not take the recommended dosage it says on the bottle. I saw more wrinkles than on a Shar-Pei puppy.

Wait, did you laugh aloud or to yourself? Let me know somehow. I would appreciate it. Okay next:

DISCUSSING, DRINKING LIMITS:

I've never been to a party that didn't have alcohol front and center. I mean, let's be honest people aren't exactly passing around bottles of Fiji water trying to loosen up. And truthfully, I've only dated one alcoholic. Other than her, I usually don't worry too much about a partner's drinking habits. But here's some free advice: If your partner enjoys knocking back a few, both of you need to talk about your drinking limits beforehand. Trust me, it saves you from that awkward moment where someone's too drunk to hold a conversation—or worse, too drunk to do anything else later.

And, of course, let's not forget the most important part: Don't drink and drive, you two lovable degenerates. Now, one of the wives I met at a party once told me, "We women usually shake off our nerves after a few drinks." I get it. Sometimes that confidence boost comes in a shot glass. Especially if she's not feeling her best about how she looks that day. But let me tell you about this one dude I saw at a party—four shots of vodka, no chaser. I just shook my head.

Unless that man swallowed a blue pill beforehand, there's no way he was worth having sex with later. (No judgment, just calling it like I see it.) Let's step off topic for a second. I've watched men drink like fish and wondered, "Why is she still married to him? Especially when she doesn't even drink herself?" I can't answer that one. I didn't grow up married to an alcoholic, but I did grow up raised by one. My dad. And Lord knows what else he was mixing with it prescriptions, street meds, who knows?

Whatever force in the universe kept me from following in her footsteps, I owe it a big thank you. I could honestly write a whole chapter about that, but I think you get the picture.

CONDOM OR RAW:

This will be an intriguing topic to discuss. Would you agree? So, buckle up because I am about to push down on the accelerator. It is obvious that you should discuss this rule before even considering the lifestyle.

Just so we are clear, there are always risks without condoms, and that's a fact. This subject, whether condom or raw, has been one of my all-time favorites. There was one time I wore a condom in high school. Wait just a moment, ...I can't believe I am unloading my memories like a pregnant woman giving birth to a 20-pound baby! If you are still listening to this audiobook, I have included a few missing details from "Vanilla Sheets".

I am not sure why the universe spared me from so many horrible situations I participated in; here, I am disease-free. Anyway, for me personally, I can't feel anything, and I can't have an orgasm. Now that I am writing about it, I will admit that there were times I needed to wear one anyway. So, I wasn't as careless as I thought. In the chapter "Pimpin Ain't Easy," I recall picking up prostitutes (ladies of the night).

During those whore search encounters, I wore condoms, and not with anyone I was dating. I realize I have strayed a bit from the topic of why it is essential to wear a condom while engaging in this lifestyle. The parties I attended in Tampa, Florida, were with like-minded people who did not like to wear condoms either.

Hi, reader. Do you require condoms from your partner? Isn't it awkward to discuss that subject just be fucking? All of us have struggled with this subject at one time or another, right? Personally, I try to clarify or discuss that right away. At times, I trust that the person I am about to have sex with is okay without using a condom. Are we playing Russian roulette? Of course, we are. Consider this question for a moment.

Has a condom ever slid off while fucking and didn't know it? Has one ever busted while fucking? etc. etc.!

(S) ANAL: Since I have already mentioned this subject a few times, David I am leaving this paragraph for you, so go ahead!

(D) Say lady! Why do you require your partner to wear a condom during anal sex but not when you are sucking his cock? That does not make any sense, does it? That's like ordering a triple-meat burger with extra sauce and large fries with a diet soda because you are watching your calories. In conclusion, I find it humbling walking up to the counter to purchase regular-sized condoms rather than magnums.

Ladies, if you are afraid to ask the size of a man's penis before you fuck him, then ask him to bring some condoms, and whatever he shows up with, will tell you everything you need to know. Anyway, discuss anal sex before you considering go to a party. To fuck, or not to fuck, that ass is the question! There is an additional topic to discussing anal sex in a chapter called: "Anal Sex Technician" before engaging in sexual activities with others.

(C) Occasionally, I will meet someone's wife at a party, and she will only have anal sex with her husband. That's not a turn-off for me. Ladies, you, and I know men come in all shapes, sizes, and thicknesses if that's your number one concern. My experience suggests that she can choose a partner with the right size and technique for anal sex. Several husbands have expressed gratitude to me for helping them explore this option with their wives.

TO KISS, OR NOT TO KISS:

You decide whether to kiss, but it would be awkward to not do so during intense passion. However, it is essential to discuss this matter before engaging in sexual activity with anyone else. Kissing can be very intimate, and I completely understand when someone's wife at a party chooses not to kiss me. Again, you should discuss this before attending a lifestyle party and engaging in sexual activity.

SAME ROOM VS. SEPARATE ROOM:

The level of trust and comfortability makes this a simple choice. In fact, if you have doubts about your relationship, it is advisable to seek advice and refrain from proceeding until you have addressed this seriously. Otherwise, I am confident that it will eventually become a distraction or far worse. I will explain the difference between the two if you are scratching your head like you are looking at Algebra on the chalk board.

SAME ROOM:

It just means all parties involved are in the same room having sex with their own partner. In some cases, if they have been together before, both couples already know what is acceptable and what is not. My preference is separate rooms. I like this because it makes me feel alone with her when actually I am not. You may be saying to yourself, "Isn't that like cheating while in the lifestyle?" To answer your question, I would say "no," as being in the lifestyle allows you to live out your imagination in a way that can be enjoyable, provided you maintain a balanced perspective. If you have never experienced this before, I am certain this is confusing for you.

SEPERATE ROOMS:

Two couples privately in a room having sex with the other person's partner. Sometimes, being around your partner may make you nervous, and you can't relax without worrying about what your partner is thinking. I have said this before, you both should not be in the lifestyle if that is the case. Or you want to share a private moment without interruptions. Whatever your reasons are, they will determine whether it benefits both of you. Remember what I said earlier: if there are hidden or obvious trust issues, please seek professional advice. Moreover, this lifestyle is not suitable for you. I have personally witnessed misinterpretations of this choice, leading to divorces or separations between couples. You should only say or do something with your partner's knowledge. I am a hypocrite because in a chapter titled "In the Swing of Thangs," I revealed a secret I have not told anyone, until now.

FULL SWAP WITHOUT PENETRATION:

Usually, this is for newlyweds or beginners testing their lifestyle. They have come to a mutual understanding and decided on their preferred mode of participation. I want to compare it to analyzing voyeurism and observing another couple in the same room. Personally, I refer to this as soft swapping, where you could sit in the same room, fully clothed, and engage in a personal and intimate conversation with the other's partner.

That's my opinion, because no matter what, do what makes you happy. If either party has experienced performance issues, please discuss this before experimenting with the lifestyle. It will only be fair to everyone involved if we discuss or address this. Trust is essential, no matter which one you choose for your fantasy. You will be comfortable with the above. Peace!

What the Hell Do I know

I don't drop names, so let us call her Maria because this woman has family and just recently moved.

I don't want to do anything that jeopardizes her security. Now that I have made that clear, let us go. I knew this one thick black woman in her sixties, and she knows who she is from what I write in this chapter. At first, Maria's dating profile did not pique my interest.

Even though she was around five feet nine in height, she was slightly larger than most women I have slept with. I liked her personality and the way we communicated through our messages online. Eventually, we exchanged cell numbers, and she sent me some G-rated photos. I told myself, she is a nice-looking woman, and I liked her hairstyle. She and I talked about everything, from the swinging lifestyle to what we both enjoyed sexually. I enjoyed talking to her on the phone, and I am being straight up with you as the reader. I forgot about Maria's size.

That judgmental attitude disappeared with her personality. As we continued conversing, we made sure to be honest with each other before we met with no expectations. I also told Maria why there should not be expectations. I wanted to be honest about her weight, or should I say size? Do you think what I told her was offensive? She did not, but she thanked me for being honest.

I also did not want to mislead her by assuming there would be a relationship or anything sexual at the outset. I was never a man who slept with someone unless there was a connection. In her case, it was our conversation, her smile, her honesty, our sexual similarities, and la1tly, just the way she spoke to me on the phone that was unexplainable and comforting.

Let us take a slight detour. You ladies need to know there have been countless times I have passed on sleeping with someone I just met. If the vibe is not right on the phone, then I pass. I **love** an excellent candid conversation that is free of judgment. We should be able to talk about everything under the sun without assumptions or leading to sex.

At some point, I decided to put my differences aside; it is not like either of us is discussing marriage. We both decided to take one day at a time, and that made her comfortable continuing to talk to me. After some weeks had gone by, it was time to meet. She drove to Orlando and visited me instead.

When Maria arrived, I watched her slowly get out of her car, and she looked in my direction, where I was standing, waiting for her. While I was watching her walk towards me, I had all sorts of ideas running through my head. When she approached me, I hugged her and was glad she made it. When I opened the door and she walked past me, she had on some kind of snake-charming perfume that made my cock hard immediately. Once she was inside my apartment, I wasn't about to waste any time talking to her.

While walking up behind her, I looked at her like I had on a pair of those 1960s X-ray glasses they advertised.

Honestly, I wasn't attracted to what she wore to see me, and since it was a long drive, I assumed she needed to be comfortable. Still, her submissive and nurturing personality and our shared interests in the swinging lifestyle also played a significant role in continuing. The more we talked, the more Maria's weight did not make any difference to me; Maria turned me on in every other way imaginable.

Now that I have provided you with some mundane details about her, "Let's Get Crackin'" by Shock. After no more than a few more steps in, I commanded her to stop. And she did exactly that. She had no idea I was about to make me cum in my pants. I thought before she arrived, I had better be prepared. I pulled out my blindfold from my pocket while walking behind her.

She still had a purse in her hand, and I told her to drop it beside her on the floor. Again, she did exactly that. Just so you know, I was smiling from ear to ear. She was slightly shaking from anticipating what I had planned for her.

I told her to walk towards my island countertop and lean slightly over while I removed her dress from her shoulder. Now, her breasts and stomach were exposed to me. Damn, she had a mocha-colored complexion that also turned me on. There were enough imperfections on her body to know she was a real woman and ready for my hands to slightly graze across her body.

While she was comfortably leaning over with the palm of her hands on my island countertop. I blindfolded her and said in a commanding voice, "Spread your fucking legs wide open as you possibly can." She did exactly as she was told. So, I reached around from behind her and started playing with her pussy and breasts while she moaned passionately.

I whispered in her ear, "You better not take your hands off my countertop, and they are to remain in place until I say you can remove them." If Maria had disobeyed me, I would have told her to get dressed and go home; it is just that simple. She understood and trusted me enough to do as she was told without hesitation. Do not hold this book and judge me; I do things according to the person I am with. She could tell me to kiss her ass too!! But the question would then be why? I guess she did not want to take the chance of me sending her home.

Like a good girl, Maria submitted herself and kept her hands on the counter.

I watched her legs shiver while she stood with her legs spread apart. The dress that I removed from her shoulders was gathered up around her waist, so from the bottom, I lifted the dress just past her ass. Standing behind her, all I could see was this big, juicy caramel-colored ass ready for the palm of my large hands to slap it.

Remember, she completely trusts me, even with the blindfold on. Never mind the fact that this was our first meeting. While Maria was standing there naked, she did not know what was about to happen next. The blindfold activated all her senses, including touch, hearing, and the hair on her skin, indicating that it was turning her on.

When her senses kicked in, I barely touched her back with one finger, and she jumped. I caught her off guard because she wasn't expecting it. Another reason I knew I was turning her on was because she was shaking again with excitement. The woman is my undivided attention. Personally, penetration is the last thing on my mind when I am with someone I care about.

I have mentioned this before, and I am saying it again. Lying and trying to run a game is easy and lazy. That's why I say it is easy to stick my cock in her pussy, mouth, or ass, but it is more satisfying to arouse her first subtle foreplay. So, while her hands are still on the countertop, I slowly rub her nipples in a circular motion. I would begin by rubbing one nipple, then move on to the other while whispering in her ear. I don't say the same fucking thing to every woman who places her hands on my countertop. Every woman is unique, regardless of the vibe I feel around them or what I see.

As I touch specific parts of her body, I also observe her breathing and legs; if they are trembling, it indicates that she is highly energized and unable to maintain a straight posture. That is when I place my hands between her thighs, and I don't touch the pussy. I enjoyed running my hands up and down inside her thick thighs, keeping her guessing what I was about to do next.

I just grazed her pussy before moving on to her beautiful, large caramel stomach. Then I rubbed her breast again and kissed her on the back of her neck. I reached around and played with both of her nipples, this time very softly. I could tell she wanted her nipples pinched. I also sensed she wanted them pinched slightly harder. Her breathing increased when I pinched her nipples harder, indicating that she enjoyed what I was doing, prompting me to squeeze them even harder. I watched her body language to determine when to back off from how hard I was pinching her nipples. The reason I know when to back off a bit is because I give a damn about her, and I am paying attention to all the signs.

Okay, it was time to step it up, so I turned her around to face me and put my hand slightly around her neck like I owned her. Because we talked about it, I already knew I could lightly choke her, and most importantly, she trusted me. I suggest not to perform choking unless you have already discussed it. Before you put your hands around her throat, make sure you've clearly established trust. I can guarantee that if she does not have confidence in you, she will tense up and not enjoy herself.

Gotdamnittohell, if you know me well enough by now then you also know I am about I'm going to suddenly throw this in while

I am thinking about it. This is a message to all of you: avoid playing with a woman's pussy when your hands are dirty.

Wash your hands thoroughly before putting your fingers inside the woman's body otherwise, she can develop an infection. I knew this one nasty muthafucka who did not care about cleanliness. Here is the best example I can give you. I watched a man playing with a friend's dog outside at a swinger's party. At the time, I thought nothing of it with him playing with the dog and it seemed harmless, right? In all honesty there wasn't anything wrong unless well, KEEP READING....

He finally stopped playing and petting the dog walked in and made a beeline straight towards my friend **Kaylee and asked her** to party with him. She nodded yes and after some time had passed, she came out from one of the bedrooms and sat next to me. Being the nosey man I am, I asked her if she had a good time with him and what happened after they went into one of the bedrooms. She explained he played with her pussy then ate her out for a little while and that was it.

I asked what do you mean he played with your pussy, played how? She said well he put a couple of fingers inside me and tried to force an orgasm. I asked how it was she said it wasn't fun. I wanted to tell her about what I had seen but chose not to say anything, fearing she would think I didn't like him.

A month later there was another party I attended and of course guess who showed up, Kaylee. She had this blue mini skirt showing ass cheeks with black strapped Stilettos with nipple clamps. Of course, she had my attention the moment she walked through the door. And just like before she sat next to me and our conversation turned my stomach inside out. I asked her if she planned on having fun at this party and the look on her told me everythang I already knew.

She mentioned a few days after that last party, she developed an infection, and her husband rushed her to the nearest ER While telling me what happened she could tell something was wrong with me during our conversation. She and I were close enough that it was guilt written all over my face and she asked what's wrong. I made up a lie saying I felt sorry for her, and I was just glade she was ok. Well, me and you as the reader, parts of that is the true right?

Anyway, none of that would have happened to Kaylee if that nasty ass mutha fucka would have washed his hands before playing with her pussy.

Are you questioning why I did not warn my friend in the first place? If I had known, I would have stood up for my friend and told her not to fuck that asshole. Nevertheless, please wash your fucking hands and clean under your nails before playing inside of a woman's pussy. I can't believe I even have to say this in the first place. Time out bitches!!! I have an important message to keep in mind while reading this part of the chapter...

ROLE-PLAY CHOKING:

Watch her breathing and body language; it'll tell you everything you need to know, but only if you give a damn that is. And if you don't care, keep your fucking hands away from her neck. I bet you don't even lick the pussy, and if you do, it is only going to lick it a couple times before you stick your cock in. Selfish cocksuckers are the primary reason I wrote this book in the first place.

I have talked to enough women and heard that a good majority of men don't take the time nor give a damn about a woman's feelings. Some men don't bother to prepare a woman, preferring to rush into sex without applying any lubrication, especially if she is over fifty.

Returning to the chapter "What the Hell Do I Know?" Maria still had both hands on the counter, legs spread, obeying my commands.

With my hands around her throat, I rubbed her clit slowly. She experienced an orgasm unlike anything she had ever felt before, she mentioned. In fact, the intensity of her orgasm nearly caused her legs to buckle and drop to the floor. I stood back and watched her legs shake like my mom used to say, " shaking like a leaf on a tree." Just to think, I was doing this to a big, beautiful black woman, and I must admit, sex with her was incredible.

The parallel nature of our lives made a significant difference fucking her. She is the only black woman I have met to this day who lived a swinging lifestyle. She had a subservient mentality, yet her coworkers respected her and did not need to know her personal business.

One evening, I blindfolded her in my bedroom and instructed her to spread her legs as far as she could while I stood on the side of the bed. I used my right hand to play with her pussy, which caused her to squirt all over my bed and face. She apologized for wetting up my damn bed, saying she had never had that happen in her entire life. I am thinking: She is in her sixties, telling me she has never had anyone play with her like I did. In fact, because of her squirting, I had to make my bed squirt-proof. I thought to myself, all the guys she has fucked at the parties, I am the person who understood her thoroughly.

What the hell is up with these guys not even taking the time to do half the things I have done with her? I would play with her to such an extent that she would always fall asleep snoring, leaving her pussy sloppy wet after I finished.

One Saturday afternoon, she squirted so much that I filled my hand with her juices and showered her orgasm all over her stomach. Another time, there was so much of it on my fingers that it dropped all over her body, face, and breasts. Eventually, that ended, but based on what I said, she knows who she is, so I thought I would mention her in this book. I completely understand if this is read like another chapter in this book.

With all the women my cock has entered, it is always possible that I have repeated certain acts on different women. There are only so many positions a man can perform without repeating them with someone new. **Peace!**

What If's

Many what-ifs are swirling around in my head. There are moments when I wonder what my life would have been like if my parents had shown love, kindness, and respect to one another.

What if my father did not have a drinking problem that I witnessed? What if my father had never been unfaithful to my mother? What if my lying ass brother-in-law had been faithful to his wife and kids? What if my lying ass cousin was faithful to his wife and kids that I witnessed?

What if my mom's so-called best friend had never flaunted her affairs in my mom's home? What if another one of my Gay Azz cousins would not have tried to fuck me in the ass? What if I had liked it? What if that same cousin had not molested me? What if my father had not died?

What if teachers took an interest in me to excel at all levels of schooling? What if my teachers paid more attention when I cried for help? What if I had been allowed to express my sensitive side without being misinterpreted? What if the adults in my life did not exploit my innocence? What if those police officers had planted drugs in my car when I was pimping?

What if I had stopped my cousin from sucking my cock? What if I had gotten every girl, I fucked pregnant in high school? Especially when I did not believe in condoms. What if one of my hoes had ratted on me while I was in jail? What if I had stayed another night at that hotel where I left behind all the money one of my hoes had made that evening? What if I had not continued going to school and became a dropout? What if I had gone to my high school graduation? What if I had believed in God? What if I.... Sorry can't say this one? What if I had a bigger cock? Knowing me I would have been a porn star. Seriously!!

TIME OUT, NOW HOLD ON BECAUSE I HAVE MORE WHAT IFS BELOW:

What if my two sons had not been manipulated by their mother? What if my youngest son called me unexpectedly? What would I say? What if my oldest son forgave me? What if I was popular in school instead of a nerd? What if I wasn't so shy in high school?

LOOK MUTHA FUCKA I AIN'T DONE YET. TAKE A BREAK IF YOU NEED TO. (LAUGHING OUT LOUD)

What if I had not married my first wife? What if I had pulled out when I had sex with my first wife? What if I had never cheated on any of my wives? What if my biological mom had not allowed my aunt and Uncle to adopt me? What if I had become addicted to crack after trying it? What if pimps and hustlers did not surround me? What if drug dealers did not surround me?

What if I had not encountered pornographic material during my high school years? What if males had not referred to me as a faggot? Because I acted differently than most boys my age? What if my dog hadn't licked my face after being knocked unconscious after I fell from my avocado tree in my mom's backyard? What if no one heard the crash in Downtown San Diego after hit and run and didn't give the information to the police after I drove through the green light? I would not have had an insurance settlement.

Do not act like you have never said "What If" to yourself. Here is one for you, what if you had not read this far into this book? On that Thank You and keep up the good work. There is no right or wrong, and everything depends on your childhood support system.

I have gained knowledge about the process known as life. I am not the only one going through this you read. It is increasingly challenging to acknowledge how our world develops as time passes. People began openly expressing themselves and their opinions at the beginning of the 1960s and into the 1970s.

On the other hand, there is a current tendency to suppress our voices and diminish our status because of our uniqueness. Since the onset of COVID and its relation to our former president, DT, I have observed that people seem less inclined to allow others to be themselves. Although many people have entered and left my life, each has contributed to my growth.

Remember, without painfully reflecting, my story would not have been told. Thank you for helping me when I needed it most. In addition, I am grateful that you made the effort to read the entire book, from the beginning to the end, or, as the saying goes, "front to back." All of this would not have been possible if it were not for you. I also know that an unbelievable story within you is worth reflecting on; begin now and allow me to read yours.

I WILL END THIS BOOK BY REPEATING WHAT I SAID EARLIER TO YOU. JUST SAYING IT DIFFERENTLY.

I consider my life's events without comparing them to others and feel no one will want to read this. Before becoming discouraged, I needed to get my story off my mind and computer. Furthermore, I aimed to write this biography slash fantasy purely from my heart. Today, authenticity is in short supply, and I intend to bring it back in a pure and unfiltered manner. I am merely a man of African American/Black/Negro whatever you want to call someone as dark as I am who is sixty-five years old and is not ashamed to talk about his ideas, perilous situations, scandalous sexual experiences, and questionable sexual choices.

Additionally, I would like to express my uncensored ideas in a manner that I am confident some of you will comprehend and value. I didn't publish this book for personal enjoyment; instead, I published it because I am not the only one who feels this way and have had some of my experience's worth expressing. Do I need to reiterate that I am not a sex guru or sexologist?

When the Innocent Became Curious

J ust when I thought I was done vomiting every damn memory, every wound, every twisted corner of my past here comes 3:30 in the morning.

The pee hour. And bam— another vivid memory flashes across my mind like paparazzi at a red-carpet event. I laughed out loud. Of course, I couldn't go back to sleep. At first, I thought, "Should I even include this memory or not?" Maybe I should just keep it to myself because the risk of writing about it could easily be misinterpreted. I kept wondering, "What are people gonna be thinking after they have read, heard or listened to this?" But then again if I had no shame sharing "It Must Have Been the Dog N Me," then I might as well go all in, right? So, we shall see. And no, I haven't told you what "this" is yet. That's on purpose.

Whatever media you have chosen to listen or read this, you're just gonna have to be patient so that your eyes or ears can hear or see every word. No skipping or scanning ahead just to find it. Let's treat this like an Easter egg hunt for what this chapter is all about. In other words, You're just gonna have to sit there and listen or read every word. No skipping. No jumping ahead and definitely no scanning.

So here goes...

Here is why I called this chapter, "When the Innocent Became Curious.

    I hope you haven't forgotten what my older gay cousin did to me before I even had the words to process or understand completely what was happening. After he moved out of my mom's home, that curiosity lingered. Like a shadow in your room and you are not in there.

    And I'd be lying if I said I didn't sometimes wonder what it might've felt like if he'd finished what I stopped him from doing. Please... be patient with me. I'm still reminding myself it's okay to share this. Still asking the universe: Why me and why now? What did I do to deserve that? Why didn't you stop him? Of course, I never heard back. Just muffled screams in a pillow and a wet pillowcase from my tears I cried on. Sometimes I would wake up with piss all over my mattress because I was too scared to leave the room and afraid he'd call me in again. And now that we have revisited that a little maybe, just maybe, this next part will make a little more sense.

    As you already know I am a deeply traumatized and imaginative kid. That imagination became my survival tool. A way of making sense of things that didn't make sense. Alright, I can imagine your face right now, frowning and saying to yourself, damn man, OUT WITH IT!! So here we are. My cousin's gone. But the memories? The confusion? The curiosity? Still lingering and haunting me like a old Linda Blair movie. Eventually, I started figuring out how to please myself... without anyone else. Just me and my vivid 4K imagination.

One day, while I'm in the grocery store in the produce section, touching apples, oranges, bananas. and nearby were the cucumbers. I paused for some strange reason... stared at them and recalled why they reminded me of him. I picked up a few and a thought crossed my mind. Yup, that thought. That's all I'm gonna say. And now I'm leaving the rest to your imagination.

Wait a fucking second!! Are you saying to yourself, "how big was it?" Seriously, then you're just as warped as I am and too ashamed to admit it. Let me end this chapter with a visual you may or may not find funny: Picture a tall Black man standing in the grocery store, holding up a cucumber in the air like Rafiki lifting baby Simba in The Lion King—grinning from ear to ear. Did you laugh?

Or not, because of your own insecurities? One last truth from the heart especially to the women listening to this: I know damn well I ain't the only man who's ever thought about doing something or have done and maybe still is doing this to himself. This isn't just about me. And the fact that I dared to write about it means I've made peace with how people might perceive me. But let me say this before you go, if I hadn't shared this here, you could meet me, date me, marry me, or become a close friend... and you'd never know if you had not read, listened or heard about it.

Ladies, keep that in mind the next time you're falling for someone. The question remains: Did he, or didn't he? That's the million-dollar mystery that might never get answered. Anyway, all of what you've heard—and what's still to come—has shaped the person I am today. You just read or listened to some vague ass shit, and you know this. You were like, why am I being so vague all of a sudden, right? Because, on 10/02/2025 at around three AM, I said fuck it I am going all in on this chapter.

So here it is, raw and unfiltered like a can of molded maggot infested sardines in the kitchen cabinets. After visualizing the size of the cucumber that may or may not fit in my ass, I tossed it in my hand-held basket among the other items that I went to the store for. I am sorry, I just lied to you and myself as I was writing this. Actually, when the idea came to mind, I specifically went to the grocery store to pick one out. There you have the truth yet again, satisfied?? Let's just say, my list did not include a damn cucumber. Anyways, I will continue. While my first wife was at work the trauma revisited my mind like an unwelcome visitor.

Oh shit!! I let the cat out of the bag now, because you just said to yourself, MARRIED!! This is what you don't understand if you have never been molested It's never out of you mind totally. Just when you think it's safe, it resurfaces like herpes. Some of us are comfortable talking about it, but there are more people that won't.

Here I am 66 years old and sometimes I sit in my shower naked and cry trying to wash the memories of my cousin off me. It hasn't worked yet, so I am just going to have to die before it fades away. Now that I have given you some context here are some visuals. When I took the cucumber out of the bag, I immediately made my decision. Should I or should I not do this to myself?

Well, just like that song by McFadden and Whitehead, there was no stopping me now at this point. I had a few hours to be curious before my wife returned home from work. so, I got everything ready. The lube that my wife and I use was nearby. I took my pants off and sat down on one of the chairs in the living room and positioned myself at an angle so that my legs would be comfortable. I lubed up the cucumber and inserted it.

The fact I had never done that before, I slowly inserted it until I had a quarter of it in me. I dared to insert a little more until suddenly there was no more to add. I was very lucky that it did not slip inside me sideways, right?

Try to explain that one to my wife. While going in and out I was masturbating at the same time. Suddenly I hit a spot inside me that can only describe as the G-spot. I shot a load that hit my face and chest.

It scared me because it felt better than just plain old jacking off. That became addictive to the point that I was doing this act three to four times a week. If you are asking what I did with the cucumber once I was done, then I will answer that right now. I put it in the fridge because maybe I can save some money if I felt like doing it the very next day.

Of course, I would clean off the poop and place it in the bottom produce drawer. Please forgive me for what else I am about to throw up all over your kitchen table. I decided to leave the house one afternoon for a little while and my wife at the time returned home from work and was hungry. Of course, she made herself a salad with that shitty cucumber I had placed in the crisp produce drawer.

Yes, reader or listener, ... I cleaned it before placing it in the fucking crisp drawer, just in case you were wondering. Now that I answered that question that was bouncing around in your head, may I continue??? Of course, of all the questions she could have asked me, and it was... if I wanted some of her salad. Close your eyes and take a moment so that you can imagine the expression on my face. So, as you know,

I obviously declined that offer, wouldn't...YOU??? Just so you know this is the first and last time I am talking about it.

Cecil, you one gross ass mother fucker!!

I know, right?

So, if you happen to meet or see me on television smile to yourself and say, that mother fucker laid it all out there and certainly did not give a fuck what anyone thought or assumed about him. Be safe, ... my closeted freaky ass friends.

Wrap Her Up

W hen two people who love sex and each other. There are so many of you who are missing romance because of your long work hours, kids, health issues, weight gain, menopause, ED, drinking too much, lack of energy, sleepless nights, arguing all the time, racial tension, gas prices, food shortages, baby formula shortages, baby momma drama, pregnancy again, vasectomy failure, and being laid off.

Without a doubt, it is not easy to be sexually creative in any of those circumstances. With that being said, let us get straight to it. While reading this chapter, I need you to do me a favor. Imagine yourself walking around in your favorite local hardware store, and a sexual fantasy pops into your head, like in an X-rated cartoon.

You gaze up at the ceiling as if you can imagine how to use the object you just picked up. I am constantly thinking of ways to surprise my partner so that it does not become predictable. You can call me a dirty old man if you want to, even at the age of sixty-five. If you don't know what shrink-wrap is, you are gonna learn today. I have used shrink-wrap more times than I can remember at work, and I have never considered it for sexual purposes.

Remember, that idea that popped into my head earlier? It is the weekend, and I clocked out early from work and headed across the street to the local home improvement supply chain to buy one roll of shrink wrap. I have shopped there and passed by it a few times, so I knew precisely what aisle it was in. I did not waste any time looking for anything else. A big smile appeared when I picked it up and held it in my hand. In fact, I held up that shrink-wrap in the air like it was R holding up S (not saying the two names to avoid copyright infringement).

Hint: Holding up a lion cub in the air. Come on now, you know that shit was funny, right? Anyway, my cock grew harder as I thought of all sorts of ways to use it. If anyone watched me on the monitor while holding it up in the air and knew my plans for the shrink-wrap, I am sure they would say, "OMG."

Now, if you see me walking in an aisle with it and smile at me, I will know you are reading this book. Let us get back to shrink-wrapping up this white woman named Jackie. Before heading to her place, I never called, talked about, or mentioned the shrink-wrap fantasy. I just showed up with it one day, and she looked confused. Jackie asked me about my plans to use it, and I said, "It's a surprise." I stood up, walked into her bedroom, and sat on the edge of her bed. Naturally, the shrink wrap was next to me.

I called Jackie and asked her to come into the bedroom, where I waited for her. When she entered her own bedroom, I asked her to stand before me and not say one word.

Even though she is an alpha female, it was in her best interest to stand there, shut up, trust me, and be vulnerable for a little while. I told her to turn around so that I was looking at her back. Then I asked her to remove her blouse and her double D's bra. Despite being so small, she had big ass titties. She felt vulnerable with her bra and top on the floor, standing in front of me. Trust means everything in this situation. I asked her to take off her pants and remove her panties.

She kept asking me questions, and I had to say firmly, "Stop asking so many questions." I was shocked that she did not rebel. Jackie needs to always be in control, so I am sure this was making her uncomfortable and excited at the same time.

I asked her to turn around while she was naked in front of me. When I reached for the shrink-wrap, I asked her to put her arms straight down by her side. I reached over for the shrink-wrap and tucked it under one of her arms. As she stood there in front of me naked, I began to walk around her, wrapping her up like a five-foot-four white Christmas present.

While I was walking around shrink-wrapping her, Jackie had an idea, and it was an excellent one. She said, "Why don't you stay seated on the bed, and I'll spin myself around like a ballerina while you place the shrink-wrap where you need it?" I will be damned; that was a damn good idea, and that is precisely what I did. Are you paying attention? She was excited enough to make it easier for me to shrink-wrap her.

When she suggested the idea, I was smiling the whole time. To me, trust is better than sex because she offered me a solution. My cock was hard the whole time as she spun around in front of me. While all wrapped up like a Christmas gift, Jackie asked, "What's next?"

I wanted to say, "Shut the hell up, so badly, but instead, I smiled, stood up, faced her, and helped her onto the bed, all wrapped up. It may be challenging to shrink-wrap your partner, depending on their weight and size, and just so you know, I am being polite.

Her assistance made the process easier than if I had tried this myself. While she was lying there naked, I looked like a kid in a candy store with a wicked grin on my face. It felt like the cashier announced on the PA system that everything in the store was free, and you could take as much as you wanted. So, of course, I poked one hole in the shrink wrap.

Wait! I understand what you are thinking—one of those holes was for her anal, right? Even though I had full access to whatever hole I wanted, she trusted me and knew I would not stick my cock in a hole that we already discussed was off-limits.

If I were Satan, that would have been the best moment to take advantage of all her holes, right? I was thankful she was open-minded. While Jackie had her arms by her side, I ensured her arms were not shrink-wrapped behind her back, which would have been extremely uncomfortable.

If I had shrink-wrapped her that way, I would have had to unwrap her at once and rewrap her again with her arms to her side. That would have disrupted the mood between us. With her arms and hands by her side, it did not matter if she was face down on her stomach or lying on her back.

Either way, she won't lie down with her arms wrapped up. I just wanted her hands and arms out of the way and comfortably. I also made sure I did not shrink-wrap her above the shoulders. If a person is claustrophobic, this is not a great idea and could trigger the person.

So please be sure the two of you have talked about this thoroughly. While Jackie was standing, shrink-wrapped, I had full access to her pussy. She had a bad habit of scratching the top of my head while eating her pussy, so I had to produce something to prevent that from happening. I suddenly had a couple of choices, shrink-wrapped her or handcuffs. I chose shrink-wrap and did not realize then that it was more beneficial for me.

I decided to shrink-wrap her just enough so that she could unwrap herself in case something happened to me, and I am unable to get her out of that situation. Shrink-wrap her enough to make it fun, but not too much, in case of an emergency. You must try it once, and you should only shrink-wrap your partner after getting to know them, not on the first date. Imagine what would happen if your roommate or family member discovered you were all shrink-wrapped without knowing your kink.

How do you think they would respond? That is also why shrink-wrap is not a great idea if someone else is in the home. Personally, I would call 9-1-1. This is not a first date thing, I repeat, not a first date thing, you know what I mean. There is nothing sexier than a vulnerable woman. And if she likes anal sex, you poke two holes into the shrink wrap. Oh, man.

I am dedicating this portion of the paragraph to the men.

And if you are into rough sex and trust one another, it could be exciting for both of you. Can you envision a scenario where your partner is entirely vulnerable, allowing you to engage in any sexual activity without any resistance? You can tease her until she is ready to cum, then you stop and leave her hanging, begging you to continue. As I have mentioned four times in this chapter, trusting your partner is crucial for engaging in rough sex, which can be enjoyable for both parties. A role-play fantasy could now involve shrink-wrapping and slapping your cock against her face. I will say this one more time: trust is everything. Anyway, that is my shrink-wrapping story.

What have I learned from this chapter?

I always find it interesting to hear people's creative stories when they share them with me periodically. Now, having someone trust me enough to be vulnerable is precious.

So, don't take their trust for granted. If you decide to try this shrink-wrapping idea for fun, make sure you are paying attention to their body language and facial expressions. You may need to address any signs of discomfort before proceeding. You will thank me later. I know she and I enjoyed our time together when we first tried it, and you might, too. **Peace!**

Zum Abschluss

WRAPPING IT UP

Und würdest du mir zum Abschluss bitte einen Gefallen tun und mir eine Rezension hinterlassen, egal wo du dieses Buch erworben hast? Ich wäre dir sehr dankbar. Wirklich.

Also, hör auf zu zögern, und fang am besten gleich jetzt an!

Wenn dich dieses Buch zum Lachen, Nachdenken, Zusammenzucken oder vielleicht ein- oder zweimal zum Augenrollen gebracht hat, dann erzähl der Welt davon. Ich möchte davon erfahren, und andere sollten es ebenfalls hören. Es ist eine Geschichte, die erzählt werden muss.

Dieses Werk war keine spontane Idee über Nacht.

Es hat vier Jahre gedauert – und ja, es erforderte viel Zeit allein, manchmal begleitet von einer Flasche Lotion und einer lebhaften Fantasie –, um dieses Buch zu schreiben. Ich bin ehrlich zu dir. Behalte das bitte im Hinterkopf.

Am 04.01.2025 kam mir folgender Gedanke:
Ich weiß, der Titel lautet „**Blutige Finger**".

Und das, was du gelesen hast, zeigt, was geschehen kann, wenn jemand seine Traumata nicht verarbeitet.
Das prägt, wie man die Welt wahrnimmt.

Meine Realität entspringt einem dunklen Ort – jeden einzelnen Tag, an dem ich die Augen öffne.
Deshalb wirken meine Gedanken manchmal sprunghaft, und deshalb leide ich an ADHS sowie wahrscheinlich an einigen anderen Dingen ebenfalls.

Aber weißt du, was wirklich zählt?
Ich danke dir, dass ich dir meine Geschichte erzählen durfte.
Ich danke dir für deine Zeit.
Und was auch immer du gerade durchmachst – bleib vorsichtig und achte auf dich.

Inspired / Procrastination

Inspiriert / Aufschieberitis

Du warst der Grund, warum ich dieses Buch überhaupt geschrieben habe.

Du hast das ganze Buch gelesen? Von Anfang bis Ende?

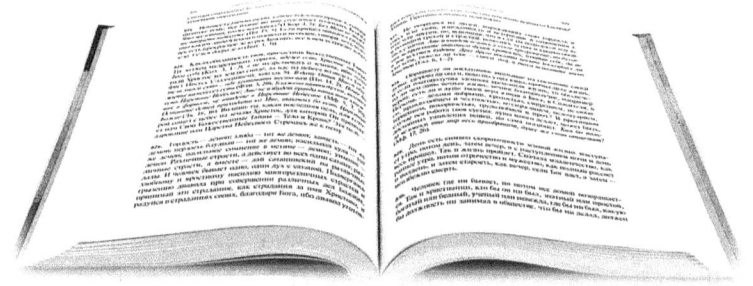

Dann schulde ich dir wohl ein bisschen Dankbarkeit – weil du mir erlaubt hast, meine Gedanken, Gefühle und völlig verrückten Geschichten zu teilen, ohne mich zu verurteilen. Na ja ... vielleicht *ein bisschen* Urteil, oder?

Aber sag mal – während du gelesen hast, sind deine Finger vielleicht ein bisschen gewandert? Wurde deine rechte Handfläche plötzlich etwas ... gleitfähig? Oder war's vielleicht das gute alte

Notfallspielzeug aus dem Nachttisch? Sei ehrlich – die meisten von euch haben es griffbereit, oder nicht?

Du hast dieses Buch wirklich ganz gelesen? Von Anfang bis Ende?

Dann schulde ich dir wohl ein bisschen Dankbarkeit – weil du mir erlaubt hast, meine Gedanken, Gefühle und völlig verrückten Geschichten zu teilen, ohne mich zu verurteilen. Na ja ... vielleicht *ein kleines bisschen* Urteil, oder?

Aber sag mal – während du gelesen hast, sind deine Finger vielleicht ein bisschen gewandert? Wurde deine rechte Handfläche plötzlich etwas ... glitschig mit deinem Lieblingsgel? Oder war's vielleicht das treue Nachttischspielzeug, das du für Notfälle bereithältst? Sei ehrlich – die meisten von euch haben es doch in Reichweite, oder nicht?

09/17/2024
Aktualisierte Gedanken seit meinem ersten Buch.

Es waren die Frauen – und mal ehrlich, die weißen Ehefrauen – die ich auf den Swingerpartys traf, die dieses überwältigende Verlangen in mir weckten, dieses Buch zu schreiben. Zu oft sagten Fremde zu mir: „Mann, darüber solltest du echt ein Buch schreiben." Immer wieder – zufällige Leute und Freunde, die mir Hinweise vom Universum gaben.

Bevor du mich verlässt, lass mich dir noch etwas mitgeben!

Eine Frau, mit der ich zusammen war, sagte: „OMG, darüber solltest du ein Buch schreiben." Und die letzte – na ja, die vorletzte – Frau, mit der ich geschlafen habe? Sie sagte dasselbe.

(Und nein, ich werde dir nicht erzählen, was passiert ist. Nur so viel: Es war genug, um mich wachzurütteln.) Ich gebe es zu – ich war mein ganzes Leben lang ein Aufschieber. Von der Kindheit bis ins Erwachsenenalter... es sei denn, etwas entfachte in mir ein Feuer – so wie dieses Buch.

Zum Beispiel – damals, als ich Super Mario Bros. 1985 spielte, Baby. Erinnerst du dich an diesen süchtig machenden Mist? Ich habe es nie zu Ende gespielt. Jede Stufe wurde härter, und als ich endlich zu diesem feuerspeienden Drachen am Ende kam, warf ich den Controller hin und ging frustriert davon.

Kennst du das?

Aber so ist das Leben, oder? Du stößt auf etwas Schwieriges – und anstatt dich dem zu stellen – gehst du frustriert weg. Übertrag diese Einstellung mal auf dein Leben. Denk kurz drüber nach. Siehst du, aufzugeben, wenn etwas unmöglich erscheint, ist einfach. Aber vielleicht war ich nicht nur ein Aufschieber. Vielleicht... war es etwas Tieferes. Ein Mangel an Selbstvertrauen. Zweifel. Angst davor, was passieren würde, wenn ich tatsächlich etwas zu Ende bringe. Ich war von Anfang an brutal ehrlich zu dir. Kein Grund, jetzt damit aufzuhören.

I Want 2 Thank You

ICH MÖCHTE DIR DANKEN

Also, hat dieses Buch meine Geschichte erzählt?
Verdammt ja. Aber es ging nicht nur um mich. Es ging um eine
Kindheit, der ich nicht entkommen konnte, und ein
Erwachsenenleben, durch das ich mich durchkämpfen musste.

**Das Schreiben hat mich gezwungen, einige verdammt
dunkle Erinnerungen auszugraben – Dinge, die ich lieber
begraben gelassen hätte.**
Aber man kann nichts heilen, dem man sich nicht stellt, oder?

Jedes Kapitel, das du gelesen hast, war meins.
Kein KI-generiertes Zeug, keine weichgespülte Version der
Wahrheit. Nur so, wie es passiert ist – oder wie es sich anfühlte, als
ich es erlebt habe. Ein Teil davon ist wirklich passiert. Ein Teil lebt
in meiner Fantasie. Finde selbst heraus, was was ist.

**Ich habe dir meine Verrätereien, meinen Schmerz,
mein Wachstum gegeben.**
Ich habe dir die hässlichen Seiten menschlicher Beziehungen
gezeigt – und die Schönheit, die man findet, wenn man aufhört,
vor sich selbst davonzulaufen. Ich habe das hier nicht geschrieben,
um dich bequem zu machen. Ich habe es geschrieben, um dich
zum Nachdenken zu bringen.

Wenn irgendetwas davon dir hilft, deinen eigenen verdrehten Weg zu verstehen – cool.

Wenn nicht, weißt du zumindest, dass ich echt geblieben bin.

Das hier ist die Geschichte von ***Blutige Finger***

Und jetzt gehört sie dir.

Don't Tell

Anyone that this is in the book, okay?

The "Dominant/ Submissive Romance" photos are real, not AI-generated. It was Lara's suggestion while taking those photos, and being her Dom was appropriate. As you have read, I lived in many different situations before authoring this book. It will be hard for you to comprehend everything you are about to read, so here goes. I met Lara on a website called Alt back then, which means alternative.

Alternative is also a code word for people who have a sexual preference for kink. Lara's way of treating the black men was different from anyone I had ever met. I remember posting an image of her kneeling to me in a Facebook group.

That image caught fire and had a minimum of a thousand comments. I read some of the comments, and you would assume Lara, as a child, was abused. Some called her a doormat, and a few mentioned it was a beautiful photo. Once the comments reached over two thousand, the group mediator had to remove them because of the controversy that had started. When I visited Lara, she made sure Oxtails with dark gravy were ready with rice. Of course, she would serve me first and her second. I am sure that's no different than how you treat your man, right? But what if I told you she sat on the floor next to me while I ate? She felt that being on the same level was disrespectful. Keep reading.

No matter where we were, if my shoestrings were loose, she would squat down to the floor and ground and tie them for me with a smile. She did not GAF where or when it happened; she tied them for me. I am not sure if she did this for shock or if it was how she was naturally. Man, I would love to know what you are thinking right now. I may have repeated some of this in another chapter, but I am sure I did not go into complete detail as I am right now.

Imagine waiting for a restaurant table, and a young white girl opens the door with a short black dress and bleached blonde hair. Right afterward, a black man walks in and waits for a table already waiting for them. As I stood outside, she walked in and gave them her name, not mine. When it came to ordering our food, I usually ordered for both of us. Occasionally, she would choose something from the menu herself. Wait! Don't you dare judge my relationship with Lara?

Treating me like this was Lara's preference, no matter what the hell you think!! I am confident right now; as a woman, you just said, "No Fucking way would you do that, right?

Good, I have your attention, and you can't stop reading what else I have to say about this arrangement. I remember this one time she and I were at Disney. She liked driving my car while I was in the passenger seat, and I did not mind it. Honestly, I had memories of my pimping days. Back to Disney because you thought I forgot. When she drove my car to be valet-parked, she would tell the guys waiting she got this, open her door, walk over to my side, and open mine. You should have seen the looks she and I were getting. The hate and disgust were in the air big time. I was used to getting the frowns from white people.

I hope I explained the (*) in "Dominant/ Submissive Romance." This is why I did not add this to the TOC table of contents. Thanks again if you made this far. Let me know either way if you did or did not enjoy reading about my adventures. By the way, if you are a white person who read this entire book without taking it personally, I want to commend you. I intend to have a meaningful, uncomfortable conversation between you, the reader, and myself.

No one wants to have these conversations anymore, would you agree? If you took offense to anything you read at any point, it means you are carrying some hidden guilt that you are ashamed of.

Do me a favor; start paying attention to your surroundings and the people you come in contact with.

Whether at a grocery store, your doctor, lawyers, managers, the CEOs of corporations, bank tellers and managers, district managers, CFO, CEO, or media owners such as Facebook/Instagram, X, and YouTube are all owned by white people. Fuck!!

Let's not forget when it comes to entertainment and sports, owners are primarily white or Jewish folks. Netflix, Amazon, and BET are not owned by folks who look like me. So, before you throw stones inside a glass house, breathe and accept the bottom line; you'll get it all, and you are still unhappy. Happy and content people do not give a damn about what other people are doing with their lives.

They should not care about what race or religion others believe in. And most certainly would not care about what they identify with. One last thing I want to leave you with. Just close your eyes for one fucking moment and imagine everywhere you went and everyone you spoke to was a black person; just imagine every show on television exclusively black people in them.

Reverse everything, I said above all of a sudden, right now, this very second. **WHAT WOULD YOU DO?**

Wortdefinitionen

Definitions Of Words

- A.F. (as fuck)
- Ain't – don't have
- BDSM (bondage and discipline, dominance and submission, sadism, and masochism)
- Betta (better)
- B.T.W. (by the way)
- Dafuck – the fuck
- F.Y.I. (for your information)
- H.N.I.C. (head nigga in charge)
- IDGAF (I don't give a fuck)
- L.O.L. (laugh aloud)
- M.O.B. (mind our business)
- M.Y.O.B. (mind your own business)
- O.M.G. (oh my god)
- P.O.S. (piece of shit)
- S.M.H. (shaking my head)
- STFU (shut the fuckup)
  - S.Y.H. (shaking your head?) W.T.F. (what the fuck)

Danksagungen

ACKNOWLEDGMENTS

Zuallererst muss ich mich bei denen bedanken, die an mir gezweifelt haben.
Ihr habt mich härter angetrieben als irgendjemand sonst es jemals könnte.

An meine engen Freunde – egal ob ihr mich unterstützt, inspiriert oder richtig wütend gemacht habt – ihr habt den Mann mitgeformt, der hinter diesen *Blutigen Fingerns* steht. Ich liebe euch dafür, auch wenn wir heute keinen Kontakt mehr haben.

An die Frauen, die meinen Weg gekreuzt haben – egal ob für eine Saison oder einen Grund – ihr habt mir Geschichten gegeben, die ich nie vergessen werde. Manche von euch haben mir das Herz gebrochen. Manche haben es geheilt. Manche ... haben mich einfach völlig verwirrt zurückgelassen. Wie auch immer – danke.

An alle, die mein erstes Buch unterstützt haben – ob ihr es gekauft, geteilt oder jemandem davon erzählt habt – ihr habt dieser Geschichte Leben eingehaucht.

Ich habe eure Unterstützung nie leicht genommen – und werde es auch nie tun.

An meine Leser:
Egal ob ihr dieses Buch aus Neugier, Schmerz, Wut oder Durst in die Hand genommen habt – ihr seid die Echten. Ich hoffe, meine Geschichte hat euch zum Nachdenken, Lachen, Weinen oder

innerlichen Fluchen gebracht. Wenn ich irgendeine Reaktion in euch ausgelöst habe, dann habe ich meinen Job gemacht.

Und an diejenigen, die meine Worte falsch verstanden, aber trotzdem bis zum Ende gelesen haben:
Ihr habt gesehen, was ihr sehen wolltet.
Ich habe geschrieben, um die Wahrheit zu sagen – nicht, um allen zu gefallen.

An mein früheres Ich – den gebrochenen Jungen, der noch nicht wusste, wie man sich selbst liebt – danke, dass du überlebt hast. Dieses Buch ist auch deine Geschichte.

Und schließlich an den Allerhöchsten ...
Du hast mich lange genug atmen lassen, um sie zu erzählen.

Bleib mit mir verbunden

Website
BLUTIGEFINGER.COM

Social Meda:

TIKTOK

FACEBOOK

YOUTUBE

Wenn dich dieses Buch zum Lachen, Nachdenken, Zusammenzucken oder zu dem Satz
„Verdammt... er hat das wirklich gesagt" gebracht hat,
tu mir einen einfachen Gefallen:
Hinterlass eine Bewertung.

Sie muss nicht tiefgründig oder poetisch sein — nur ehrlich.
Deine Worte helfen diesem Buch, den nächsten Menschen zu erreichen, der es braucht.
Und glaub mir... irgendjemand da draußen tut es.
Danke,
Cecil Hicks

www.ingramcontent.com/pod-product-compliance
Lightning Source LLC
Chambersburg PA
CBHW071625140626
46555CB00021B/2